THE FRENCH WAY ■

Richard F. Kuisel

THE FRENCH WAY

How France Embraced and Rejected

American Values and Power

PRINCETON UNIVERSITY PRESS   *Princeton and Oxford*

Copyright © 2012 by Princeton University Press

Requests for permission to reproduce material from this work
should be sent to Permissions, Princeton University Press

Published by Princeton University Press, 41 William Street,
Princeton, New Jersey 08540

In the United Kingdom: Princeton University Press, 6 Oxford Street,
Woodstock, Oxfordshire OX20 1TW

press.princeton.edu

Library of Congress Cataloging-in-Publication Data

Kuisel, Richard F.

The French way : how France embraced and rejected American values and power /
Richard F. Kuisel.

   p.   cm.

   Includes bibliographical references and index.

   ISBN 978-0-691-15181-6 (hardcover : alk. paper) 1. United States—Relations—
France. 2. France—Relations—United States. 3. France—Civilization—American
influences. 4. Anti-Americanism—France. 5. United States—Foreign public
opinion, French. 6. Public opinion—France. I. Title.

   E183.8.F8K85 2011

   327.73044—dc22   2011012261

British Library Cataloging-in-Publication Data is available

This book has been composed in Garamond Premier Pro

Printed on acid-free paper. ∞

Printed in the United States of America

10 9 8 7 6 5 4 3 2 1

For Sally McCarthy Kuisel

1947–2008

She met life with grace, kindness,

courage, and a beautiful smile.

CONTENTS ∎

LIST OF ILLUSTRATIONS ∎

PREFACE ■

By the end of the twentieth century America was the object of French fascination, anxiety, and scorn. If the New World had been observed by the French since Jacques Cartier's explorations of the St. Lawrence River in the 1530s, it was not until over four hundred years later that America became the foil for national identity. By the 1980s America had become the standard by which the French measured their progress or decline. Success in foreign affairs meant acting as the partner of the United States yet keeping a comfortable distance and counterbalancing the U.S. government's hegemony. The "good society" was defined by rejecting mainstream American notions of work and leisure. Similarly, a modern economy did not imitate the "wild capitalism" of the United States; if some borrowing of American practice was necessary, it had to be adapted or repackaged as French. And culture, the nation's pride, needed to be protected against the onslaught of Hollywood movies, American English, and fast food. Viewed from France, the United States was engaged in a transatlantic competition whose stakes were national identity, independence, and prestige. Viewed from the United States, France was of little account except when it got in the way. It was an asymmetrical rivalry.

This study examines how, why, and with what consequences America served as a foil for France in the final two decades of the twentieth century. It is the story of France's effort at designing its own path to modernity, a path that moved at a tangent from the one represented by America.

Perceiving America as a model to be emulated or avoided did not start during the most recent fin de siècle. Beginning as early as the eighteenth century, travelers, intellectuals, journalists, and others observed and commented on transatlantic developments creating a veritable "discourse," much of which was anti-American. The tempo of commentary accelerated between the two world wars, but it was only after 1945 with the advent of the United States as a superpower, an economic-social model, and a cultural juggernaut that America came to be a major concern of policy makers and the public alike. Nevertheless, one would not say that the French in the early postwar decades were yet obsessed with America. They were not yet persuaded that America represented a form of modernity that had to be reckoned with and countered. French businessmen, for example, who visited the United States as guests of the Marshall Plan, were unconvinced that they either could, or should, try to transfer what they observed in American factories, offices, and shops. Similarly, French filmmakers and directors believed they could make movies as they did before the war and hold their own against Hollywood—if only they had adequate government assistance. And engineers and scientists were confident they could develop high-technology sectors like high-speed trains, nuclear energy, and even nuclear weapons without the Americans. After 1958 President Charles de Gaulle thought the French could move ahead without depending on American investments and without knowing English. As late as the 1960s many intellectuals believed America was irrelevant and could be ignored.

By the final decades of the century, however, America could no longer be kept at a distance and it had become a pressing issue of both public concern and government policy. The allure of the model and anxiety about its power had escalated beyond any previous level: America had become a national fixation.

It is my principal task to examine how the French perceived America, why they came to measure themselves against the Americans, and how they designed policies in response to this model in the final decades of the century. This inquiry leads to the larger question of whether or not they found a divergent "French path" to modernity in contrast to that of the American way. Had the French, by the end of the century, charted a distinctive and viable alternative to what their transatlantic cousins championed as the only way forward?

America, for the purpose of this study, imposed itself on the French in three ways: in international affairs, economics, and culture. These three arenas often overlapped and interacted and thus, when appropriate, will be treated concurrently rather than analyzed separately. What these three dimensions of America all connoted was power and modernity. Simply stated, America raised two questions for the French: How can we avoid American hegemony and remain independent? How can we be modern and yet remain French?

The final two decades of the twentieth century offer something of a contrast in perceptions and attitudes among both the French elites and the populace about America. If widespread interest and concern, against a background of indifference, characterized both decades, the overall balance tipped from positive to negative in the 1990s. Whereas the 1980s featured a veritable belle époque of transatlantic harmony, one in which the French in general admired American society and economic prowess; eagerly embraced American fads in fashion, music, and food; and warmed to Presidents Ronald Reagan and George H. W. Bush, the 1990s, in contrast, witnessed a degradation of views. After the end of the Cold War, the French grew increasingly disenchanted with the U.S. government's triumphalism, with what came to be called the American hyperpower and, to a certain extent, with America itself including its values.

Were the French unique among Europeans in focusing their attention on their transatlantic cousins and on systematically trying to find ways at keeping their distance? Without attempting to explore this comparison in depth, the obvious answer is "yes." The British, Germans, Italians, Belgians, Dutch, Poles, and others (Yugoslavia aside) did not treat the United States as did the French at the end of the century. They all had their differences with the Americans, but they did not, for the most part, measure themselves against the New World. None of these other Europeans officially tried to prevent the spread of American English. None went so far as the French in trying to contain American television programs and movies. None trashed a McDonald's franchise. None burned the Stars and Stripes as did French farmers. None tried consistently to use the European Union as a counterweight to Washington. None defined their identity in opposition to the Americans as did the French. There was something peculiar, if not unique, about the French.

Gallic fascination with the New World raises an obvious paradox—that of a nation that, in many respects, embraced America and at the same time rejected it. France was seduced by America after the Second World War: it Americanized as much as any other European country. The spread of McDonald's outlets, the ubiquitous Coca-Cola bottles in cafés, and the construction of Euro Disney outside Paris all illustrate how the French fully shared in the European-wide process of Americanization. At the same time they mounted a shrill effort at resisting and criticizing it. Gallic anti-American attitudes, compared to those registered by other Europeans, remained relatively potent. This paradox of the simultaneous advance of Americanization and persistent anti-Americanism requires an explanation. It is my contention that a historical perspective helps understand this phenomenon. If one examines the last half of the twentieth century there seems to be a pattern to anti-American perceptions: they have been cyclical; they surge and recede according to certain variables. One can also see this pattern at work both in the rather benign 1980s and in the more acerbic mood of the late 1990s. Hopefully a historical analysis of this perennial, yet cyclical, phenomenon will help explain it.

Comprehensiveness, for this topic, is an unattainable aim. It would be impossible to examine all the ways in which the French measured themselves against America: such an effort would require more skills and learning than I possess—not to speak of hundreds of additional pages that would test any reader's endurance. My investigation has three dimensions: international relations, economic policy, and popular culture. Other topics are for other scholars. Thus I shall refrain from addressing a host of other issues where America may also have acted as a foil, such as immigration policy, multiculturalism, race, feminism, science and technology, education, high culture, or scholarship.

One might ask, Why would a historian address such a contemporary topic? Few of the essential records like government archives and private papers are available, and historical perspective is limited. In fact, historians can consult copious secondary, and even some primary, sources for the period. The available historical record is surprisingly rich. There is, in addition, a compelling issue of historical and contemporary dimensions that deserves our attention.

This study will offer reflection on a hypothesis about what some analysts see as a significant trend in European-American relations—their drifting apart. One Italian scholar has boldly asserted that "there is no longer an Atlantic or a Euro-American community."[1] Despite convergence around democracy, a market economy, and American-led globalization there have been long-term developments that point to a growing estrangement between Europe and the United States, toward a widening of the Atlantic. The American model that dominated the transatlantic community during the Cold War, in this view, is being supplanted by the European way. The dispute over the beginning of the Iraq War in 2003 demonstrated not only a new assertiveness among Europeans about international affairs but also exposed even more fundamental differences over political, economic, social, and cultural practices. America and Europe seem in recent years to have diverged over such essentials as the role of government in social and economic life, social solidarity, lifestyles, and the value of cultural diversity while expressions of anti-Americanism persist. Distancing also takes the form of growing uneasiness about the imbalance in the Atlantic Alliance and differences over issues like the role of international organizations in peacekeeping, environmental protection, recourse to military force, and globalization. Europeans appear more confident, even smug, about the superiority of a continent where life is more humane, more communitarian, and more enlightened—for example, in the turn away from capital punishment and religious-based morality. In a word they think of themselves as more *civilized* than their American cousins.

To be sure, this collective perception of divergence contains some wishful thinking, and Europeans do not speak with a single voice. And what some see as a trend may be little more than appreciation of a historic and enduring transatlantic distance that recent events have simply highlighted. There may not be a trend, just recognition of a gap. Moreover, there has been a counterpoint to drift, for, as this study will demonstrate, in many ways France and America were growing together at the fin de siècle. France may be an example not of continental drift but of the dynamic of globalization/Americanization that makes nations defy growing interdependence and uniformity by asserting difference. In fact, this simultaneous homogenization and assertion of national identity forms the crux of this study.

Only time will tell whether French resistance to America was a temporary deviation in the grand narrative of an ever closer transatlantic community or if it represents growing estrangement. If the latter is confirmed, then France was at the forefront of this trend, it was Europe's leader. As this study argues, the French at the fin de siècle used America as a foil for change, as a way to chart their own path toward modernity and to assert their independence. *The French Way* describes how and why and with what consequences—some meritorious, others unfortunate—France marked out its distance from its transatlantic ally. This study frames the recent history of transatlantic relations around the notion of competing conceptions of social and economic modernity, cultural status, and political power with America serving as a standard of measurement for Europeans.

ACKNOWLEDGMENTS ■

I am most grateful to those who read all or parts of my manuscript and made recommendations for improvements. My helpful and generous consultants were Frédéric Bozo, John Kim Munholland, Janick Marina Schaufelbuehl, David Ellwood, Sophie Meunier, and Robert Harvey, as well as the two anonymous readers for Princeton University Press. Other forms of scholarly assistance came from Hélène Volat, Paul Gallis, Seth Armus, Harvey Feigenbaum, Sherrill Wells, Donald Lamm, Martin Schain, Justin Vaïsse, Philip Mooney, Erin Carriere-Kretschmer, and Mary Demeri. This work owes much to the rich intellectual environment that combines policy and history created by the BMW Center for German and European Studies and the History Department at Georgetown University. The BMW Center and its director, Jeff Anderson, also provided me with resourceful and dependable research assistants—namely, Efthymia Drolapas, Chantal Clement, Kristin Melby, Stacey Chappel, and Marie Harding. Brigitta van Rheinberg, Sara Lerner, Sarah Wolf, and Brian Bendlin at Princeton University Press paid close attention to my manuscript and made important contributions.

Most of all I want to express my personal debt to my late wife, Sally McCarthy Kuisel, to whom this book is a tribute. Sally, who was an artist and an archivist, encouraged my scholarship, but, more important, she made both of our lives joyful and fulfilling. Her remarkable esprit merits memorializing, and to evoke it I propose one of her favorite pieces of music, Franz Schubert's "Trout Quintet," which expresses her warmth, optimism, vivacity, and beauty. As my grandson said of Sally, "she sparkled."

Washington, D.C., March 2011

A NOTE ON ANTI-AMERICANISM ■

For readers who are scrupulous about terminology I shall at the outset define the elusive term *anti-Americanism* and explain how the expression will be used. Scholars who have faced the definitional question tend either to emphasize intellectuals, political extremists, and discourse or they stress the general public and polls. The first conceptualization narrows and hardens the cohort; the second makes it diffuse and volatile.[1] My exposition employs both approaches while noting the distinction.

The restrictive usage conceives of anti-Americanism as a predisposition, a reflex, or a bias that automatically assumes the worst about anything associated with America, in which America appears to have no virtues, only vices. It is metaphorically described as a disease—and a contagious one at that. It is fueled by a discourse about America dating from the nineteenth century, if not earlier, and it relies on stereotypes, images, tropes, and accusations that belittle everything associated with America and treats America and Americans as malevolent and dangerous. And it is a constant seemingly impervious to events or other developments. Accordingly, America is a dystopia with connotations of rampant consumerism, vulgar mass culture, social conformity, violence, and a will to world dominance. This stance, often labeled *anti-américanisme primaire*, which could be translated as "primary" or "primitive" anti-Americanism, conveys a confrontational intent and treats America as an ideology. The notion that America is an "-ism" makes this usage comparable to other ideological expressions like "anticommunism" or "anti-imperialism." "Primary anti-Americanism," including outspoken protagonists, captured a sympathetic audience of no more than 10 or 15 percent of the population. It is most commonly identified with intellectuals and extremist political and movements. The phrase *anti-américanisme primaire* came into vogue during the late 1970s and early 1980s as a reproof to ideological extremists on both the left (e.g., communists), and the right (e.g., the New Right).[2]

Dystopian anti-Americanism has a right-versus-left inflection though both sides converge on basics. From the right America is a standardized, mass society rooted in materialist values and lacking either true culture or spiritual transcendence; from the left it is a capitalist monstrosity built on inequality, greed, and exploitation and pays no heed to social welfare, community or the environment. Both right and left agree that Americans have always been slaves to the "Dollar God" and are consumed by consumerism. Both view American society as feminized yet racked by violence. Both regard American culture as akin to trash. Both also see American foreign policy as unreliable—vacillating between imperialism and isolationism—and driven by moralistic and messianic aspirations as well as economic advantage. Both are disposed toward condemning America for what it is as well as for what it does. Defective policies originate less from flawed political decisions than from who Americans are and what they value.

Once the historian looks beyond the texts of writers and party programs and a hard-core minority and addresses attitudes among the general populace, anti-Americanism takes on a different color: here perceptions and assessments are less reflexive or totalizing; they oscillate and are more responsive to circumstances. There has been a kind of historical pulse as criticism ebbed and flowed, sharpened and softened, that requires understanding how changing contexts explain the dynamics of the phenomenon. The fluctuation of collective attitudes toward America appeared in polling data and the media. Opinion surveys regularly reported a small bloc of the populace that identified itself as holding strongly unfavorable views of Americans and America; but, in certain circumstances, such views could swell to half or more of the populace. These popular attitudes, unlike those aired by the dystopians, were highly volatile and often policy-specific, subject especially to transatlantic affairs like disputes over politics or trade. When a surge occurred, many of those surveyed attacked not only the U.S. government's policies, but also the shortcomings of American society or Americans. Analytically it is thus difficult to distinguish objections to "what America does" from "what America is" because they tend to overlap. At some level what America does, and who it is as a country interact—or, at least, are perceived to interact. For example, in the eyes of many French men and women, Ronald Reagan's tough anti-Soviet stance in the early years of his presidency or his harsh socioeconomic policies represented who Americans were. Popular surges of antipathy form the second dimension of anti-Americanism alongside the far smaller cohort of dystopians.

The end of the twentieth century is an example of such a surge, when large numbers of the population, prompted by their leaders and the media, not only voiced criticism of American policies but also professed views about Americans that could be termed anti-American. For example, more and more of the French during the 1990s associated America and Americans with disparaging terms like *violence, racism,* or *domination.* I shall refer to this phenomenon as "growing anti-Americanism" with the understanding that this attribution is quite different from that represented by "primary anti-Americanism."

In brief, I shall use the term *anti-Americanism* in two ways: it will occur in its restrictive sense when discussing the dystopians who prejudged and belittled everything attributed to America; but it will also be used more expansively to identify critical attitudes expressed by the general populace of America, of Americans, and of policies, both domestic and international, associated with the United States. In this study the French have often scolded America for acting as a hegemonic power and for taking the wrong path toward modernity. In this way anti-Americanism encompasses both the small minority of reflexive haters as well as mass attitudes and perceptions that censored important aspects of America and its policies.

THE FRENCH WAY

1.

America à la Mode: The 1980s

America, and much that was associated with America, was in vogue in France during the 1980s. Ralph Lauren fashions, California wines, Hollywood blockbuster movies, and venture capitalists were all chic. One Parisian couturier served McDonald's hamburgers at the opening of his fashion show. The socialist president of France, François Mitterrand, paid a visit to California's Silicon Valley and also admitted that he was a fan of the television show *Dallas*. U.S. president Ronald Reagan, after initially facing a cool reception, became so popular that many French wanted him reelected in 1984. President George H. W. Bush, especially after the success of German reunification, was even more highly regarded than his predecessor. And anti-Americanism, which once was synonymous with the cognoscenti of the Left Bank, was now unfashionable. By the end of the decade America, Americans, American society, and American popular culture were more warmly received than at any time since the GIs marched through a liberated Paris in 1944.

This narrative of French perceptions of America at the fin de siècle begins with an era of relative good feeling from the early 1980s to the early 1990s. The major aims of this chapter are, first, to describe and explain the warmth of these years as a prelude to the creeping chilliness in perceptions and relations that followed while watching the underlying rivalry that generated controversies and, second and more specifically, to examine how the French responded to the American model—principally Reagan's domestic policies.

Why were the two decades of the fin de siècle apparently different? The answer lay in an unusual conjuncture of circumstances in the 1980s. Among the reasons for transatlantic amity was the admirable way Washington navigated the end of the Cold War. The splendid performance of the U.S. economy in the mid-1980s and the personal appeal of Reagan enhanced America's reputation. French domestic politics also contributed when the attempt at advancing socialism crashed and "Reaganomics," at least to some French conservatives, briefly seemed attractive. Then there was the craze for American popular culture, especially among young people, and the spectacle of the French government courting the Walt Disney Company and showering awards on Hollywood stars. But one should not be deceived by appearances: these were not two completely different decades.

The contrast at the fin de siècle cannot be described simply as a shift from the balmy 1980s to the chilly 1990s or from America as a model to America as a pariah. This story is too complex for such simplifications because history, in this case, did not occur in neat decadelong packages; because perceptions were complex, nuanced, and fluid; because attitudes varied among different social and political groups; and because when it came to specific issues—such as American television programs—there was a range of responses, some of which were quite hostile. Amiability at the level of state-to-state relations, which itself was rather staged, existed only for brief periods, such as the years 1982–85 or 1989–91, and even these times were marred by serious quarrels. Moreover, Reagan's popularity was ephemeral and his domestic policies failed to inspire. At the same time transatlantic rivalry obstructed French efforts at combating the AIDS epidemic and cost over a thousand lives. Finally, favorable opinion was often informed by basic ambivalence about America and even about Americans. In short, the historian should be cautious in making generalizations about the decade, with one important exception: that of the public's general welcoming posture toward America,

Americans, and American popular culture. This seems indisputable. If the general mood was more comfortable during the 1980s than either before or after, it was nevertheless fragile and, as we shall see, easily upset.

■ Before France could become more welcoming to America there had to be fundamental changes in politics and society. The French had to be liberated from two older narratives about their destiny and they had to come to enjoy the benefits of a more open consumer society. Political change as well as deep socioeconomic transformations opened the way to an appreciation of the American way in the 1980s.

Up to the 1970s Gaullism and communism—two entrenched political ideologies that defined what loyalists believed constituted France's identity, and both remnants of the early postwar era—together commanded the loyalty of roughly half the French electorate. Both, in their own ways, were pillars of anti-Americanism. The peaks of French anti-Americanism following the Second World War occurred in the early 1950s and the during the 1960s: the first was largely the work of the communists and the second that of the Gaullists. The 1970s were something of a transition as these two sources ebbed: their demise was crucial to the transatlantic affability of the Reagan/Bush/Mitterrand years.

Gaullism lost much of its allure after General Charles de Gaulle retired as president of the Fifth Republic in 1969. His call to grandeur seemed rather passé once France had lost its empire, and his plans for remaking Europe lost credibility. He was unable to persuade either the United States or the USSR to end their bipolar hegemony and his effort at reinforcing the Paris-Bonn axis stumbled over the preference of West Germans for the Atlantic Alliance. De Gaulle's attempts at reshaping the incipient European Community, even though he succeeded in vetoing admission of the British, had not brought France the leverage he sought. From the U.S. government's perspective the general was notorious for removing France from NATO's integrated command and challenging the *pax Americana*. After his departure the Gaullist credo based on national independence, an autonomous nuclear force, bal-

ance among the superpowers, and continued presence in traditional
French preserves like Africa survived and formed a consensus among
the French political class, but there was little enthusiasm for appeals to
grandeur, threats to withdraw from the Atlantic Alliance, pronouncements aimed at embarrassing Washington, D.C., or pretensions that
France should be present at every international crisis. Ironically, once
de Gaulle had restored some distance between Paris and Washington
there seemed to be less need to taunt Uncle Sam. The French people
slowly accepted the reality that their country had become a middling
power rather than a competitor with the superpowers and a candidate
for grandeur. By the early 1980s less than a quarter of the French believed their nation was any longer a great power.[1] De Gaulle's successor
Georges Pompidou quietly retreated from the Gaullist creed by admitting the United Kingdom into the European Community; and Valéry
Giscard d'Estaing, who followed Pompidou to the Elysée in 1974, was
not even a Gaullist. Giscard refrained from baiting the Americans and,
in the eyes of diehard Gaullists, abandoned France to Atlanticism.

The decline of the Gaullism carried with it a domestic message—
that state direction of the economy or *dirigisme* had reached its limits.
The Gaullist approach to macroeconomic management and modernization, a strategy that was in great part responsible for the reconstruction
of the economy after World War II, seemed to many to have become
heavy-handed and out-of-date by the 1970s. De Gaulle's presidency featured national economic planning; tightly regulated financial markets;
protection of "strategic sectors," especially from American takeovers;
the elevation of "national champions" (i.e., high-tech companies that
could show the tricolor in global competition); resistance to the hegemony of the dollar; shelters for agriculture and certain noncompetitive
industries; and an integrated Europe closed to Anglo-American influence. Critics from the center and right of the political spectrum and
much of the business community had come to see Gaullist economics
as flawed. France, in their view, needed relief from suffocating state dirigisme that curbed healthy competition, denigrated private profitability,

subsidized lame-duck industries, distorted investment, and stifled entrepreneurship. The pendulum of political economy needed to swing
back toward deregulation and the free market—the direction Margaret
Thatcher and Ronald Reagan were to head. This, however, was not the
view of Gaullism's other critics, Mitterrand's socialists—as we shall see.

A moderation of Gaullist dirigisme was underway in the 1970s.
Presidents Pompidou and Giscard d'Estaing advanced deregulation,
marginalized economic planning, and made state intervention con-
form more closely to market criteria of profitability. Giscard infuriated
traditional Gaullists by exposing vital industrial sectors to American
multinationals. During the administrations of Pompidou and Giscard
the French economy benefited from the expansion of trade within the
new European Community and rapidly opened to markets outside the
continent. When De Gaulle came to power at the end of the 1950s the
share of imports and exports in gross domestic product (GDP) was less
than 10 percent, but by 1980 these shares had climbed to 25 percent.[2]
The realities of the global economy would, in time, teach the socialists
that France needed to streamline dirigisme and take a dose of market
medicine.

To a great extent Gaullism depended for its verve and appeal on the
status and vision of a heroic wartime leader, and the cause lost momentum once the great man left the political scene. The Gaullist party survived, but as a conventional right-wing organization, one among several
conservative parties run by career politicians like Jacques Chirac rather
than as a national movement above partisanship, a rally of all French
men and women, which had been the general's intention. Like an old
Napoleonic battle flag in a military museum, the colors in the banner of
Gaullism had faded by 1980.

The rival grand narrative to Gaullism, that heralded by the French
Communist Party, which formed the hardcore of anti-Americanism on
the far left, was also in disarray by the 1970s. The red star symbolized
by the Soviet Union was no longer at the apex of the firmament: it had
dimmed as the hope of progressives. Revelations of Stalinist gulags and

economic failures, repression of dissent, and sclerotic political leadership had tarnished the reputation of the Soviet way. Equally damaging was Moscow's oppressive control over other communist regimes in Eastern Europe including armed intervention in Czechoslovakia in 1968. Even the vaunted Red Army was humbled in Afghanistan after 1979. In France the Communist Party suffered from similar sclerosis under the leadership of Georges Marchais and from the weight of a nineteenth-century political program featuring the dictatorship of the proletariat. As France deindustrialized—that is, closed coal mines, docks, textile mills, and iron foundries—the industrial working class, the proletariat of Marxism, shrank. Radical student activism and the events of 1968 made the party appear to a young generation as a leftover of a Stalinist past. For intellectuals alignment with the communists was no longer de rigueur. Locked in a sociopolitical ghetto the party suffered from sagging electoral support and in the 1970s faced a revived rival on the left, the rebuilt Socialist Party of François Mitterrand. Because he was afraid of it becoming a junior party, Marchais abandoned what appeared to be a winning electoral alliance with the socialists in 1977. The heroic days of communism were long past.

By the 1970s the ability of traditional Gaullism and communism—two pillars of anti-Americanism—to intoxicate the French polity had crumbled. The path was open to alternatives. The Jacobin socialist model advocated by Mitterrand would be tried in the early 1980s, but it would fail to inspire economic growth and the socialists would be forced to make a right turn toward the market. The American model, our subject, was the other alternative. It became more attractive not only because Gaullism and communism had waned but also because of long-term economic and social changes—in particular, the arrival of consumer society.

What had been derided and dreaded by anti-Americans of earlier generations had become French social reality by the 1970s. The signs were everywhere: consumers possessed the purchasing power to buy consumer durables like automobiles and the latest home appliances. For example, in 1960 only one of four households owned a refrigerator, but fifteen years later nine of ten did; they spent less of their income on necessities and more on comforts, health, communications, and leisure; they shopped at supermarkets, franchise stores (including American outlets), and discount marts; bought on credit; and enjoyed vacations abroad including tours to the United States. And advertising, much of it speaking in American English, was ubiquitous. Affluence, which arrived in the late 1960s, also brought American brand products like Tide detergent, Levi's jeans, Hollywood chewing gum, Marlboro cigarettes, Tupperware, and Hertz rental cars. To the dismay of at least one American couple, by the mid-1970s the French had sacrificed their quaintness: they had adopted frozen food, carpeted floors, dishwashers, shopping centers, and Kleenex.[3] Social mobility accompanied consumer society making the old class distinctions of *bourgeois* and *paysan* seem like archaisms of the last century. Distinct social stratification—though far from absent—had eroded, and sociologists spoke of the new French society, one that was more informal, open, and fluid.[4] *Classe moyenne* replaced *bourgeoisie* just as *agriculteur* ("farmer") replaced *paysan*. Advances in transportation and communication like television brought new physical mobility and easy access to national and world events to the rural populace and eroded parochialism. What modernizers criticized as "the stalled society" of the 1950s was on the move. Traditional markers of identity like the village, the peasantry, and the Catholic Church lost ground, and in this new French society of openness and movement American society seemed closer to home than ever before. Social status, according to the chic set who flirted with Americanization, consisted of the muffled sound of a closing car door. As the Atlantic narrowed, the American model became more relevant.

The clearing of the way for increasing interest in America as sketched here formed the background for amiability. In the foreground, as we shall see, were developments in international affairs, economic policy, intellectual life, and popular culture. The net result was a decade or more of relaxed attitudes.

■ In the 1980s the French said they liked Americans, their society and culture, and they also approved of the United States as an actor in world affairs—even if they harbored reservations and made distinctions among Washington's policies. How the French perceived America was registered in opinion surveys as well as in newspapers, magazines, and other forms of the media. But surveys are the best source for what the public thought given the representative nature of their sampling, the specificity of questions, the connection of attitudes with categories like age and occupation, and the professional and systematic way the material was usually collected. These surveys were mainly conducted by local polling organizations often under contract with newspapers or U.S. government agencies.

When asked to describe themselves, approximately three times as many of the French said they were "pro-American" as those who admitted they were "anti-American."[5] Americans, in the eyes of most, were a generous, industrious, energetic, inventive, decisive, trustworthy, and friendly people who appreciated French history and culture.[6] They were praised for their achievements in science, technology, and information processing and virtually every French person who claimed to have had direct contact with Americans—for example, through travel, education, or friendships—described the experiences favorably.

American society was appreciated much like Americans themselves, but here qualifications entered the Gallic assessment. The descriptive words most commonly evoked were all laudatory: *power*, *dynamism*, *wealth*, and *freedom*. Less complimentary descriptors such as *violence*, *racism*, *inequality*, *moral permissiveness*, and *imperialism* lagged behind. Almost absent were words like *youthful* and *innocent* that historically had described Americans.[7] Like other West Europeans the French gave high marks to American society for economic and social opportunity, law and order, political and religious freedom, and artistic diversity; they gave middling grades for providing all Americans with equal justice and an adequate standard of living; but they awarded awful scores for the care of the sick and the elderly and respect for the rights of ethnic and racial minorities.[8] The French were rather distinctive among West Europeans in finding greater differences between their values and those supposedly held by Americans.[9] Despite these reservations, when asked the hypothetical question, "If you were to leave France, which country would you like to live in?" the United States led others by a wide margin especially among those in their twenties and thirties and among those who associated themselves with the political Right.[10]

Self-professed "anti-Americans" were a durable minority hovering in the range of 15 to 25 percent in this decade, much like such minorities in West Germany, Italy, the Netherlands, and Belgium, but rather less numerous than those in the United Kingdom, Spain, and Greece. Those who held this anti-American reflex among the French diminished slightly between 1982 and 1988 by which date they were considerably less (18 percent) than those recorded in the United Kingdom. Among West European voters in general those attached to left-wing parties were two to three times more likely to consider themselves anti-American, while a tiny fraction of those associated with right-wing parties also expressed such hostility.[11]

American popular culture appealed to the public in the 1980s even though the ruling socialists and some intellectuals insisted that it subverted national identity. Majorities thought that American cinema, clothes, advertising, food, sports, literature, art, and even American English posed little or no problem, but popular music was more divisive and television programming was commonly viewed as invasive.[12] In fact, two of three said they liked American music, cinema, and sports.[13] Americanization, as a cultural phenomenon, simply failed to arouse as much opposition in this decade as it did earlier—or later.

Unlike perceptions of Americans or American society, views of the United States in world affairs were highly volatile. If most assessed bilateral relations as good and thought the United States treated France with "dignity and respect," almost two of three also found the U.S. government domineering, and substantial numbers voiced their disapproval of certain policies like the Reagan administration's unbending adherence to the strong dollar or its aid to the anti-Sandinistas in Nicaragua.[14] The United States ranked near the top, along with West Germany, Belgium, and Canada, as one of France's closest friends while Iran, Libya, and the Soviet Union were singled out as its principal enemies. When asked specifically if they felt rather friendly or unfriendly toward the United States, a majority said friendly, a handful voiced an unfriendly opinion, and a third said "neither." Once again, expressions of friendship came more from those associated with right-wing parties and slightly more approval came from the young and from business managers and farmers.[15] In most polls unfavorable attitudes ranged from 14 to 30 percent, which corresponded closely to the number of those who professed being anti-American.

■ François Mitterrand had to wait a long time before he became the first socialist president of the Fifth Republic in 1981. He had first run for the presidency against Charles de Gaulle in 1965 and compounded this defeat with two more setbacks in 1969 and again in 1974 in a close run off against Valéry Giscard d'Estaing. Raised as a Catholic, his student affiliations were with the Right and he began his political career during the Second World War when he maneuvered between the Vichy regime and the resistance. During the Fourth Republic (1946–58), which was infamous for its instability, he served as a cabinet minister in several left-center governments, enhancing his reputation as a political survivor. Under the Fifth Republic Mitterrand became an outspoken critic of President de Gaulle, and in the 1970s joined and renovated the Socialist Party, moving it toward a steely anticapitalism and collaboration with the Communist Party. His reputation was that of the consummate politician, a clever and ruthless tactician, and an opportunist rather than an ideologue, yet a man of courage, conviction, and patience—an enigmatic figure, or, as he was sometimes labeled. "the Florentine."

As he described himself, Mitterrand was a friend of the American people. The heroes and ideals of the American Revolution, he said, had stirred him as a child and, later, as president he was thrilled to visit Williamsburg, Virginia, with its evocations of the Founding Fathers.[16] He also made several private visits to the United States after the war—the first in 1946 when the sight of New York City from the air reminded him, strangely, of a Renaissance painting. On the one hand he had an idealized vision of America, the land of freedom and creativity; on the other hand, he detested Wall Street, the Pentagon, the urban ghettos, and the war in Vietnam. But he was never interested in America it-self—for example, society or politics—or American culture except for literature: he was familiar with the adventure stories of James Oliver Curwood as well as social critics like John Steinbeck and contemporary writers like William Styron.[17]

As the fates of international politics would have it, François Mitter-rand had to work with Ronald Reagan for his entire first term (1981–88) as president of the Fifth Republic. A socialist who promised to break with capitalism, a cultivated author with philosophical pretensions, a rather provincial Frenchman who was not close to the United States, a party leader who had not been a partisan of NATO, and a politician known for his devious ways faced, in the White House, a conservative Republican, a champion of free enterprise, a patriot who intended to assert American leadership, and a former actor not known for either refined tastes or cosmopolitan interests who affected an affable and straightforward demeanor. The Florentine and the Cowboy were an unpromising pairing for a harmonious political script. Yet Mitterrand's Elysée Palace and Reagan's White House, despite mutual suspicion, some cagey maneuvering, and several public spats, managed to main-tain cordial relations.

Ronald Reagan's victory in 1980 over Jimmy Carter was more per-plexing than surprising to the French. Assessing the presidential race the French press viewed Carter as a weak candidate for reelection. The prestigious left-center daily *Le Monde* described the Democratic incum-bent as intelligent, informed, and well-meaning, but indecisive and too idealistic.[18] During his presidency the White House appeared adrift and weak; witness the continued embarrassment over American hostages in

Tehran. It was only at the end of his term, in the view of *Le Monde*, that Carter grasped the Soviet danger. In the conservative *Le Figaro Magazine* one columnist, on the eve of the election, not only assailed Carter's pursuit of détente with the Soviets but complained about the decline of culture, civility, and the virile pioneering spirit among Americans in general during the 1970s.[19] Carter's America seemed to represent the decline of American power both hard and soft. The public, as opposed to the media, had a favorable opinion of Carter as a person, finding him honest, moral, personable, and trustworthy.[20] But polls showed that a majority lacked confidence in his foreign policy and almost as many thought U.S. prestige had declined.[21] Carter's agonizing over the hostages and his innocence in dealing with the Soviets had dimmed his reputation. The French reacted with indifference to his defeat. But Reagan's victory caught attention.

The French media greeted Reagan's election in 1980 with snickers, curiosity, and apprehension. One headline from the left-leaning daily *Libération* mockingly read, "In association with Warner Brothers, the State of California, and the Republican Party, *Libération* presents Ronald Reagan in an American blockbuster 'The Empire Strikes Back.'"[22] The new occupant of the White House was inexperienced, puzzling, and unfamiliar. He had been snubbed by the government of Giscard d'Estaing when he visited Paris in 1978. The press filled columns with references to the cowboy president, the TV huckster, the aging Hollywood actor—"an old star is born," one quipped. There was apprehension about both Reagan's economic and foreign policies: Would he face up to the international economic crisis that was dragging down Europe? Would he let the market run roughshod? Would he turn back the welfare state and damage workers' rights? Would he, in his effort to make American strong, act belligerently toward the Soviets?

Why had the Americans chosen Reagan? The French media attributed it to nostalgia. Pretending to speak for the American voter, *Libération* commented, "We've had enough of Jimmy Carter. He's not a bad guy, but he doesn't understand where we want to go. He's weak and doesn't know how to lead. He thinks you can work with the enemy. . . . We don't feel safe with him. Please Ronnie take us home." "Home" meant returning to the halcyon 1950s when America was still the most powerful nation in the world, when the Organization of Petroleum Exporting Countries didn't matter, when racial tensions didn't exist, when the minimum wage didn't cause unemployment; all that was needed was "the spirit of initiative and courage, which has always been the grandeur of the American people, to put everything in order."[23] As the paper saw it, the Americans were waiting for a superhero to save them, and this explained Reagan's election.

Where one might have expected enthusiasm, on the right, there was at best cautious approval. *Le Figaro* spoke optimistically of "a new Eisenhower" and an end to years of vacillation, but worried that the president-elect was prone to simplistic answers on complex issues.[24] Right-leaning politicians welcomed a more resolute president who would not tolerate Soviet expansionism. Jacques Chirac, then mayor of Paris, said the election demonstrated that "the American people refused to fade away."[25] But no one was sure of what to expect of the new occupant of the White House.

Anxiety and curiosity marked the Left's response to the 1980 election. Without hesitation socialist leaders opened fire. Laurent Fabius, a future Socialist Party minister and prime minister, thought the new president was oblivious to the problems of the Third World, and his assertion of U.S. leadership through military strength risked confrontations. Jean-Pierre Chevènement, another future minister for Mitterrand, warned about the danger of rising international tension given the "imperialist" convictions of Reagan.[26] The Republican victory, it was feared by some socialists, opened the way to reactionaries like the Moral Majority. *Le Monde* was only slightly less worried than the socialists. The election represented simultaneously a "patriotic, interventionist, and isolationist earthquake."[27] Transatlantic relations were threatened by a president who believed you could eliminate differences by speaking loudly, taking a hard line toward Moscow, and forcing Europeans to align with the policies of Washington, D.C. There were larger issues: Would Reagan adopt a pugnacious and unrestrained form of American interventionism or retreat into "fortress America"? Would Europeans profit from a strong United States willing to face the Soviets, or would they suffer from American domination?

For the first two years of Reagan's tenure, French perceptions of the United States were no more upbeat than they had been under Jimmy Carter. A majority blamed Reagan's policies—for example, high interest rates—for harming the French economy.[28] Dissatisfaction with transatlantic economic relations ranged across the entire political spectrum.[29] As for attractive foreign prototypes, when asked in 1981 which model of socioeconomic reform would be best for France, most of those surveyed chose social democracy as represented by West Germany or Sweden while only a small number (17 percent) preferred following American "liberal capitalism."[30] The deep recession that accompanied the first two years of Reagan's administration confirmed French suspicions.

Then, rather quickly, perceptions brightened. The American success at creating jobs after 1982 and Washington's tough diplomatic stance won approval from the French. Books and articles began to appear praising the economic accomplishments of the Reagan administration. Given rising Cold War tension, the French were reassured that the United States would protect them in the event of a confrontation with the Soviet Union. Most unusual was the absence of fear of American domination. In 1984, half of those surveyed were not worried about Washington's interference in French foreign policy and slightly less expressed anxiety about interference in economic affairs.[31] Apprehension of Yankee domination faded in spite of the bolder posture of Washington.

The management of the economy under the Reagan administration attracted considerable comment and made some converts, but it also inspired skepticism and criticism. No one could deny that so-called Reaganomics had produced impressive results: gone was the depressing "stagflation" of the 1970s. The conservative media took some pleasure in listing American achievements after 1982: the creation of a million jobs, a fall in inflation, strong economic growth, a buoyant entrepreneurial spirit, lower taxes, and fewer regulations. Such glowing assessments were often made with either an implicit or explicit comparison to the poor performance of the French economy under the socialists: the Yankees were doing better.

Reaganomics inspired a few prominent French followers. Guy Sorman, a lecturer at Sciences Po and a columnist/author, was perhaps the best known. [32] Reagan's election, to him, was the turning point in a global shift toward economic liberalism. ("Liberalism" in the European lexicon has the opposite meaning of the term as used by Americans: it refers to a market oriented economy and an aversion to state intervention.) Sorman borrowed heavily from the Chicago school of economics (e.g., that of Friedrich Hayek), celebrated supply-side economics, cited neoconservatives like Norman Podhoretz, and wrote ardently about both Jerry Falwell's Moral Majority and the advent of computers. "The neoconservative ideology is at present the only Western model that successfully unites morality and the microprocessor." [33] His message was simple; he was against socialism, bureaucracy, big government, and technocrats and he was for free enterprise, individual initiative, and the market. Since the motor of the economy was the entrepreneurial spirit, which the Americans embodied, he recommended that the French deregulate their economy and adopt an "optimistic liberal ideology." [34] "Reagan the simple cowboy has become the devil for some of the Left," Sorman wrote, because "he crystallizes a coherent ideological system that is an effective counter to the socialist model." [35] President Reagan returned the compliment by citing Sorman in a 1984 speech at his alma mater in Illinois as one of the French thinkers who "are rejecting the old clichés about state power and rediscovering the danger such power poses to personal freedom." [36]

Reaganomics attracted other French fans. Philippe Lefournier, writing for *L'Expansion*, a major business review, praised the United States as "the first country to emerge from the great 'crisis' of capitalism" and spoke of the "exciting future" of the nation that had "married high-tech with the old spirit of enterprise and an awakened patriotism."[37] Louis Pauwels, the director of *Le Figaro Magazine*, paired Ronald Reagan with Pope Jean Paul II as the two great contemporary "charismatic leaders of human freedom."[38] As a disciple of American neoconservatives, Pauwels proselytized for market liberalism because it was the natural human order, because it assured prosperity, and because it was based on Christian principles. He urged the French to admit that Reaganomics worked, that socialism had failed, and that learning from America meant cutting taxes, relying on private initiative, and taking pride in national and traditional values. Even the Left, on occasion, was complimentary, or as *Libération* observed, grudgingly, "Less State, fewer taxes, more optimism: the Reagan recipe was simple, even simplistic, but it has worked."[39] A virtual tour of Parisian bookstores, conducted by *Le Nouvel Observateur*, demonstrated the popularity of titles like those by Sorman celebrating market liberalism, including translations of the "anarcho-Reaganite" Milton Friedman. Writing for this review Alain Minc, a young economist and corporate manager, warned the "French Reaganites" against expecting miracles from the market, yet he advised his socialist friends that "the Left will be liberal or it will not survive."[40]

If the press invariably pointed out the obvious shortcoming of Reaganomics like big budget deficits, it tended to evaluate these as less important than its accomplishments.[41] The only question was, Why had the Americans succeeded? And here the answers scattered. The possibilities were many: a strong dollar, lower taxes, deregulation, deficit spending, new technologies like computers, industrial redeployment, a flexible labor market, immigrant workers, an expanding service sector, and/or a probusiness atmosphere. Or, as Jude Wanniski, the originator of the expression "supply-side economics" simply answered, "Be confident in long term investment, in enterprise, and in individuals. You will see how well it works. Even Mitterrand understands it."[42]

Not all conservatives, however, were pro-Reagan enthusiasts. Sorman lamented that the "intellectual and political Right" were too *diri-*

giste to accept Reagan's liberalism.[43] A popular and otherwise sympathetic book on Americans written by the New York correspondent for *Le Figaro* disdained Reagan's social and environmental policies.[44] Some experts were not convinced that American methods were transferable to Europe. They pointed out the unique position of the dollar, the openness of the American economy, the perils of deficits, and French dependence on the state.[45] Should we imitate the Americans, even if we could? some asked. Or, as one business journal put it, "Our old country often envies the benefits of the American model while forgetting the basis on which it is built, the sacrifices and the dynamism it assumes. . . . Young Americans have bet on optimism, work, ambition, personal independence, a taste for challenge, family, and the United States," with the consequence of creating a generation of egotistical careerists.[46]

The moderate and left-wing press mocked the American "soap bubble" economy built on huge budgetary and commercial deficits, growing social inequality, cutbacks in social assistance, brutal layoffs in rust belt industries, high interest rates, "McJobs" (low-level, part-time work in fast-food outlets), and protectionism.[47] Nicole Bernheim, the correspondent in New York for *Le Monde,* indicted Reagan for shredding America's already tattered social safety net, widening inequality, and deepening discontent among minorities. The plight of the unemployed in northern cities who trekked off looking for jobs reminded her of Steinbeck's *The Grapes of Wrath.* Reagan simplified issues, like calling the USSR the evil empire, to win the support of the American heartland: he had revived the Left's caricature of Uncle Sam as rich, ignorant, and selfish. Bernheim reported that the French who had fled the socialists after 1981 to make their fortune in the United States had discovered the precariousness and expense of life under "wild capitalism" and were ready to go home.[48] The left-leaning weekly *Le Nouvel Observateur* offered a mixed assessment that, in the end, was more hostile than generous. It credited Reagan with engineering recovery, conceded that France should import America's entrepreneurial élan, and noted how the socialist government was interested in learning from the Americans—but it scorned Reaganism for its methods and its costs. In order to kick-start growth, "Reagan the ruthless" (*Reagan l'Impitoyable*), as he was lampooned, had encouraged cruel restructuring in sectors like the automobile industry, which had forced the mayor of Detroit to rely on nightly curfews to keep order. The American "miracle," as far as this review was concerned, was built on deficits, the impoverishment of the marginal, an artificially strong currency, and selfishness: "to live as an American, is, above all, to live for yourself."[49] The prototype of Reagan's economy were the "yuppies," the children of "baby boomers," whom the Left, updating the historical stereotype of Americans, caricatured as overly planned, materialistic go-getters who had no time for vacations, enjoyment, or marriage and possibly preferred physical exercise to sex.[50]

International affairs will be discussed in detail in chapter 3, but a brief note is helpful here. At first the French thought poorly of the Reagan administration's international posture; a majority in late 1982, mainly among socialists and communists, but also some associated with the Right, volunteered a very, or rather, "bad opinion" of America's position in world affairs.[51] But attitudes improved dramatically between 1982 and 1984 among men and women, among all ages and occupations, and for those associated with both the Left and the Right, and this image remained flattering, in the range of 70 percent, through the early years of the administration of President George H. W. Bush. On the eve of the fall of the Berlin Wall the French viewed the United States as warmly as did the West Germans and the British.[52] But this pretty picture needs shading. The French welcomed the assurances given by the Reagan administration that the United States would come to their assistance if the Soviets threatened, but this appreciation was hardly novel: the French had about the same level of confidence in Jimmy Carter in 1977.[53] And Reagan's international stance never commanded a majority. In 1984 he won less support for his overall policy than had Carter.[54] Reagan's strong stand against the Soviet Union divided the French into thirds: for, against, and no opinion.[55]

The electoral campaign and eventual reelection of Ronald Reagan in November 1984 offered the French an opportunity to assess his achievements. In that year Reagan's reputation peaked; early disdain had virtually disappeared. Still, skepticism remained the rule.

President Reagan's standing within the Hexagon by 1984 was marginally better than that of his immediate predecessors in the White House and certainly higher among the French than it was among other West Europeans. When asked in late October for whom, if they had the vote, they would cast their ballot, 38 percent of the French selected Ronald Reagan and 25 percent preferred his opponent, Walter Mondale—but 37 percent gave no response.[56] In other words, those who were indifferent were almost as numerous as those who "voted" for him. This choice was, nevertheless, relatively strong compared to the tepid support given Presidents Richard Nixon, Gerald Ford, and Jimmy Carter before him—though Carter had his advocates—and to that awarded George H. W. Bush in the 1988 election. And Reagan's 38 percent backing was uniformly firm among men and women, among all age groups, and for almost all occupations; the anomalies were relatively higher support among businesspeople, from shopkeepers to top managers, but relatively low approval from farmers. A comparison among West Europeans revealed much cooler attitudes among West Germans and the British, who split their "votes" almost equally between Mondale and Reagan.[57] More French men and women in 1984 thought of themselves as pro-American, as opposed to anti-American (44 percent versus 15 percent) than did West Germans (35 percent versus 19 percent) or the British (39 percent versus 20 percent). But this international comparison can be readily explained: it was Reagan's foreign policy. Far more of the West Germans and the British than the French thought his policies had increased the chance of war.[58] Reagan's strong stance against the Soviets, as we shall see, was more welcome in France.

Analyzing Reagan's reelection, *Le Monde* editorialized that Americans wanted an "homme sympathique," a seemingly kind, good-humored leader, and likened him to "a grandfather of their dreams" who, though a bit old-fashioned and even doddering, offered order and stability in a rapidly changing world.[59] In fact, Reagan also appealed on the personal level to many French men and women. They liked his rosy demeanor, and his message of "morning in America" traveled easily. The press wrote approvingly of Americans' enthusiasm for their president's amiability, optimism, good sense, self-assurance, and courage. Columnists contrasted the new mood of confidence in the United States in 1984 with the vacillation and soul-searching of Carter and with the morose mood of the Nixon and Ford years. One news magazine drew the contrast this way: the seizure of American hostages in Tehran had lost Carter the trust of many Americans and opened the way for Reagan, who represented "the Zorro of justice and vengeance."[60]

"The French prefer Reagan to Reaganism," as *Le Monde* put it.[61] If the French tended to approve of the president, they were far less enthusiastic about his domestic policies despite his achievements, such as creating jobs. For most, Reaganomics—given its partiality for the market and its harsh treatment of the less privileged—was not seen as an antidote to French economic or social problems. Only one in four of those polled in 1984 wanted France to imitate Reagan's social and economic policies.[62] Virtually every social category, from managers and professionals to workers and farmers, turned thumbs down on adopting such programs. The French thought the aspect of American society that had deteriorated most between 1982 and 1987 was that of the care of the sick and elderly, and this deterioration was attributed to retrenchment in social spending.[63] Reagan's economic success could not convince many of the French to tamper with their social model.

The most compelling explanation for Reagan's popularity in the mid-1980s is also the simplest: it was largely a matter of political partisanship. His "voters" were mainly, but not exclusively, French conservatives. Reagan's economic and social policies generally made the French apprehensive except for those aligned with the Right. Partisanship determined positive and negative answers to a survey that asked about opinions of the United States in the world; it was those aligned with the two conservative parties that most eagerly nodded their approval.[64] Jacques Chirac, the head of the Gaullist Rassemblement pour la République (RPR), hailed the American electorate for rejecting the mood of doubt and decline and electing "a man who by his convictions, actions, and style represents a voluntaristic and dynamic conception of the United States" and added, "The economic and military renewal of American power is going to continue and permit France and Europe to count on a respected ally conscious of its responsibilities."[65] This partisan response found an echo in the conservative press with one editorialist in *Le Figaro* anticipating Reagan's reelection, noting, "France and Europe will be thrilled at a Republican victory, not just because of the very sympathetic personality of Reagan, but because we will see in his success proof that the United States remains committed to a renewal of "American values" like "courage, the spirit of enterprise, and individualism linked to a sense of civic duty."[66] The right-wing press lavishly praised Reagan for his contribution to his country's recent economic recovery, which undoubtedly reflected some backlash against Mitterrand's failed interventionist economic policies that had rebounded in Reagan's favor. By 1984 France and the United States seemed headed in opposite directions, and Reagan's team looked far better than the socialists did as economic managers. Thus, when polled about the "ultraliberal" or Reaganlike policies, referring specifically to a reduction of state intervention, it was supporters of the Right who gave the strongest affirmative responses.[67] French conservatives liked the Reagan message: "Government is not the solution to our problems, it *is* the problem." The head of the national federation of employers applauded Reagan's victory as an inspiration for France from a people who knew how "to roll up their shirt sleeves" and the center-right Union pour la Démocratie Française (UDF) called the election results a victory for economic liberalism and private initiative rather than the state.[68] Jean-Marie Le Pen, head of the extreme right-wing party, the Front National, stated that "his model" was Reagan.[69]

In contrast, Lionel Jospin, the secretary-general of the French Socialist Party, disparaged Reagan's reelection, calling attention to the
high number of abstentions, and admonishing, "The conservative and
puritanical America of Reagan in the next four years better take into account others, others at home and others in the world."[70] *Le Monde* held
back any endorsement and gave a balanced accounting, calling Reagan
a "Super Pinay" (referring to the conservative French prime minister of
the 1950s) who brought down inflation and created jobs, but at the price
of large deficits that might undermine his achievements.[71]

It would be unfair to confine President Reagan's support in France
to political and economic conservatives. To some extent he commanded
admiration, or at least grudging respect, in the mid-1980s from a wide
swath of the population who might not have "voted" for him but who
liked his persona as well as certain aspects of his policies—especially
how the American economy flourished under his tutelage and, to a
lesser extent, how he dealt with the Cold War. Whereas almost half the
French population thought the United States had overcome the economic crisis in early 1984, virtually no one thought France had done
so—including most on the left.[72] Economic performance mattered. The
socialists' faltering management of the economy in the early 1980s unintentionally boosted Reagan's image. But political reputations are tran-
sient and Reagan's stock would fall before the end of his second term.

■ Reagan's economic model was largely irrelevant to the policies pursued
by French president François Mitterrand—at least initially. Yet within
two years the socialists took notice and once the conservatives under
Jacques Chirac regained the premiership in 1986 free-market liberalism was in vogue. But Reaganomics was not a major reference for either
Mitterrand or Chirac. French economic and social policy, as one would
expect, was almost entirely driven by domestic issues, internal politics,
and economic developments while Anglo-American market liberalism
remained suspect even to Chirac and the Gaullists. Nevertheless, America was watched, and it functioned as a standard of measurement for

economic performance. Mitterrand's government wanted, according to Diana Pinto, to demonstrate that "real socialism" could offer an alternative to "flabby social democracy," Soviet totalitarianism, and "American economic imperialism."[73]

After his election in 1981 Mitterrand set out to introduce "socialism with a human face"—hardly a program to endear him to the America of Ronald Reagan. After decades of sitting on the sidelines of the political life of the Fifth Republic, the newly elected socialists, along with their communist partners, were eager to introduce their agenda, which featured a daring effort to relaunch the economy and an ambitious social program that would mark a "rupture with capitalism." The stagnation of the 1970s—triggered by the energy crisis, which had brought sagging growth and unemployment—could be reversed, or so the Left thought, with ramped up public spending, extensive nationalizations, aid for the least favored members of society, and strengthened labor at the plant level. "Reflation," or pumping up demand, meant, among other tactics, raising the minimum wage, cutting the workweek to thirty-nine hours, adding a fifth week of paid vacation, encouraging early retirement, raising social benefits, and adding to the public payroll. The wealthy would contribute to recovery by paying a special tax. The driver of recovery would be a vastly enlarged public sector encompassing almost the entire banking system. Among the newly nationalized firms were investment banks like Paribas and nearly a dozen major industrial groups, including high-tech firms like the aeronautics manufacturer Dassault-Breguet and the Compagnie Générale d'Electricité. These nationalized companies were to receive large capital inputs, streamline their structures, and raise France to the top of international competition in the most advanced sectors of industry. Mitterrand's France was heading in the opposite direction of the Anglo-Americans in 1981: where Reagan and Thatcher took aim at inflation, Mitterrand targeted unemployment and growth. The former embraced tight money, deregulation, and tax relief; the latter preferred spending, nationalizations, and a tax on the rich.

Mitterrand's team assumed the world economy was about to bounce back and that France could count on rising exports and lower interest rates. This was a losing gamble. By mid-1982 it was evident that the international economy was still in the doldrums. Foreign imports—especially expensive dollar-denominated petroleum products—poured into France, and exports found few buyers. As a consequence there was a galloping deficit in trade, steeply rising budget deficits, price inflation, and stubborn unemployment. Even a series of devaluations had little effect. The government under the premiership of Pierre Mauroy (1981–84) had to face the prospect of abandoning its brave program of a rupture with capitalism and instead embrace austerity. By 1983 tax increases, price controls, spending cuts, business profitability, and a strong franc had become the way out. As one authority has described it, "the year 1983 . . . marked the end of the socialist economic project both as ideology and as policy."[74]

A new socialist prime minister, Laurent Fabius (1984–86), who formed a government without communist participation, advanced economic liberalization—with a socialist face—even further. He hailed modernization and entrepreneurship and helped business expand so it could create jobs. Fabius, who had been Mauroy's minister of industry, openly expressed his interest in developments in the United States. To some on the left, his button-down shirts marked him as an Americanizer. Stronger evidence of his sympathies came when he initiated negotiations with the Walt Disney Company in 1985 to bring its proposed leisure park to France. Fabius also commissioned an extensive report on comparative technology policies: it used the example of Silicon Valley to recommend greater reliance on the private sector for developing technologies like those in the information sector.[75] He boldly asserted, "The private sector is predominant in France and it is going to stay that way."[76] Fabius reflected the country's new mood. Entrepreneurship, profits, and CEOs, according to opinion surveys, were increasingly favored: one management consulting firm found that virtually everyone believed that an improvement in the economy required first that French enterprises become more competitive, and a large majority thought that regulations on companies had to be reduced.[77]

The socialists under Mitterrand and Fabius were eager to do whatever was necessary, even if this meant borrowing from Reagan's America and embracing entrepreneurship, to avoid defeat in the 1986 legislative elections. "America, even among the Socialists, that's what's chic," *Le Nouvel Observateur* proclaimed.[78] The government was thrilled to learn that surveys showed that two million French citizens wanted to start their own companies. Jacques Attali, Mitterrand's adviser, visited Washington, D.C., and spoke with officials like Donald Regan, the secretary of the treasury, about American success. Jacques Delors, the minister of finance and principal adviser on economics to Mitterrand, in 1984 called for "a French modernization à l'américaine." Wholesale imitation was not in order, but a healthy dose of American competitiveness, carefully applied, was. Thus, Fabius tolerated massive layoffs at the Citroën and Talbot plants, but they were to be gradual and accompanied by job training because the government refused to apply what some called the "American logic" of massive firings.

The most explicit expression of interest in the American economy, muted by a stout defense of socialist policy, came during Mitterrand's formal state visit to the United States in March 1984. In Washington, D.C., he spoke to a joint session of Congress where, after praising the American War of Independence and the Atlantic Alliance, he appealed to his audience by describing the French economy as competitive, one that "preferred risk—good risk, modernity to comfort," and noted that brakes had been applied to inflation and state intervention. After a visit to the White House and a stop in Atlanta, Mitterrand flew to California for his now famous visit to Silicon Valley, where he and his team inquired about venture capital, start-ups, scientific and technological research, academic and industrial linkage, and solar energy. One reason for this visit, according to his staff, was to impress the French on the need for scientific research and investment.[79] After a visit to a farm in Illinois where he displayed his agricultural savoir faire by posing with a baby pig, Mitterrand addressed the Economic Club of New York; to this assembly of business leaders he presented the French economy as more open and dynamic than his audience probably imagined. Mitterrand was on the defensive because France faced serious inflation and deficits despite—or more likely because of—his aggressive interventionism and massive nationalizations. Trying to calm his audience's concerns he wryly announced, "We [socialists] have not burned the churches, closed factories, or dropped the iron curtain."[80] Nor, he noted, had they collectivized the economy; in fact, they had created 80,000 companies recently and now welcomed American investors. To American businesspeople who owned companies in France and were, for whatever reason, unhappy, he said, "Come see me. We'll take care of you." Even though he asserted there would be no further nationalizations, he still encountered skepticism among his listeners, who asked him about the weak franc, state intervention, protectionism, and the difficulties of hiring and firing employees.

Liberalization and modest borrowing from the Americans was in Mitterrand's view consistent with socialism, but America was not a model. Modernization and industrial restructuring, he argued after his return from the United States, aimed at supplying the domestic market and gaining international competitiveness had long been his goal.[81] He said he had no grief with entrepreneurs and "just profits"—meaning gains made by innovation, work, and savings that created wealth for everyone—but he did not concede on his larger agenda: nationalizations marked a "rupture with capitalism" and the "mixed economy" was a transition to socialism. The balance between the public and private sectors in the mixed economy meant France would not subscribe either to "English ultraliberalism or Chinese collectivism." In the course of his tour of the United States, Mitterrand had taken a swipe at the Reagan administration's economic policy—especially the budget deficits and high interest rates that harmed Europeans. When asked what lessons he found applicable to France, he responded coyly by complimenting the American people on their energy and inventiveness, singling out, as an example, the cooperation between academic research and private entrepreneurs. But he took issue with calling America a model economy because it benefited from a privileged situation—the size of its market and role of the dollar—and because "the American recovery has been accompanied by considerable disorder and is based on a few tricks [*quelques artifices*]." "I admire the virtues of these people," he concluded, but the lesson was that France needed to reorganize its own way and not imitate America.

Efforts at turning the economy around, which included stimulus via market incentives, gradually began to show results, but they were not sufficient to convince the French that the socialists were good managers. Mitterrand's reputation plummeted, even among fellow socialists who felt betrayed by *rigueur*, making him the most unpopular president of the Fifth Republic to that date. By the mid-1980s the vocabulary associated with the Left—words like *socialism* and *nationalization*—aroused more hostility than approval, while terms like *competition* and *free market* that were favored by economic liberals were fashionable. Polls showed that the majority of those surveyed, including most socialists, now wanted the development of private enterprise rather than the public sector and that the people also placed the health of businesses ahead of raising individuals' standards of living.[82] Majorities wanted to privatize industrial groups that had been recently nationalized and preferred easing social charges on businesses—even at the cost of some social protection. A plurality asked for a reduction of state intervention in economic and social affairs. One business journal crowed that the French seemed finally to have discovered economic orthodoxy as a reaction to socialist failure.[83]

Disappointment with Socialists' efforts at economic revival led directly to their defeat in the legislative elections of 1986. Mitterrand was forced to name Jacques Chirac, the leader of the Gaullist RPR, as his prime minister, and the Fifth Republic embarked on its first experiment with "cohabitation"—that is, with a president and prime minister belonging to opposing parties. The socialist president stepped aside and allowed Chirac, with a few exceptions, to pursue an antisocialist program that undid much of what had been introduced between 1981 and 1982. Leading the way was the sweeping privatization of many of the firms that the socialists had nationalized, along with tax cuts, including abolishing the new wealth tax; deregulation; the easing of rules on hiring and firing; and a general turn toward bolstering private enterprise and invigorating the market. Economic liberalism was in vogue as interest in the Anglo-American model peaked. What had begun with the socialists during 1983–85 as a grudging concession to the market now became a principle of good governance.

Within Chirac's governing coalition, which included the UDF and its affiliates, were some eager free-market ideologues. Younger UDF leaders, like François Léotard, occupied the Ministry of Culture and Communication while Alain Madelin became head of the Ministry of Industry; he rather overreached by proclaiming that "today, everyone is a liberal."[84] The RPR also had a few true-blue liberals, like Philippe Séguin at the Ministry of Social Affairs. But the ideologues were not the dominant faction in the new government; that role belonged to more moderate, or pragmatic, liberals like Chirac himself and his finance minister Édouard Balladur, who represented the dirigiste strain in the Gaullist party derived from their mentor Georges Pompidou; they were less committed in principle to the self-regulating market, but viewed reforms that advanced competitiveness and private enterprise as politically and economically useful. As Balladur famously remarked, "Good sense should temper liberalism."[85]

Laissez-faire, laissez-passer as a basis for economic policy has a long history in France even though, ironically, its most fervent advocates have always been the Anglo-Americans. It was no different at the end of the twentieth century when Reagan and Thatcher led the way and Chirac limped behind. The rebirth of what was called "new liberalism" during the 1970s and '80s was almost entirely a product of French concerns and traditions and owed rather little to the Anglo-Americans except for a few popularizers like Sorman who, as we have seen, opted to import the Chicago school. The new liberals, whose reputation soared in the mid-1980s—mainly economists close to the employers' movement like Michel Drancourt and Octave Gélinier or businesspeople like Yvon Gattaz—were largely homegrown. These Gallic true believers, according to Suzanne Berger, arrived at their convictions from an aversion for socialism and communism, a distrust of technocrats, and a concern about an ambient anticapitalism.[86] They received an enormous boost from widespread frustration with the interventionist reforms and economic disappointments of socialist governance after 1981. Internal political and economic dynamics created the liberal moment of 1986–88 while the successes of Reagan and Thatcher served, at most, to embolden French proponents.

If the causes of a resurgent liberalism were entirely French, so was the content of their program; it was not a bland copy of that of either the American or British conservatives. For example, French new liberals accepted a far larger role for the state as the guardian of the general good over private interests than did the advocates of Reaganomics or Thatcherism. They assumed that the market, if left unattended, would logically end up in *libéralisme sauvage* and thus attributed a substantial role to government for addressing social problems like poverty and income inequalities.[87]

The French public endorsed the liberal turn as long as it was strongly flavored with dirigisme and deferred to Republican solidarity. A week after the 1986 election a national survey demonstrated the electorate was prepared for only a modest turn toward the market and remained strongly attached to social protection: if a majority was ready for an end to price controls and privatization of big firms, an equal number or more wanted to retain administrative regulation of layoffs, the new tax on wealth, and endorsed increased aid to large families.[88] Even businesspeople, who opted for denationalization and deregulation, wanted to retain the minimum wage.[89]

Economic liberalism within Chirac's governing circle, except for a tiny cohort of ministers, displayed little of the ideological zest of the new liberals. In the hands of Chirac and Balladur, liberalism was more a practical approach to problems than it was a matter of principle or dogma: it could get a stalled economy moving and function as a powerful weapon against socialist rivals. Chirac himself never subscribed fully to the liberal credo and employed market-oriented policies opportunistically. One should be skeptical about his pronouncements as prime minister, such as his claim that "statism and bureaucracy are in the past. The future belongs to free and independent private enterprise" or his earlier endorsement of Reagan and Thatcher declaring that "the only problem with liberalism is that in France it has never been tried."[90] Yet when the government's economic policies faltered, Chirac blamed Balladur for being "too liberal."[91] Years later, at the end of his long career, Chirac would tell an interviewer that liberalism, like communism, was a perversion of human thought, led to the same excesses, and was destined to failure.[92] Even a loyal disciple of the Anglo-Americans like the Gaullist Philippe Séguin was circumspect about the market. As minister of social affairs Séguin promoted studies of the American economy aimed especially at finding answers to unemployment. Séguin managed to open the labor market with legislation that, among other reforms, softened the requirement of administrative authorization for layoffs. But even he was reluctant to import Reaganomics, pointing out the risks of tactics like deregulation.[93] The truest of the ideological liberals, Alain Madelin, went to such an extreme in refusing to rescue embattled firms and pruning his own budget that he ended up isolated among Chirac's ministers, who liked to mute their Reaganesque impulses with activism like subsidizing ailing industries and aiding companies in hiring young workers. If the most important liberal departure of the 1980s was the privatizations of industrial firms, banks, and television stations, the way Chirac and Balladur managed the process—for example, by apportioning shares of denationalized firms—was far more interventionist than the way Thatcher achieved the same goal.[94] Stanley Hoffmann wrote at the time, "The state is loosening the screws, not removing them."[95] Dirigisme was alive, if rather anemic, even when the liberals ruled.

Well before the presidential election in 1988 the French flirtation with free-market liberalism had flagged. It had brought only mediocre economic results—for example, failing to reduce unemployment or revive growth—and it had antagonized many with its apparent favoritism to the wealthy. It had also left many indifferent because its reforms were so cautious that Chirac seemed little different from his "liberalized" socialist predecessor Laurent Fabius. Then in 1987, Wall Street collapsed, and that collapse carried with it much of the prestige of the "American way" and its French fans. One beneficiary of Chirac's stumble was Mitterrand, who worked his magic, regained popularity and the presidency in 1988, and returned a socialist—Michel Rocard—to the head of government. Opponents of Chirac's liberal turn massively backed Mitterrand and the socialists.[96]

For the rest of the decade (1988–91) economic policy was in the hands of Rocard, who practiced a sober, if not austere, kind of socialism that was closer to the policies pursued during 1983–85 than to the "rupture" of 1981–82. The new premier attracted a formidable following among American experts on French affairs. In fact, the Radical Left tried to denigrate Rocard by associating him with America. But he was no economic liberal; as Mitterrand's agriculture minister he had been an outspoken critic of Reagan's economic and trade policies.[97] Rocard was a cautious socialist who aimed at solid, incremental gains. Ideology and ruptures, whether in the form of socialism or liberalism, gave way to pragmatism and the "mixed economy" that featured participation for entrepreneurs, the state, and the "social partners" as well as an industrial policy to promote sectors like information technology.

By the end of the 1980s the faint glow of Reaganomics had been extinguished and Ronald Reagan's record, though he had left the White House, continued to be smeared by Gallic critics, many of whom had once been associated with the liberal turn. Among the socialists, Laurent Fabius, now head of the National Assembly, insisted that Reagan might have spoken about shrinking the state but actually expanded it and spurred growth with the biggest Keynesian style boost in U.S. his-

tory.[98] The former head of economic planning, the liberal economist
Michel Albert, warned against the consequences of following the flashy
"casino economy" of the Americans—for example, the loss in social
services. The self-proclaimed Reaganite Jean-Marie Le Pen, who had
applauded the free market and privatization and found U.S. global economic domination justifiable in the 1980s, abandoned liberalism and
moved toward a protectionist, anti-American stance. In fact, the leader
of the Front National had never embraced liberalism in principle: Le
Pen regarded it at best a useful economic strategy in certain circumstances.[99] The Reagan model had lost its glitter and attention turned
to alternative experiments like the "Rhineland model" or to Japanese
methods.[100]

The tepid interest in Reaganomics was only one way in which French
policy makers watched, and then rejected, trends in America. Below
the surface of Franco-American amity during the Mitterrand-Reagan
years there was intense rivalry: it ranged over politics, trade, culture,
and even medicine. Rather unexpectedly, medical research and practice
generated controversy and scandal and marked the most tragic episode
of this rivalry. Settling this dispute eventually required the personal intervention of President Reagan and Jacques Chirac, the French prime
minister.

The deadly AIDS epidemic, which emerged during the early 1980s
among Americans, threatened to envelop Europe and spurred researchers in both France and the United States to find its cause. A team of
virologists at the Pasteur Institute in Paris led by Dr. Luc Montagnier
and another at the National Cancer Institute in Maryland under Dr.
Robert Gallo claimed almost simultaneously, between 1983 and 1984,
the discovery of the culprit, what later became known as the human im-
munodeficiency virus, or HIV. At first there was transatlantic scientific
cooperation: the Pasteur team provided the Americans with specimens
and research data, which the latter used to isolate and reproduce the
virus. Identification of the virus led to research for techniques to curb

the disease and especially for a test that would screen blood supplies and donors. Patent rights for such a test, given a viral outbreak that could become a pandemic, had the potential of generating revenues on a global scale. The French and the Americans soon became embroiled in a controversy—which lasted almost a decade—over who had discovered HIV and who deserved the patent rights. In 1984 the U.S. Patent Office ignored a request by the Pasteur Institute for rights to a prototype diagnostic test, which it had licensed to a Seattle company, and instead awarded a patent to the Gallo team on behalf of the U.S. government. At stake were not only millions of dollars in royalties but also the scientific prestige of discovery—which was keenly felt by the Pasteur Institute because its reputation had been eclipsed. Some speculated (correctly, as it turned out) that a Nobel Prize might even be awarded the researchers.

The transatlantic rivalry inflected the way France confronted the AIDS epidemic in three ways: patent rights, blood transfusions (i.e., treatment with heated versus unheated blood products), and testing blood donors and stocks. In the latter two cases the contest had deleterious consequences for hundreds of French patients.

Administrative control of the blood supply in France was complicated. This bureaucratic tangle played an important part in this sad affair because it hampered communication and clouded responsibility. The Centre National de Transfusion Sanguine, or CNTS (National Blood Transfusion Center), was "national" in only a limited sense: it monopolized the import of all blood products from abroad, represented France internationally, and acted as the principal technical adviser to the government. As a major fractionating, or separation, center it also supplied plasma and concentrated blood products for Paris and much of northern and western France. But the CNTS had no authority over either 160 other transfusion centers, which also collected blood from donors and distributed products to users like physicians and hospitals, or the several regional fractionating centers like the one at Lille, which sometimes cooperated with, and sometimes competed against, the CNTS. The CNTS itself was divided into two sections: one for production and distribution and another for research. It received advice from numerous consultative boards composed of hematologists and other medical researchers, and in turn reported through various bureaucratic routes to the Ministry of Health and, above all, the Ministry of Social Affairs, which subsidized the CNTS, set prices for products, and bore the ultimate responsibility for the national blood supply. The point person for the administration was the director of health, a post held at the time by Jacques Roux.

At first, French officials regarded AIDS as a sexually transmitted infectious disease confined mainly to American homosexuals; it was not long, however, before cases appeared among those receiving transfusions in both countries, suggesting that blood could be a carrier. French authorities were confident that their blood stocks were "pure," certainly compared to those in the United States. Blood donations in France were given freely, without reimbursement, and were thus presumably less likely to carry disease than donations enticed by payment from marginal members of the populace. The best protection then appeared to be stopping the importation of blood products from the United States.

If recipients of transfusions were in danger, hemophiliacs were even more vulnerable because they needed regular treatment with anticoagulants that were especially susceptible to HIV contamination. Anticoagulants derived from blood lots donated by thousands of donors multiplied the risk of contamination. If blood could transmit HIV, then donors required screening and blood needed treatment before it could be used. France relied entirely on unheated blood products, but over the course of 1983–84 studies showed that heating blood products reduced the possibility of contamination. Preliminary findings, reported at an international conference held in Munich in the summer of 1984, tentatively confirmed the effectiveness of heating blood products and testing donors. When an American company, Travenol-Hyland Laboratories, offered to sell heated products to the CNTS in early 1984, the center ignored the proposal on the grounds that imports would cause a panic among French users who would think that they had been exposed to

infection by the use of unheated products.[101] Confidence in the safety of
the French blood bank precluded American imports.

By then France—and Paris, in particular—was in the grip of the
AIDS epidemic and it was becoming increasingly clear that one of its
target populations was that of hemophiliacs. But the CNTS, which was
directed by Dr. Michel Garretta after October 1984, harbored doubts
about the effectiveness of heated products in deactivating both HIV
and a certain type of hepatitis. There was also the fear of incurring huge
financial loss from the unsold French blood bank and causing a panic,
especially among those dependent on regular transfusions.[102] Garretta
elected to continue using unheated concentrates, including Factor VIII,
which was one of the anticoagulants used by hemophiliacs that were
easily contaminated by the dreaded virus. Dr. Garretta, who was under pressure from the Ministry of Health to make France self-sufficient
in blood products—in part to avoid imports that might be contaminated—accelerated the production of Factor VIII without waiting for
the development of heating techniques and without increasing imports
of heated products from outside sources like the United States. But the
director of the CNTS did take precautions: he signed a contract with
an Austrian firm to use its heating technology in a new plant that would
come on line in 1985.

By early 1985, evidence gathered by French researchers demonstrated that the national blood supply was probably contaminated and
that there was a grave risk of infection from the use of unheated products. Meanwhile, Dr. Montagnier's team confirmed that heating blood
concentrates deactivated the virus. Those responsible for the blood supply had to choose: they could recall previously distributed products, destroy the rest, and turn to the Americans or other suppliers for heated
products, or they could continue monitoring the situation and depend
on the Pasteur Institute, which was on the verge of perfecting its own
heating process, and wait for the opening of the new CNTS plant that
would rely on Austrian technology. They chose to wait. Opting for a
recall and turning to American or other suppliers of heated blood prod-

ucts would incur heavy financial loss for the CNTS, which was under instructions from the Fabius government to control costs. Moreover, foreign laboratories, principally American, would most likely replace French suppliers. There was a third alternative, but because of rivalries among the transfusion centers the CNTS also rejected turning to local fractionating plants like the center at Strasbourg, which Travenol-Hyland Laboratories was assisting in developing its heating process, and the center at Lille, which had designed its own technique. In April, Dr. Garretta attended an AIDS medical convention in Atlanta; he later admitted that he should have begun purchasing American products then: "I should have bought massive amounts of heat-treated blood from abroad. I didn't do it. It was a mistake."[103]

Advisers to the CNTS in the spring of 1985 were giving contradictory advice: some recommended that "the stock of 'contaminated' products be distributed entirely before proposing the substitution of heated products"; this might mean, they acknowledged, selling their stores at discount on the French market or exporting them.[104] Others urged that all stocks be recalled immediately and destroyed. At a fateful meeting of the CNTS on May 29, Dr. Garetta acknowledged that all the Paris center's stocks were, at least in a statistical sense, contaminated. One scientist in attendance estimated the probability of any lot of CNTS blood being safe was 1 in 22,000. Nevertheless, Dr. Garretta cited administrative, judicial, and practical obstacles for a recall, especially noting "serious economic consequences."[105] Estimated losses for halting the distribution of Factor VIII alone were over a million dollars a month while destroying the large store of unheated blood and importing concentrates would cost $10 million or more. Dr. Garretta chose to continue the current practice of distributing unheated supplies and passed responsibility, including the financial losses, for changing course to the ministries.[106] But recommendations to the ministries from the CNTS about modifying existing policy were often ambivalent: they cited costs and uncertainties about obtaining supplies and managing a recall, and these reports, once forwarded, seemed to get lost in the bureaucracy. Without intervention by the supervisory ministries, the practice of depleting the unheated stores continued throughout the summer and early autumn of 1985. Budgetary constraints, bureaucratic fumbling, and holding off the Americans trumped medical ethics and safety.

Meanwhile, inquisitive and often critical articles in medical journals and the press urged the government to act promptly to secure the blood supply. But Dr. Garretta received no instructions from the ministries to recall or destroy existing blood stocks. On June 26 he informed his colleagues in charge of transfusion that sufficient heated blood products from domestic providers would not be available for at least a month, and concluded, "The distribution of nonheated products remains the normal procedure, so long as they are in stock."[107] He later argued that he had to wait on French suppliers because available imports were inadequate, but this argument has been challenged: it seems foreign suppliers, like the Americans, were willing and able to meet French needs.[108] Moreover, the regional fractionating center at Lille, which had acquired the technology, claimed it could fill much of the demand itself.[109] As a precaution the CNTS, which now was fully aware of the risk of contamination, urged using remaining unheated French products for those already infected with HIV and reserving the heated supply for patients without HIV. Yet without readily available screening tests, it was impossible to know which patients were HIV-positive.

Screening tests were a second missed opportunity that turned on the rivalry with America. Until 1985 there was no reliable way to check donors or the blood supply for HIV. Researchers at the Pasteur Institute were working on such a technique when in February 1985 the Americans perfected a process and offered it to the French. Abbott Laboratories, which marketed the test, contacted the CNTS and sent representatives to local French transfusion centers selling their technology. Thus the Americans forced another decision on the CNTS and the responsible ministries: importing the Abbott test would rob the Pasteur Institute of its French market valued at $11 million and possibly its global market.[110]

In early May, at a meeting of representatives of the ministries, the scientist representing the prime minister's office decided to delay licensing the Abbott test, even though it was less costly and simpler to use, in order to protect the French market for the Pasteur Institute.[111] The American rival was on their minds. Officials were told to do what they could to save the national market, which was "already in large part captured by the American test," for the Pasteur test.[112] As Jacques Roux, a key official in the health administration, stated later, "It appeared utterly normal that they tried to help Pasteur whose financial weakness handicapped it industrially and commercially compared to an American industrial giant."[113] A month later, on June 18, 1985, Dr. Montagnier confirmed that the Pasteur Institute had perfected its screening technique; the next day Prime Minister Fabius promised the National Assembly he would make checking for HIV mandatory for blood donations. The Pasteur test was immediately licensed while the Abbott test did not receive its certification until the end of July. During the intervening weeks the principal transfusion centers equipped themselves with the Pasteur test. The Fabius government continued to dally. It was not until July 23 that the Ministries of Health and Social Affairs ordered mandatory tests, but they postponed the start date until October 1 and did not require the destruction of existing blood stocks.

Together, hesitant and divided officials from the CNTS and the ministries delayed introducing screening tests and continued providing unheated products, which were most likely contaminated, during the spring and summer of 1985 to anyone who would buy them; this deadly practice continued until October. The CNTS and the supervisory government officials had passed up importing American heated products and the Abbott test in order to avoid financial losses and to protect the French from dependence on the United States. They did not want to undermine confidence in French medicine and medical research, to give an advantage to the Americans in the competition for medical markets including France itself, especially in patenting and selling the tests and treatment that might control the epidemic, or to boost their transatlantic rivals' claim in the legal contest over who discovered HIV. But this unseemly rivalry had its costs. Between April and August 1985, when the risk of communicating the virus was obvious, over a million units of unheated factor VIII alone were sold and, it has been calculated, over 1,000 recipients—mainly hemophiliacs—were infected with AIDS.[114] France continued distributing unscreened blood products for more than six months after the United States, Canada, and several other countries had stopped the practice. The transatlantic rivalry was more than a battle of words and policies; in this case it cost hundreds of lives.

To be sure, competition with the United States was not the only, and probably not even the principal, reason for French mismanagement of the AIDS epidemic in 1984–85. There were several problems, such as the complicated administrative hierarchy that obscured responsibility, generated turf battles, and compartmentalized information; the concern over budgets and financial losses; the illusion of a pure national blood supply; the uncertainty among medical experts about the infection and its treatment; and the monopoly of imports that prevented access to foreign suppliers by transfusion centers as well as some incompetence and moral obtuseness. Nevertheless, the Americans offered an alternative in the way of screening tests and heated products that the French spurned; here is where the rivalry turned into tragedy.

The introduction of safeguards like mandatory testing did not end the quarrel over patents. In 1985 the Pasteur Institute sued the U.S. government: the French insisted on recognition of the institute's claim to the discovery of HIV and the right both to sell its tests in the U.S. market and its share of royalties from the American tests.[115] At this point the world market for screening AIDS was valued at $150 million per year. The Pasteur Institute also tried to burnish its reputation by introducing a trial drug in 1985 that seemed to have some success in halting the infection. AIDS victims from all over the world, including Americans like the actor Rock Hudson, flew to France for treatment. For a moment France seemed to have regained the lead in the search to contain the epidemic. Nevertheless, the quarrel continued. It was only in 1987 that the transatlantic dispute was settled, but it required intervention at the highest level of government. Once the Montagnier and Gallo research teams had reached an agreement about their respective roles, President Reagan and Prime Minister Chirac officially resolved the issue by meeting in Washington, D.C., and declaring both the United States and France shared in the discovery of HIV and that they would divide patent rights.

Even the Chirac-Reagan agreement did not end the controversy. There were further inquiries in the United States into Dr. Gallo's research methods, and in 1991 the French realized they were facing a major medical and political scandal. Investigators charged that government officials and their medical advisers knowingly continued to distribute contaminated blood products in 1985. Trials in 1992 and again in 1998–99 ended in jail sentences for several of the leading participants, including Dr. Garretta; a suspended sentence for others like Jacques Roux; reprimands for officials in the ministries; and acquittals for others, including Prime Minister Fabius on the more serious charge of "complicity in poisoning." President Mitterrand's role in the scandal remains a mystery. At the root it was French and American competition for medical prestige and lucrative markets. It was one of the most shameful chapters in this narrative.

What one day may be construed as the grand finale to this story came in 2008 when Dr. Montagnier and his fellow virologist Françoise Barré-Sinoussi shared the Nobel Prize in Medicine for discovering HIV. Dr. Gallo was passed over, though Dr. Montagnier stated the American was equally deserving of the award. Some experts continued to believe that the French and American teams deserved to be honored as codiscoverers.[116]

■ As the presidential election approached in the autumn of 1988 the French used the juncture once again to assess Ronald Reagan—and America. The stock of the "great communicator" fell from its peak four years earlier because of his troubles in the Middle East—especially the fiasco surrounding Iran, shortcomings in his domestic policy, and the rise of a new star in the East, Mikhail Gorbachev. But the actor-turned-president was still popular. There was considerable admiration, especially on the right, for Reagan. "Who have been the two greatest presidents of the United States since the war?" one French survey asked. John F. Kennedy, who had achieved legendary status in France by then, was selected first. In a virtual tie for runner-up, though far behind JFK, were Ronald Reagan and Dwight D. Eisenhower. Even farther behind were Richard Nixon, Jimmy Carter, and Harry Truman.[117]

Reagan was less of a pop hero in 1988 than he had been because he had to share center stage as peacemaker with Gorbachev. When asked to name the two most important statesmen of the 1980s, the French placed Mitterrand and Gorbachev at the top, followed by Thatcher; Reagan finished fourth.[118] Other questions that compared the United States and the Soviet Union as peacemakers or advocates of arms control showed that Gorbachev had closed the gap that existed before he came to power in Moscow.[119] The press tended to credit Reagan with adopting a more vigorous stance in international affairs, especially for negotiating with the Soviets from a position of strength, but journalists also detailed his setbacks in foreign policy, like the forced retreat from Lebanon, the misguided interventions in Central America, the fantasy of the "Star Wars" defense plan, and the scandal over trading arms for hostages with Iran.

In domestic affairs Reagan received mediocre grades as manager of the American economy. "Was the presidency of Ronald Reagan in economic affairs more or less a success?" was the question. In 1988 slightly more than one-third of those surveyed thought him rather successful, but 44 percent said he was neither a success nor a failure or they had no opinion. What is apparent, and more important for long-term trends, was the emergence in the media of an indictment of American society. By 1988, at least according to the press, Reagan was leaving America in a sorry mess. Readers' attention was drawn to the spending cuts mandated by the Republicans in social programs like public health, education, and child care. A collage composed of the homeless, poverty, drugs, and crime presented a grim picture of American cities. *Le Monde* tried to show both sides of the Reagan legacy, crediting him with ending the pessimism of the 1970s, spurring economic growth, stemming inflation, and creating jobs, but also exposing his legacy of social inequality, indifference to the underprivileged, "colossal" budget deficits, and urban decay.[120] A more sympathetic paper like *Le Figaro* regretted that Reagan had done nothing to help the three million U.S. homeless.[121] A leading business review, which had once embraced Reaganomics, now drew a vivid contrast between a country in full expansion yet burdened with huge deficits, concluding that Reagan's legacy was an economy "rejuvenated but ruined."[122] One weekly, referring to the budget deficits, declared "the party's over" and that Reagan's successor would have his hands tied in addressing social issues like alleviating poverty.[123] Despite attacks on the federal government, the press pointed out, bureaucracy had grown. Despite promise of a moral renewal, the Reagan administration had been racked by scandals. More than one journal either labeled the Reagan administration as "corrupt," listing scandals and dwelling on "Irangate," or at least criticized the Republican White House for failing to deliver on its promise of moral rectitude.[124] In 1988 the media were ahead of the public in perceiving America's social problems. The social critique that would dominate French opinion in the 1990s was already apparent, at least in the media, because of the stern social policies associated with eight years of Ronald Reagan.

The U.S. presidential election of 1988 itself did not elicit much interest in France. Had the French been able to participate, they would have "voted" by a small margin for George H. W. Bush rather than Michael Dukakis (24 to 19 percent), but more than half had no opinion. The press that supported the Republican candidate praised Bush for his wide experience in international affairs and his pragmatic approach, contrasting him with the more ideological and less reliable Reagan.[125] In fact, President Bush was going to surpass Reagan in Gallic esteem.

The year 1988 recorded the most favorable postwar poll for America.[126] Queried about their overall impression of the United States, 54 percent in France said they were sympathetic, and a meager 6 percent registered their antipathy (while one-third said neither one nor the other). The vocabulary most often associated with the United States was one of *power*, *dynamism*, *wealth*, and *liberty*. Only one-fourth of those surveyed cited violence, racism, or social inequality.[127] Over half dismissed the economic influence of the United States on France. But there were some shadows. Respondents continued to disapprove strongly of Reagan's economic policies, and American culture—referring mainly to television programming, cinema, and music—seemed excessive to a majority. America set a good example for free enterprise, the media, political institutions, and education, but less so for its treatment of minorities.[128]

■ As an economic model, Reagan's America won the attention of many in France but failed to win many adherents. The socialists went so far as to make a pilgrimage to Silicon Valley, study American economic practices, consult American officials, and endorse entrepreneurship and private enterprise, yet in the end Mitterrand and his ministers rejected any transfer of Reaganomics as a betrayal of their socialist mission and republican principles. At the same time left-wing editorialists ridiculed the accomplishments of Reaganomics and exposed the deceptions and social costs. The right-wing press was more laudatory, and there were even a few true believers among economists, businesspeople, and politicians, but they were never in charge of policy. During the brief liberal moment when Jacques Chirac was prime minister (1986–88), the cohort of Americanized liberals remained marginalized and the dominant party of Gaullists, led by Chirac and Édouard Balladur, designed their own version of market reforms without ever subscribing, or even paying much attention, to Reagan's policies. The public, much like the political elite, found little merit in transporting American practices across the Atlantic. Reagan may have been more popular than his predecessors, but his appeal did not translate into enthusiasm for his policies. In the end, French ideals of Republican solidarity informed both left and right and insulated the French public against adopting either free-market principles or the tough social policies associated with the Reagan administration. Reagan's version of the American model was not for the French.

In retrospect the rosy glow that radiated across the Atlantic during the 1980s was fleeting, and it also concealed much. It is erroneous to conceptualize the decade as some halcyon past. There was a Reagan "bubble," a brief period when Paris and Washington, D.C., became anxious about a renewed Soviet threat and America's economic prosperity made the United States seem admirable. But the bubble dissipated quickly and the more typical pattern of bickering and competition emerged. The good feelings of the middle years of the Reagan/Mitterrand relationship obscured an unrelenting and disruptive transatlantic rivalry—a rivalry felt more keenly by the French than by the Americans. It informed the two nations' economic and social policies and even the two medical communities—in the case of combating HIV, acting as competitors rather than partners—with tragic consequences.

The government of Laurent Fabius during the mid-1980s illustrates the underlying rivalry. Fabius may have endorsed American-style entrepreneurship and sought to emulate Silicon Valley, but only to serve his socialist agenda; he courted the Walt Disney Company to win the theme park from other Europeans; he permitted shameful practices during the AIDS epidemic rather than turn to American medical companies; and when Reagan faltered, he attacked Reaganomics. He remained a French socialist despite his Brooks Brothers shirts.

The rivalry that emerged over economic policy and the HIV contagion also surfaced in cultural affairs. The socialists attempted to ward off what was labeled as "American cultural imperialism," and this effort ignited a lively dispute over anti-Americanism—a dispute that exposed a significant trend among French intellectuals. These controversies are the subject of the next chapter.

2.

Anti-Americanism in Retreat: Jack Lang,

Cultural Imperialism, and the Anti-Anti-Americans

First came the snub; then the broadside; then the programs. That is how France's new socialist minister of culture, Jack Lang, went on the attack against American popular culture. He refused to attend the American film festival at Deauville in September 1981; several months later he gave a notorious address denouncing American cultural imperialism at a UNESCO conference in Mexico City; and then he tried to organize a global "crusade" to combat cultural imports from the United States. Lang, the key actor in this story, was a flamboyant young politician whose movie-star good looks, iconic pink jacket, dramatic initiatives, and hyperactive ways won him both admiration and ridicule. He presided over the Ministry of Culture from 1981 to 1986 and again from 1988 to 1993.

Lang forged his strategy against American cultural imperialism in the late 1970s as a way of distinguishing socialist policy from that of the Right—in particular from that practiced during the administration of Valéry Giscard d'Estaing, and as a means of assisting François Mitterrand: it would curry favor among the more *gauchiste* party members and intellectuals and separate Mitterrand from his party rival Michel Rocard. Lang hosted luncheons for Mitterrand with scientific, artistic, and literary luminaries like Roland Barthes to elevate the candidate's stature. His plan was to play to the Third World at a moment when the ideology of *tiers-mondisme* still captivated many socialists. American mass culture, from his perspective, placed the independence of all nations, not just France, as well as the principle of cultural diversity, at risk. But culture had a certain economic dimension. American multinationals—for example, Hollywood's large studios—threatened the existence of the world's artistic industries such as cinema, television, publishing, and music. Before the presidential election of 1981 Lang staged festivals, gave interviews, and issued press releases attacking both Americanization and the Right: the true Left, he proclaimed, opposed "the penetration of a cosmopolitan and pan Atlantic culture."[1] At a symposium he organized at Hyères, which attracted film celebrities like Bernardo Bertolucci and Bulle Ogier, the participants petitioned the European Community to protect the national cinemas of Europe from "colonization" by American multinationals. Lang filled the air with grand promises about a socialist victory: all of France would become a festival of creativity.

A few months after the socialists' electoral triumph, Lang, as the new minister of culture, turned down an invitation to attend the annual American film festival at Deauville, claiming, "A minister must choose between the exploiters and the exploited. The role of the minister is not to participate in fashionable receptions financed by American companies, but to be where there is life."[2] He told an interviewer that he was not opposed to American culture, only to its excessive penetration—pointing out that in 1980, of 235 foreign films distributed in France, 195 were American, 30 were European, and a mere 10 came from the rest of the world: "Do you think the government and parliament can accept this caricature when we are engaging in a new North-South dialog?"[3] The new minister defended his refusal: "Don't count on me to promote American movies. We are not diehard anti-Americans, but we must recognize that the American cinema is backed by a powerful, world-wide distribution network" and he urged a European counterattack. "We want to defend our art of living and not allow an impoverished and standardized external model be imposed on us."[4]

If the Deauville snub was a sensation within France, the speech in Mexico City in July 1982 grabbed global attention. The occasion was a UNESCO conference on cultural policy at which Lang elaborated two themes. Coining the slogan "economy and culture: the same struggle," he tried first to connect culture with economic development. It was a rather fuzzy notion about culture acting as a source of economic dynamism. Encouraging creativity in culture, he argued, would stimulate innovation, inventiveness, and enterprise. It was a second theme, however—his sharp attack against a standardized, globalized culture made in America, even though he did not explicitly name America— that excited his audience. Lang orated about "certain great nations" that once taught the world freedom now seeking profits by imposing a homogenized culture on the planet. "Today cultural and artistic creativity are victims of a system of financial, multinational domination against which we must organize. . . . Our countries accept passively, too passively, a certain invasion, a certain submersion of (both) images manufactured elsewhere and standardized music." Reviewing global television programming, Lang observed that most of it comprised standardized productions that "naturally plane down (*rabotent*) national cultures" and transmitted a uniform style of life. He asked, "Is it to be our fate to become the vassals of the immense empire of profit?"[5]

The French minister enjoined the delegates to launch "[a] real crusade against—let's call things by their name—this financial and intellectual imperialism which no longer, or rarely, appropriates territories. It appropriates consciousness, it appropriates modes of thinking, it appropriates styles of living. . . . We must act if we don't want tomorrow to become sandwich-men for the multinationals."[6] Underlying this "crusade" was Lang's conviction that standardized—that is, American—movies and television programs, forced on others by American multinationals, stifled the development of true creativity that he believed was rooted at the national, regional, local, and municipal levels, and possibly within everyone. He assumed the natural creativity of people needed to be encouraged, released, and expressed as a way of stimulating cultural growth and diversity. This was best accomplished, he said, with like-minded nations banding together to ward off uniformity. France, for example, should league together with other Europeans, with the Francophone world, and with other Latin nations.

It was reported that most of the delegates from Third World countries approved of Lang's tangy speech, that it raised diverse reactions among the Europeans, and that it exasperated the Americans.[7] One member of the American delegation was so infuriated by the address that he challenged the Frenchman to a public debate; it was refused. The American delegation was incensed not only by the accusation of imperialism and the incitement against American audiovisual products, but also by Lang's laudatory comments about Cuba. On his way to Mexico he had visited Cuba, gone lobster fishing with Fidel Castro, and spoken of his "natural sympathy" for the Cuban experiment and his admiration for Castro's successes in education and health care. Cuba and France both refused "the international dictatorship of a great power as well as the standardized and industrialized monoculture."[8] According to Lang, "Cuba is a courageous country that is building a new society. Its socialism is not like our own (but) we respect it."[9] In a rather obvious taunt aimed at the Americans, he affirmed the right of the Cubans to live under the political system of their choice. In Mexico Lang gave full voice to socialist tiers-mondisme, to courting the Third World especially the population of Latin countries, and to chiding U.S. policy in the Caribbean and Central America. Only a few months earlier President Mitterrand had addressed a north-south summit in Cancun, Mexico, also attended by U.S. president Ronald Reagan, on the merits of international economic assistance for the Third World.

The Deauville boycott and the Mexico speech sparked a sharp debate among French intellectuals about cultural imperialism, national identity, and anti-Americanism. Lang had his fans. The most outspoken, representing the Third World, contended that liberation from colonialism depended on asserting cultural identity. Tahar Ben Jelloun, a Moroccan writer living in Paris, assailed American cultural imperial-

Figure 1. Wolinski's parody of Jean-François Millet's painting *The Angelus*: contemporary farmers pausing to pray are told to "hurry up" because *Dallas* is beginning. Courtesy Maryse Wolinski.

ism for its latent racism and its scorn for other cultures. Americans, he wrote, sold weapons and images in the name of freedom: "[O]ne could say that the family in *Dallas* is objectively an accomplice to the massacres being committed in Lebanon at this moment by the Israelis." (The American TV show *Dallas*, with its lead character J. R. Ewing, was commonly evoked as the prime example of American television in the 1980s.) Among homegrown writers, the novelist Hervé Bazin encouraged Lang to check the Americans before they completely overran French culture.[10] The movie director Gérard Blain, who had once worked in Hollywood, applauded the Deauville incident and inveighed against "the poison" of American films that "crushed or cretinized" creativity, lowered morals, invaded the subconscious of children, and turned the French into "miserable clowns" who imitated the American way of life. Blain did not spare America itself, "a country of invertebrate zombies."[11] Using less brutal language, the newly organized Committee for National Identity—which included such celebrities as the actor-director Jean-Louis Barrault, the playwright Eugène Ionesco, the author Albert Memmi, the editor-philosopher Jean-Marie Domenach, and the historian Philippe Ariès—endorsed Lang's actions. Committee members complained about Hollywood exports taking over theaters and television screens not only in Europe but also in the developing world. The committee's manifesto asserted that "cinema is a faithful reflection of a national identity and its abandonment to foreign interests leads inevitably to a certain deculturalization especially among young people."[12] For example, French children, it was charged, knew more about the American Civil War than the French Revolution. The committee called for more restrictive quotas on Hollywood movies in order to make room for films from France, from Francophone countries, and from other Latin and European nations on television and in the theater. Lang adopted the committee's recommendation of quotas for both the large and small screen and made it central to the debate over Americanization in the 1980s. But he was careful about discriminating among Hollywood's talent; thus, in 1981, he honored the American film director King Vidor, distinguishing his work as that of an artist from others whom he belittled as hustlers.[13]

If enthusiasts of tiers-mondisme, representatives of the audiovisual industries, and a few major writers approved of Lang's campaign, he received a cold shoulder from a host of prominent intellectuals. Many were simply indifferent to his appeal. Some pointed out the hypocrisy, given a French past that included Napoleon, of damning Americans for cultural imperialism. Others took exception to fighting outdated battles with ham-fisted tactics aimed at the wrong enemy.

A typical response came from author and screenwriter Guy Konopnicki, who mocked the diehard defenders of national identity. Because of globalization, the myths of contemporary French youth, he
argued, were not about Gauls or the French Revolution but came from
Walt Disney and the American West. To inhabitants of the contemporary urban world, what America exported was more relevant than
Jean Giono writing about peasants. American capitalism was simply
more proficient at creating and marketing mass culture: socialism, he
warned, was not going to be built by rejecting what capitalism did better.[14] It seemed misguided to Konopnicki and others to fault Americans for French shortcomings and futile to try to build walls against
imports from across the ocean. Alain Finkielkraut chastised Lang for
demagoguery in blaming the Americans for what the French were doing to themselves: "Don't unload our mediocrity on the transatlantic
Great Satan."[15] Yes, "Uncle Sam dumps grade B products on the world,"
noted Finkielkraut, but the French, according to this prominent philosopher, simply preferred *The Godfather* to domestic films and had
loved watching drivel on television long before *Dallas* appeared. Almost all of Lang's critics agreed that cultural protectionism was not the
answer. André Glucksmann, one of the highly visible "New Philosophers," thought Lang was heading in the wrong direction altogether.
Glucksmann denounced Lang's "cultural protectionism" along with
the "archaic" program of the socialists.[16] The actor/entertainer Yves
Montand thought the minister's policy smelled a bit like the reactionary nationalism of wartime Vichy. He agreed with the writer Michel
Tournier that what was needed was an offensive strategy, that "if you
really want to counter United States 'hegemony' the best response," according to the latter, was "to inundate it with French culture."[17]

Many disapproved of Lang for, intentionally or not, reviving anti-
Americanism. Georges Suffert, a writer and editor at *Le Point*, took him,
and others like him, to task for preaching "primal anti-Americanism,"
calling the minister a "third-world dilettante" (*tiers-mondiste de salon*)
while Jean Daniel, the editor of the *Nouvel Observateur*, weighed in

against the "reappearance of a nationalist left" and objected to socialists adopting anti-Americanism.[18]

Most intellectuals dismissed the supposed American threat and
distanced themselves from Lang's aggressive policies. Claude-Jean Bertrand, writing in *Esprit*, systematically dissected the errors of the cultural imperialist school, such as assuming that importing cultures passively received American products or that they were so fragile that they
were easily overwhelmed. Bertrand also noted that much of so-called
Americanization was superficial: "jeans on the backside of a young
Russian don't make him Americanized."[19] Another newsweekly ran an
inquiry among the cognoscenti asking who thought Mickey Mouse
was "a danger" to French culture.[20] None of those surveyed liked Disney's cultural merchandise, yet no one thought it was a serious threat.

A few reproached the socialists as frauds. They singled out Serge
Moati, a friend of Lang and Mitterrand, who had once declared, "We
don't want to be the audiovisual garbage can for the United States," but
as director of FR-3 Moati won an award for broadcasting the Disney
Channel as the best "French" TV program for children.[21] Journalist
Jacques Julliard attacked the socialists as hypocrites who complained
about the new barbarians from across the Atlantic yet feted the invader
and courted Disney. The selection of France for Euro Disney was a
symbol of capitulation—or worse, of powerlessness—according to Julliard, exposing the lack of creativity among the producers of French
culture. What is the contemporary French equivalent of Donald Duck
or Mickey Mouse, he asked? The animals of La Fontaine? Of Buffalo
Bill? D'Artagnan? But they date from the distant past. "Today," he
asked, "where is our Rambo?" The fault lay not entirely with the socialist government, he concluded, because French creativity seemed to be
waning. Citing Umberto Eco's position that Disney was the kingdom
of illusion, the triumph of the fake, "we will soon have in France a copy
of the fake."[22]

Still other intellectuals thought Lang was playing into the hands
of the communists because he neglected Soviet imperialism—which

Lang stoutly denied. Pierre Daix took exception to the minister's failure to mention the "cultural genocide" facing Eastern European nations like Czechoslovakia and Poland, and omitting any mention of the physical and moral destruction of artists in the Soviet empire.[23] Bernard-Henri Lévy chided Lang for his "natural sympathy" for Cuba, "the tropical gulag," and asked why he had ignored how the United States offered a safe haven for hundreds of intellectuals escaping totalitarianism. Lévy found the Mexico address "comical" with its musty Marxism and "reactionary" in its evocation of cultural protectionism. He asked how a government that flattered itself with its "youthfulness" thought it could block American culture from generations "who learned to read, think, and feel with Warhol, Cunningham or even the Rolling Stones."[24]

Lang's efforts in Deauville and Mexico City not only failed to win an endorsement from the intellectual community but prompted a good deal of dissent and mockery. This reception was consistent with how left-wing intellectuals had failed to rally to the socialists after their victory.[25] The cool response awarded Lang was an expression of this distancing of intellectuals from socialist political practice.

Under siege Lang protested that he was neither anti-American nor a protectionist. He admired much about American culture, especially its vitality and relevance to contemporary life, and insisted that he had personally "discovered" many American artists.[26] As minister he welcomed talented Americans to France, awarded honors to some, and refused to engage in protectionism, although France, he insisted, was justified in defending its cultural independence from American multinationals in any way it could. His Mexico City speech, he complained, had been distorted by the media as anti-American, when its aim had been to appeal to all UNESCO nations to stimulate their creative forces and resist the multinationals who would suffocate diversity. Lang denounced the charge that the socialists engaged in "poujadist-chauvinist policies, when our ambition is to attract artists from all over the world." Posing as a responsible minister against irresponsible

detractors, he explained that the socialist government—facing an economic crisis—had to mobilize all the nation's productive forces, including culture, to "reconquer the domestic market." Why, for example, he
asked, should France, which was once the principal exporter of musical
instruments, now import them? Today's economic wars were fought
with innovation and creativity, so "France and Europe would only sustain their vitality and their independence if they were up to the mark,
for example, in winning the battle over audiovisual programming."

There was, to be sure, an apparent contradiction between a minister who made American popular culture his adversary yet claimed he
admired much of it, attended rock concerts, and gave awards to the
likes of Sylvester Stallone and Sharon Stone. Lang thought there was
a distinction. As he explained in an interview in New York, "There
should be no confusion between living culture and . . . standardized

Figure 2. Jack Lang awards Sylvester Stallone the honor of Chevalier
des Arts et Lettres, 1992. Courtesy James Andanson/Corbis.

products, [which] are invading the media. . . . Instead of choosing an easy solution and disseminating ordinary products we should disseminate living products."[27] The distinction between which American exports were "living" or creative and which were "standardized" or commercialized pap may not have been obvious to Americans, or even to the French—the television host Bernard Pivot, for example, said Stallone represented the worst of American movies.

Ignoring his critics, Lang proceeded to stage a lavish international colloquium at the Sorbonne in February 1983 inviting hundreds of celebrities from all over the world. In attendance were economists, artists, intellectuals, scholars, and movie directors including the Italian philosopher and novelist Umberto Eco and the film actress Sophia Loren. Lang rewarded many Americans, including William Styron, John Kenneth Galbraith, Francis Ford Coppola, Susan Sontag, and Norman Mailer, with a flight on the Concorde to Paris. Their collective task was to examine the relationship between creativity and current economic and social problems. Since the government under the premiership of Pierre Mauroy (1981–84) had made economic recovery its priority, Lang adapted. He articulated an expansive conception of culture that encompassed a wide range of creative tasks like industrial design and advertising, allowing him to present culture as relevant to the economic crisis. He spoke specifically about how industries like publishing, cinema, television, design, or haute couture could bring benefits in international trade. Other speakers offered less practical suggestions: Norman Mailer made an obtuse recommendation of taxing all plastic products because they symbolized consumer society. The popularity of *Dallas*, invoked by several participants, was offered as evidence for the danger posed by American television. François Mitterrand gave the closing address at the Sorbonne extravaganza, which seemed, for a moment, to make Paris once again the cultural center of the globe. But some of the attendees were not thrilled when the president asked his audience to assist in problem solving. The philosopher of deconstruction, Jacques Derrida, worried about being co-opted while Umberto

Eco asserted that the task of artists like himself was "not to cure crises"; rather, he said, "I instigate them."[28]

The French press was unimpressed with the notion of treating economic problems as an issue of creativity. It was rather implausible to argue that invigorating creativity would energize the economy and spur innovation and enterprise. Commentators ridiculed Lang's expansive definition of culture as *le tout-culturel*. And what Lang meant when he declaimed at the Sorbonne colloquium that "culture is poets plus electricity" seemed like flim-flam.[29] Some journalists dismissed the colloquium as little more than daydreaming, while others demeaned it as a socialist effort at employing culture to burnish Mitterrand's reputation.[30]

In the midst of this Parisian cultural festival the *Wall Street Journal* ignited a fire storm when its arts editor Raymond Sokolov intruded, writing, "Instead of worrying about *Dallas*, Jack Lang should spend his time wondering why France is a nullity in contemporary, active world culture. Instead of posing as the savior of planet wide culture, he should ask himself why France has produced no novelists of real importance in twenty years, except Michel Tournier, why France has slipped out of view in the visual arts. . . ."[31] Attacking *Dallas*, according to Sokolov, was "a perfect example of classic anti-Americanism, that mixture of envy and scapegoating, that anti-Semitism of the Left."

The Left responded by disparaging the *Wall Street Journal* article as a Reaganite assault on the socialists. As a rebuttal *Le Matin* ran a special dossier in which Lang said he was astonished by the "childishness" of the "provocation," adding sarcastically that it came from an American newspaper not known for being "very cultural." Emmanuel Le Roy Ladurie, the historian, called Sokolov "ignorant" and noted the prestige of French luminaries like Michel Foucault and Claude Lévi-Strauss among American academics. Others refuted Sokolov by citing contemporary French notables like Nathalie Sarraute and Marguerite Duras, by mocking the culture of *Dallas* and its central character J. R. Ewing, and scorning American pretensions—"since Vladimir Nabokov," who was a Russian émigré with an American passport, "whom do you have in the Pantheon of letters?"[32]

What fueled the Sokolov controversy was French pride and anxiety about cultural status. It also exposed doubts about Lang's grand strategy of reasserting French and European culture at the expense of America. Sokolov expressed, as Diana Pinto has explained, what many Frenchmen actually thought in private, that "French culture now existed mainly as a beacon for a desperate Third World and as an opposition to American cultural imperialism. Politicized cultural voluntarism was replacing genuine cultural creativity."[33] Not everyone was pleased with the socialists ostentatiously parading national culture for political ends and exciting anti-Americanism.

Resisting American commercial pap and assisting the culture industries were central to Lang's ministry, but they were not his only aims. The frenetic minister wanted, among other goals, to democratize culture, help President Mitterrand complete his *grands projets* like building a new opera house and the new national library, guard the national *patrimoine*, and, foster creativity of all sorts at all levels. Such an agenda forced him to fight continuous political, budgetary, and bureaucratic battles while his flamboyant showmanship, courtship of celebrities, and gaudy festivals caused a stir. The media joked about "Disneylang" and *la gauche-caviar*.[34] His programs extended over the entire decade despite the brief turn to the right in 1986–88 because the conservatives did not succeed in overturning his initiatives and Lang returned to direct cultural affairs for a second term from 1988 to 1993.

His most aggressive efforts at curbing Americanization focused on the audiovisual industry. The French cinema, which had been suffering from declining admissions, had nevertheless managed to retain a respectable 45 percent of box office receipts well into the 1970s before it fell victim to a more youthful audience and a wave of Hollywood blockbusters like *Star Wars*. Spectators stayed away from theaters and the American share of the domestic market soared; by the mid-1980s Hollywood films were selling as many tickets as were French movies.

Facing similar trends Italian filmmakers like Bernardo Bertolucci and Federico Fellini warned that European cinema faced "cultural genocide" and asked the French to take the lead in seeking redress through the European Community (EC). Lang took the issue to Brussels in 1984 and persuaded the European Commission to investigate the growing power of American films; eventually, as we shall see, it took action.

The socialist government also assisted the industry at home in 1982–83. Lang raised subsidies to the cinema, paid for in part by new taxes on television stations, and introduced tax incentives to private investors for financing the audiovisual industry.[35] Every branch of the industry—producers, distributors, and theater owners—benefited from his largesse. The Ministry of Culture, along with several other ministries, also tried to protect the cinema by obstructing the use of videocassettes. In 1982, Lang, to the satisfaction of filmmakers and theater owners, required a one-year delay after its initial showing before a film could be sold as a video. Meanwhile Michel Jobert, the minister for foreign trade, invoked the trade deficit to block the entry of imported VCRs, mainly from Japan, by making them pass through customs at the tiny office in Poitiers, thus reducing the import flow to a trickle. Jobert, a notorious critic of America, justified his ruling with the wacky claim that "[t]he French really don't need VCRs."[36] The Ministry of Finance did its part by adding a stiff annual fee to owners of VCRs and raising the value-added tax on prerecorded videocassettes. Lang further helped by tightening regulations on television stations so that they favored local over foreign (i.e., American) materials.

Television, like the cinema, struggled with American imports. Yet unlike the cinema, television was growing by leaps and bounds in the 1980s and the socialists, seeking to encourage decentralization, aided this surge by opening what had been a virtual government monopoly to several new private channels like Canal Plus and La Cinq. But these private stations came to rely heavily on American shows, which cost a fraction of locally produced programs, to fill their schedules. And on major TV channels in 1983, one-third of movies shown and an even larger share of serialized dramas and game shows came from the United States. It took, for example, just six months for *La Roue de la fortune*, a French version of *The Wheel of Fortune*, to surpass the number of viewers for the more traditional and more intellectual game show *Des Chiffres et des lettres*.[37] Such developments contradicted Lang's grand proposal of making French television "the best in the world." In order to inspire more creative programming and avoid being swamped by cheap American imports, in 1984 Lang created a fund supplied by a new tax on the income of television channels. He also imposed stiff quotas of 50 percent for French films on the new private channels, but these were difficult to enforce.

Matters took a turn for the worse between 1986 and 1988 when conservatives assumed control and Lang had to watch from the sideline as François Léotard ran the ministry. Deregulation, favored by prime minister Jacques Chirac and Léotard, seemed only to escalate programming of inexpensive American game shows or variety shows and Hollywood films. Private channels like La Cinq and M6 filled their airtime with American imports, provoking some critics to complain that television was being Americanized. Worse still, La Cinq, against Lang's wishes, was awarded to a private group headed by Silvio Berlusconi, the Italian magnate whom many thought had ruined Italian television with American shows. *Le Monde* ran a cartoon depicting a pair of American tourists watching television in Paris: the man, wearing cowboy boots and a Stetson, proclaims "I love French TV," to which his obese wife responds, "It's so American."[38] The socialists charged the Right with selling out to the Americans, and as the French presidential election campaign began in 1987 Lang made limiting American television programs an issue. Now the problem would be addressed at the higher level of Europe.

At Brussels he labored to get the European Community to adopt quotas. Many Europeans, besides the French, worried that American television exports would soon dominate their programming. Jacques Delors, Mitterrand's former finance minister who was now president of the European Commission, observed, "I would simply like to pose a question to our American friends: do we have the right to exist? Have we the right to preserve our tradition, our heritage, our language? How will a country of ten million inhabitants be able to maintain its language—the very lynchpin of culture—faced with the universality that satellites offer?"[39] In April 1988 the European Commission adopted the controversial Television without Frontiers directive that called for devoting a majority of programming to European products "where applicable." Its aim was to facilitate intra-European exchange of television broadcasts and also protect the community from American imports. It would take another year of negotiating, which featured some intense European/American jostling before the directive became law. Lang justified the action: "We are not doing this in order to be hostile toward the United States. We are in favor of competition, but it must be fair." He thus won the adoption of European quotas in principle, but the "where applicable" clause inserted by opponents, led by Margaret Thatcher, undercut the victory by leaving implementation to individual countries. Lang complained about the watered-down directive: "This is only one step, and a timid one at that."[40] The French cinema industry denounced the socialists for backsliding on quotas, and Max Gallo, the writer and friend of Mitterrand, demanded "real protection" against "the shadow of Batman."[41] Parading their opposition, a delegation of French movie directors headed by Bertrand Tavernier marched before the European Parliament in Strasburg protesting the "colonization" of the audiovisual sector.

American trade officials were furious, calling the new directive "outrageous" and warning that quotas would lead to a commercial war between "fortress Europe" and the United States.[42] The chairman of the U.S. House Ways and Means Committee called the directive "censorship"; other congressmen threatened retaliation; and the U.S. House of Representatives adopted a resolution denouncing the European Commission's initiative.[43] A miniature trade battle erupted, with the Americans and the French threatening to block each other from filming movies in their countries. President George H. W. Bush joined the scrum, asking the General Agreement on Tariffs and Trade to condemn the directive. In fact, American programs rarely exceeded the 49.9 percent level for any network within the EC, rendering the directive rather superfluous. Lang soldiered on at trying to win the EC to tougher quotas, but without much support from other Europeans. No one seemed satisfied—not the Europeans, not the French film industry, and certainly not the Americans. France imposed its own rules under the Television without Frontiers mandate, requiring broadcasts of at least 50 percent of the French-made and 60 percent of the European-made films that were shown. Among the member states of the EC there was, following the directive, a gradual decline in the number of U.S. programs shown on television; most countries observed the 50 percent ceiling.[44]

These modest efforts could not stem the flow of American imports and failed to stimulate sufficient French or European production to supply television's voracious appetite. In fact, television production declined in France in the mid-1980s while transmission of foreign programs grew.[45] One of the most serious problems in raising domestic output was the fact that the purchase of an American show was far less expensive than producing one. Monitoring quotas also proved difficult, and television stations found ways to evade them. Similarly, Hollywood's share of the big screen continued to grow. Between 1980 and 1993 the box office share of American films soared from 35 to 54 percent while the market for French films fell in almost the same proportion.[46] Audiovisual issues were arguably the most important aspect of French cultural policy in the 1980s, and combating America was neither successful for Lang nor satisfying for the industry or the political Left, some of whose members continued to campaign against the Americanization of television.

Limiting American audiovisual imports also meant developing French or European alternatives in music. The taste of French youth for rock music added millions of francs to the trade deficit through the import of recordings and foreign manufactured musical equipment.[47] As a countermeasure, Lang's ministry heavily subsidized local popular musicians including jazz, blues, reggae, and rock artists. He helped build rehearsal studios, renovated a building in Paris to serve as a concert hall for rock music, and made a show of attending rock concerts. In 1985 as part of the socialists' youth employment program Lang allocated five hundred jobs to the association Réseau Rocks, run by Bruno Lion, making it the largest employer of rock musicians in the country. In 1989 the unconventional and always imaginative Lang appointed the twenty-seven-year-old Lion to his ministry to promote French rock music.[48]

One cannot give Lang's ministry high marks for developing a coherent strategy for invigorating the audiovisual sector, much less for matching it with the government's diplomacy. It did not go unnoticed that while Lang was attacking American popular culture, he and Mitterrand were handing out honors to Hollywood celebrities (the president gave the Legion of Honor to Orson Welles, and Lang made similar awards to Jerry Lewis and Warren Beatty), or that the socialists were courting the Walt Disney Company. Moreover, cultural initiatives and foreign policy were not aligned during the early years of Mitterrand's presidency. At the very moment Lang was challenging American cultural imperialism in Mexico City before an American delegation headed by Jean Kirkpatrick, a trusted foreign policy adviser of Ronald Reagan, Mitterrand was doing his best to win Reagan's confidence by acting as a Cold Warrior. In fact, Lang had not consulted Mitterrand about his UNESCO address, and the Elysée believed that the minister was simply reporting the facts about the Americans, even though he had done so in a "maladroit" way.[49] The most persuasive explanation for this incongruity is that the Mitterrand team arrived in power eager to advance tiers-mondisme and combat multinationals as central features of a socialist foreign policy, and they assumed these goals would not compromise their efforts toward improving relations with the U.S. government. They never intended to align themselves fully with the United States and sought to open a dialog with the Third World, to

curb the power of multinationals, and to challenge Washington's policies in Latin America. Mitterrand's team believed they could win the
U.S. government's confidence on other issues like fighting the Cold
War while quarreling over the Sandinistas in Central America and inciting cultural anti-Americanism.

Lang quietly retreated from anti-American posturing without ever
relinquishing the cause of combating American standardized culture.
He did not retract his belief that American imports stifled creativity
and identity, but he became more conciliatory. On a visit to New York
in 1984 for the opening of a French film festival the minister admitted
he had made an error in his Mexico address: he said he should not have
used the word *imperialism* because it carried different meanings to
Americans—that is, where the French might think of imperial Rome,
Americans associated it with communist anti-Americanism. Trying
to placate his audience, he revealed that François Mitterrand watched
Dallas, that "he knows the story line and he knows every character." As
for Cuba, Lang admitted he now had mixed feelings about Castro; but
"I could not say Cuba is a total failure."[50] A year later, instead of boycot-
ting the American film festival at Deauville, he hosted a party for it.

Given the tepid domestic reception to his early attempts at raising the demon of American cultural imperialism, the shifting priorities
of the socialists, and the huge and varied agenda of the Ministry of
Culture, such as expediting Mitterrand's *grands projets* and fostering
creativity, fighting the Americans receded as a priority. Lang, however,
never abandoned his struggle against cultural Americanization. The
row over the Television without Frontier directive in 1988–89 and the
continuous baiting of the Americans demonstrated his determination.
Later, during his second tour at the Ministry of Culture, Lang, in an interview with an American magazine, affirmed his distaste for America
as "the mass culture superpower" that threatened to replace cultural
diversity around the world with "an international mass culture without
roots, soul, color, or taste."[51] Would technology, he was asked, create
diversity through more channels of artistic expression? His answer was,

not likely: "the higher the satellite, the lower the culture." He refused to retract what he had championed almost a decade earlier, that "it is criminal to destroy or dilute a culture."

In retrospect Jack Lang tried to arouse some passion for the socialist program by exploiting French fears of cultural loss and stirring up anti-Americanism. The ploy largely failed. It awakened as much opposition as it did enthusiasm and the support was often ugly. Moreover, his audiovisual policies, which ranged from increasing aid and employing quotas, accomplished little toward forcing an American retreat. The tidal wave was unstoppable and Lang lacked the budgetary resources and political support, both domestic and European, to build an effective bulwark. Given the appeal of American popular culture, Lang lost to a formidable opponent.

■ Is Anti-Americanism Passé? The Intellectuals Debate

Jack Lang's offensive against American cultural imperialism prompted a major debate about anti-Americanism itself. Central to this discussion was the question of finding an appropriate response to the American "invasion"—especially that of the media. What is historically significant about this conversation is that the balance shifted perceptibly against the anti-Americans. They were drowned out by the voices of those who insisted *anti-américanisme primaire*—that is, "primal" or "primitive" anti-Americanism—was passé. Of course, such ranting continued and gained fresh partisans, such as those of the New Right, and took on different forms like that of postmodernism while less virulent forms of the disease persisted. It was still chic at Parisian dinner parties to ridicule Americans. Christine Ockrent, the television news anchor, in comparing how French and American officials celebrated Christmas Eve in Beirut—the former attended church services while the latter opted for a party hosted by a comedian—caustically commented, "To each his own cultural level."[52] And schoolchildren still read texts about how Americans who lived in a consumer paradise were slaves to comfort and conformity and lacked culture in a European sense. Nevertheless, a new chapter in this centuries-old discourse emerged in the 1980s. Journalists and other intellectuals led the rebuttal in condemning old ways, and they were joined by academics who wanted to use their critical tools to confront a bad habit before banishing it. By the end of the decade some former antagonists of America reassessed their position. Indeed, a decade earlier the scaffolding that supported those who lived off attacking America had already begun to collapse and a trend toward a more modulated appraisal had emerged. A brief look back at the 1970s reveals how and why the authority of anti-américanisme primaire began to dissipate.

Figure 3. "To each his own cultural level." On August 15, 1987, French Catholics organize church processions on the Feast of the Assumption while thousands of Americans crowd Memphis to commemorate the tenth anniversary of the death of Elvis Presley. Courtesy Plantu, "Les Célébrations du 15 août." In *A la soupe!* Paris: Éditions La Découverte/Le Monde, 1987, 135.

It would be a fool's errand to try to analyze the complicated world of French intellectuals in these decades given the diversity of views, the numerous cliques and reviews, the friendships and rivalries, the shifts in perspectives, and the subtleties and intensities of the discussions.[53] Then there was the *non-dit*, or meaningful silence, about America that is impossible to chart. All that is necessary here is to draw out a few observations about how the way opened to launch attacks on anti-américanisme primaire and, to a lesser extent, to express some sympathy for America. In broad terms, primary anti-Americanism had rested during the early Cold War on three pillars: the antipathy of leftist intellectuals and the unholy alliance of communists (some socialists) and Gaullists.

One of the major props of the anti-American structure was the network of left-wing intellectual circles in Paris who, during the early postwar years, had made hating America a credential for membership and aligned themselves with the Parti Communiste Français (PCF). There was a wide range of attitudes within this community toward the PCF and the Soviet Union, but even the noncommunists or independents, like those around the journal *Esprit*, hoped that the Soviet Union would become the promised socialist Eden while they shunned America as the citadel of capitalism, consumerism, and militarism. But the Left's faith had begun to ebb during the 1950s, given the inexcusably repressive behavior of the Soviets in Eastern Europe and the revelations about Stalinism, so that they distanced themselves from the PCF and worked instead to ensure that the coming of socialism would bring freedom and democracy rather than the dictatorship of the proletariat. Many turned to alternative socialist models in the Third World, like those of Cuba or China. Some of the younger partisans on the left, known as the *gauchistes*, who sparked the so-called student rebellion of 1968, embraced notions of direct democracy and rejected both state power and party politics in principle. That year exposed the base opportunism of the PCF and its enmity toward the student movement as well as the antidemocratic habits of Moscow when the Warsaw Pact nations forcefully intervened to crush reform in Czechoslovakia. It became obvious by the early 1970s that the communists were not the champions—but instead the enemies—of freedom, human rights, and democracy. This growing disenchantment erupted into an open press war in 1974 with the translation of Alexsandr Solzhenitsyn's *Gulag Archipelago* and its revelations about Soviet labor camps. When the communists and their fellow travelers tried to discredit Solzhenitsyn a galaxy of major intellectuals, many on the left, rallied to his side to attack the party for its Stalinist behavior. They refused to be intimidated. Solzhenitsyn's allies against the communists included, from the left, Jean Daniel and Jacques Julliard of *Le Nouvel Observateur*; Jean-Marie Domenach and Michel Winock at *Esprit*; Philippe Sollers at the review *Tel Quel*; and two young *engagé* intellectuals, who were later labeled as the "New Philosophers," André Glucksmann and Bernard Henri-Lévy. Major journals like *Libération* and *Le Monde* from the left or left-center joined—though the latter did so cautiously. Solzhenitsyn also found backing from Jean-François Revel at *L'Express*, and closer to the center, from Georges Suffert at *Le Point* and Raymond Aron at *Le Figaro*.[54] All of these names, reviews, and journals would figure prominently in the debate about America a few years later. At the same time the independent Left became wary of the electoral alliance between the communists and the socialists who expected victory in the 1978 legislative elections: journalist/intellectuals like Daniel, Domenach, Julliard, and Revel worried that the communists in power might strong-arm their socialist allies, restrict civil rights, and impose their Stalinist form of socialism.[55] By the mid-1970s the anticommunist Left had taken up the fight against totalitarianism wherever it might be found: within the PCF, among the communist regimes of Eastern Europe, in the Soviet Union, and even embedded in the revolutionary tradition itself. Part of this story involved historians like François Furet, who reassessed the French Revolution, debunked its Marxist historiography, and uncovered the roots of totalitarianism within the revolutionary project. Now the French Revolution, the very foundation of leftist politics, was implicated. Historians and political theorists also began reexamining the American Revolution; the goal was to reinsert France in the age of democratic revolutions of the eighteenth century. The revolutionary project was giving way to a resurgent Republicanism.

If the antitotalitarian campaign of the 1970s marked a turn toward liberal democracy, civil society, and human rights among independent intellectuals on the left, cheered on by their more centrist colleagues, they were not necessarily converted to philo-Americanism. But they were becoming both more open to America and less tolerant of those on the left—not just the communists, but also elements of the Socialist Party, who still adhered to the Marxist inspired revolutionary credo that condemned American imperialism, overlooked the oppressiveness of the Soviets and other communist regimes, fetishized tiers-mondisme, and preached French cultural exceptionalism. Attacking this menu became the trademark of the New Philosophers, who became darlings of the media. The shift was also visible among former Maoists like Philippe Sollers and Julia Kristeva, who had become regulars on the American academic circuit. They, along with many other stars of the French intelligentsia like Jean-François Lyotard, were discovering America in the 1970s.[56] In 1977 Sollers, Kristeva, and company devoted an issue of their journal *Tel Quel* to America, arguing that the New World could offer solutions to the impasse in Europe over political and social injustice.[57] The newspaper *Libération* also became more receptive to America; it had begun in 1973 as a subversive gauchiste newspaper sponsored by Jean-Paul Sartre, among others, but quickly evolved into a more conventional journal of the Left. By the late 1970s, *Libé*, as it was nicknamed, was mocked for its appeal to a youthful, not-so-radical, audience and for expressing itself in "French-*Américain*." Similarly the satirical journal *Canard Enchaîné* ran an amiable series on "the American connection" in 1977.[58] The movement toward liberal democracy could also be found in the proliferation of moderate, anticommunist reviews like *Commentaire* and *Le Débat*.

America itself came under reexamination by the Left.[59] One of the discoveries was that America spawned radicals who were not mere copies of European Marxists or social misfits. Edgar Morin found the "other" America, the one that did not resemble the stereotypes of conformity, racism, militarism, materialism, or puritanism and produced its own homegrown radicals, especially in California.[60] Revel saw America as the true land of revolution, and identified Europe's future with the American Left while attacking anti-Americanism as a symptom of the French Left's paralysis.[61] And America, according to *Le Nouvel Observateur*, turned out to be more of a friend of "liberal socialism" than the Soviet Union.[62] The New World also looked better to those searching for democracy when they observed how the Watergate scandal demonstrated the system was capable of self-correction. These reassessments benefited from frequent transatlantic visits of French academics and intellectuals, especially to American universities; such experiences opened eyes to the vitality and diversity of American democracy and to the nation's scholarly eminence and achievements in high culture.[63] Michel Crozier, for example, after a year at Stanford University, contributed a stinging critique of the French bureaucratic state, stressing what it might learn from America.[64] Many of these visitors, and there were many—men and women like Crozier, Julliard, Daniel, Domenach, Furet, Kristeva, and Michel Serres—would participate in the 1980s conversation about America.

Even the militants of the PCF, the noisiest cheerleaders for anti-américanisme primaire during the Cold War, lowered the volume. In the 1970s the party suffered from a steady loss of its electoral base and a dwindling ability to intimidate the noncommunist Left—many of whom believed the party had exposed the emptiness of its revolutionary cant and its political incompetence. Détente and the coming of Eurocommunism led the party to mute its ideological dogmatism, including its attacks on America. The PCF might still badger Giscard about capitulating to American multinationals, but it also acknowledged American achievements, like enjoying the highest standard of living in the world. Following his first visit to the United States, Jean Ellein-stein, a party historian and proponent of Eurocommunism, marveled at American freedoms and the prosperity of some African Americans.[65] The party newspaper admitted Americans enjoyed opportunities for personal advance and considerable freedom, even if, it also pointed out, these liberties were often illusory.[66] At least the PCF was willing to grant some concessions to American society and economy. But it was the communists' political failings, the emptiness of their message, and their unwavering defense of the Soviet Union that made them vulnerable should they try to play the anti-American card.

The Gaullists, the third pillar of what was once a formidable anti-American coalition, continued posturing against Uncle Sam, but they surrendered their commanding political position in the 1970s and curbed their attacks. Their hold on the presidency came to end in 1974 with the election of the conservative non-Gaullist Giscard, and they would not regain the Elysée for twenty years. Factionalism splintered the party so that it ran three candidates for the presidency in 1981 and all lost. Jacques Chirac, after briefly serving as prime minister (1974–76) reorganized the party and cast it as Giscard's rival. Some Gaullist hard-liners like Jean-Marcel Jeanneney, Michel Debré, and Michel Jobert attacked the "Atlanticist" and globalizing tendencies of Giscard; and Chirac criticized Giscard for leaning toward the market and away from the "voluntarist" or Gaullist way of national economic planning. Charles De Gaulle's disciples also continued to inveigh against the superpower division of Europe: in 1978 Chirac expressed regret that France had fallen under an American protectorate.[67] Behind this bombast, the Gaullists were mellowing in the 1970s: they were on their way to becoming the most pro-American political party, along with the Union pour la Démocratie Française, the conservative backers of Giscard, in France. In a few years Chirac would rather abruptly move the party strongly toward an Atlanticist posture while other prominent Gaullists began to urge more American-style competition in the economy and society.[68]

The Anti-Americans

Despite these signs of waning enthusiasm for anti-Americanism, some intellectuals and politicians continued to vituperate about Uncle Sam in the 1980s. Leading the assault on American culture were Lang's faction of socialists, and these hard-liners were joined by newcomers who twisted the discourse into novel shapes. Ideologues, as usual, provided the most intense firepower. The extreme Right and Left joined forces, or at least praised one another, in campaigning against America. For example, the New Right endorsed Lang's battle against cultural imperialism—at least at first. And one prominent Gaullist, Michel Jobert, served as a minister in the socialist government and gave full-throated support to Lang. Similarly the communists cited conservative tracts about the dangers of Americanization. Anti-Americanism brought the far reaches of the political spectrum together and provided backing, meager as it was, for Lang's policies.

Lang spoke for a potent faction of the Socialist Party that held posts in the government of Pierre Mauroy (1981–84), which served under President Mitterrand. Lang represented the rush of tiers-mondiste enthusiasm and stubborn resistance to American imperialism in all its forms that informed the stance of the party in the 1970s and colored the early years of Mitterrand's administration. Lang enjoyed at least passive backing from the president and more explicit encouragement from members of the Elysée team like Régis Debray and Jacques Attali. He was assisted by the so-called Jacobin socialists, led by Jean-Pierre Chevènement, who streaked their socialism with nationalist and protectionist colors and wanted to act even more aggressively than the minister of culture in guarding French culture and shutting the door to American imports. Chevènement, who was minister of research and industry in the Mauroy government, consistently opposed American policies, whether the issue was television programs or the war in the Persian Gulf. In a 1983 *Le Monde* article he grieved over the fate of the French language, noting, "Never since the Hundred Years' War have our people known such an identity crisis. Our language is threatened with extinction for the first time in history. America has become the last horizon of our young because we have not offered them a great democratic design."[69]

Those in the party, the moderates who dissented from such zealotry, clustered around Michel Rocard. In the eyes of the Jacobin socialists, Rocard's clique stood condemned, infamously, as *la gauche américaine*. The Communist Party, which held four portfolios in the Mauroy government, also backed the Lang-Chevènement hard-liners in resisting American cultural imperialism. Even though the communists had moderated their stance toward the United States in the 1970s, they had continued to attack Giscard's "American party" for its mistaken effort at entering the American-run global market at the cost of smothering French identity. One of Mauroy's communist ministers, Anicet Le Pors, warned Americanization brought "ethnocide."[70]

In short, the triumphalist Left, following its stunning electoral victory, led the charge and heartened the partisans of anti-Americanism. And, of course, there was the unrepentant radical intelligentsia of an earlier generation, those celebrities like Jean-Paul Sartre and Simone de Beauvoir, who ridiculed opponents with the anti-American label. For example, they assigned the worst sin possible to the New Philosophers: the Americans had co-opted them.[71]

The discourse of primal anti-Americanism also persisted among some Gaullists, as well as socialists and communists. Jacques Thibau, a former director of the public TV station Antenne 2 (now France 2) under de Gaulle and an authority on the media, described his country's predicament as "colonized France" and analyzed in detail how America had occupied the French mind and economy and turned the country into a political dependency. Evoking a common critique of imperialism—that the most advanced form of cultural dominance occurred when the colonized shared the colonizers' views of themselves—Thibau argued that the French had accepted the stereotype of themselves as provincial and backward while the Americans were supposedly the model of global modernity. Unmasking Americanization by showing ways in which American films, television programs, and advertising colonized the French imagination, or how American multinationals exploited dynamic economic sectors like computers, or how "modernization" was a trap relegating France to weakness in the global division of labor, ran rampant in the pages of his diatribe. By submitting to American manipulation and homogenization, he concluded, France was committing "ethnocide."[72] But Thibau's rant contained no prescriptions on how the French could escape this fate except that they should not try to imitate the inaccessible American model—advice he did not follow himself. Despite his disgust with the Americanization of his peers, Thibau acknowledged that he had sent his son to the Harvard Business School and owned California real estate. A more conventional Gaullist swipe at the United States came from Georges Pompidou's former foreign minister and Mitterrand's foreign trade minister (1981–83), the irascible Michel Jobert, who advised Americans to accept the alleged loss of their exceptional position in world affairs.[73] What piqued Jobert was what had disturbed de Gaulle: the U.S. government cloaked its self-interest and will to power in the guise of altruism and libeled anyone who opposed it not as just mistaken, but as evil or traitorous. When it came to the twin imperialisms, American and Soviet, Jobert found the American variety more dangerous because it was more insidious.[74]

If there was some continuity on both the right and the left in anti-Americanism rhetoric in the 1980s, new variations on old tropes about America also emerged: one came from what was deemed the New Right; the other appeared in the garb of postmodernism.

The New Right

The *Nouvelle Droite*, or New Right, as used here, refers to the study group Groupement de Recherche et d'Études sur la Civilisation Européenne (GRECE) and its affiliated reviews like *Nouvelle École*, which

were formed in the wake of the Algerian War and the events of 1968—
that is, its members were advocates for keeping Algeria French and opponents of the gauchiste students who sparked the disorders of May 1968.[75]
Formed from a small group of young politically engaged intellectuals,
many in their twenties and thirties, the New Right labored at designing a comprehensive political, social, and cultural agenda—or what they
termed "metapolitics"—aimed at invigorating France, global cultural diversity, and the "European empire." Among its activists were numerous
educators, students, journalists, intellectuals, and professionals as well as
at least one member of Giscard's government. GRECE sponsored conferences, founded a publishing house, and published or assisted several
reviews; for a time, some of its members held editorial positions in the
mass circulation weekly *Le Figaro Magazine*.[76] The star of the movement
was Alain de Benoist, one of whose essays received an award from the
Académie Française. Numbering only a few thousand members but, at
least briefly, reaching possibly hundreds of thousands through channels
like *Le Figaro Magazine*, the New Right attracted considerable attention, much of it hostile, from the late 1970s through the 1980s.

These counterrevolutionary intellectuals compiled a formidable
negative agenda. They weighed in against the Enlightenment, Judeo-
Christian cosmopolitanism, socialism, communism, egalitarianism,
liberalism, the Jacobin nation-state, religious fundamentalism, consumerism, globalization, and, most notably, came to be stridently anti-
American; indeed GRECE was the only major political or intellectual
organization of the time that made America its principal enemy. It
sought to revive France without returning to the nationalist, exclusion-
ary, anti-German, or Catholic themes of the traditional far right. Their
goal was to enhance cultural diversity in particular to renew European
civilization as an alternative to a uniform, Americanized, Atlantic pseu-
docommunity. For GRECE an ideal community was organic, rooted
in an inherited culture, racially homogeneous, and hierarchical—one
led by "natural" elites who performed "heroically." When the organization spoke of a "European race" it referred to Northern Europe,—to

Celts, Vikings, and Germans. Benoist refuted charges of racism and fascism—but not to everyone's satisfaction. He proclaimed his support for immigration and "the right to be different" and he embraced Third World peoples as the natural allies of this new Europe, a stance that was dubbed *tiers-mondisme de droite*. After all, Benoist insisted, it was not immigrants who had spoiled French culture or hawked the commercial values of *la société marchande*. GRECE refused to align itself with any political party keeping its distance from the ruling right-wing parties and attacking Jean-Marie Le Pen's Front National as political opportunists running on a reactionary, anti-immigrant platform.

Americanization in the late 1970s, as viewed from the New Right, became even more than Marxism the principal threat to European and global cultural diversity. Any attempt at installing a universal culture, as the Americans supposedly intended, would lead to convergence and entropy or the death of living, national, regional, or local cultures. Or, as these newcomers to the far right phrased it, "American-Western civilization" spread egalitarianism and a uniform, hedonistic, and consumerist culture that had little to do with true European culture. Culture, they contended, had boundaries, national or continental, and one such boundary—surely an eccentric proposition—was the Atlantic. American and European ways were supposedly essentially antagonistic. It would be best if Europe disengaged from American culture and intensified exchanges with Third World societies. After all, from their perspective, Europe and the Third World were both victims of the Americans' market ideology. Advancing global diversity, which was the cause of all peoples, would stop the spread of *Homo economicus américian*. As for Europe, Benoist declared, "it will be made against the United States or it will not be made."[77]

The New Right readily borrowed from the standard Gallic repertoire of stereotypes: Americans were Bible-toting preachers who worshipped the dollar; they were consumers immersed in a "gadget culture"—and they were obese. They preached morality to the rest of the world after they had exterminated the Native Americans and dropped atomic bombs on the Japanese. While they pretended to be worldly, they were intensely parochial: half of the sophomore geography class at a Florida university, according to one account, could not place Spain on a blank map of Europe.[78] Benoist claimed that 90 percent of Americans had never read a book.[79] What America sold was a "global mass culture" that "annihilated" naturally distinct—meaning hereditary— cultural communities. The French people, according to the New Right, were enduring "the staggering progress of the Americanization of our ways of thinking and living."[80] Should American English advance any further among the French, an alarmist article in *Le Figaro Magazine* warned, they would lose their heritage, their soul, and would "soon accept the American way of life" and become colonized "gallo-ricaines."[81] The toxic effects of Americanization could be seen when American movies were so recognizable that there was no need to translate their titles, or when televised news awarded more coverage to the United States than to France.[82] The coming of cable and satellite television and videocassettes made the television monitor the central front in the fight for cultural independence. Benoist wrote that in their entire history France and Europe had never been so profoundly "occupied" as they were in the 1980s: "France has never been less French and Europe less European" than today because of Americanization.[83] GRECE concluded that if there were two "totalitarianisms" facing France—Soviet communism and American liberalism, both advancing egalitarianism and homogeneity—the greater danger came from the United States because it was closer to realization. Benoist pushed this choice to its logical conclusion and reluctantly advanced philo-bolshevism: "The East imprisons, persecutes, bruises the body and suppresses individual freedom. The West breaks up organic structures, depersonalizes peoples. It creates happy robots; it air conditions hell; it kills souls."[84] Or, as he once infamously declared, if he had to choose between the two evils, he would prefer to wear "the Red army cap" than have to live and "eat hamburgers in Brooklyn."[85] Not everyone within GRECE endorsed Benoist's bizarre choice, and some defected. Consistency, coherence, balance, and even common sense were not the strength of someone who had so many hates and whose agenda rapidly evolved.

One could not expect any relief from intellectual or political elites; according to these young partisans, they had sold out to the Americans: "In the space of twenty years the majority of the [French] intelligentsia has succumbed to its [America's] siren call."[86] Nothing in the way of protecting French culture from the Americans would come from the politicians of the Fifth Republic. The parties of the Right were constrained from protecting French culture either by their market ideology or by fear of appearing antimodern. Indeed, some of them were mistakenly enamored of Americanization and Reaganism. On the left, they charged, the ruling socialists courted Disney, and Mitterrand paid homage to the lords of Silicon Valley. In response GRECE hosted a conference in 1986, "The Challenge of Disneyland," at which Benoist called for the extermination of Mickey Mouse and a cultural war against the United States.[87]

After initially welcoming Mitterrand's cultural watchdog Jack Lang, the New Right was disappointed: he, and the socialists, proved inept at invigorating and protecting French culture.[88] Lang wrongly treated culture, like books, as merchandise, something that generated profits or economic growth. All he accomplished, according to GRECE, was radio broadcasts of French *chansons*, gaudy colloquia at the Sorbonne, and new flower pots at the Grévin Museum. He offered no coherent or vigorous program to revive national culture. What the New Right failed to mention was that its recommendations for cultural policy—more protection and exchanges with the Third World— were precisely what Lang championed. The New Right urged both the Right and the Left to overcome their historic rivalry and make resistance to Americanization the unifying issue, and to construct a "European Monroe Doctrine" against the American empire.[89] Such a plea underestimated how complicit both the Right and the Left had become in Americanization and how inadequate primal anti-Americanism was for generating a new politics.

As complements to the New Right there were similar right-wing sermons like the one by Henri Gobard, a professor of literature, who warned that the French were submitting not to another culture but to a negation of culture, one that mixed the arts, styles, and religions of various countries into an "undefined hamburger that was not American but simply *usaîque*."[90] Another conservative academic, former diplomat and member of the New Philosophers, Jean-Marie Benoist, who later converted to Reaganism, drew parallels between the Soviet gulags and the American media: both imperial powers imposed their tyrannies of normality or uniformity.[91]

But it would be tedious to review all this repetitious and corrosive right-wing literature. What deserves more attention, despite its egregious flaws, is the popular, yet odd polemic, by Jean Baudrillard.

■ *Amérique*

Baudrillard's *Amérique*, which was published in 1986 and appeared two years later in a trendy, illustrated English translation, was possibly the most widely advertised and reviewed anti-American text of the decade, one that belonged to no particular political persuasion but leaned vaguely toward the left.[92] At the time Baudrillard enjoyed a following in American artistic and academic circles as well as considerable prominence at home.

Amérique may represent the nadir of a Gallic literary/philosophical genre, one that began with Baudelaire, that uses America as a metaphor for (post)modernity. In this long essay Baudrillard, a sociologist-cum-philosopher, reworked clichés about America employing a postmodernist vocabulary and exposition along with Marxist sentiments and categories. The result is a pretentious, self-indulgent, impenetrable, jargon-filled, maddening, random collection of sometimes inane but always gloomy observations—not to speak of the factual errors: Minneapolis is supposedly located "on the edge of the Rockies" (13).

Amérique infuriated most American reviewers and did not impress many French critics.[93]

It is modernity itself, Baudrillard exclaims, not "just a gap between us, but a whole chasm of modernity" that divides America from Europe (73). America "is the original version of modernity. We are the dubbed or subtitled version" (76). In America everything is possible: it simulates affluence, freedom, sexual gratification, and justice and in so doing has become "the absolute model for everyone" (77). The whole world dreams the American dream, less because of American power than because of its (un)culture, especially its cinema. Americans, he asserts, have no past, no identity, and live only in the present: the future belongs to such people with "no origins and no authenticity" (76). Europeans, he writes, "shall never catch up," can imitate and parody the Americans, but "do not have either the spirit of audacity for what might be called the zero degree of culture, the power of unculture" in order to be modern in the American sense of the term (78). He adds, "From the day when that eccentric modernity was born in all its glory on the other side of the Atlantic, Europe began to disappear" (81).

To be sure, America is also a culture of hyperreality or virtual representation, a complex of artifice, lies, false promises, and broken dreams; it is as empty as the desert—Baudrillard's favorite postmodern landscape. Americans, he opines, "have no sense of simulation. They are themselves simulation in its most developed state..." (28–29). Having elevated, or disparaged, America as the epitome of postmodernity, Baudrillard proceeds to rehearse the standard tropes about a society of conformity, inequality, crime, and violence; about "vertical" cities without centers or pedestrians; about the genocide of Native Americans; and about the Calvinist work ethic. Americans appear as some anonymous mass: only two individuals are named in his essay, Ronald Reagan and Walt Disney—a censorious selection. There are nasty comments about the ubiquitous American smile—the contraction of the facial muscles that hides emptiness and indifference. Speaking of New York, he wails, "It is a world completely rotten with wealth, power, senility, indifference, Puritanism and mental hygiene, poverty and waste, technological futility and aimless violence," yet, he continues, it represents the world's future "because the entire world continues to dream of New York" (23). Baudrillard is paranoid about American cities: Santa Cruz, California, as part of "the post-orgy" world, seems like paradise, but "a change of just a few degrees would suffice to make it seem like hell" (46). Squirrels in urban California appear like cute, furry Disney friends, but, he writes, "behind these smiling eyes there lurks a cold, ferocious beast fearfully stalking us" (48). There is little point in cataloging the inanities that purport to be profundities in *Amérique*, but it is difficult to resist the temptation to mention a few: in Los Angeles "the only real society or warmth" is on the freeway (53); "there are no cops in New York" (22); and "Manhattan was built according to the architectural conceptions that were laid out for Coney Island."[94]

To this postmodernist theorist America is simultaneously a "utopia achieved" and an "anti-utopia being achieved" (97). But is this achieved utopia, he asks, paradise? Yes, he answers, in the sense that Santa Barbara, Disneyland, and America itself are all paradise, even if this paradise is "mournful, monotonous, and superficial" (98). It is also an anti-utopia because America represents the end of European values and culture: it is a society without reflection or introspection, without reverence for cultural heritage, without depth or a sense of the tragic, without any aspirations for meaning or identity. According to this French theorist, culture in America has no aesthetic pretensions; it is merely kitsch, advertisements, diversion, hyperreality, and simulation. Because he thinks "the cinema and TV are America's reality" (104), Baudrillard dismisses American high culture. One wonders if any French writer has made more obtuse statements about America than these.

Time and again Baudrillard bares his fixation with California, equating this western state, this "mirror of our [European] decadence," with America (104). But California is "not decadent at all. It is hyper real in its vitality, it has all the energy of the simulacrum"(104). It is "the world center of the inauthentic" but only in a European sense: Europe has disappeared in America, and what remains is the authenticity of Disneyland. "When you leave Disneyland and enter so-called real America, you realize that all of America is Disneyland, that all its characteristics are gathered there in a virtual matrix. . . ."[95] That America could not be Europe's future because it represented "the disappearance of Europe" seems in a perverse way to give Baudrillard pleasure: "There is something fascinating, dizzying, about feeling the very sources of one's own culture disappear."[96]

Baudrillard cannot end his tour without ridiculing American political life. California returns yet again in the guise of Ronald Reagan, whom he sees as a symbol of a nation that has taken refuge in "a triumphal illusionism" (108), that has lost its past hegemonic power and substituted "power as a special effect" (107). Reagan has made America into California, where paradise has been realized and the have-nots are abandoned or banished, and he has transformed the presidency into a kind of cinematic performance. If Reagan is the symbol of contemporary America, then, he asks, is the superpower now "at the face-lift stage"? (115). Exhausted from his deconstruction of the continent Baudrillard concludes, "The country is without hope. Even its garbage is clean . . . . life is so liquid . . . the bodies and the cars so fluid, the hair so blond, and the soft technologies so luxuriant, that a European dreams of death and murder, of suicide motels, or orgies and cannibalism to counteract the perfection of the ocean, of the light, of that insane ease of life, to counteract the hyper reality of everything. . ." (121–22).

■ Anti-anti-Americanism

When the Left came to power in 1981, the socialists and communists tried to play to anti-American sentiments and beat the drums of cultural imperialism, but they found most of the intellectual community was deaf to their appeal and impatient with their revolutionary credo, their cultural exceptionalism, and their tiers-mondisme. Jack Lang's speech in Mexico City provoked a storm of dissent rather than applause. The enemy, according to his critics, was to the east, not the west. The Solzhenitsyn affair, the atrocities in Cambodia, the plight of the Vietnamese boat people, the Soviet invasion of Afghanistan, and repression of the Solidarity movement in Poland made attacks on America seem misdirected. Primal anti-Americanism seemed backward and irrelevant, particularly among independent leftists, the New Philosophers, and moderate political journalists.

Politically, anti-Americanism was "the socialism of imbeciles," trumpeted Jacques Julliard.[97] Writing in *Le Nouvel Observateur* in 1986 Julliard was among the most outspoken journalist/intellectuals who denounced the anti-Americans, including those on the left. He welcomed what he believed were signs that the socialists had abandoned their full-throated attacks on America. To Julliard, anti-américanisme primaire in a cultural sense represented: "the revenge of failed writers and mediocrities of Francophonie. Since the collapse of the communist ideal, political anti-Americanism is no longer a winner in France. It is only a shady meeting place frequented by Communists, the fascistic extreme Right, anti-Semites and neo Machiavellians." Or, as he elaborated, this kind of anti-Americanism represented a "sad procession of poujado-communists, vengeful Maurrasians, failed writers, or false left-wing Gaullists who have found America the ideal scapegoat of modern times."[98] One must admit, as we shall see, that Julliard's brutal interpretation was on target.

Was anti-Americanism passé or, at least, should it be? This was the principal issue discussed by independent leftist and moderate political analysts.

The most important journal for the intelligentsia, *Le Monde*, which had a long history of being hard on the United States, changed its colors: it joined those who endorsed the retreat of anti-Americanism and wished it would disappear. As early as 1980 Guy Scarpetta, a literary critic for the daily, wrote of anti-américanisme primaire as "a veritable French sickness that consists of being able only to affirm our identity by opposing the United States."[99] He went on to describe the persistence of this malady among hard-line socialists like Jean-Pierre Chevènement, who had blamed the events of May 1968 on the "Californians," or the director of the Pompidou Center, who refused to host a retrospective of two American artists. Scarpetta insisted it was time to resist these "old xenophobic demons." And early in Mitterrand's term the paper featured columns mocking those like Jack Lang who advocated protectionism against American mass culture.[100] A few years later, under the title of "Uncle Sam's French," Nicolas Beau proclaimed that "anti-Americanism was sick" and that *Le Monde* itself had "turned away from its anti-American stance."[101] How could one be anti-American when America was everywhere you looked—it was *banalisé*—he asked? If the *branché* of the 1960s identified with the American counterculture, in 1984, according to Beau, they embraced the more upwardly mobile, the "*Dallas* esthetic" of making money and striving for success. Jean Cocteau may have once asserted America killed dreams, the columnist concluded, but the time had come to forget Cocteau and say "bonjour l'Amérique." And when Baudrillard published his anti-American polemic, *Le Monde* sneered at him.[102]

Among journalists or experts writing for more moderate publications like *Le Point*, *Le Figaro*, and *L'Express* or reviews on international affairs there were even more vehement denunciations of the old phobia. Dominique Moïsi, the foreign policy analyst, argued that the decline of anti-Americanism was permanent; it could not survive because its underlying political structure had fallen apart, the youth of France embraced the American style of life, and both young and old were fascinated with high technology and entrepreneurship.[103] Alain-Gérard Slama, a historian of ideas who was also a columnist, wrote that the French had become realistic about America: they now thought it and Europe to be facing similar problems. "If this observation is accurate," he predicted, "the semi-eternal debate [between] Americanism and anti-Americanism will soon interest only some dinosaurs on the extreme Right or in the Communist Party." Europe, once freed from defining its fate in terms of dependence or independence from the United States, would be forced "to make a new start in order to become its own model, its own America."[104] It was no coincidence that the early 1980s also marked the apogee of Raymond Aron's reputation among the intelligentsia. Aron, a stout defender of Atlanticism, then writing for *L'Express*, had long been shunned by the Left. But this scourge of ideological politics and critic of anti-Americans like the New Right finally enjoyed national respect before his death in 1983. Two newcomers to these discussions were *Commentaire*, which featured luminaries like Marc Fumaroli, Alain Besançon, and Jean-Claude Casanova and owed its inspiration to Raymond Aron; and *Le Débat,* founded and directed by Pierre Nora and Marcel Gauchet. These publications, the first coming from the moderate Right and the latter from the moderate Left, were at the heart of French intellectual life in the 1980s, and both refrained from anti-Americanism. These reviews engaged America in all its forms, but always as interested observers. They frequently relied on American experts for enlightenment about transatlantic developments. The tone was that of learning and comparing rather than of condescension or derision. They consciously turned against the Old Left and embraced what Nora called "intellectual democracy." Thus *Commentaire* published Francis Fukuyama's essay "The End of History?" and *Le Débat* ran a series, "The Opacity of the United States," that featured authorities on American culture like Robert Bellah and Michael Kammen.

The Academics

Scholars joined in to study anti-Americanism and in so doing further discredited it. The phenomenon had not been a topic of serious academic inquiry, at least not among the French, prior to the 1980s. A few Americans had addressed it, usually in the form of doctoral dissertations in history or as conference papers, but it was hardly a major topic of scholarly inquiry.[105] Foreign policy experts in Washington, D.C., had always been concerned, but that was a separate world. All this changed in the early 1980s as the question became, What did anti-Americanism represent in the past and was it fading, perhaps even disappearing? The historian Michel Winock initiated the discussion, writing of the resurgence of the phobia in 1980–81 and scorning it.[106] Sciences Po hosted the first Franco-American scholarly conference on anti-Americanism in 1984, presenting social scientists and historians like Winock, Denis Lacorne, Marie-France Toinet, Jacques Rupnik, André Kaspi, and Pascal Ory. As the scholarly conversation developed it generated colloquia in Paris and New York that featured authorities like Philippe Roger and celebrities like Régis Debray, Jean Baudrillard, Michel Crozier, and Pierre Bourdieu. In their wake came major scholarly studies by French and American researchers who mapped the historical phenomenon in depth.[107]

This academic attention diminished, even belittled, anti-Americanism by exposing both its vagueness and imprecision as an analytical category and its sources in irrationality, envy, ignorance, narcissism, antimodernism, and political extremism. It also confirmed its decline, though views differed about whether this was circumstantial or irreversible.

Finding an acceptable definition of the phenomenon was elusive. Delineating the category strictly seemed to exclude most everyone, including the likes of Jean-Paul Sartre, but a broader classification might include those like Alexis de Tocqueville, who did not seem to belong. There was also the difficulty of clearly categorizing most discourse, groups, or individuals as either anti- or pro-American.[108] Attitudes often evolved or were mixed or even contradictory so that America simultaneously fascinated and repelled. Equally perplexing was how adversaries and admirers often used the same images, but attributed opposing values to them.

Despite such classification problems, the experts agreed the phenomenon could be explained by the fears and passions of the French. Some scholars contended perception of threat varied according to

what ideals or interests seemed at risk. Concerns about Cold War affairs—for example, what was more dangerous (the Soviet Union or the
United States) or about the domination by American multinationals—
aroused anxieties about French independence or status, while those
antagonized by American mass culture worried about protecting national identity or the traditional role of intellectuals. Other academics
analyzed anti-Americanism as less about ideals or interests and more
about the irrational and the imaginary: they offered psychological explanations like envy, projection, or stereotypical thinking.[109] Scholars
frequently located anti-Americanism within the Franco-French debate
about modernity, placing the anti-Americans in the camp of enemies
of economic, technological, and scientific progress. And it was common to perceive the phobia generated by a clash of two universalisms,
or twin narcissisms, with the Americans championing democracy and
the French *civilisation*.

Researchers made further distinctions. They detected a cleavage
between the elites and the public and made intellectuals or extremist politicians on both the right and left responsible while arguing the
public endorsed most American cultural imports.[110] And systematic
anti-Americanism, or anti-américanisme primaire, according to these
scholars, was rare and virtually nonexistent among certain groups like
business managers or elite civil servants.

But the major question posed by the academics, as the historian
André Kaspi put it, was, "Has French anti-Americanism finally ceased
to exist?"[111] Kaspi may have responded negatively, but the fact that he
and other scholars raised the question suggests that the pattern was
one of decline. Social scientists surveying trends in public opinion
concurred: they speculated France might have become "the most pro-
American country in western Europe" and one expert argued that the
phobia was on its way to becoming a parlor game.[112] The voice of anti-
Americans, Michel Crozier concluded, no longer stirred an "important
echo."[113] The weight of this scholarly discussion in the 1980s further
damaged the authority of anti-Americanism.

■ The Philo-Americans

As we have seen, by the mid-1980s, America—or most everything associated with America—was chic, whether it was jogging or the preppy look. America as a fashion for the status-conscious extended even to left-wing journals like *Libération* and *Le Nouvel Observateur*, in which readers found articles celebrating a yuppie-cum-American style.[114] More of the same was to be found in conservative journals like *L'Expansion* and *Le Figaro*. But there was more than status and fashion involved in this discussion; there were those who praised American society and culture: the "philo-Americans," or the most ardent anti-anti-Americans. On the periphery of these admirers were the liberal ideologues and the pragmatic modernizers, those who selectively borrowed from their American cousins.[115]

Outspoken praise for America, even at the fin de siècle, was exceptional among the intelligentsia. There had been only a handful of enthusiasts like Jean-François Revel through the 1970s, but in the next decade they spoke out more confidently and their ranks grew modestly. For example, two political moderates, Léo Sauvage and Georges Suffert, joined the small chorus. Sauvage, who had been bureau chief for *Le Figaro* in New York through the mid-1970s, collected hundreds of sympathetic stories, interviews, and anecdotes in an entertaining book titled *Les Américains* that aimed at debunking myths about France's transatlantic cousins. He made fun of Gallic fears about American urban crime, for example, by recalling an incident in Brooklyn in which the police arrested a man accused of breaking the windows of parked cars. This perpetrator, as it turned out, was not a thief or vandal but the co-owner of a local shop specializing in replacing automobile windows.[116]

Georges Suffert issued a more forceful attack. His background was that of a left-wing Catholic; he had directed the technocratic Club Jean Moulin as well as serving as editor-in-chief at Servan-Schreiber's *L'Express* before covering the United States for the moderate weekly *Le Point* in the 1970s and early 1980s. He confessed openly to love America. His book *Les Nouveaux Cowboys* was an explicit attack on anti-américanisme primaire. Sensibly, Suffert conceived of America as a vast storehouse in which an outsider could find what he or she wanted. Yet, he argued, however one evaluated America one must nevertheless admit its dynamism, its willingness to invent, change, and adapt. "The new cowboys" were the technological whiz kids and venture capitalists of Silicon Valley who created "an aristocracy of intelligence and informality which has no equivalence in my very small and very dear Europe."[117] Speaking to a typical Frenchman, Suffert counseled, "I am going to tell you why you don't like Americans: they play, they putter about assembling a world, and before long you will no longer know how to play in it."[118] When Suffert tried to explain primal anti-Americanism he identified the usual suspects, such as humiliation and jealousy; the French could neither pardon the Americans for liberating them in 1944 nor for making them feel so small, parochial, and backward—especially in technology. Then there was simple ignorance as well as the legacy of communism, and, to a lesser extent, Gaullism. Probing more deeply he found a disturbing basis for his people's historic irrationality: "one discerns vaguely a pathetic refusal of change, camouflaged under the colors of various progressive ideologies, envy of an [American] empire that invents one renaissance after another like a child blowing soap bubbles, [and] nostalgic heartache of dethroned kings...."[119] Suffert had exposed the roots of primal anti-Americanism.

On the periphery of the philo-Americans were those who found much about America that France should imitate or borrow without necessarily posing as enthusiasts. We have already encountered the French Reaganites, the economic liberals, analysts like Guy Sorman and Louis Pauwels who advocated a wholesale adoption of American economic policies and practices and saw Ronald Reagan as the anti-Mitterrand. More numerous than these free-market ideologues were the pragmatists—the descendants of a long tradition of French industrialists, labor leaders, intellectuals, and other reformers that dated back at least to the 1920s—who saw importing certain American practices and values as the way for France to remove obstacles, such as the state bureaucracy, that blocked the way to modernity. Jean Monnet, the architect of the postwar reconstruction period was part of this tradition, as were the productivity enthusiasts of the Marshall Plan era,. In the 1980s those who advocated selective borrowing—and thus either explicitly or implicitly rejected anti-Américanisme primaire—included familiar faces from earlier years like Michel Crozier and Jean-Jacques Servan-Schreiber; the latter being the author of the 1960s best-seller *The American Challenge*, gathered like-minded commentators at *L'Express* that included Revel and Suffert.[120] Latecomers to the fold of pragmatic modernizers were the likes of Michel Albert and Alain Minc, who embraced America for its spirit of innovation and risk-taking or its linkages between research and industry.[121] Albert worked at the planning commission while Minc, a prominent corporate manager and government adviser, wrote extensively about information technology and economic policy. He identified Silicon Valley with the rise of individual entrepreneurship and the vogue of the market. The roster of American-inspired modernizers could be extended to many business managers and government officials.

■ Reappraisals

For many intellectuals anti-Americanism in its "primal" formulation had become retrograde: it could be dismissed as a product of illusions, emotions, or ignorance. Nevertheless, a certain hauteur remained in their assessments of American culture. The itineraries of three prominent figures, Pierre Nora, Jean-Marie Domenach, and Régis Debray, are our evidence.

In the 1980s Pierre Nora was in the midst of editing and publishing what became the most influential history of France of his generation, the monumental *Les Lieux de mémoire* (Realms of Memory), which reconstructed the nation's memory and sense of identity. He was also directing the review *Le Débat,* teaching at the École des Hautes Études en Sciences Sociales, and serving as history editor at the venerable Éditions Gallimard, where he championed translations of major works in American social science and history. Nora described himself as a disciple of Raymond Aron and a supporter of *la gauche américaine*. He stood at the center of the myriad of networks that crisscrossed French intellectual life. Entry into the Académie Française in 2001 was to crown his career.

Among his diverse historical and intellectual interests, Nora harbored a certain fascination with the United States. In 1963 he toured the country and wrote about its people and history. He found a dynamic society but one marred by racism, consumerism, inequality, and distrust of intellectuals. What dominated his thought about America was its distance or separation from France and Europe; he accepted the notion of American exceptionalism—or, at least, the American construction of its uniqueness. Persistent mutual incomprehension followed from this transatlantic gap. In 1966 he wrote about how American historians tried to escape the "weight of the past" or a European sense of history with its ruptures, ideologies, and conflicts and substitute a narrative of consensus and progress.[122] At the core of their narrative was a faith in the universal anti-ideology of "Americanism."

A decade later, writing in *Daedalus*, he firmly asserted that American and French intellectuals could not understand one another because they had different conceptions of social science and their own roles in society. American researchers thought their French colleagues sacrificed their objectivity by straying into politics, especially Marxism, while the French saw their American peers as "docile" and given to ratifying the status quo. Or, as Nora put it, American intellectuals invested themselves with a "function" while the French practiced a "ministry." Even more important in accounting for their mutual incomprehension was their different conceptions of revolution. Where the American Revolution built a national consensus around the country's founding—"the national ideal absorbed the revolutionary ideal"—and marginalized the Left, the French Revolution destroyed consensus and made guarding the flame of revolution the *mater et magistra* of the Left's intelligentsia, lending it prestige as the counterforce to established power: "Revolution is the eternal future of a country with a long memory, in America it is the eternal past of a nation which has no memory. It is this symmetry which makes for the incommunicability of the two cultures and sets the terms of the impossible dialogue."[123] Thus American intellectuals had trouble understanding why French youth preferred to be wrong with Sartre rather than right with Raymond Aron—that is, being anti- rather than pro-American.

There was a dismissive, if not condescending, tone in Nora's writing about America in the 1970s, as if American intellectuals were a conservative lot who sought refuge from reality in empiricism, parochialism, or an illusion of a happy past and a happier future. When they attempted to study France, they could not master the assumptions or intricacies of its cultural life. As for the French, except for a handful of brilliant exceptions who, in his eyes, never had much influence, "the United States has never occupied the central position in the mental geography of French intellectuals which England held in the eighteenth century, Germany in the nineteenth, or the Soviet Union and the Third World in the twentieth. A reflection, an offshoot of Europe: that is how America is always seen; the intelligentsia of the Old World has not yet discovered the New World."[124]

During the 1980s Nora directly addressed the French public's view of America, but he shifted from condescension to detached analysis and concern. In his introduction to a special issue of the popular magazine *L'Histoire* devoted to "The American Adventure: From Lafayette to Reagan," he continued to portray America as "incomprehensible" where common terms like *state*, *freedom*, or even *God* had different meanings so that "America is more foreign to us by being so close." How, he asked, could the two societies understand one another when one nation was built on Catholicism, a peasantry, a monarchical and centralized past that entered modernity via a wrenching revolution while the other was a continent peopled with minorities, framed by a puritan and colonial background, a federalist structure, and a political consensus about its origin? Such a historical and cultural gap, Nora argued, was at the root of anti- and pro-American feelings: "Without readily understanding [one another] people take refuge in passion. A deep rooted anti-Americanism lies dormant here alongside a flamboyant pro-Americanism."[125]

Nora concluded both "-isms" were superficial because they expressed fantasies and circumstances like shifting appreciations of the international roles of the Soviet Union and the United States rather than true mutual understanding. He doubted that the facade of Americanization or the ease of travel and communication would enlighten the French about the American experience: "We do not willingly renounce the America of our mythology. Our natural rapport with the United States is not knowledge, but fascination. We only tolerate strong images, a spectacle on the big screen, the eternal other of old Europe. And we keep, for better or worse, this unreal America."[126] Nora the skeptic approved of serious historical research about America, but concluded that anti-Americanism, as well as pro-Americanism, were resistant to rational investigation because they expressed illusions and emotions.

A second figure standing at the center of Parisian intellectual life was Jean-Marie Domenach, the journalist turned public philosopher. The former editor of *Esprit* was a professor of humanities and social studies at the École Polytechnique in the 1980s. Twenty years earlier he had provided an acerbic commentary on American consumer society from the perspective of the Catholic Left, denouncing it for debasing human beings and human relations, noting how the pursuit of material comfort begat a spiritual and moral crisis represented by covetousness, waste, crime, and drugs. But he admired the American universities that had been his hosts. To Domenach, the events of 1968 represented Europe's first counterattack against the consumerism and cultural flattening transmitted by America, though he later reflected that the upheaval failed to slow Americanization. Speaking to an American academic audience in 1979 he reminded them that one topic all French intellectuals, both on the right and the left, agreed on was that France was a model of a balanced, rational, happy civilization that could be destroyed by an American inspired "technical frenzy. " They also shared a horror of the United States as a country without memory, marred by "odious mechanization" and a mass society that crushed any hint of social hierarchy.[127] Yet Domenach now distanced himself from his former anti-American vocabulary, muted his misgivings about American society, and focused on the failures of the French people at coping with the new age of the media. In his writings and talks from the late 1970s on, America became a laboratory or reference for the coming of mass culture rather than an external enemy.

Americanization, according to Domenach, had inspired some rather stupid commentary, especially that of anti-américanisme primaire. Even though he retained reservations about mass culture, he no longer held America responsible for its global reach, only for initiating and proselytizing it. If Americans introduced blue jeans, Coca-Cola, and reality TV shows, the world eagerly embraced them. (Though, in fact, Europeans originated reality TV.) Europeans had only themselves to blame, was Domenach's reproach. They had neglected their own national cultures, had lost their creativity, had accepted the superficial global culture, and allowed their collective imaginations to atrophy. "It's not the Americans who have prevented the French from writing good novels," he wrote.[128] The threat was not, as some held, from a media saturated with American images; it came from a collective passivity about culture that preferred inferior creations like insipid television programs or Disney's industrialized leisure. "Passivity is a determining element of our cultural life": this, rather than some transatlantic imposition of a banal mass culture, was the source of *le mal français*.[129]

To be sure, Americans, according to Domenach, had certain advantages in producing and spreading mass culture. Hollywood films, for example, profited from big budgets and America's special place in the European imagination—a dreamlike landscape that was both familiar and exotic. More profoundly, Americans, far more readily than the French, expressed the modern imagination. America, Domenach argued, was born in the age of democracy and large-scale industry, and its artists and writers were at ease in inscribing the modern—for example, the megapolis or technology—in what they created. The French imagination, in contrast, dated from Joan of Arc or the court at Versailles, so that "a bulldozer in Touraine is a dangerous monster" for a French reader.[130] Moreover, Domenach contended, Americans retained an Enlightenment confidence in human progress coupled with religious faith. These certainties provided them with sources of creativity that Europeans—the French, in particular—had abandoned.[131] "French intellectuals have difficulty in excusing Americans for maintaining a faith they have lost," he noted.[132] According to Domenach, the French could learn from Reagan's America, where "God is modern."

What should be done about the flood of mass culture associated with America, he asked? After endorsing Jack Lang's efforts in principle, Domenach distanced himself from a nationalist or protectionist reflex. Although he had signed the petition of the Committee for National Identity, Domenach clarified his views, observing, "The worst service we can render our culture would be to defend it as 'national culture' . . . . French culture is grand because of its universal vocation; it becomes impoverished when one treats it as an expression of a national particularity and it would accelerate its decline if one were to make it an instrument of anti-American nationalism. . . . Let's stop 'defending,' let's try to promote and assist. Let's stop denigrating other cultures, let's try to love and fortify our own. . . ."[133] In his studies of French and European cultural decline Domenach castigated his own people rather than the Americans. It was Gallic linguistic and cultural laziness that accounted for the success of the American media. The French needed to reacquaint themselves with their history and culture as well as learn about the art, literature, music, and cinema, of their fellow Europeans. He noted that, as a teacher in Paris, almost all his students had visited the United States, but a majority of them had not seen the nearby cathedral at Chartres. Domenach recommended that French elementary schools teach English because it was vital in fields like science, technology, and business, but that secondary schools should require a second

European language so that French children could have access to another European culture. Above all, the French, and the Europeans, had to recover their creativity and use it to enter the world of mass culture: "When our cinema and television are capable of producing a series like *Dallas* or films of the type that Americans made about the war in Vietnam, then the French will make a valuable contribution to European audiovisual production. French identity will be in step with Europe only if it begins to assert itself boldly and only if it agrees to enter the era of mass culture without hesitation."[134]

The third figure in this trio who banished anti-américanisme primaire was Régis Debray. As Mitterrand's confidant and onetime companion of Che Guevara, Debray, in what he called his "confession," provided a lively and candid account of his itinerary.[135] Yes, he acknowledged before an audience at New York University, he had been anti-American and, in a certain sense—that of opposing American cultural imperialism—he still was; but he then proceeded to deny the label for himself by distinguishing his views from the partisans of anti-américanisme primaire and trying to convince his audience that his current stance was reasonable.

His anti-Americanism was generational, Debray declared. He came of age (b. 1940) when U.S. support of dictatorships in Latin America outraged a young radical. All that remained of his guerilla days was his moustache, he playfully added, and that facial hair would deny him a job at Euro Disney. In fact, he insisted, he opposed all forms of imperialism whether it was that of the French in Africa or the Soviets in Eastern Europe. The American empire emerged not, as some Marxists contended, because of capitalism or because of an evil conspiracy, but simply because the United States was unopposed by other countervailing forces. Today, according to Debray, the problem was still the fight against American imperialism—not trying to topple the *caudillos*, as in the 1960s, but stemming the flood of American culture: "I fight the present hegemony exercised by American power on consciences and peoples . . ." (206). The struggle was not between France and America, but between "culture and subculture" (*sous-culture*), and it was every-one's battle (212). The source of American power was the television set in everyone's living room that colonized imaginations. As a colleague of Jack Lang, he defended the minister's protectionist policies while at the same time explicitly condemning anti-américanisme primaire. The battle was against American kitsch, against the aesthetics of mass media that simplified life, reduced experience to sentimentality, and turned politics Manichean. *Homo americanus*, the creature of the mass media, could be found everywhere in Europe. As an antidote to this mentality Debray offered one suffused with ambiguity, complexity, and uncertainty.

Anti-américanisme primaire, in his view, was beneath contempt; it was a kind of pathology or hysteria, an essentialism, an ahistorical stereotype that refused to try to understand either the complexities of America—citing Las Vegas, but not Harvard University—or what was facing France. It simply assigned all the sins of modernity to America. Such prejudice was common among old-fashioned intellectuals, but did not exist within the business community or the media. Debray re-fused to have his views identified as "anti-American" in the sense of this phobia (202). How, he asked, can you be anti-American when America makes us all dream, when it creates the imaginary? This was America's greatest triumph. One had to be a killjoy, or a Trappist monk, to be anti-American today. Debray affably reminded his audience of how much he liked Americans, how he envied their freedom and openness, their universities, museums, and libraries. If he had to go into exile, his choice, he revealed, would be between Italy and the United States. The other object of scorn, besides those who hated America, were those who idolized it. These philo-Americans, in his view, failed to under-stand America any better than those who deplored it. They ignored the widening gap between the American dream and the reality of shabby cities, high infant-mortality rates, disastrous pollution, low political participation, and ubiquitous religious practice.

Debray added a note on international affairs to his confession that praised Charles de Gaulle for curing him of his former small-minded, bilious, reactive anti-Americanism by giving the French back their self-respect so that they no longer needed the American scapegoat. Don't, he alerted his New York listeners, expect France always to align itself with the United States because (citing de Gaulle again) France wanted allies, not masters. The fundamental aim of French foreign policy, in an age of increasing global interdependence, was still to reduce dependency to as low a level as possible.

Debray ended his confession by expressing his disapproval of how the mass media had dispossessed the intelligentsia—how the TV anchor had replaced the poet. And he worried about how France had become "wired" to America via the media so that the average Parisian felt closer to New York or Houston than to Hamburg or Madrid. This middle-age radical exposed his cultural traditionalism and republican values when he coyly expressed the wish that he would not be condemned as anti-American because he still believed in a civilization where one reads books; respects Sundays and the circumflex accent; honors citizenship and a republic that is elective rather than ethnic; esteems *laïcité* and the school as a transnational community rather than a pluralistic community; and believes that people are more than the sum of opinion polls (218).

Anti-américanisme primaire retreated to the margins of the debate over America in the 1980s. There may have been some strident believers of the old religion whom Jacques Julliard derided as political extremists, dissident Gaullists, vengeful traditionalists, and assorted intellectual mediocrities, but, unlike the early postwar decades, they no longer dominated the discussion. Among the implicit, if not explicit, critics of anti-américanisme primaire were the opponents of Jack Lang's "crusade" against American cultural imperialism; these included the likes of Alain Finkielkraut, Guy Konopnicki, Michel Tournier, André

Glucksmann, Pierre Daix, and Bernard-Henri Lévy. It was the anti-anti-Americans who gained in confidence and status. From Jacques Julliard on the left to Georges Suffert at the center it became de rigueur to lampoon those who tried to give intellectual or political legitimacy to the scapegoating of America. Within the world of political journalism, former American baiters either lost their appetite for the fight or enlisted in the cause of giving America a fair assessment. This was true of such established leftist, or left-center, publications as *L'Express*, *Le Nouvel Observateur*, *Le Point*, *Esprit*, *Libération*, and *Le Monde*, and weighty newcomers like *Le Débat* and *Commentaire* joined in. These were the most read publications. Circulation of weeklies like *Le Nouvel Observateur*, *L'Express*, and *Le Point* ranged from 300,000 to 500,000 copies, in contrast to the small run of the New Right's reviews, whose subscribers were less than 5,000. Notables like Pierre Nora, Jean-Marie Domenach, and Régis Debray, who stood at the center of French intellectual life and had (in the case of the Domenach and Debray) earlier expressed anti-American sentiments reappraised their stance and invited balanced and nuanced assessments of America while the academic community dissected and embalmed the phenomenon.

Cultural snobbishness still prevailed, and one could make fun of Americans and American culture, but this was far removed from a past when intellectuals like Jean-Paul Sartre and Simone de Beauvoir could intimidate Saint-Germain des Près with their anti-American posturing. In the 1980s, when Alain de Benoist tried to elevate the phobia to a megapolitical ideology or Jean Baudrillard attempted to transform it into a postmodern discourse, their efforts simply fell flat. Circumstances, of course, would change in the 1990s, and the old tropes about America would surface especially among the political class and in popular attitudes, but anti-américanisme primaire had lost its standing within the intellectual community. It would appear only in insufferable polemics.

3.

Reverie and Rivalry: Mitterrand and Reagan-Bush

According to Evan Galbraith, the American ambassador in Paris, Franco-American affairs in the early 1980s were "probably the best they had been since 1918."[1] Many contemporary observers viewed relations as a kind of reverie. François Mitterrand and Ronald Reagan, even if the two presidents were a study in contrasts, were usually congenial, while Mitterrand and George H. W. Bush respected each other and enjoyed what might, with only slight exaggeration, be termed friendship. Transatlantic relations were arguably better in this decade than at any time since the end of the Second World War. They were surely more relaxed than in the troubled years of the Fourth Republic, when the allies quarreled over most everything from Germany to Indochina, or the early Fifth Republic, when Charles de Gaulle removed France from the integrated command of NATO. And there was far less turmoil than the early 1970s, which witnessed the hostile crowds in Chicago assailing President Georges Pompidou and mutual recriminations about the war in Vietnam. Troubles eased somewhat later in the decade after Valéry Giscard d'Estaing became president and Jimmy Carter won cautious approval from the French for his pursuit of détente and his advocacy of human rights, but his vacillating policies and his failure to recover American hostages in Tehran tarnished his reputation. There was marked improvement after 1982, and by 1984–85 the United States and, to a lesser extent, Ronald Reagan, were genuinely popular.

If the 1980s were, in comparison to what preceded and what followed, a kind of transatlantic reverie, like all daydreams they masked reality—and they had to come to an end. Despite the TV coverage of cheerful statesmen attending summit meetings and the upbeat polls for Reagan and Bush, there were sharp disagreements, mutual mistrust, and even some nasty spats—which occurred mostly off camera. For example, in 1981, Evan Galbraith publicly insulted President Mitterrand, who ranted in private that if Galbraith weren't ambassador he would have expelled him from the country.[2] Some officials in the Reagan administration never flagged in their expression of dislike for Mitterrand. The quarreling between the two allies that persisted throughout the seemingly decorous 1980s exposed a fundamental Franco-American rivalry that turned on American unilateralism, opposing conceptions of the Atlantic Alliance and the French quest for autonomy within that alliance.

Independence for France and for Europe was, as is usually pointed out, the fundamental goal of French diplomacy. There were several reasons for this pursuit of autonomy, such as the security that comes from being master in one's own house. But, as this chapter stresses, the American Gulliver also served as a foil for the nation's identity in the world. The degrees of separation from the United States, more than the strength of the partnership, determined self-esteem and France's role as a major player in global affairs. Independence helped define what it was to be "French" on the international stage, and it was the U.S. superpower that deprived France of attaining this status.

Mitterrand's France employed various strategies aimed at channeling or curbing the energies of the superpower, ranging from acting as the U.S. government's confidant to resorting to obstructionism. Nothing worked—except when other European countries joined in and faced the United States as a solid front. At international summits France often felt both isolated and dominated, and on one occasion Mitterrand threatened to stay away altogether. Frustration became most apparent when he had to yield to President Bush and watch the Americans and the West Germans manage German unification.

This chapter will blend the narrative of relations between Paris and Washington with the response of the French media, elites, and public. Before embarking on this story it is important to sketch a picture of French attitudes toward American power, policy, and leaders on the eve of the elections of Presidents Reagan and Mitterrand.

As evidence for perceptions, the principal sources are opinion surveys and the print media. The two were tightly related. As one expert has pointed out, opinion in this case was "an echo of an echo"—meaning that surveys reflected largely how the media informed the public.[3] And the press and television acted as the principal conduits of information about international affairs. Elites depended more on the press, and the public more heavily on the little screen.[4] A historian must be careful about survey data because attitudes could be ephemeral and inconsistent, respondents were often poorly informed, and answers depended on wording and context. It made a difference if pollsters asked about views of the United States as opposed to those about Ronald Reagan. It made a difference when polls were conducted—for example, during or after major incidents—and what choices were allowed. Nevertheless, there is a sufficiently large body of survey data, some of which are continuous, as well as print materials, to provide a fair idea of how people viewed Franco-American affairs.

A distinction must be drawn between elites and public opinion. Among the elites there were policy makers who were directing relations with Washington; intellectuals, mainly situated in Paris, debating the relevance of America for France; and other opinion makers like journalists and television reporters. Then there was everyone else. Sometimes elites and the public were aligned, as they were during the mid-1980s, but at other times they were at odds. In principle, one should also expect inconsistency, ambivalence, and contradictions when either elites or ordinary French citizens expressed themselves about America.

The United States had lost its luster in the 1970s as a world power because of the sad end to the war in Vietnam and the turmoil surrounding the Watergate scandal. Then came the Soviet buildup. Beginning in the early 1970s, less and less of the French viewed the United States as the most powerful country in the world, and by 1977 twice as many believed the Soviets, rather than the Americans, were ahead in total military strength. In tandem came dimming perceptions of American economic advantage, which declined to the point that by 1980 almost as many thought the Japanese and the West Germans were economically as strong as the United States.[5]

None of this rebounded to the advantage of the other superpower. Over the same years the Soviet Union suffered from a deteriorating reputation; it steadily lost its standing, even among the French Left, as a progressive country that was committed to peace. The so-called Gulag effect was operating here. Accompanying this darker image was growing concern about expansionism, especially after the Soviet Union's interventions in Africa and Afghanistan, as well as deepening anxiety about Moscow posing a military and political threat to Western Europe. On the eve of the French presidential election in 1981 a majority believed the military might of the Eastern bloc was greater than that of the West; and more of the French, after the declaration of martial law in Poland later that year, believed the USSR was the greatest danger to world peace.[6] But the scowl from Moscow did not mean the French wanted a return to the Cold War. It may have led some to welcome a more assertive America, but many in France remained committed to détente, or at least expressed a strong preference for negotiation, rather than adopting a confrontational posture vis-à-vis the Soviets. And it certainly did not recommend that they lean more heavily on the Atlantic Alliance. Yes, the Soviets were more threatening, but the danger seemed abstract and remote rather than real and immediate. The French in the late 1970s worried almost as much about the danger to international peace emanating from the United States as they did that represented by the Soviet Union, while they were also apprehensive about other problems like instability in the Middle East. In fact, many continued to prefer "a nonbinding relationship" with the

United States and a path that fell between the superpowers; some even wanted strict neutrality in the Cold War. A 1979 survey on the Atlantic Alliance indicated that most of the French hoped for an independent stance in the Cold War and, surprisingly, only one in five opted for a military alliance between Western Europe and the United States.[7]

America's faltering power was only part of its diminished reputation. When asked to select between favorable and unfavorable views of the United States, the latter grew from the early 1970s and continued to increase during the early years of the Reagan administration. By late 1981 unfavorable views were as high as they had been at any time during the Fifth Republic.[8] To be sure, the British and the West Germans recorded a similar pattern. If the question posed in surveys was more narrowly circumscribed as whether or not the respondent had confidence in U.S. leadership, the trend was the same. From the nadir, which came in 1975 at the end of the war in Vietnam and the Watergate scandal, the level of confidence rose under President Carter, but remained low; it then declined again in 1981–82. The arrival of Ronald Reagan at the White House did not, at least at first, stem this downward trend in French perceptions of how Washington managed world affairs.

■ State-to-state relations were essential to the cozier atmosphere of the 1980s. Governments set the mood and, to an extent, the public followed their lead. Thus, any explanation of this belle époque of transatlantic relations must address policy makers—especially François Mitterrand, who managed how France dealt with the United States for five years after he became president. Even after 1986, when legislative elections brought a conservative majority, thus forcing Mitterrand to share power with Jacques Chirac, the president permitted the Gaullist prime minister little room for defining transatlantic policy. In short, the historian must look first to Mitterrand and his foreign policy team for answers.

When speaking of "French" or "American" policy one must be aware that such terms homogenize often conflicting views among those making decisions. While President Mitterrand, for example, may have been the most important player, he and his team at the Elysée had to work with the prime minister and his or her government; the military or defense establishment, which was generally keen on closer ties with the Americans; and the foreign ministry or Quai d'Orsay—an agency that was reputed to be the least amenable of all policy-making bodies toward working with the Americans. Nor did unanimity reign within these circles of power even among the Elysée staff. For example, not all of the president's advisers agreed with the radical agenda of Régis Debray, who subscribed to the principle that "there is more power in rock music, videos, blue jeans, fast food, news networks and TV satellites than in the entire Red Army" and wanted to promote revolution in Central America.[9] Mitterrand also had to take into account socialist leaders, who watched closely lest he betray the party's ideals by aligning too closely with the United States and international capitalism, as well as his communist governing partners. As for public opinion, Mitterrand paid close attention to it, but he was not subservient.[10] Similarly, the White House made policy with the advice of the National Security Council, the State Department, the intelligence community, the Treasury, and the Pentagon, among others; it should not be assumed these actors always held the same views in dealing with France, because the Reagan administration was notorious for its infighting over the control of foreign policy.

Mitterrand, as we have seen, thought of himself as a friend of the American people. Whatever affection he may have had for Americans, however, did not, prior to his presidency, translate into admiration for the American dominated Atlantic Alliance. "I like Americans," he wrote, "but not their policy. Under the Fourth Republic I was exasperated by the climate of submitting to their least desires. I did not recognize their right to pose as the world's gendarmes."[11] During the 1967 legislative elections he spoke for a negotiated, step-by-step elimination of both the Atlantic Alliance and the Warsaw Pact. In 1972 the Socialist Party's program called for the "renunciation" of France's nuclear deterrent and denounced NATO because it tied "all signatories to American imperialism and . . . expose[d] them to preventive attacks." Moreover, Mitterrand as party leader complained that the alliance facilitated France's "economic colonization by the United States."[12] He wrote in 1980 that he felt "no more attached to the Atlantic Alliance than a Rumanian or a Pole did to the Warsaw Pact."[13]

As the presidential elections of 1981 neared, however, the socialists muffled their reproaches, endorsed the force de frappe, and accepted NATO while still warning about aligning with "imperialist"—that is, American—positions in world affairs. Political reality had forced the socialists to adjust. If the Left had any chance of coming to power in the Fifth Republic by attracting moderate voters, it had to accept the fact that France's independence and prestige depended on maintaining its nuclear deterrent and that NATO, if in need of reform, was increasingly vital to national security. The prime mover behind this shift was the growing threat in the 1970s from the Soviet Union, which had been building up its conventional forces in Central Europe and deploying intermediate-range multiple-warhead missiles (SS-20s) targeted at countries like France. The Cold War balance in Europe had tilted against the West. Soviet intervention in Third World hot spots like Angola heightened the sense that the Russian bear was on the prowl. But it was the Soviet invasion of Afghanistan in 1979 that confirmed suspicions that communism was on the move again. The read from Paris was that the Cold War had returned and détente was on hold. The United States, meanwhile, distracted by Watergate and adhering to détente under Presidents Richard Nixon, Gerald Ford, and Jimmy Carter, seemed to be meekly committed to Europe's defense. To make matters worse, West Germany, as it pursued its *Ostpolitik* in the 1970s, appeared to be embracing its own form of détente with Eastern European regimes and the USSR. The arrival of SS-20s, or the popularly named "Euromissiles," on their borders intensified the appeal of neutrality among the German populace, and President Carter's decision to compensate by deploying American intermediate-range Pershing II and cruise missiles in Western Europe (though not in France) roused open opposition among many members of the Social Democratic and Green Parties, both of whom called for nuclear disarmament. The fear was that the West Germans were losing their commitment to the Atlantic Alliance and seeking security by dealing with Moscow. As Mitterrand famously quipped about the Germans, "The missiles are in the East, but the pacifists are in the West."[14] He believed France needed to bolster the Atlantic Alliance both to keep Germany from slipping away and to offset the Soviet threat.

During the presidential campaign Mitterrand criticized his rival, the incumbent Giscard, for being too accommodating to the Soviets, especially for meeting Leonid Brezhnev after the Afghanistan invasion. As early as 1977 he had warned that the SS-20s would lead to decoupling the United States from Europe. NATO, in his estimation, had always rested on the dubious assumption that the United States would automatically intervene with strategic nuclear weapons in the event of Soviet aggression. Soviet intermediate-range missiles would make what was already suspect unlikely, because Washington might hesitate at crossing the strategic threshold in the event of a tactical missile strike and ground attack by Moscow. By 1979–80 Mitterrand had come to accept the need to reinforce the Atlantic Alliance because a second Cold War had emerged. But this did not mean he would propose reentering NATO's integrated military command structure, endorse an extension of NATO's reach, accept the U.S. government's "bad habit" of avoiding consultation with its allies, sacrifice France's independent nuclear deterrent, or freeze relations with Moscow. The "new Atlanticism" would, as we shall see, resemble Gaullist balancing among the superpowers rather than a break with the past. As his adviser on international affairs phrased it, Mitterrand wanted to move France closer toward the United States and NATO, toward a policy that made France an "ami, allié, pas aligné."[15]

Just as François Mitterrand was ready to cross the Atlantic, Ronald Reagan was anxious to scrap the policy of détente because he believed it sustained the Cold War rather than ending it. The White House was determined to pursue a far more aggressive agenda against the Soviet Union, including spending heavily on arms, competing for advantage in the Third World, and doing whatever was necessary to weaken the Soviets. There was a happy convergence, with Reagan and Mitterrand moving in the same direction.

To the surprise and joy of the Left, Mitterrand became president in May 1981; the legislative elections that followed gave the socialists and their communist allies a majority, and the new government of Pierre Mauroy included four communist ministers. Now a socialist government in Paris would have to deal with a conservative administration in Washington.

As soon as he became president Mitterrand began courting the Americans—a typical pattern for incoming French heads of state.[16] He was not only eager to implement his "new Atlanticism" as a riposte to the Soviet buildup but was also anxious to head off the major free-market liberal countries, the United States and the United Kingdom (where Margaret Thatcher was then prime minister), from "marginalizing socialist France."[17] There was good reason to be anxious. The Reagan administration expected trouble with what some labeled the "socialist-communist government" in Paris. They wondered, Would it be soft on communism and hard on NATO? U.S. Ambassador Galbraith said he couldn't stand "the word socialism" and thought of Mitterrand as "an opportunist."[18]

The new president gave his first interview to the *New York Times*, telling James Reston of his "kindred feeling for the American people," his interest in visiting the United States, his misgivings about SS-20s, and his intention not of collectivizing the French economy but simply restoring to "national ownership what belonged to the nation."[19] Reagan immediately sent Vice President George H. W. Bush to Paris out of concern about the communist ministers. Mitterrand assured Bush that he had brought them into the government in order to weaken them and that they would not affect his foreign policy or the Atlantic Alliance. The communists, the new president told his visitor, had "introduced a totalitarian poison" that was incompatible with the humanist traditions of French socialism.[20] It was a good start for Bush and Mitterrand.

Mitterrand went further in wooing the Americans. He approved what was called the "dual track" strategy—that is, accompanying arms talks with the deployment of Pershing II and cruise missiles, which President Carter had begun and Reagan had now advanced, in order to balance Soviet intermediate-range missiles. From the French perspective, however, such deployment would only be a last resort should superpower negotiations over arms control being conducted in Geneva fail. Paris refused to let Moscow acquire the power to intimidate it on security issues and to decouple the United States from Europe. [21]

It was at the Ottawa Summit of Industrialized Nations in July 1981 that the two presidents first met. They tried to charm one another, with Mitterrand praising Reagan for his courage in facing his attempted assassination and Reagan inviting the French president to attend the two hundredth anniversary celebration of the Battle of Yorktown in October. Mitterrand tried to win Reagan's trust by passing important information gleaned by a French intelligence "mole" in Moscow about several Soviet projects, including revelations about the extent of Soviet espionage in the United States. Stunned by the intelligence, Reagan supposedly exclaimed, "That's the biggest fish since 1945."[22] He took his French colleague aside and explained how he had distrusted the communists ever since the Kremlin had supposedly trained a priest and sent him to Hollywood to take control of the screen actors' guild. When Mitterrand expressed some skepticism, Reagan informed him that there were many people in the United States who were unidentified communist spies. Mitterrand confided to an aide that Reagan had watched the TV series *The Invaders* too often.[23]

The French president visited North America three times during his first year in office, including the celebrations at Yorktown. Whatever differences existed over issues like American high interest rates or the Sandinistas in Nicaragua were papered over. Mitterrand and Reagan were bent on courting one another. Mitterrand found Reagan, as he told the German chancellor Helmut Schmidt, "a man without ideas or culture . . . but underneath this exterior, you will find a man who is not stupid, who has abundant good sense and who is basically kind. And what he doesn't make out with his intelligence, he grasps innately."[24] Reagan was pleased that the French seemed on board; he was now convinced that their leader was a stout anticommunist.[25] In fact, Reagan admitted that when he first met Mitterrand he did not realize there was a difference between socialism and communism.[26]

Pierre Mauroy's government took aim at the Soviets. The Ministry of Defense under Charles Hernu broke with tradition and singled out the USSR as "the primary threat to French security."[27] Mitterrand suspended regular summit meetings with the Kremlin as long as France was subject to blackmail by the SS-20s. In the spring of 1983 the minister of the interior expelled forty-seven Soviet officials from France, most presumed to be KGB agents, accused of scientific and military espionage. Later that year the Soviets inadvertently stoked the fire by shooting down a Korean passenger airliner. But the Elysée believed that the Kremlin didn't want war, that it instead wanted to threaten war to get what it wanted—or, as Mitterrand observed, "they play checkers, not poker."[28]

The socialists had to act tough in order to persuade Moscow to negotiate a de-escalation of tension. The Mitterrand-Mauroy-Hernu team raised defense spending, overhauled conventional military forces, and enhanced strategic nuclear deterrence with programs like refitting its submarine fleet with multiple warhead missiles and developing longer-range tactical nuclear weapons (such as the Hadès missile).[29] The most novel addition was the creation of the Force d'Action Rapide (FAR) of 50,000 well-equipped troops capable of fighting on the German front line in case of a Soviet attack.[30] France appeared to be moving away from reliance on nuclear deterrence toward engaging in conventional combat with NATO. As one defense expert concluded, the fear was no longer that the United States would draw France into an unwanted conflict as in the days of de Gaulle but that it might not honor its obligation to its European allies should the Soviets attack. And the French acknowledged openly that Europe's defense depended on the Americans. Mitterrand reiterated time and again that France wanted the United States in Europe: "I continue to believe that the worst danger for us at present, as for our neighbors in Western Europe, would be that America withdraws from the shores of our continent."[31] ("At present"—*présentement*—of course introduces some ambiguity to this affirmation.) Foreign minister Claude Cheysson admitted that "the guarantee of European territories that do not have nuclear weapons therefore can come only from the integrated command of NATO, that is to say, in fact, the U.S."[32] Nevertheless, the Mitterrand administration insisted it alone controlled the use of its military forces, including its nuclear deterrent. Furthermore, it argued, since the force de frappe was strictly defensive, it was not comparable to the huge nuclear arsenals of the two superpowers and should not be counted in arms limitations talks like those underway in Geneva that were aimed at curbing the new Euromissiles.

France, according to one defense official, "has no more complexes with respect to the [Atlantic] Alliance. . . . We contend that there is no discrepancy at all between our resolve for independence and our desire for solidarity."[33] Contact between the French military and NATO command was closer in the mid-1980s than ever before under the Fifth Republic.[34] In addition to planning for the FAR there were many forms of cooperation, including joint naval maneuvers, access to French hospitals to treat American casualties, and the use of French airspace for the refueling of U.S. bombers. Out of the public eye, American and French experts were collaborating on nuclear weapons development. The program named Apollon, which began under Presidents Carter and Giscard, was covert because the Americans did not want to appear that they were violating their own law against sharing nuclear technology and the French sought to guard their image of nuclear independence.[35] Reagan's administration would exploit this secret program to coerce Mitterrand to stop aiding the Sandinistas.

In a formal, diplomatic sense, as well as in its defense posture, the Fifth Republic warmed to the Atlantic Alliance even if it continued to remain outside its military command structure and limited its participation in its policy-making organ, the North Atlantic Council. Where Giscard had downplayed alliance formalities, in 1982 Mitterrand attended meetings of the alliance. The next year, for the first time since the 1960s, France hosted the annual meeting of the North Atlantic Council.[36] Mitterrand proclaimed that the Atlantic Alliance and the force de frappe were the "two pillars of our security."[37] Outside the alliance France cooperated with the United States in Lebanon, Chad, and Iraq.

Reconciliation with Washington enjoyed far more domestic support on the right than on the left. Among the political class, Jacques Chirac, head of the Rassemblement pour la République (RPR) before he became prime minister in 1986, backed the socialists' endorsement of the dual-track strategy and preferred even closer consultation with NATO while Giscard, the leader of the Union pour la Démocratie Française (UDF), tried to prove he was a better ally of the United States than was Mitterrand.[38] But there was grumbling within the Socialist Party: Lionel Jospin, the secretary-general, insisted socialists had reservations about the new Atlanticism and the party's goal remained the dissolution of both NATO and the Warsaw Pact; other spokesmen criticized the United States as a country that had never conceived of a comprehensive international design except containment.[39] To be sure, the communists were not pleased with the chummy Atlanticism of their own government. They accused their socialist partners of abandoning Gaullist principles of independence and security that assumed that French forces served only the goal of national defense.[40] The media, meanwhile, were sharply divided about Reagan and, implicitly, about Atlanticism. If conservative, and even some moderate, journalists praised Reagan for abandoning the illusions of détente, columnists on the left were less indulgent, stressing his failures like the retreat from

Beirut after the attacks on U.S. and French servicemen in 1983.[41] At the same time Washington's policies toward Central America and the Middle East were almost universally ridiculed in the press.

The French public was not enthusiastic about either the new Atlanticism or the stationing of Euromissiles. Whereas in other West European societies "stronger U.S. leadership" in the alliance was deemed desirable, in France half of both elites and the public believed it was not. Polls indicated that as little as a third of the respondents favored American deployment, and most preferred that arms negotiation take precedence over deployment.[42] Almost half opposed stationing Pershing II missiles even if the Soviets maintained their stock of SS-20s.[43]

At Bonn in January 1983 the French rapprochement with the United States made world headlines. In an unprecedented address to the Bundestag, the president of France lectured the legislators on the need to support Chancellor Helmut Kohl and the Christian Democrats who had endorsed the deployment of Pershing and cruise missiles. Mitterrand the socialist spoke out against the pacifist tendencies of the German Social Democrats and asked the West Germans to back the Atlantic Alliance, arguing that it was the Soviets who had wrecked the balance in Europe. Ronald Reagan wrote to thank Mitterrand for his speech: "Your Bonn speech reinforces the Alliance at the very moment when European countries are admitting their impotence, or at any rate their anxiety, in the face of public opinion. I fully share your judgment about the risks of decoupling between Europe and the United States. Your speech is an important contribution to our mutual efforts at reinforcing Western security . . . it is of inestimable value."[44] The analyst Philip Gordon concludes that "the Mitterrand government went further to cooperate with NATO than any French administration for more than twenty years including that of the so-called Atlanticist, Giscard d'Estaing."[45] It would be over a decade before a French president would come so close to embracing the alliance again.

The climax to the conciliation of the Reagan administration came during the formal state visit of the French president to the United

States in March 1984. The limits of the new Atlanticism and Mitterrand's allegiance to Gaullist principles of balance between the superpowers were also apparent. Since the economic and cultural aspects of this tour were discussed in chapter 1, attention here will be directed to the diplomatic agenda.

Mitterrand began with a meeting at the White House and a speech to the U.S. Congress in which he praised the heroes of the American War of Independence for representing the principles of freedom, law, and respect for others and oneself.[46] If there were allusions to some differences, like those over Central America, Mitterrand impressed everyone with his courtesy. Speaking of the Atlantic Alliance the French president made the usual reference to Gallic independence and insistence on full partnership. He noted that the alliance's success depended on candor, consultation, and the acceptance of different points of view: "[I]t's in remaining themselves that France and the United States understand and respect one another. It is essential that the two countries can count on each other."[47] He reminded the members of Congress that each member of the Atlantic Alliance determined its own relations with the Soviet Union and, with a bow toward renewing détente, that allies should not be afraid of reopening conversations with Moscow about reducing nuclear weapons. At the state dinner that followed, Ronald Reagan said he approved of his guest's remarks.

After a stop in Atlanta to meet Mayor Andrew Young and lay flowers at the tomb of Dr. Martin Luther King Jr., Mitterrand flew to California for his now famous visit to Silicon Valley. In a telling rhetorical stumble in San Francisco Mitterrand said, "Nous aimons le peuple américain," which the translator rendered as "We love the United States," but the president corrected the translation, saying, "the American people."[48] He returned via New York, where the weeklong tour ended with a gathering at the home of his friend Elie Wiesel and other intellectuals like William Styron; some said this meeting aimed at compensating for Jack Lang's speech in Mexico City about American cultural imperialism.

Everything had gone well on the official tour, unlike the awful visit of President Georges Pompidou in 1970. *Le Monde* praised Mitterrand for the "excellent state of relations between the White House and the Elysée."[49] One American official said the U.S. State Department now "saw fewer problems between the United States and France than between the United States and Britain."[50] And Secretary of State George Schultz stated to the French press that France was "a very reliable friend" and that "we don't have a better one."[51] A close adviser who had accompanied the French president assessed the visit as a complete success and called 1984 "an idyllic year" for Franco-American relations.[52]

Despite such applause, all was not well between France and the United States during the early 1980s; insiders knew it, and the public caught glimpses of trouble. France was indeed a friend and an ally, but it was not aligned. The story is one of continued attempts at redirecting the superpower or, at times, obstructing it—usually with little success.

Mitterrand was always something less than the "new Cold Warrior" that the Reagan administration sought, according to historian Frédéric Bozo.[53] The Elysée continued to believe in détente as the best way of loosening Moscow's grip on Eastern Europe. Poland's imposition of martial law, encouraged by the Kremlin, only underscored this problem. More generally, Paris had never relinquished its geopolitical goal of ending the superpowers' division of Europe symbolized by Yalta. "All that will help leaving Yalta is good," Mitterrand declared on television on New Years Eve 1981. His diplomatic team, moreover, soon learned that embracing the Atlantic Alliance compromised their independence and encouraged Washington's bad habit of dominating its allies, forcing its interpretation of agreements on others, and trying to extend NATO's scope and functions. Transatlantic solidarity had its disadvantages. In 1982 Mitterrand politely rebuked Reagan for "not respecting national personalities" within the alliance.[54] By 1984 the French president was ready to visit Moscow and resume détente.

The earliest trouble between France and the United States surfaced over the Sandinista government in Nicaragua. The French socialists, with their dedication to *tiers-mondisme*, sought to aid this embattled leftist regime that the Reagan administration was trying to suffocate.[55] In the eyes of French diplomats, the White House, in its anticommunist ardor, mistakenly assumed that the Soviets intended to create a new Cuba in Nicaragua and U.S. support for rightist movements like the contras—that is, anti-Sandinistas insurgents—as well as authoritarian regimes in Central America would only inflame the entire region and play into the hands of Moscow. Speaking in Mexico in 1981, Mitterrand chided Washington for introducing Cold War politics into countries that were trying to emerge from backwardness while insisting his efforts at easing the north-south divide did not contradict his rapprochement with the United States.[56] In December of that year France agreed to supply the Sandinista government with economic aid, arms, and helicopters. The French public, in general, supported their government on this issue and strongly disapproved of U.S. policy in Central America.[57]

In Washington the Republicans, eager to overturn the Nicaraguan government by helping the contras, were upset by France's meddling in the region. State Department officials complained, "Central America is an ideological freebie for the French. They can be as leftist as they want there. Whatever happens can do them no harm. . . ."[58] The White House, sensing communism on the march in the region, objected vehemently to the arms deal and suspended Apollon, the covert program that assisted French development of nuclear weapons. Mitterrand had to fly to Washington in March 1982 to patch matters up personally with the White House. Reagan said he could not tolerate communism "south of the Rio Grande" and warned gravely that the arms deal placed Franco-American strategic cooperation at risk.[59] Mitterrand responded that American policy in Central America was "counterproductive," yet he drew back because he was unwilling to antagonize the White House over a minor matter and sacrifice nuclear cooperation. The Elysée suspended further sales of weapons to the Sandinistas; a month later Apollon was revived. In the end Paris submitted to Washington's coercion. It also lacked the means and the determination to bolster the Sandinistas: France had only modest resources for foreign aid, and priority went to Francophone Africa. Yet French officials continuing to criticize the U.S. government over Central America and other issues prompted the White House in October 1982 to send a special emissary to the Elysée who insisted that France tone down its "anti-American campaign." Once again Mitterrand stepped back rather than jeopardize relations with Reagan, and he urged both sides to turn down the volume. In the early 1980s the socialists had to retreat from helping the Third World even if they never relinquished the cause in theory.

American monetary and economic policies aggravated the Europeans—especially the French. There was friction over tariffs and agricultural subsidies, but the biggest problem was America's high interest rates and the overvalued dollar exchange rate, which contributed to inflation and unemployment in France as well as to trade deficits and hindered the socialists from stimulating the French economy. Mitterrand found the U.S. government uncooperative: he said obliquely that the dollar appeared "not to have understood its duties" and its increasing value represented "a practically intolerable" situation for the rest of the world.[60] The Reagan administration, when pressed by the French, cited the need for an elevated dollar to fight inflation and blamed the Democratic-led U.S. Congress for deficits; otherwise it ignored their entreaties about staging an international monetary conference to address the problem.

The primary transatlantic grievance was American financial policy.[61] Large majorities saw the United States as uncooperative and unconcerned about helping improve European economic conditions. Objections ranged across the political spectrum with—unusually—the UDF and RPR supporters registering even stronger criticism on this issue than the socialists or communists.[62] The media excited opinion by blaming the Americans for refusing to rein in the dollar. The public thought that during his presidency Jimmy Carter had taken better account of West Europeans than Ronald Reagan was presently.[63] Then came trouble with the Soviets.

The imposition of martial law by the Polish government in December 1981 prompted the Reagan administration to retaliate with trade sanctions against Poland and the USSR. A combination of concerns, such as the need to offset the Soviet military buildup; to thwart Soviet efforts—including espionage—at technological catch-up; and ultimately to bring the USSR to the negotiating table, convinced the U.S. government that the West needed to curb exports of technology and credits that might strengthen its Cold War rival. Some hard-liners on the Reagan team, though not the president himself, wanted to launch all-out economic warfare against the Soviets in order to create stress that might topple the regime.[64] The specific issue was the proposed Euro-Soviet pipeline, which would bring natural gas from Siberia to Western Europe; the United States feared it would give Moscow hard currency, Western technology, and leverage with which to control its European customers.[65] But West Europeans—including the French—who were dependent on the Organization of Petroleum Exporting Countries wanted to diversify their energy supplies: they were willing to extend credits and sell advanced technology in order to construct a pipeline that would stretch from Siberia to the Czechoslovak border and then transfer natural gas to West European consumers. The Reagan administration sought a coordinated Western policy that would apply sanctions, curb credits, and effectively kill the pipeline. The West Europeans submitted to Washington's pressure over some penalties, but balked at the prospect of giving the United States control over trade with Eastern Europe and the possibility of scuttling the Siberian project. On this issue a majority of the French people backed their government, believing that buying energy from the Soviets would not make them vulnerable to political pressure from Moscow.[66] Trade with the Soviets, the pipeline, and American interest rates became the top agenda items at the G7 meeting held at Versailles in June 1982.

Mitterrand dazzled Reagan and the other heads of state by staging an opulent and carefully choreographed conference at the palace of Louis XIV, but disputes over dealing with the Soviets upset the pageant. Mitterrand and his West German counterpart, Helmut Schmidt, objected to Reagan's attempt at using the G7 for political purposes, particularly for, as they put it, creating a "political directorate" that would control exports and credits with the Eastern bloc according to political criteria.[67] American negotiators at Versailles pushed their agenda so hard that their French counterparts complained of the "brutality of unilateralism." They also charged the United States with holding back financial help for the defense of the franc, which was facing another humiliating devaluation, as a form of diplomatic blackmail.[68] Behind his back French officials scoffed at Reagan's ignorance of issues and ridiculed his boasts—based on his experience in Hollywood with the Screen Actor's Guild in the 1950s—about knowing how to treat communists.

At the end of the summit the statesmen tried to conceal their bickering with an embarrassingly vague final communiqué. A disappointed French president lashed out at the United States in the press for its "insupportable attitude of political and economic domination."[69] On the left the press spoke of basic differences that divided the two countries over dealing with the Soviets, describing Reagan as indulging in "simplistic anticommunism," mistakenly attributing disorder in the Third World to Soviet subversion, and demanding "blind loyalty" of Europeans while neglecting their interests.[70] American hypocrisy also seemed evident when the Reagan administration, after admonishing the Europeans against subsidizing the communist bloc, ended former president Carter's grain embargo and resumed shipments to the Soviet Union.

The Europeans, as it turned out, wrongly believed they had conceded enough on trade and credits to merit American softening on the pipeline. Shortly after the Versailles Summit the quarrel escalated when the Reagan administration, instead of relaxing the pressure on its allies, unilaterally extended the scope of sanctions to include retroactively foreign subsidiaries and licensees of American companies. It appeared that European firms would suffer for providing equipment based on American know-how to the Soviets. The French manufacturer Alsthom-Atlantique, which was scheduled to supply rotors patented under General Electric, was singled out for penalties if it disregarded the embargo. The Americans were insisting that the Europeans violate their contractual agreements, a tactic that even bothered Secretary of State George Schultz.[71] France was joined by other Europeans, including the United Kingdom, West Germany, and Italy, in formally taking exception to the way the Americans were usurping their rights as sovereign nations.[72] Prime Minister Mauroy's office, referring to the sanctions, announced that the government "cannot accept the unilateral decisions taken by the United States," noting that this was also the view of other members of the European Community. Hubert Védrine, an adviser to the Elysée, called the turmoil surrounding the Soviet pipeline the "most serious crisis since 1973."[73] In private, Mitterrand assailed the sanctions: "There is no question of accepting this American approach according to which everything that is economic is strategic, thus military, thus within the scope of the Alliance. Taking this path would be to admit that there can no longer be independence for France. Reagan is completely oblivious of his allies' needs, ushering us into hard times."[74] And outspoken foreign minister Claude Cheysson rather dramatically warned on national television that American indifference to the problems of the Old World was leading to a "progressive divorce between Americans and Europeans."[75]

Reagan relented when it became clear that his administration had gone too far. The sanctions had disrupted the alliance: the Europeans had, for once, stood together and defied the embargo in order to honor their contracts. But the way Reagan lifted sanctions in November 1982, connecting this action with an announcement of renewed consultation over transferring strategic materiel and credits, antagonized the Elysée. In a huff Mitterrand refused to return Reagan's phone call about the matter and the French formally disassociated themselves from the announcement. Cheysson could not restrain himself: "We signed the [NATO] Washington Treaty," he exploded, "not the Warsaw Pact."[76] The irony of the pipeline affair, as Anthony Blinken has pointed out, was that Reagan's policy had made adversaries out of his European allies, who in turn supported the Soviets.[77]

At the heart of these disputes was the heavy-handed anticommunism of the Reagan administration that slighted West European interests and advice. Given their extensive trading with East Europeans, given the likelihood sanctions would impose further suffering on the Polish people, and given their hope for détente, the French and many other West Europeans were not eager to face down the Kremlin or risk an all-out trade war to fight communism.

In the eyes of the French, Reagan and his policies were, at first, unwelcome. After nearly a year in office they thought he was nearly as great a threat to world peace as was Leonid Brezhnev.[78] Almost two years after he came to the White House over half of the French had a bad opinion of U.S. policy in world affairs. To be sure, the most potent naysayers lodged on the left including two-thirds of those supporting Mitterrand's own Socialist Party.[79] Despite the government's new Atlanticism there was public outrage, above all, because the Reagan administration proved unwilling to assuage French grievances over America's high interest rates and the elevated exchange rate of the dollar while the dispute over the Soviet pipeline only intensified feelings that the United States was ignoring French and European economic interests and trying to rule by fiat. In 1982 the most common adjectives applied to the U.S. government were "interfering," "arrogant," "insufficient" and "inconsistent." There was little difference between right and left, with almost as many supporters of the RPR finding the Americans "arrogant" as did Socialists.[80]

When the G7 gathered in Williamsburg, Virginia, in the spring of 1983 the principal issues were inflation, global economic recovery, and American interest rates. Paris had advised Washington to confine the summit to such economic topics, but Ronald Reagan insisted on adding a resolution on security that presented a solid Western front to stop Moscow from obstructing the arms limitation talks at Geneva. He also wanted to add Japan, which in theory could become a target for the SS-20s, to the alliance under the rubric of "global security." Mitterrand took strong exception and, to Reagan's dismay, critiqued his resolution word by word. "Global" was inaccurate since, he reminded his host, "the Atlantic Alliance is not universal."[81] If Japan were to be included, the French president argued, solidarity had to be limited to the Euro-missile danger. In the background was the French fear that Reagan's proposal for "global security" would bring France so close to the alliance that the Soviets could legitimately insist that the force de frappe be counted in the arms talks; French nuclear forces could then be negotiated away by the superpowers. Mitterrand whispered, "If I don't stop this text, France won't have any nuclear weapons in ten years."[82] He held firm, vetoing any communiqué that might endanger the French deterrent, and creating a tense scene at Williamsburg: Reagan in frustration threw his pencil on the table; he later admitted, "I got angry."[83] Margaret Thatcher and Helmut Kohl tried to persuade a testy Mitterrand to compromise, and Reagan's security adviser, unbeknown to Mitterrand, threatened one of the latter's aides with breaking all military relations with the French, including assistance in developing nuclear weapons, if they refused to sign.[84] Isolated, Mitterrand gave in, but not before he had softened the language of the resolution so that it created some space between France and "global security."[85] The French president, according to his aides, was "furious": he called the Williamsburg Summit "a trap" and later openly railed against Reagan's behavior as "more dangerous and more unpredictable" than he had ever believed.[86] To the press Cheysson described the talks as "lively" rather than acrimonious, but his answers to journalists' questions exposed the intensity of the disagreements.[87]

Mitterrand's team came to view such summits as perilous because France was often put in a minority position and had either to give in to the Americans or be treated as an obstreperous ally. According to Hu-

Figure 4. Smiles conceal bickering: Presidents François Mitterrand and Ronald Reagan at the Williamsburg Summit, 1983. Courtesy Ronald Reagan Library.

bert Védrine, "For France, each year, under Reagan, the G7 is *Apache Canyon*."[88] He likened the Reagan White House to a "bulldozer" and found Reagan himself to be unsophisticated and prone to telling anecdotes rather than to serious negotiation. Yet Védrine believed it was a mistake to underestimate "the former actor's powerful charisma," his deep convictions, his pragmatism, and his intuitive sense of the American people.[89] Jacques Attali, another member of the Elysée team, was more severe. He was not seduced by Reagan's optimism and happy talk, which only concealed "the extraordinary emptiness of his conversation" punctuated by stories about his career in movies and silly jokes. During summits, Attali observed, the American president could only "read from tiny note cards that he took from his left inside coat pocket" which usually ended with a question.[90] To French diplomats Reagan seemed unable to develop coherent arguments and preferred to extract information from others.

Williamsburg demonstrated the precarious position in which Mitterrand had placed France: by crossing the Atlantic he had put at risk French independence, especially in security matters. He could not square the circle by trying to close the gap with NATO yet stay aloof. Nor could he satisfy his own backers. Many socialists remained skeptical and the French Communist Party, his governing partners, attacked the Williamsburg Resolution, accusing Mitterrand of aligning France with the United States.[91]

While the heads of state quarreled—mostly behind doors—at their summits, the French public warmed toward Reagan and the United States. The balance of opinion shifted rather dramatically from negative to positive at the end of Reagan's first term. Between December 1982 and June 1985 the overall favorable opinion of the United States jumped from 48 percent to 70 percent and remained near this high level until 1987.[92] And this improvement contrasted sharply with diminishing confidence among both the British and West Germans in the same period.[93] Similarly "good" rather than "bad" opinions of U.S. global policies advanced smartly from 1982 to early 1984 and progressed further by late 1985; in fact, they improved among all age cohorts, occupations, and political parties as well as both genders.[94] The mid-1980s were the halcyon days of the Reagan administration in France. In 1987, among eight West European countries, France, along with West Germany and Italy, ranked highest for holding favorable views—as well as the fewest unfavorable views—toward President Reagan.[95] Among those expressing positive attitudes, Reagan was accepted as friendly, trustworthy, and inspirational.

Explanations for the heightened popularity of U.S. policy and President Reagan in the mid-1980s are several. Some of these have been discussed in chapter 1, like the eye-catching performance of the American economy after 1982. There was also the gradual abatement of some controversies, like those over Central America and the Soviet pipeline. At the same time Reagan's assertiveness, accompanied by his affable ways, seemed to please those in France, especially on the right, who had grown anxious about the Soviets. The apprehensions that greeted Reagan in 1981–82 subsided once he demonstrated firmness without belligerence. Mitterrand contributed by trying to cultivate Reagan and by putting a smile on relations with Washington, and this was topped off by his state visit in 1984. In a small way he mollified dissent from the left. Finally, there was the Gorbachev factor: in 1985 the Soviet leader initiated a relaxation of Cold War tension, and this improved the image of not only the USSR but also the United States because Reagan seemed to be amenable to a sincere pursuit of nuclear arms control; this pleased that large body of French opinion that continued to favor détente.

During 1985–86 the meltdown of the Cold War created a new situation for Franco-American relations. In 1985 Mikhail Gorbachev took charge in the Kremlin and adopted a far more conciliatory stance toward the West, including expressing interest in resolving the dispute over the Euromissiles and scaling down the nuclear arsenals of the superpowers. At the same time Ronald Reagan took up the cause of nuclear disarmament and the construction of an antimissile defense as ways of ending the danger of an atomic Armageddon. He also champ-ioned the "double zero option," which proposed the elimination of all intermediate missiles instead of deploying American launchers to balance the SS-20s. "How should France respond to these initiatives?" became the question.

As the Cold War entered a new phase socialist domination of the French government ended; in 1986 the Right won the legislative elec-tions and Mitterrand had to partner with Jacques Chirac as his prime minister. "Cohabitation," as this power-sharing was dubbed, undercut the consensus on foreign policy. Differences between the socialist pres-ident and the Gaullist premier made headlines—but, in the end, the Elysée prevailed.

The American bombing of Libya exposed both the insouciance of the Reagan administration toward currying French support and the loss of consensus in Paris. It also showed that the French people were more disposed toward backing the United States over taking the fight to terrorists in the Mediterranean than was the Mitterrand team.

On the night of April 14–15, 1986, American F-111s based in the United Kingdom, along with carrier-based aircraft, bombed several sites along the Libyan coast and killed, among others, the adopted daughter of its president, Mu'ammar al-Gadhafi, and nearly hit him. Reagan wanted to strike a blow against a notorious sponsor of inter-national terrorism and to retaliate for Libya's alleged involvement in the bombing of a West Berlin nightclub that had taken the lives of two American servicemen and wounded hundreds. The French agreed with the goal of removing Gadhafi: they had clashed militarily with Libya over Chad and would have liked to see an end to Gadhafi's terrorist activities, which threatened them even more than they did the Ameri-cans. But Paris was not consulted about the operation and worried, once informed of Washington's intentions, that a mere show of force would put at risk France's relations with the Arab world while failing to remove Gadhafi from power.[96] Reagan told Chirac he intended to kill Gadhafi, but the French prime minister expressed his doubts about such a mission.[97] Advisers in the Elysée also worried about making Gadhafi a martyr to the Arab world.[98] The Quai d'Orsay joined in expressing skepticism about the operation and worrying about the safety of French hostages in Beirut. Chirac and Mitterrand agreed to refuse to cooperate with the U.S. government.

The European allies were informed, rather than consulted, about the action and the French government was officially asked to allow use of its airspace less than two days before the raid. Mitterrand balked, and denied the Americans fly-over rights, forcing the F-111s to travel almost twice as far to hit Libya. In general, West Europeans were unimpressed by the strike, seeing it as an ineffective, Rambo-like gesture by Reagan. Most governments shunned it, and Spain also refused use of its airspace. In the end only Margaret Thatcher, against the will of the British people, openly backed the attack.

The snub from Paris touched off another anti-French spasm in the United States. Not only did the Republican administration blame France for making American pilots fly a more dangerous route but Democratic leaders in the U.S. Congress openly expressed their disappointment with their ally. In the press and on television the French were vilified: American tourists planning European vacations were advised to skip France. On the *Tonight Show* Johnny Carson threw a pie at an actor portraying a Frenchman while on French television Vernon Walters, the special envoy who had toured European capitals in behalf of Washington's plan, complained of the country's ingratitude while reminding the audience of the aid the United States had given them after World War II. Some in the French press took exception to this vilification. One weekly retaliated by invoking the well-known American inferiority complex: "Could they be jealous of our culture, our sophistication, our taste, our subtlety?"[99]

The French public, despite their government's refusal to let the Americans use its airspace, supported the raid—-far more than did other West Europeans. Where roughly two-thirds of the French approved the operation, just as many West Germans and British disapproved. And half the French, unlike the Germans or the British, endorsed another American attack if the Libyans continued to sponsor terrorism.[100] There were anti-American demonstrations in the streets of London, Bonn, and Rome, but not Paris. In taking military action against Gadhafi, the French people sided more with Washington than with Paris. Chirac faced dissent from within his parliamentary majority when leaders of the UDF, including former president Valéry Giscard d'Estaing, backed the Americans. *Le Figaro* gave a full-throated endorsement of the bombing, arguing that madmen like Gadhafi only understood force and reminding its readers where appeasement led.[101] On the left, *Libération* said the raid was justified, but the West needed to address the roots of terrorism—with which *Le Monde* agreed, writing that terrorism would not be stopped by bombs from the sky.[102] Neither the public nor the media gave much support to their government's refusal to cooperate with the Americans, so in this case Mitterrand and Chirac were at odds with their own electorate.

The main diplomatic arena of the period 1985–87 was not fighting terrorism but arms control—especially combating Reagan's move to protect against the devastation of a nuclear war, his Strategic Defense Initiative (SDI), first broached in 1983, which centered on the construction of a protective "shield" in space that could destroy attacking ballistic missiles. France, at first, did not take the scheme, dubbed "Star Wars," seriously, but by 1985 it was clear that the Americans were acting in earnest and Paris had to decide whether or not it would participate in the project's development.

The SDI challenged the basis of mutual deterrence and threatened to render French and British nuclear forces obsolete.[103] The threat of retaliation, not defense, was the key to deterrence. "Star Wars" raised several questions for the French. Would Western Europe be as well protected by this "shield" as the United States? Once the United States could protect itself from Soviet missiles, would it be even less reliable as Europe's defender? Here was the bogey of decoupling.[104] There were also technical problems that cast doubt on the scheme's feasibility. And if it were effective, wouldn't it leave West Europeans at risk from Soviet short-range missiles and conventional forces? Furthermore, French officials thought it "inopportune" to alarm the Soviets when the superpowers were in the midst of serious disarmament negotiations: the Soviets might retaliate with new offensive weapons and thus relaunch the arms race. Signaling its adherence to the principal of nuclear deterrence, in 1985 France launched its sixth nuclear submarine.

At the annual meeting of the G7 at Bonn in May 1985, President Reagan again ignored French insistence on limiting such summits to economics rather than turning them into a "global political directorate." He directly asked Mitterrand to sign on to the SDI, using the language of "subcontracting" to describe Europeans' participation in designing the technology. Mitterrand, after expressing his objections, responded just as directly: "It's no." The notion of acting as "subcontractors" especially irritated him. As the summit progressed, disagreements continued over Nicaragua and American reluctance to call an international monetary conference, but then Reagan forced another issue on Mitterrand, proposing a new round of the General Agreement on Tariffs and Trade. The French had warned the U.S. government against setting a date for new trade talks before preliminary negotiations were complete fearing renewed pressure on France to dismantle its agricultural subsidies. Commercial talks with the United States, Mitterrand confided to his government, forced France to make concessions because one could not reject everything: "that's why the 'no' must precede . . . negotiations."[105] The debate intensified with the British, Germans, Italians, and even Jacques Delors, the (French) president of the European Commission, siding with Reagan. Mitterrand, in the words of his aide, "exploded." As Mitterrand exclaimed at the time, "It's not healthy that allies dictate our policy. Certain [countries] accept it. Not me. . . . I hear it said that no one wanted to isolate France. Very well. But that's what's happened in this room. It's not healthy. Just as it's not healthy that European affairs are judged by countries far from Europe. I'm ready to open a public controversy if this continues. . . . If these summits don't return to their initial form, France will no longer attend [them]...."[106] The United States had its way on opening trade talks and at dinner that evening the heads of state got into storytelling and, as Reagan later observed, "a good time was had by all–(all except Mitterrand)."[107]

"Star Wars" bewildered Mitterrand. He told Gorbachev that "Reagan's conception of SDI is a product either of humanitarian reverie or [it's] propaganda."[108] French analysts attributed the scheme to domestic politics like Reagan's need to pass his defense budget.[109] Mitterrand received conflicting advice from his experts about the feasibility of the SDI, but in the end France, alone among the allies, officially refused to cooperate in developing the project—although French firms were permitted to compete for SDI contracts. Chirac disagreed with the Elysée and argued that France should participate and avoid being left aside— to which the president replied, "If you insist, I will call a referendum about it and I will win."[110] At first a majority of the French wanted their country to participate in research, though many misunderstood the project's purpose, but opinion shifted as opposition in the media mounted and by 1986 they accepted government policy. Almost two of three French people wanted their nation to take the lead in developing an independent space defense; less than one in five opted for the American version.[111] Mitterrand turned to Europe and urged creating a cooperative high-technology program called Eureka as a way of coordinating research and development. Eureka was to provide Europeans, especially the West Germans, with what was, at least ostensibly, a civilian alternative to the SDI's military research.

Despite the appearance of a more conciliatory leader in Moscow, the French remained deeply skeptical of the Soviets and proved less amenable to Gorbachev's charms than did other West Europeans. When asked to compare Gorbachev and Reagan in 1985 the French public gave the American president higher grades than most other West Europeans for trustworthiness, flexibility as a negotiator, understanding European problems, and desiring peace—yet all of these endorsements were tepid, with only a quarter or a third awarding high marks to Reagan and most saying neither leader deserved them or registering no opinion.[112]

In October 1986, the French government received a reminder of its marginal status in the Cold War. At the Reykjavik Summit with Gorbachev, the U.S. president appeared so eager to reduce the superpowers' nuclear arsenals, and perhaps eliminate all nuclear weapons, that he raised the possibility of negotiating away the French deterrent—or at least making it obsolescent. Reagan and Gorbachev agreed tentatively to sharp reductions in their strategic missiles and to the double zero option for Euromissiles. Trying to allay Soviet fears about the SDI, which Moscow opposed, Reagan offered the technology to the Soviets. Even though the talks collapsed because Reagan refused to relinquish his "Star Wars" project and Gorbachev's doubted American promises to share the new technology, it seemed like the Americans and the Soviets were up to their old tricks—deciding the fate of Europe without the Europeans. The fear of a superpower condominium had returned. From a European perspective the Reykjavik Summit also raised the specter of the superpowers, secure behind their shields, fighting with conventional or nuclear weapons on the European continent. Chirac worried that "decisions vital to the security of Europe could be taken without Europe really having any say in the matter."[113] Unlike his prime minister, Mitterrand was, in a subdued way, favorable toward Reykjavik for advancing disarmament and the double zero option—which he had come to embrace. The summit appeared to the French press as a major setback—especially for Reagan, who some thought may have been outsmarted by Gorbachev.[114]

In the aftermath of the summit in Iceland, Chirac's government and the Elysée engaged in a long duel over the double zero option for Euromissiles. The prime minister thought Gorbachev intended to "Finlandize" Europe in order to hold it "hostage" and cautioned against any action that might lead to the withdrawal of American nuclear forces from Europe.[115] The Quai d'Orsay noted Soviet advantages in conventional weapons and short-range missiles and warned, rather wildly, against the "denuclearization of Western Europe."[116] Mitterrand acknowledged that removing intermediate-range missiles raised the old bogey of decoupling, but he countered that he, and his fellow socialists, had always favored reducing the nuclear arsenals of the superpowers and the double zero option did not directly touch the force de frappe.[117] Moreover, deterrence, in the form of superpower strategic forces, remained in tact.

On this issue the French president enjoyed the public's support because it did not view the Soviet Union as an immediate threat and was inclined toward disarmament and détente. They backed the double zero option more strongly than did their government, even if they were rather cynical about Reagan's motives and skeptical about Soviet compliance.[118] A majority even wanted France to follow the lead of the superpowers and reduce its arsenal of nuclear weapons.[119]

It was not until 1987 that the decadelong debate over Euromissiles ended. The signing of the Washington Treaty in December of that year, negotiated by the Americans and the Soviets, adopted the double zero option and eliminated all intermediate-range weapons; it won massive public and media support in France as well as Mitterrand's endorsement.[120] Yet Chirac and some French military leaders disapproved of the treaty because it seemed to weaken deterrence. Mitterrand ignored them; he vowed that France would maintain its strategic nuclear capability, arguing that the goal of deterrence was "to prevent war, not to win it."[121] As for "denuclearization," he argued, should it happen, that would be far in the future.

At this point Mitterrand, according to one of his biographers, had lost confidence in Reagan, whose rash approach to negotiating with the Soviets and his unilateral treatment of France convinced Mitterrand that the U.S. president was visibly "losing his grip."[122] Mitterrand worried less about Gorbachev's proposals about totally eliminating superpower nuclear weapons some day than he did about the White House: "the principal danger is the dream and madness of Mr. Reagan, who accepted at Reykjavik the complete withdrawal of nuclear forces.

We came close to catastrophe."[123] In fact, the Reagan administration had largely ignored both Mitterrand and Thatcher in negotiating with Gorbachev over arms control.[124]

Then came a debilitating scandal. On November 13, 1986, "the great communicator" went on television from the Oval Office and informed the American people that his administration had been secretly selling arms to a sponsor of international terrorism, the Iranian Islamic Republic. The president denied that the United States had sent weapons to Iran as "ransom" for Americans held in Lebanon, yet he admitted that one of the reasons for the transfer of arms was to win Tehran's help in obtaining "the safe return of all hostages." He trivialized the sales, saying the weapons were strictly "defensive" and so few that they could all have been transported on a single cargo plane. Reagan seemed clumsy and ill at ease. French journalists, like much of the American public, were not impressed with his performance. They recognized blatant hypocrisy and incompetence in the White House, contrasting the image of Reagan in 1979 ranting against then president Jimmy Carter's attempt at negotiating with the Iranian revolutionaries with Reagan's humiliating admission that he had been secretly working with Tehran. *L'Express* reminded readers how the Reagan administration had advocated a hard line against states that supported terrorism and had exhorted its European allies to do the same—yet, when it wanted, it not only negotiated with Tehran but supplied Iran with sophisticated weapons, submitted to blackmail, and bargained for hostages. The hostage swap, according to the weekly, was only the latest in a series of diplomatic faux pas, such as the "muddle" at the Reykjavik Summit and the clandestine delivery of weapons to the contras in Nicaragua that "called into question Reagan's competence."[125] *Le Nouvel Observateur* declared that "the president's cowboys have gone too far," referring to the clandestine program "run by a team of amateurs from within the White House itself."[126] In Paris a spokesman for Chirac's political party smirked, "Those who give morality lessons would do well to sweep in front of their own door before criticizing others."[127] Toting up Reagan's foreign policy *Le Monde* could identify only a few successes, like the invasion of Grenada, while listing many "reverses and setbacks," including the headlong flight from Lebanon, the amateurish efforts at backing the anti-Sandinistas, the Reykjavik fiasco, and now Iran.[128]

The scandal deepened in 1987 with new disclosures about the complicated dealings with Iran, including the revelation that profits from the weapons sales had been used to subsidize the contras. In an embarrassing television address in March 1987, Reagan acknowledged his responsibility and conceded that his policy had "deteriorated" into an exchange of arms for hostages. By then a large majority of the French thought the scandal had compromised Reagan's ability to lead the alliance.[129]

As Ronald Reagan neared the end of his presidency, his image, but not that of America, lost its glow. The romance with Reagan cooled from late 1986 on after the stumble at Reykjavik and news of the Iran Contra Scandal; at the same time as Reagan's stock fell, Gorbachev's climbed. At the end of his administration Reagan's popularity was substantially lower than it had been.[130] A combination of bungled international initiatives and skepticism about the social costs inflicted by his management of the American economy had reduced his stature. What appeared especially impetuous and capricious was Reagan's attempt at disposing of nuclear deterrence and promoting the SDI. According to Dominique Moïsi, a pro-American analyst, it seemed to many in France that "not only were the Americans unpredictable and adventuristic, their diplomacy was unreliable and probably incompetent."[131]

Yet the image of America remained pleasing. In April 1988 the French posted an overwhelmingly positive view of the United States at levels similar to those for the United Kingdom and West Germany.[132] If a majority of the French thought Washington did not try to understand their problems and two-thirds said that it expected France to give in to its wishes—expressing a constant anxiety over unilateralism—virtually everyone opined that bilateral relations were good and that the United States treated France with "dignity and respect." By a margin of three to one, those surveyed described themselves as pro-rather than anti-American.[133]

During the final years of Reagan's presidency the integration of the European Community (EC) surged forward after a decade or more of lethargy. Spurred by Jacques Delors, the European Commission's president, it adopted the Single European Act (SEA), which, once ratified in 1987, set in motion the construction of a single market by eliminating remaining obstacles like nontariff barriers to intracommunity trade by 1992. The nonchalant attitude of the Reagan administration toward the effects of its macroeconomic policies on Europe was one, among many, motives for the SEA that also gave impetus toward monetary and political union and strengthened Europe's ability to defend its common interests. After a nod in favor of a market liberating initiative, Reagan's team greeted the SEA with inattention and some distrust. The EC appeared as little more than a talking shop—incapable of concerted action—that was at best marginalized; the U.S. government preferred managing its economic relations bilaterally. One top Reagan official admitted that the administration did not understand what was happening in the EC and did not care.[134] Moreover, America's leverage in Europe came through NATO rather than the EC, and for the Reagan administration security issues and the Iran Contra Scandal trumped transatlantic commerce. British prime minister Margaret Thatcher, furthermore, shared her growing skepticism about the future of the SEA with her close friend in the White House. After ratification, however, anxiety mounted among some officials, the U.S. Congress, and the American press about a future "Fortress Europe" that might close opportunities and discriminate against American corporate interests.[135] Trade experts spoke of the need to be "vigilant" about the trend toward a "Europe for Europeans" while France was singled out as the leader of the protectionist clique that could manipulate the EC.[136] Once Europeans began implementing the SEA with specific directives, including the Television without Frontiers directive (discussed in chapter 2), transatlantic disputes grew. Reagan's successor would have to deal with a more assertive EC, and big troubles lay ahead.

Nineteen eighty-eight was a presidential election year in both countries. The French reelected Mitterrand to a second seven-year term, and in the U.S. George H. W. Bush succeeded Ronald Reagan. At a White House dinner in September, Mitterrand complimented the outgoing president, to which Reagan responded, "We are friends. We are like an old couple. It's always difficult to separate. . . ."[137] But the president-elect later confided that Mitterrand and Reagan "were not close" and he intended to improve relations with the French. In May 1989 Bush invited Mitterrand to his home in Kennebunkport, Maine, where the two heads of state got on well. Bush later reflected that the "deep trust" they had established there helped them cooperate in the coming years over trying issues like German reunification. Mitterrand "proved to be a dependable ally and friend."[138]

With Mitterrand's reelection the socialists regained control of the government from the right and France tilted away from the Atlantic Alliance, toward Europe, for security. The new defense minister Jean-Pierre Chevènement, a fierce Jacobin, stated, "It is time that Europe thought about ensuring itself its own defense. . . . Today, the aim must be to replace the American defense of Europe with an autonomous European defense."[139] Mitterrand had never given up on Europe, even when he was embracing Atlanticism, and during the late 1980s he was on the move again toward constructing a powerful European Community. He actively promoted economic integration by backing the ambitious SEA, and by 1989, thanks to the prodding of Jacques Delors, the European Commission was preparing intergovernmental conferences that would create financial unity through the Economic and Monetary Union (EMU). Mitterrand had also sanctioned a proposal, initiated by Chirac, to work with the Germans to rehabilitate the Western European Union (WEU), a hidebound vestige of the 1940s, as a first step toward constructing a European defense—which the U.S. government resented.[140] The WEU was not taken seriously among some American diplomats, who joked that it was little more than a place to shelve retired Italian admirals.

When Mitterrand hosted the G7 meeting in Paris in 1989, despite this new European tilt, he made a special effort during the lavish ceremonies to honor the new president of the United States, George H. W. Bush. Celebrating the bicentennial of the French Revolution was linked conspicuously with the American Revolution. Harmony reigned at the summit, according to the French press, and Mitterrand seemed pleased that his presidential colleague was Bush rather than Reagan.[141] It was during the first years of Bush's presidency that perceptions of the United States climbed to stratospheric levels with the euphoria generated by German reunification and the end of the Cold War. In November 1989 the French viewed the United States as favorably as did the British or the West Germans. Multiple surveys conducted in the years 1987–89 recorded significantly higher appraisals of the United States than comparable polls from the years 1981–82.[142]

The shift in the White House to Bush from Reagan did not mark any flagging of American pretense to direct Europe. In his State of the Union Address the new president spoke of America's destiny to lead and organize a "new world order," and his secretary of state, James Baker, insisted on NATO taking the lead in European security.

■ Within months of the G7 extravaganza in Paris, events in Central and Eastern Europe faced France and the United States with a major international crisis: How were they to respond to the collapse of the East German regime and the political upheaval underway in other communist states, the signals of reform emanating from Moscow, and the effort by the West Germans to seize the opportunity to realize the great ambition of German reunification?

The remainder of this chapter explains how the Mitterrand and Bush administrations dealt with the German question. Other major issues confronting them, like the Gulf War and the creation of a European security alternative during 1990–91, will be discussed in chapter 5.

Long before the events of 1989–91 that marked the end of the Cold War, François Mitterrand had said he was not afraid of German reunification and thought it was historically inevitable. But he, like most, was surprised in the autumn of 1989 at both the rapid pace of events and Soviet acquiescence. While some contemporary officials and scholars, especially Americans, contend that Mitterrand tried to retard reunification, at least until the spring of 1990, the most authoritative recent studies assess him more positively. In particular, Frédéric Bozo proves that Mitterrand, although initially anxious about the possible unsettling consequences of a powerful, united Germany, collaborated with all the principal players—especially West German chancellor Helmut Kohl—to advance the process of reunification. "At no moment did French diplomacy seek to slow down, let alone impede, German reunification," he writes.[143] The French facilitated German unity even if, at times, they irritated the chancellor by trying to shape the new Germany—especially its boundaries with Poland.

The Bush administration was equally surprised at the sudden dissolution of communist rule, but, it gradually overcame its apprehensions about the turmoil in Central Europe, realized the process of East Germany's disintegration was irreversible, and worked closely with the West Germans to help manage the transition. On the essentials of German reunification the French and Americans converged. Both, if at first cautious, accepted the Germans' right to choose unity, and then sought to advance the cause without destabilizing the continent or jeopardizing Gorbachev's position in the Soviet Union. Both also wanted the new Germany anchored in NATO. But convergence, as we shall see, did not mean unanimity.

Mitterrand's initial response to the rush of events leading to the fall of the Berlin Wall in November 1989 was passive and philosophical—American officials found his statements "elliptical." At a press conference in November he stated he was not alarmed by the prospect of reunification: "History is there. I take it as it is. . . . If this is what [the Germans] want and they can bring it off, France will adjust its policy so as to be able to act for the best in Europe's interest and in its own interest. . . . The answer is simple: insofar as Eastern Europe is evolving, Western Europe must itself grow stronger, strengthen its structures and define its policies. . . . Reunification poses so many problems that I shall make up my mind as the events occur."[144] In fact, he was apprehensive that the rapid pace of events in Germany would destabilize Gorbachev and return Europe to the fragmented world of 1913. French diplomats were slow to accept reunification because they remained convinced until the end of 1989 that Moscow was not ready to relinquish its grip on Central and Eastern Europe and that the way out of the bipolar division of Europe was to strengthen European integration, especially the Franco-German partnership, rebuild the Atlantic Alliance, and create a European security structure that would engage the Soviet Union as well.[145] Among the French public, almost three of four accepted the prospect of a unified Germany in November, believing it dangerous to oppose it but fearful of German economic power.[146]

Despite his anxieties about the destabilizing effects of a united Germany the French president during the winter of 1989–90 conferred with all the major participants—Bush, Thatcher, Gorbachev, and Kohl—about channeling the process. He informed the German chancellor that France would not stand in the way of unity, but he insisted that reunification must also serve the purpose of European integration—in particular, to advance the goal of the EMU. In December 1989 Kohl bent to Mitterrand's request. The chancellor's concession was less a quid pro quo for French approval than it was a ratification of the importance of the Franco-German tandem in the construction of Europe.[147]

The cascade of events in Central and Eastern Europe raised the possibility of the end of the Cold War and the need for channeling developments. *Encadrement*, or framing, was the French solution. The diplomats' motives for encadrement stemmed from several fears and hopes. There was the fear of reverting to the divisive nationalisms and ethnic rivalries of pre-1914 Europe as well as anxiety about a powerful

Germany cut loose from its mooring in the EC. And there was a desire to support reform in the USSR and the communist bloc and the hope of ending the bipolar domination of the continent and constructing a new European order run by Europeans. The French project focused on binding a united Germany within an integrated EC, using the Conference on Security and Cooperation in Europe (CSCE) to manage disarmament (the CSCE, a product of the Helsinki Accords of 1975, was a thirty-five-nation organization that included the USSR and the United States), renovating the Atlantic Alliance, and initiating a new pan-European confederation, which would exclude the United States, to preside over the new map of Europe. Encadrement in its grandest scope meant building an independent Europe outside the Atlantic Alliance. The premise of the Elysée and other French policy makers was that the end of the Cold War would, and should, lead to America's retirement from Europe. It seemed inevitable that as the Soviet danger subsided, the United States would withdraw its forces from Germany and gradually diminish its commitment to Europe. The imminent withdrawal offered an opportunity to overhaul NATO as well as define a new security system for the continent. One U.S. diplomat who was privy to French thinking wrote, "The most striking impression I derived from my many conversations is the nearly total absence of the U.S. in the mid- and long-term calculations of French policy makers. So convinced do the French seem that the U.S. will rapidly withdraw its forces from Europe that they are thinking, and at times acting, as if we were already gone."[148] The French pressed the United States for a fundamental reassessment of the Atlantic Alliance, thinking this would lead to Europeanizing the structure. NATO would survive, but only as a kind of insurance for continental security; it certainly would not enlarge its role. The Americans had other plans.

The United States was anxious that NATO, without the Soviet threat, would inevitably wither away—as the French expected. But the Bush administration was determined to stay in Europe: the president stated forcefully that the United States would remain "a European power."[149] This Atlanticist vision, a formula to which the British also subscribed, assumed, according to one U.S. diplomat, that American power was necessary "to balance continuing, if diminishing, Soviet military preponderance, serve as a counterweight to a newly powerful Germany, and lend a general stability" to Europe as the Warsaw Pact disintegrated and the Soviets withdrew.[150] According to one insider, "No idea was more strongly and deeply held in the upper levels of the [Bush] administration than the core conviction that the American presence was indispensable to European stability and therefore to vital American interests."[151] Or as National Security Adviser Brent Scowcroft put it to one French official, Jacques Attali, American aims were to prevent Europeans from returning to the old ways that had led to two wars and to combat isolationist forces at home that would bring an American withdrawal.[152] What Scowcroft did not admit was that the United States also wanted in principle to continue to have a say in European politics: it was determined that the United States and NATO would remain the pivot of European affairs and not be confined narrowly to providing security.

Washington and Paris were pulling in opposite directions over NATO's role in post–Cold War Europe. Where the Americans sought to expand its functions, extend it eastward, and heighten its multinational character, the French thought the alliance would begin to shed responsibilities and that the Americans would, sooner or later, disengage. For the Americans a united Germany should be firmly situated within the Atlantic Alliance; for the French it should also be embedded in the EC. It is no surprise that once negotiations began over institutional reform, the Americans found the French were "always the most problematic."[153]

In December 1989 Secretary of State James Baker spoke boldly about a new Atlantic Alliance that would be more political in nature, negotiate relations with the democracies emerging in Eastern Europe, and operate outside the Euro-Atlantic zone. Paris interpreted the proposal as a way to maintain American preeminence in the alliance and Europe while expanding its scope. The Mitterrand administration expressed its reservations about Baker's scheme and pursued its own project of reinforcing the French/German tandem within the EC, and channeling the process through the CSCE and a new pan-European confederation. The Americans were annoyed.

Such annoyance remained out of sight at first. When Presidents Bush and Mitterrand met at Saint-Martin in the Antilles in December, the former insisted on Germany remaining in NATO and the latter recommended moving slowly lest events destabilize Gorbachev. Mitterrand did not press his projects, like holding a CSCE summit. The French public assumed all was well when they were treated on television to images of the two presidents in shirtsleeves walking together on the beach.

In early 1990 political leaders and diplomats including the Soviets and the Germans, both West and East, moved ahead toward resolving the questions surrounding a united Germany. Margaret Thatcher could not conceal her misgivings and continued to issue warnings about going too fast. Mitterrand was deeply engaged in the process, but to American officials he appeared aloof, talking abstractly about a unified Europe re-

Figure 5. The European leader that George H. W. Bush most respected. Presidents George H. W. Bush and François Mitterrand at the Elysée, January 1993. Courtesy George H. W. Bush Presidential Library and Museum.

gaining its place in the world. They chided him, unfairly, for thinking about "distant horizons, not the compelling issues of the moment."[154]

Personally, Bush and Mitterrand remained on good terms, though the latter confided to Gorbachev that Bush "has a very big drawback—he lacks original thinking altogether."[155] In contrast, Secretary of State James Baker and his French counterpart Roland Dumas were often testy with one another. Before the Key Largo Summit in April 1990 the American president wrote Mitterrand about the "critical importance" of Franco-American relations to European stability and conveyed his esteem for his colleague: "There is no European leader today whom I respect more than you."[156] Yet Bush cautioned, "I am convinced that the United States must remain profoundly engaged in Europe and in the midst of the Atlantic Alliance. . . . If one leaves NATO only a narrow military function, its importance and the support it receives from western public opinion are certain to diminish as the Soviet military threat eases," thus undermining America's commitment to Europe. He posited that the French president should accept a "strengthened political role" for the United States. One overly cynical adviser to Mitterrand interpreted Bush's letter as "the threat is clear: either the entire reorganization of Europe goes through NATO or the United States stops supporting Europe. Certainly Bush is fixated by the [European] Community. He doesn't support it; like his predecessors he wants [the United States] to be in a weak Europe."[157]

When the two presidents met at Key Largo, Florida they avoided any skirmishes and relations remained genial. Mitterrand tried to dispel any suspicion that France wanted to exclude the United States from Europe while Bush denied charges, which had appeared in the press, that he had any intention of trying to force France into rejoining the integrated command. But he did state, "The support of the American public for our presence in Europe would collapse if the U.S. did not appear involved in European affairs. Thus it is advisable to extend the role of NATO giving it a greater political role."[158] Mitterrand simply responded that it would be wise for the alliance to stay within its traditional geographic scope and function, that of defense. Despite the friendly atmosphere of this Florida summit, these tensions were bound to surface.

The Bush White House, instead of curtailing its role on the continent, was busy in the spring of 1990 reshaping the Atlantic Alliance to fit the newly emerging European order. In particular, it had to find some way to overcome Gorbachev's resistance to incorporating a united Germany into the alliance. In an attempt to placate the Soviets by proving that NATO was no longer a threat to them and that the Cold War was over, Secretary Baker proposed renouncing the seemingly aggressive doctrines of "flexible response" and "forward defense," substituting the concept of "last resort" for nuclear weapons—that they would only be used in the hypothetical case that the West was losing a conventional war. He also advocated recasting NATO as a political organization and opening diplomatic contacts between the alliance and former members of the Warsaw Pact. There was, in addition, a proposal to reinforce the integrated command by adding multinational units like a new rapid reaction force. In response Mitterrand politely gave his approval to reinforcing the defensive character of the alliance, but reiterated France would remain outside the integrated command and was not bound by the new "last resort" doctrine. From the French perspective, he explained, for dissuasion to be effective it had to be "early" (*précoce*), meaning the purpose of the force de frappe was to prevent war, not to win one. At a special NATO summit meeting in London in July 1990 the Bush administration literally forced its new conception of the Atlantic Alliance on its partners.

In London the strains among the allies over the effects of German reunification on NATO became visible. Margaret Thatcher raised objections, as did Mitterrand, to the doctrine of "last resort," and he also took exception to "politicizing" the alliance. His chief military adviser had reported earlier that it was probably necessary to modify the image of the alliance in order to appease the Soviets, but the American proposals served to tighten the integrated command structure and reinforce their privileges at the expense of the Europeans. Nevertheless the adviser recommended against openly opposing the London resolutions because the Europeans were going to replace the Americans who were sure to disengage militarily.[159] Defense minister Jean-Pierre Chevènement was more brutal, denouncing the agreement as an underhand way to strengthen "the integrated command and American leadership."[160] In the eyes of one French diplomat, the Americans at London demonstrated their "barely concealed indifference" to French views.[161] At the closing press conference Mitterrand indirectly expressed his displeasure with the Americans and their high-handed ways by announcing that France would withdraw its military from Germany after unification.

For its part the State Department expressed irritation with the French for placing obstacles in their path toward maintaining U.S. leadership; these officials, in turn, disparaged French statesmanship as "erratic" and born out of a "sense of frustration."[162] They were, nevertheless, confident that the French would come around. Once again, trying to redirect the superpower by playing up to it and muting differences failed.

In fact, the French were fully engaged in the process of reunification. They were central, for example, in mediating German and Polish differences over boundaries and helping persuade Gorbachev to allow a united Germany to remain in NATO. French diplomats, however, were less successful in making the thirty-five-nation CSCE serve as the forum for dealing with Germany's—and Europe's—future. Gorbachev spoke warmly of the organization as "a common European home" and several newly liberated Eastern European nations looked to the institution as an alternative to the Warsaw Pact. French diplomats envisaged a grand conference staged in Paris in 1990 that would preside over the reunification of Germany and the birth of post–Cold War Europe; it would also invigorate the CSCE as an alternative to NATO as a security forum. But the White House and the Kohl government kept the German question off the CSCE's agenda out of fear of losing momentum with extended deliberations in this large body. When the conference did meet in November, events had outrun it. The terms of German reunification had already been negotiated, robbing Paris of its moment of glory; the conference did little more than preside over a treaty on the reduction of conventional forces in Europe.

During the summer of 1990 the basic terms of reunification were negotiated between East and West Germany and ratified by the four wartime Allies. If the French did not get their way with framing much of the new order, at least they made certain that Germany remained anchored in the EC. From the outset Mitterrand had made his coop-eration in the unification process dependent on keeping a united Ger-many committed to the EC and in particular to have it sign on to the EMU. The monetary union was elaborated in subsequent negotiations, and figured as part of the Maastricht Treaty drafted at the end of 1991. Mitterrand's major achievement was preserving rapport with the West Germans and winning Kohl to the principle of advancing the construc-tion of Europe.[163]

From the French perspective, one last option for redesigning the new Europe was a proposal for a new continent-wide confederation— a project first vetted at the end of 1989. Mitterrand and his foreign minister Roland Dumas, who were the strongest advocates of a con-federation among French policy makers, saw the scheme as a way of bringing the two parts of Europe together as well as lending support to reform in the Soviet Union. They also thought the newly freed coun-tries of Eastern Europe were not ready for membership in the EC; the pan-European grouping was a way to mollify them and delay admis-sion. Within the proposed confederation, which included the USSR but not the United States, Europeans both east and west could confer on political issues and cooperate in fields like economic development and the environment. In the end only Mitterrand and Gorbachev gave the project serious backing. The supposed principal beneficiaries of the scheme, the former Soviet satellites in Eastern Europe, refused the kind offer from Paris. Led by the Czechs, who were to host the inaugural session of the confederation in Prague in June 1991, several of the East Europeans saw the plan as a subterfuge to keep them from joining the EC. They wanted to turn west, not east, and were not pleased with the presence of the Soviets. They preferred quick admission to the EC and NATO over the French scheme. Mitterrand harmed his own cause by mentioning the word *decades* as waiting time for East Europeans to enter the community because of their rundown economies. Germany was not enthusiastic either. In general, Europeans, other than the French, wanted to be close to NATO, especially since the summer putsch against Gorbachev in Moscow suggested chaos and violence to the east. The United States let it be known that it refused to be "used by the Europeans for security and held apart from other domains."[164] The Anglo-Americans lobbied to disrupt the project, prompting Mitterrand to complain about Washington pressuring the Czechs. Before the conference met in Prague, the pan-European confederation was dead.

By 1991 Mitterrand could only try to salvage what was left of his plans for post–Cold War Europe by turning his attention toward the major EC summit at Maastricht and nursing his hope for constructing a European defense capability. The Americans had had their way in expanding the scope and functions of the Atlantic Alliance, embedding the Germans in it, maintaining U.S. primacy over European security, and subverting both the CSCE and the pan-European confederation. But the French, the Germans, and the rest of the EC would adopt the EMU, which defined the process for instituting a common currency and a European central bank. A united Germany would remain firmly anchored in the EC and reunification would occur without damaging Franco-German relations. And France had several lesser achievements in determining the outcome of unification. If Mitterrand could have been proud of some results of the process, he proved unable to steer it away from the Atlantic Alliance. In the end the United States imposed its Atlanticist vision, subverted Mitterrand's alternative European encadrement, and frustrated his hope of pushing the United States to the edge of the new European map. But accelerating the construction of Europe that transpired at Maastricht was compensation.

■ The reverie of the 1980s that featured the French public's approval of the United States and amiable relations between Presidents Ronald Reagan and George H. W. Bush on the one side and François Mitterrand on the other was fading as the Cold War ended. Strains between Paris and Washington became apparent from the mid-1980s with the quixotic and incoherent diplomacy of the Reagan administration and the advent of Soviet leader Mikhail Gorbachev. The demise of communism in Europe and the collapse of the Soviet Union brought the Franco-American rivalry over the shape of a new European order, a rivalry that had been barely suppressed, into sharp relief.

Transatlantic harmony, or its appearance, reflected an eagerness for comity, shared interests and values, and extensive cooperation. But the show of cordiality concealed continuous disputes, mistrust, and occasional explosions of anger by the presidents of both countries and their staffs. This tension was not always visible to the public because statesmen wanted to behave as good allies and cover up altercations with smiles and conciliatory press releases. And the media was often complicit in reporting flattering accounts of summits. What accounted for the prickly relations behind the apparent reverie?

From one perspective France and the United States occupied separate places in the global political order. They had dissimilar national interests, endowments of power, historical experiences, and approaches to many international issues. These differences were exacerbated by the sharply contrasting political ideologies, styles, and personalities of Mitterrand and Reagan (and to a lesser extent Bush). Such differences help explain certain episodes in this rivalry. For example, given limited resources for foreign aid, the secondary priority and absence of historical ties to Central America, France abandoned the Sandinistas and the cause of tiers-mondisme to the mercies of the superpower. Or, in contrast—given the importance of developing a new energy source for Western Europe, the strong historical and economic links with Eastern Europe, the unwillingness to use trade for political ends, and the preference for détente with the Soviets—France, with the help of other Europeans, forced the superpower to stand down over the Siberian pipeline.

Disparities in power and distinctive experiences and perspectives, however, do not entirely explain how, during the denouement of the Cold War, the two nations addressed important issues. There is an alternative interpretation, the one that this study stresses: as the Cold War waned, U.S. policies and unilateralist tendencies became the principal obstacle to French and European independence. The French tried, without much success, to assert their autonomy within the Atlantic Alliance—very few in positions of authority harbored the more extreme aim of excluding the United States—for several reasons. First they believed their nation was more secure when making decisions and defining policies for itself. Or, as a corollary, independence, according to Stanley Hoffmann, served as "a kind of *tous azimuts* insurance policy against future perils."[165] Second, France was uneasy about both the U.S. commitment to Europe's security and Washington's leadership, which, as the superpower rivalry faded, seemed to veer between unilateralism and withdrawal. Third, overcoming history drove the quest for autonomy. By the 1980s, the past to be exorcised was the shadow of Yalta, the superpower condominium, and the division of Europe. Finally, the French sought greater freedom from the United States as an end in itself. Separation from America expressed French status as an important player in international affairs and confirmed national self-esteem. A sense of cultural and diplomatic superiority, corroborated by a perception of Reagan's ineptness in international affairs, nourished this pride.

For the most part Mitterrand's transatlantic policies enjoyed wide domestic support—more so after he turned away from his early Atlanticism. Public opinion was not, generally speaking, in an Atlanticist mood in the 1980s: it did not favor moving closer to the United States, or desire leadership from Washington, or accept a greater role for the alliance. It was anxious about American domination. At most the public tolerated Mitterrand's flirtation with the alliance because it appreciated a strong posture from Reagan during the early 1980s toward a Soviet Union that had disturbed the equilibrium between East and West. It also preferred the Americans' tough stand on terrorism compared to that of their government. And the French public displayed a passing infatuation with the amiable Reagan. Otherwise its preference was for détente, for avoiding confrontation with Moscow, for arms control, for a mediating role between the superpowers, and for French independence. Mitterrand was largely in sync with his voters.

"When they manage their national interests, the Americans become hard to bear," one French diplomat has noted, "and [they] don't hesitate treating us as vacuum cleaner salesmen."[166] Fundamentally the problem for Mitterrand's France was how to redirect the energies of its overbearing ally. Trying to curb American domination, France attempted three not entirely distinct strategies. None worked. The Mitterrand administration attempted to cozy up to Reagan and Bush, to play down differences and act as loyal Atlanticists, and then exploit its access to persuade or cajole its big brother. This failed because the United States then took the French for granted, manipulated them, or ignored them. For example, at the Reykjavik Summit Reagan and Schultz simply overlooked their allies. Similarly the Bush-Baker team assumed that the French, despite their misgivings, would eventually accept the U.S. approach to negotiating German reunification. The French discovered that acting as Atlanticists they had lost, not gained, leverage. An alternative, which was used when the Americans pushed too hard, was to just say "no." This was the Gaullist obstructionist posture. But this tactic only worked if France could control the situation, as it did in refusing fly-over rights for the attack on Libya, or if, as in the case of the Soviet pipeline, it enjoyed the support of other major allies like the West Germans or the British. When France found itself isolated, as it did at several summits, it was embarrassed and had to back down. The third, or "official," option was for the French to declare simultaneously that they were loyal members of the alliance yet independent. But they learned that by trying to straddle the problem they would still lose most battles with the Americans and end up appearing like inveterate troublemakers and whiners—or, as Schultz described Mitterrand at Williamsburg, looking "sour and imperial."[167] Unwilling to act either as a true Atlanticist or a Gaullist, Mitterrand often had to settle for being ineffectual and resentful.

France measured its security and its status by the degrees of separation from the United States as much as it did by its partnership with it. Thus François Mitterrand, when convened by Ronald Reagan for a conference in New York, responded much like Charles de Gaulle had when summoned by President Franklin Delano Roosevelt to Casablanca during the Second World War. Mitterrand in 1985, like the general four decades earlier, protested that "one doesn't summon France" and stayed home.[168]

4.

The Adventures of Mickey Mouse, Big Mac,
and Coke in the Land of the Gauls

When President Bill Clinton visited Lyons for a G7 meeting in 1996, local schoolchildren designed posters presenting their impressions of America. Their drawings featured Mickey Mouse, McDonald's Golden Arches, Coca-Cola bottles, and the World Trade Center. American businesses—in particular, Disney, McDonald's, and Coca-Cola—functioned as private ambassadors of the United States. One way to understand how America functioned in France at the fin de siècle is to examine the experience of these companies looking closely at the selling of American forms of entertainment, food, and drink.

The setting of this narrative is the final two decades of the twentieth century, the moment when these businesses, which had been present for some time, changed strategies and moved into high gear. It was also the period when the French response was most dramatic. For example, opponents of Euro Disney threw tomato sauce and eggs at Disney's CEO; farmers sprayed a government building with a fusillade of Coca-Cola; and antiglobalization militants trashed a McDonald's site. I use the word *adventures* to describe the story of Mickey Mouse, Big Mac, and Coke in France because the term suggests tales in which the protagonists, in their quest for fortune, faced perilous predicaments and suspicious, and at times even hostile, natives in a foreign land.

The basic plot is this: even if these Americans encountered serious difficulties in expanding their businesses; even if they had to face scorn, denunciations, and public demonstrations that destroyed their property; and even if they encountered interference from government regulators, in the end the French came to accept Mickey Mouse, Coca-Cola and McDonald's. In spite of their troubles the Americans were successful; the French were seduced by these iconographic American products.

My account of these American enterprises addresses three issues. First, did Coca-Cola and the others directly export their products, techniques, and strategies to France, or did they modify their ways to suit the locals? Did they impose or adapt? A second issue is an assessment of the impact of these American multinationals: What kind of reception did they get from French consumers, and what effects did they have on their French competitors? These questions lead toward a third and more general issue—the importance of culture and identity in determining French reaction. Were the perils of these outsiders caused by American managers' misunderstanding or disregard of French values, traditions, and sense of identity? Did culture hamper American business or did it prove so supple that it was of little consequence?

If these are the general interpretive issues, one might fairly ask—given the vast number and variety of American enterprises operating within the Hexagon at the end of the century—Why select Disney, McDonald's, and Coca-Cola? There are several reasons.

First, these multinationals, more than most American corporations, carried the flag—they were businesses and products that the world associated with America. For example, according to one corporate official in Atlanta, "Coke is a part of the American lifestyle that people everywhere want to emulate to some degree."[1] As global enterprises these companies exploited whatever positive connotations America may have conveyed abroad to sell their merchandise. Main Street USA in Euro Disney outside Paris offered a fantasized version of America to Europeans. Freedom itself was invoked when Coke promoted its famous bottle alongside a facsimile of the Statue of Liberty. Americans also took pride in these enterprises which, in turn, paraded their patriotism; for example, Ray Kroc, the founder of McDonald's, insisted that each of his American units erect a flag pole to display the Stars and Stripes.

For the French it would be difficult to identify companies that were more distinctively American than these three. The logos of these globalized firms represented America to the French and to others around the world—and thus have often been targets for anti-Americanism. When French farmers protested U.S. trade policy in 1992, they sealed off access roads to Euro Disney, demonstrated in front of McDonald's franchises, and occupied a Coca-Cola plant in suburban Paris. The French were not alone in using these companies as symbols of what they disliked about corporate America or U.S. policies; people as different as the Swedes and the Koreans have attacked McDonald's for disrupting national culture, and Coca-Cola and Disney have long histories of such troubles in foreign countries.

Exploiting their cultural associations with America was one of several common strategies employed by these companies. They also attempted to appear as local businesses. They tried to balance between acting as indigenous enterprises and maintaining an American allure. The franchise system employed by Coca-Cola and McDonald's lent itself to this strategy. McDonald's claimed it was not an American corporation, but a loose federation of independent local retailers who marketed the same product. A third common strategy employed by these multinationals was to appear as global, as well as American and as local, enterprises. Coca-Cola, for example, created the first global television commercial in the 1970s and for years the *Economist* has employed the "Big Mac Index" as a lighthearted way to determine whether or not the currencies of the world were correctly valued. For its part Disney appropriated national cultural artifacts like fairy tales and presented them as Disney creations. When its theme park came under attack by French critics, one company executive responded, "It's not American, it's Disney."[2] If the products of these American giants became global, so did their profits. Thus, where Coca-Cola received only 25 percent of its profits from international sales in the mid-1950s, by the 1990s it earned over 75 percent overseas.[3] This trio played in all three registers: American, local, and global.

A second reason for selecting these businesses is the fact that they simultaneously expanded their positions in France at the fin de siècle. By the 1980s it was the world market (and that of Europe in particular), not the saturated home market, that became the new frontier. The anticipation of a Europe without trade barriers by 1992, following the adoption of the Single European Act, was a huge incentive for these three firms to expand and invigorate their businesses on the continent. In 1988–89 Coca-Cola acquired direct control over its bottling and distribution network in France, invested in new facilities, and launched an aggressive marketing campaign. In the 1980s McDonald's, after years of virtual paralysis brought on by a dispute with its French franchisee, seized control of its operations, initiated massive expansion, and quickly became the leader in the French fast food industry. Disney, under the leadership of CEO Michael Eisner, negotiated an agreement with the French government in 1987 to construct a theme park outside Paris. The park, called Euro Disney, later renamed Disneyland Paris, opened at Marne-la-Vallée in 1992. (For the sake of consistency I shall, with a few exceptions, refer to the park as Euro Disney.)

A third reason for this selection is that Walt Disney, Ray Kroc, and the founders of Coca-Cola constructed similar reputations for their products. They built their companies by stressing wholesomeness: Coca-Cola began as a tonic that purportedly cured a host of ills; Disney started as a producer of films for children and families; McDonald's made its reputation providing fast food for suburban families. Ray Kroc, intent upon preventing his restaurants from becoming "hangouts," as was the case for many drive-ins, banned cigarette machines and jukeboxes. "Our theme," Kroc liked to repeat, "is kind of synonymous with Sunday school, the Girl Scouts, and the YMCA. McDonald's is clean and wholesome."[4] All three of these businesses took pride in offering their customers reliable, predictable, "safe" food or films. Ray

Kroc and Walt Disney were compulsive personalities. Cleanliness was part of wholesomeness. Both men were notorious for personally policing the sites of their businesses. Disney leisure parks became famous for their tidy appearance, which separated them from the bawdy and often tacky amusement parks that preceded them. And McDonald's bathrooms are famous all over the world for their hygiene. Wholesomeness excluded sex or exotica. The Coca-Cola Company featured fetching young women in its ads even before 1900, but there was no hint of sleaze; they were "bewitching sirens who lure us to Coca-Cola."[5] If Disney's theme parks displayed some exotic amusements they were carefully sanitized. The rigorous dress code for its theme park employees— for example, for women no flashy jewelry, no unnatural hair color, no dark or patterned stockings—prompted the snide observation, "The Mormons ask less than this."[6] Children, or at least the young, were the favorite customers of the big three. Disney captured the imagination of many French children with its comics and television shows long before it built its park at Marne-la-Vallée. When McDonald's needed a mascot, management selected a childlike clown named Ronald McDonald. Even the hamburger chain's principal charity is for children: Ronald McDonald Houses provide low-cost or free housing to families with seriously ill children at nearby children's hospitals. And Coca-Cola targeted the youth of the world in its advertising as in its famous hilltop commercial of the 1970s that featured a crowd of idealistic young people dressed in national costumes clutching Cokes and singing, "I'd like to teach the world to sing in perfect harmony."

A fourth reason for examining these corporations is that they eventually developed informal business alliances to promote faster growth especially in global markets.[7] These interlocking relationships were usually marketing arrangements. Coca-Cola has been the sole supplier of soft drinks to Disney theme parks since 1955, including Euro Disney, and the two companies initiated a general marketing alliance in 1985. And Coke and McDonald's have worked together for decades. When Ray Kroc began his burger business in the mid-1950s he persuaded Coke to supply his restaurants. And since Coca-Cola was sold in far more countries than McDonald's, the Atlanta giant helped its partner set up restaurants around the world. McDonald's, like Coca-Cola, was a major sponsor of Euro Disney. McDonald's also had a formal arrangement whereby the hamburger chain had exclusive rights to use Disney film characters in its promotions. In exchange it promoted Disney productions. Thus, a French customer was likely to encounter all three brands simultaneously. A visitor to Euro Disney might be transported around the park on a railroad sponsored by McDonald's and eat at Casey's Corner restaurant hosted by Coca-Cola. A stop at a McDonald's in Paris would acquaint a French customer with the latest Disney movies while he or she ate a Big Mac and downed a Coke.

A final, if less serious, reason to select this trio is that they claimed to have some special links to France. Walt Disney and Ray Kroc served as Red Cross drivers in France during, or just after, the First World War and may have even met there. Moreover, according to company lore, Walt Disney received his inspiration for *Snow White* at a Paris cinema in 1935 where he first saw his short subjects shown independently; this gave him the idea of producing the first full-length animated feature. Productions like *Snow White and the Seven Dwarfs* later won him France's Legion of Honor. There may even be some Gallic blood in the Disney family. In the early 1990s, when the company's theme park in Marne-la-Vallée found itself in trouble, Walt Disney's nephew claimed ancestry from the town of Isigny-sur-Mer in Normandy.[8] Coca-Cola also has a Gallic flavor, or at least some background: the predecessor of the modern soft drink was Pemberton's French Wine Coca, which itself was modeled on Vin Marinari, a concoction of Bordeaux wine and extract from the coca leaf. Dr. Pemberton later modified his drink, removing the wine and adding other ingredients, and it thus became Coca-Cola.

As a preface to these adventures it may be useful to recall these companies' histories and their entry into France. McDonald's was founded by Ray Kroc, a salesman from the Midwest, who bought the rights to a rationalized hamburger operation from the McDonald brothers in California. Kroc built his first restaurant in Illinois in 1955 and established his headquarters in the Chicago suburb of Oak Brook. He proceeded to sell franchise rights to other small entrepreneurs who bought the assembly-line methods of food production and the company logo. Oak Brook provided certain services like designated suppliers, management training, site selection, and detailed instructions for operations, while the franchisee expended capital, added local initiative, and paid fees.[9] Relying on this franchise system and extensive advertising, McDonald's rapidly became the number one hamburger chain in the United States during the 1950s and '60s.

Coca-Cola, compared to Ray Kroc's chain, was much older, dating back to the 1880s, when Dr. John Pemberton introduced a new cola tonic in Atlanta. The Coca-Cola Company also employed a franchise system for its bottlers and relied heavily on advertising to sell its soft drink. By 1900 this regional enterprise had become a national company, making its owners and bottlers rich.[10]

Walt Disney, like Ray Kroc, was a small-time Midwestern entrepreneur with an idea. He founded a film company producing animated short subjects in the 1920s. Within a few years the Walt Disney Company, located in Burbank, grew into a major movie studio and by the late 1930s it had become a wildly successful producer and distributor of full-length animated films.

These enterprises were established, profitable, high-profile companies at home before they ventured abroad. Coca-Cola entered the international market in the 1920s, but waited (except in Germany) until after the Second World War to expand operations in Western Europe. In France the soft drink had been sold in a few cafés as early as 1919, but it only became a major competitor in the soft drink market during the 1950s. Walt Disney tentatively entered the overseas market in the 1930s. A few Parisian cinemas were showing his movies during the Depression, but the French became familiar with Disney films, comics, and television programs only after 1945. McDonald's was the last entrant into overseas markets. It opened its first restaurant outside the United States in 1967 and the Golden Arches first appeared in France in 1972. All three companies became major players in France only after the Second World War.

The adventures of Mickey Mouse, Big Mac, and Coke began as soon as they landed in France. In retrospect all made costly errors. There was also arrogance that provoked anxiety and resentment about American corporate power. Of the three Disney faced the most perils.

■ Disney

The Euro Disney Resort, created at Marne-la-Vallée outside Paris, experienced a difficult start-up: it riled most everyone involved in its construction and operation; provoked aesthetic, political, and philosophical debates; and within two years almost went bankrupt. Yet it not only survived but led France toward becoming the principal European site for theme parks.

Michael Eisner, the CEO of the Walt Disney Company (WDC), wanted to replicate the successful theme parks in Orlando, Florida, and Tokyo while avoiding their mistakes.[11] At Tokyo Disneyland, for example, Disney had assumed no equity and little control and ended up with meager revenue. In negotiating with the French in the mid-1980s the WDC sought a different contract. Eisner's team knew that they had the upper hand because the French government wanted the park to create jobs, stimulate tourism, and attract foreign spending, and because officials worried that Disney would select another site like Barcelona. Politicians did their best to lure Mickey Mouse to Paris. Prime Minister Laurent Fabius, a socialist, signed the letter of intent with the WDC in 1985 and Jacques Chirac, his conservative successor, completed the negotiations and endorsed the voluminous contract in 1987. Estimates of job creation ranged between ten and twenty thousand on-site positions, with tens of thousands more for related work like construction and off-site services. Government officials spoke of tourists spending a billion dollars a year in France. The public was enthusiastic: in one survey four out of five polled supported the project,[12] and the newspaper *Libération* added mouse ears to its logo when the agreement was signed. Disney exploited its advantage to win generous concessions including tax breaks, a low-interest loan, an extension of the suburban railway, a rock-bottom price for land, a percentage of all revenues, and total control for only a tiny part of equity.

What Eisner's team had in mind was more than a new theme park. In the first stage, there were also plans for six hotels with 5,200 rooms as well as a campground, a golf course, and a shopping mall. In the second stage there would be another theme park modeled after the MGM Studios as well as additional hotels, apartments, office buildings, a major convention center, and more. In short Euro Disney was but the beginning of an enormous, and enormously expensive, real estate development sprawling over five thousand acres and costing over four billion dollars. Its aim was to transform European notions of leisure. The Disney project was going to offer a complete vacation resort rather than just a park devoted to day-trippers.

French entrepreneurs smelled opportunity. If Disney calculated that the country was ready for an expensive theme park, then there should be room for them. But they needed to hurry and beat the Magic Kingdom to the punch before the planned opening in 1992. There was also the appeal of millions of tourists coming to Europe for the Barcelona Olympics the same year. Six major parks opened while Euro Disney was under construction, as did several small ones, making France the European leader in the new leisure business. Of these Disney challengers, however, only two proved successful; the others either closed or barely survived from year to year. Mirapolis, based on Rabelaisian themes, opened in 1987 near Paris, but floundered when its attendance was less than half of what was expected. Big Bang Smurf, featuring Belgian cartoon characters, started two years later near Metz and had the same fate. Both faced bankruptcy after one or two summers. Others, like Planète Magique, an indoor family fun center, and several aquatic parks, lasted but one season. What went wrong? There was a combination of exaggerated aims, misspent or inadequate capital, poor design or location, sparse attractions, neophyte managers, errors in marketing, and weak advertising.[13] And French customers were hesitant about paying pricey one-day admissions.

Two other parks showed more potential. Parc Astérix, which was based on the famous French cartoon stories that featured the wily Gaul Astérix and his sidekick Obélix who outwit the bumbling Romans—opened to crowds of 20,000 per day in April 1989. It enjoyed a favorable location just north of Paris, solid financing from investors like Barclays Bank and the Accor hotel chain (although initial investment was only $200 million compared to $4.5 billion for Disney), some sound advice from California consultants, and smart marketing that utilized the media. It featured historical sites like a Roman city and tableaux with depictions of such events as the storming of the Bastille. In its initial two years the annual gate was $1.4 million. But management held its breath over the impact of the coming of the Magic Kingdom. The other new park, whose self-description was that of an "image park," was Futuroscope, which began in 1987 and built its attendance to 1.2 million by 1991. While Parc Astérix was a private venture, Futuroscope was part of a technology, research, and educational complex built and owned by the regional government with the aim of reviving the economy of the area around Poitiers.[14] A new high-speed rail connection made the area easily accessible. Public funds ($180 million in its first years) constructed and developed the complex while a private concessionaire operated it. Futuroscope featured attractions like 3-D cinema and an IMAX theater, futuristic architecture, and exhibits and shows on the "Enchanted Lake."

The leisure industry in Europe anxiously awaited the arrival of Mickey Mouse in the spring of 1992. At a conference in Germany some theme park officials expressed their fear that Disney would set unaffordable standards for them and steal their customers.[15] Others, like

Olivier de Bosredon, the director of Parc Astérix, believed Europeans could compete, but they must "fight back." He pointed out the weaknesses of their Yankee competitor: high prices and long waits. "Europeans won't want to queue up for two and a half hours. They are not used to that." A former Disney consultant was optimistic. He reminded his apprehensive listeners that Disney would help them in the long run by promoting greater public awareness of their industry: in the United States and in Japan, he pointed out, Disney had been a boon because it induced higher levels of investment, raised operating standards, and sparked product innovation. His advice to Bosredon and his colleagues was to reinvest and rejuvenate their enterprises.

Meanwhile, Eisner's team encountered trouble.[16] If republican politicians paid a king's ransom for the park and the public seemed welcoming, there were some noisy dissenters from the outset. One union claimed the company had gouged the French government and won such privileges that the Magic Kingdom had become the "fifty-first state." Nor was the entire political class on board. Environmentalists attacked the project for despoiling good farm land; communists disapproved of the squandering of taxpayers' money; radical rightists regretted the subversion of French culture, and even a few socialists like Jean-Pierre Chevènement stood against their own government.[17]

Eisner's managers provoked opposition by insisting on a comprehensive contract and then proceeding to enforce every detail—to the point of antagonizing government agencies, contractors, trade unions, local residents, and employees. Government officials and contractors grumbled about imperious treatment, and farmers about the low price paid for their land; and many of the newly hired employees, labeled "cast members" in "Disneyese," complained about just everything: they objected to the stringent dress code that proscribed anything that detracted from the clean-cut Disney image—no beards, mustaches, or earrings for men.[18] They disapproved of their training, pay, working conditions, and housing, and they carped about the strict surveillance from the company's monitors, who carried clipboards and wore headsets. Cleaning women were among the first to protest because they could be made to work at night, sometimes every night. There were charges of racism because blacks and North Africans were confined to cleaning the park. Trade unions, including the communist connected Confédération Générale du Travail, joined in to try to force Disney to obey the French labor code, which required paying for overtime and granting sick leaves. Over a thousand trainees quit just after the park opened, and sporadic strikes including hotel workers, cleaners, and musicians interrupted the resort's operations. There is some evidence that the French, who made up about two-thirds of the hires, were more difficult to train than other Europeans.[19] Disney retaliated with tighter surveillance of its employees and layoffs for troublemakers. One scholar, Marianne Debouzy, has concluded that Disney's "brutal methods" made "a clean break with French work culture."[20] A satirical journal inverted Disney magic: "Mickey invents the exploitation of man by mouse."[21]

To many the Californians seemed not only aggressive but arrogant. One executive told a French newspaper, "There is a world of difference between Disney and the others. . . . We are already the best." Another likened the park's construction to the pharaohs building the pyramids: "We're building something immortal."[22] The communications manager for the project was only half joking when he said "Paris will be one of the attractions of Euro Disneyland."[23]

Some journalists disparaged the project even before it opened with charges that the Americans wanted to industrialize leisure, murder fantasy, denigrate the French language, and lower cultural standards.[24] *Le Nouvel Observateur* ran articles like "Mickey's Long Teeth" and one of its editors, Jacques Julliard, noted that the last popular action hero for the French was D'Artagnan (from Alexandre Dumas's *The Three Musketeers*) and pleaded, "[W]here is our Rambo?"[25] When Eisner and other company officials appeared at the Paris Bourse to launch the sale of stock in 1989, signs called for "Uncle Scrooge" to go home and a handful of leftist protesters pelted the Americans with tomato sauce and eggs.

Figure 6. Farmers' tractors block the opening of Euro Disney,
June 1992. Courtesy Yves Forestier/Corbis.

On opening day, April 12, 1992, Disney's quarrel with trade unions
erupted in a transportation workers slowdown that disrupted access to
the park. Contractors claiming unfair treatment threatened to picket.
Local residents complained about traffic and the nightly fireworks. By
June "Operation Mickey" found hundreds of tractors blocking roads,
with farmers protesting the "colonization" of agricultural land. The new
park's reputation was awful. And the early crowds, which management
worried would be too large to accommodate, fell below expectations in
spite of an extravagant media blitz. Worse was to follow. Robert Fitzpatrick, the first president of Euro Disney, would not live down his infamous prediction: "My biggest fear is that we will be too successful."[26]

Disney managers compounded the problem with numerous business errors.[27] They overestimated the need for overnight accommoda-
tions and set prices too high for admissions, hotel rooms, food, and

merchandise. They also underestimated the effects of nasty weather and, above all, they misjudged the state of the French—and the European—economy. The Americans expected booming prosperity in 1992 because of the big step forward by the European Union when in fact they faced Western Europe's worst postwar recession. And they made smaller mistakes like ignoring travel agents and restricting the sale of alcoholic beverages.[28] There were complaints about prices, queues, and slow service. The first season was a major disappointment: admissions, expenditures on food and merchandise were all below expectations, and the hotels were only half full. The recession prevented the company from selling its real estate while, at the same time, it had to pay heavy financial charges on its debt. The resort was hemorrhaging money. It lost over $35 million in the first fiscal year and losses continued to mount into the next year. British tabloids ran articles like: "Hi ho, hi ho, it's off the cliff we go." Fewer than eleven million entrants, which was at the low end of the target for admissions, had come by April 1993. Of these, 36 percent were French. The price of stock collapsed. Officials announced losses of $87 million for the first three months of the 1993 season, or almost a million dollars per day. By the summer it was imperative for the company to restructure its finances, cut prices, and reduce its payroll. Attendance slumped below nine million. Eisner threatened to close the park if his partners, a consortium of banks and investors, refused concessions.

Euro Disney was on the brink of bankruptcy during the winter of 1993–94. A rescue package negotiated in March 1994, which included givebacks by both the WDC and the banks, and a huge investment of a Saudi prince, began the turn around. But losses continued, reaching $1.5 billion. Only in the summer of 1995, in its third year of operation, did the park's operations turn a profit.[29] But the heavy debt would continue to weigh against the resort's finances while its annual attendance stabilized around twelve million.

Years later a successor to Fitzpatrick as president would admit that the park was initially larger than it should have been and that it had assumed too much debt.[30] In harsher language a British analyst alluding to the 1994 restructuring concluded, "Pride, conceit, greed, and over-ambition lie at the heart of Euro Disney's downfall."[31] Too much was spent, for example, in hiring six famous architects to design six different theme hotels. Costs spiraled out of control and in the end the park struggled with a crushing financial burden of billions of dollars in loans. By trying to avoid the mistakes made in Tokyo, Eisner, in this view, had gone too far in constructing a vast, expensive, highly leveraged complex whose profits went mainly to the WDC.

An alternative, but not convincing, explanation for the problems of the Magic Kingdom argues that it was Disney's fault for refusing to adapt to France and to Europe. Disney planners decided that what Europeans wanted was an American theme park, not some hybrid Europeanized Disneyland, so they rebuilt Florida's Disneyworld on the River Marne. Michael Eisner announced that he intended to make his Paris park "every bit as American as Tokyo Disneyland and our domestic parks—meaning fast food instead of smoky bistros, Coca-Cola and lemonade in preference to wine, animated movies rather than film noir."[32] Main Street USA, according to Eisner, was to be purely American, just as Frontierland captured the American West and Big Thunder Mountain recalled the Gold Rush. Or, as Shanny Peer has observed, "Disney concentrated more efforts on commodifying Americana in France than on Frenchifying the Disney experience. . . ."[33] A French spokesperson for the resort explained, "We are bringing a naïve, simple view of America reflecting the idea of America that Europeans have."[34]

What concessions did Disney management make to Europeans in its Magic Kingdom? There were many, but all were minor and did little to "Europeanize" the site. Planners added one French restaurant, adopted French as one of the two official languages, and modeled Sleeping Beauty's castle after illustrations from *Les très riches Heures du duc de Berry* and the chateaux of the Loire. They also made a few of the attractions appear European. For example, the Visionarium, which featured a circular movie screen, did not show the *American Journeys* film as it did in Florida and California but presented a panorama of European sites like the Hofburg in Vienna and used European actors like Gérard Depardieu and Jeremy Irons as narrators. And once the park opened, or shortly thereafter, most of the Americans went home, including its first president, Robert Fitzpatrick, who was replaced by a Frenchman, Philippe Bourguignon.[35] Eventually the resort also abandoned its ban on alcoholic beverages. Disney went further in trying to win the natives' approval. After the financial restructuring of 1994 Eisner renamed the reborn park "Disneyland Paris," in order, he explained, to identify it with "Walt's original creation and with one of the most romantic and exciting cities in the world."[36]

But the park remained a fantasized version of America.[37] The entrance to the Magic Kingdom was through Main Street, evocative of small-town America, and the park was divided into categories like Adventureland and Fantasyland that had been imported from Disney World in Orlando. "Cast members"—that is, all employees who had contact with "guests"—had to speak English, while many of the park's signs and the announcements of the Disney railroad were in English (the other "official language"). Hotels like the Sequoia Lodge and the Hotel Cheyenne catered to European fantasies about the Far West. The food served in most of the park's restaurants, like The Gibson Girl Ice Cream Parlor, was American, while the music and the costumes of the "cast members" all served up an imaginary construction of America in the 1890s. The Auberge de Cendrillon served true French cuisine like *pâté de foie gras* on toasted brioche, but a guest could also order hamburgers and fish fingers. Few Europeans would confuse Sleeping Beauty's castle with a Loire chateau; it was pure Disney. Yet it is difficult to dispute this strategy. Europeans wanted to eat American food like barbecued ribs and hot dogs. As Eisner commented, "the French don't want us to come over and do crêpes."[38] An early survey of 30,000 European families had shown the way. "Almost all of them," according to Fitzpatrick, "wanted Disney to be the same as in the United States. The Mickey that we will come to see shall not be half Schtroumpf and half Astérix."[39] What the French wanted was an American theme park; Eisner and his fellow planners were right.[40] Imposing America rather than adapting to France was not the principal reasons for the park's initial stumble—even if it contributed. The problem was one of poor business decision making.

Still, the locals did not troop to see Mickey as expected. Instead of the anticipated 50 percent of the gate, the French provided only 40 percent on average. In 1998, when receipts were up, 38 percent of the visitors were French. And the locals, at least in the eyes of American tourists, earned a reputation for violating rules, especially for failing to stand in line. In fact, French visitors used the park differently than Americans. For example, instead of staying multiple nights, they tended to spend a single overnight. They also used travel agents to schedule their trip, but Disney refused to work with such intermediaries. And they were shocked by the high initial entrance fees (which included the rides): $41 for adults and $27 for children. As a result, the majority of those wandering through the Magic Kingdom were not French.

Once observers could actually view the new Disney creation, the intellectual debate sharpened with attacks from across the political spectrum. Alain Finkielkraut wrote that it was "a terrifying step toward world homogenization." A rightist pamphleteer, Jean Cau, scorned the site as "a horror made of cardboard, plastic and appalling colors, a construction of hardened chewing gum and idiotic folklore taken straight out of comic books written for obese Americans."[41] To some, national identity was at risk by letting Americans impose their form of imagination and creativity on French children. After visiting the resort one scholar labeled it the "slaughterhouse of dreams" and called it "a canker in Europe, in the heart of the Ile-de-France."[42] From the New Right Alain de Benoist described the Magic Kingdom as the dream world of Americans—tranquil, soulless, infantile, commercialized, and homogenized.[43] *Le Monde* described the park as a "slice of the American dream": it evoked images of abundance and antiseptic happiness that were "a long way from the real America."[44] Others scoffed at Euro Disney for its aesthetics, its cultural theft, its sanitized artificiality, its sweet sentimentality, its passive form of fun, its visual rather than literary character, its "hyperreality," its commercialism, and its pretense that entertainment was "culture."[45] One of the more infamous comments came from Jacques Julliard, who expressed hope that a fire might destroy the park.[46] But the most notorious denunciation came from the theatrical director Ariane Mnouchkine, who called the park "a cultural Chernobyl." Fitzpatrick said he nearly fell off his chair when he heard Mnouchine's barb because she had accepted his invitation to visit the California resort where she had posed with Mickey Mouse. As for lowering cultural standards, Fitzpatrick responded sarcastically, "Diversion is also a form of culture. The French know it well. Have they forgotten?"[47]

Jack Lang, the incumbent minister of culture whose disdain for American culture we encountered in chapter 2, said he was too busy to attend the park's opening and regretted that the park afforded so little room for attractions from Europe. Yet the minister softened his snub by expressing his admiration for the technical capacity of Disney and admitting he had found his visit to Disneyworld in Florida "quite fascinating."[48]

The American press mocked the French for their anxieties and their carping. The *New York Times* carried articles like "Defy Disney, the Unmitigated Gaul" or "Only the Elite Scorn Mickey's Debut" while one review, drawing on the story of Snow White, referred to a France "Where All the Dwarfs are Grumpy."[49]

But the grumps did not monopolize the discussion: the Magic Kingdom had its defenders, including some familiar anti-anti-Americans. Michel Serres, the philosopher, chastised the critics by arguing, "It is not America that is invading us. It is us who adore it, who adopt its fashions and above all its words." Jean-François Revel added, "If French culture can be squashed by Mickey Mouse or more exactly by simply moving Mickey geographically, it would have to be disturbingly fragile."[50] Revel pointed out that culture circulates, and in this case California was simply repackaging for European such European stories as Cinderella and Pinocchio. André Glucksmann chided the "aristocratic disdain" of critics for "popular pleasures": "The fact that Mickey and Minnie manage to draw against them the holy alliance of right-thinking progressives and conservatives ought to bring them the Oscar for humor."[51] One writer, after visiting the park, thought Euro Disney—like hell—was also "paved with soft caramel," yet he admitted that he enjoyed his day, wearing Mickey Mouse ears, eating popcorn, and going on rides.[52] Weekly magazines agreed. "Who's Afraid of Mickey Mouse?" was how *L'Express* greeted the park's opening.[53] *Le Point* concurred, "Culture: Let's not fear America."[54]

The critics soon grew silent, the media mellowed, and by 1993–94 the press sounded rather positive. "Disney is fashionable among us," *Le Monde* reported.[55] Defenders reminded the arrogant elite of St. Germain des Prés that the park was just fun for the family. "American culture swings," according to a contributor to *L'Express*; "Merleau-Ponty has a certain value, I'm convinced, but, tomorrow, I am going to Disneyland."[56] Disney's spokespeople also counterattacked by portraying themselves as victims of mean-spirited snobs.[57] The fact that Euro Disney sparked a debate rather than a monologue indicates the faltering hold of the anti-Americans over the intellectual community.

If the French did not come in the numbers the WDC expected or wanted, they did keep the turnstiles moving. Once attendance stabilized, they arrived at a rate of between four and a half to five million customers per year. The younger generation, who had been raised on American mass culture including *Le Journal de Mickey* and Disney animated films, were strongly attracted to visiting the Magic Kingdom.[58] Hotel occupancy reached near 90 percent while spending on merchandise and food climbed. And most visitors seemed pleased with their experience—apparently unimpressed with the warnings of the intelligentsia. Disney products were popular as well. The Disney Store on the Champs-Elysées, which opened in 1993, moved more merchandise than any of its counterparts worldwide. And the government lent its blessing: six months after its opening Pierre Bérégovoy, the socialist prime minister, awarded Michael Eisner the Legion of Honor. Even President Mitterrand relented. He had previously refused to come to the park, but Eisner used his political connections to persuade former U.S. president George H. W. Bush to invite him to dine there in 1994. Facing the press Bush noticed the somber expression of his dinner companion and said "Smile, come on, François, smile!" Photographs of the two cheerful presidents made the front page the next day and Eisner had his symbolic endorsement.[59]

By the end of the decade the Magic Kingdom appeared, at least in some respects, to be prospering. According to the Paris tourist office it had more visitors (12.6 million) than the Cathedral of Notre Dame (12 million), making it the most popular tourist site in the region. But attendance was still less than what was needed for profitability, and the price of the resort's stock remained pathetic. Nevertheless, Gilles Péllisson, the CEO in 1999, announced plans to build a second park devoted to the movie and broadcasting industry at the cost of 4.5 billion francs: Walt Disney Studios was scheduled to open in April 2002, the tenth anniversary of Euro Disney. Once again the socialist government, in this case the minister of economy and finance, Dominique Strauss-Kahn, welcomed the new site, relishing the investments and jobs.[60] Once again, however, Disney overreached and once again its timing was unfortunate—terrorism was in the air. Two years after Walt Disney Studios opened, it attracted only two million visitors, less than half of what had been expected, and did nothing to improve the park's financial situation.[61] Dragged down by debt and still struggling to become profitable, Euro Disney had to refinance a second time. Still it bragged it was the number one tourist destination in Europe. Mickey had arrived when the Tour de France finished the race at the resort in 1997.

The coming of the Magic Kingdom disrupted the French leisure industry. Parc Astérix was the hardest hit: attendance dropped to one million in 1992–93 and like Euro Disney refinancing was required. But the slump was brief and management, led by Olivier de Bosredon, refused to surrender: they invested $10 million, introduced new attractions like "Nationale 7," a miniature car ride on the old highway that took vacationers to the south—and spruced up the park. Bosredon likened the competition to the struggle between the Gauls and the Romans: "Astérix was a fighter against massive invasion, and so are we. The Romans insisted their soldiers not wear beards, much as Disney does. There are some interesting parallels."[62] By 1995 the park's managers were declaring victory: attendance had recovered to 1.5 million and so had profits. Two years later the gate reached 2 million and the park sold shares on the bourse. The marketing manager Nicolas Perrard declared the reason for victory was that Astérix was "a French theme park and not an American concept." "Disney is based on fantasies, we are based on realities," he added. "They are not based on national culture, but on fairy tales."[63] One might question, however, both the "reality" and the national character of Astérix. In fact, what accounted for Parc Astérix's "victory" was as much its cloning of Euro Disney as its exploitation of French history. It had drawn on the Americans for its design and advertising and it learned how to refurbish with new attractions like Le Grand Splatch, a water ride inspired by attractions at Marne-la Vallée. Like Disney it offered theme merchandise in its stores and built its own hotel. Perrard admitted that the staff that had opened Parc Astérix had had little understanding of theme parks, but "by watching Disney the company transformed the park from a passive form of entertainment almost like a public park, to a participatory operation. Thanks to Disney, our people now know what the product is."[64] Parc Astérix also went continental—teaming up with other European parks to coordinate marketing and investment. Bosredon was right when he predicted back in 1992 that French parks would benefit in the long run from the arrival of Disney.[65]

By the end of the 1990s Disneyland Paris was the only park in Europe bringing in more than 10 million admissions annually. Between 12 and 13 million "guests" arrived at the year-round theme park while Futuroscope (with 2.8 million visitors) and Parc Astérix (with 2 million visitors), though prosperous, trailed far behind. Several other parks, like Le Puy de Fou, located in the Vendée, which re-created French history through such shows as a reenactment of the Hundred Years War, were expanding, and others like Vulcania, which exploited the volcanic terrain near Clermont-Ferrand, were in the planning stage. Then there were the numerous aquatic parks on the coasts and many smaller sites inland. Theme parks had become a big business, and Disney had led the way. It demonstrated how such parks could flourish, trained the public in the habits of routine day trips and vacations at resorts, and forced French competitors to keep up. Marne-la-Vallée left plenty of room for French entrepreneurs to find their niche. Before Mickey Mouse settled in, leisure parks in France counted 1.5 million visitors annually. By the mid-1990s there were over sixty such parks attracting more than 20 million people per year. France had become the largest market for theme parks in Europe.[66]

■ McDonald's

The McDonald's Corporation experienced a miserable setup phase.[67] In 1972 it awarded an exclusive license for Paris to a local entrepreneur, Raymond Dayan. Within a few years Dayan was operating a dozen restaurants, some of which were among McDonald's most profitable foreign performers. But when inspectors arrived in 1977 to test whether or not the Parisian units met company standards, they were appalled. They found rancid cooking oil, grease-covered walls and floors, and open cans of insect spray atop containers of hamburger sauce. Entering the branch at Gare St. Lazare, customers had to pass through the arcade of a porno movie house. The next year McDonald's sent another team of inspectors, this time accompanied by French officials, who snapped pictures of dog droppings in the stores and found Dayan charging for ketchup. McDonald's initiated legal action to terminate Dayan's franchise, but it took four years and a trial in Illinois for the firm to recover control. Dayan claimed that Chicago simply wanted to get its hands on a profitable franchise. In 1982 a judge ruled that McDonald's had the right to cancel Dayan's license. But more than a decade had elapsed before McDonald's could try to rehabilitate its French operations. Ray Kroc's company had to play catch-up in France thanks to the fiasco with its first franchise. It should be noted however, that the misadventure in France was not unusual in Europe. McDonald's had serious setup problems in the Netherlands, England, and Germany as well.

By the time McDonald's was ready to relaunch operations, it faced strong competition within a fast food sector that had been expanding quickly since the early 1970s.[68] In 1984 it had only sixteen units in France. While McDonald's struggled with its legal problems, French burger chains like Free Time, backed by the hotel chain Accor, had entered the market; it, like others, directly copied Ray Kroc's operations and marketing. Both Free Time and France Quick, the Belgian chain, had many more units than McDonald's in the mid-1980s. Burger King had also opened shop and was soon operating more outlets in Paris than McDonald's. And Dayan was still functioning: he renamed his outlets O'Kitch, modified his menu to suit French tastes—for example, adding Béarnaise sauce for his hamburgers, and went on making money. There were also a host of small homegrown competitors with names like Manhattan Burger, Love Burger, or Astérix Burger. Despite the rapid growth in hamburger vendors, a substantial share of the fast food market in the mid-1980s belonged to the *viennoiseries* that had also blossomed during the 1970s, led by chains like La Brioche Dorée serving a more traditional menu like croissants and pastries. Then McDonald's made its move.

In 1984 a company-owned unit reopened in an upscale Parisian quarter, attempting to erase the memory of Dayan's small, minimally furnished stores. Expansion would be high-profile and expensive targeting high-density urban centers and fashionable neighborhoods in Paris and provincial cities. McDonald's paid $6 million to lease its flagship restaurant on the glamorous Champs-Elysées. The new units would replicate the standard external and interior decor, employ the highly rationalized operating methods perfected in the United States, and rely on tight quality control from the U.S. corporate headquarters. The strategy worked. Within three years Accor sold its Free Time chain, saying it was too costly to compete with the Americans. By 1990 there were 110 McDonald's restaurants in France, and three years later there were 240. By then McDonald's and France Quick controlled two-thirds of the national market.[69] Within the French fast food business hamburger sales grew at the expense of more traditional fare. In 1988 burgers accounted for 48 percent of fast food consumption; by 1992 their share had soared to 81 percent. At the same time, sales at viennoiseries slumped from 29 percent to 8 percent. The latter, however, also continued to expand, with chains like La Croissanterie, La Brioche Dorée, and La Viennoisière leading the way. Sales of sandwiches grew, but trailed behind hamburgers, and "take home" fare was still in its infancy. Despite the growth in fast food, it still accounted for only 10 percent of total restaurant sales in the late 1980s.[70]

A survey of fast food restaurants in Paris and Lyons conducted in 1986 indicated that customers for burgers, compared to those who used viennoiseries, tended to be more male than female and more youthful (68 percent were under twenty-five years old).[71] Middle- and low-level managers, office staff, and the unemployed, which included many adolescents, far outnumbered factory workers. The reasons cited for choosing fast food rather than a traditional restaurant or a café were the speed of service (81 percent) and the price (41 percent), followed by atmosphere (32 percent) and taste (25 percent) while, as one might expect, the primary reason for selecting a café was ambiance.

McDonald's corporate managers in the United States, who worried that Europeans might perceive their business as an intrusive American multinational, tried, from the outset, to give their operations a measure of autonomy. Franchise owners were local entrepreneurs who enjoyed some say in marketing and product innovation, but the headquarters in Oak Brook, Illinois, kept tight rein over essentials like operations, menu, and suppliers. In Germany, at least at first, localizing went too far. In the early 1970s Ray Kroc allowed his German franchises the freedom to prepare fried chicken breast, serve beer, and make their units look "German," complete with heavy wood paneling and dim lighting.[72] They failed to turn a profit: quality control was difficult with chicken; beer encouraged young layabouts; and the dark interiors were not inviting to families. Kroc intervened: he eliminated the chicken (but kept the beer), had the units remodeled to look more American, and attracted children with techniques honed at home, such as birthday clubs. In a few years they were turning a profit. The head of McDonald's international division drew a lesson from such mistakes, noting, "McDonald's is an American food system. If we go into a new country and incorporate their food products into our menu, we lose our identity."[73] A superior strategy was to adhere to the American way and wait—if necessary, for years—for foreign consumers to accept it. Figuratively speaking, these Americans only wanted to speak *un peu de Français*.

The new French franchises, nevertheless, made some modifications to the menu like serving a mustard sauce rather than ketchup on the Big Mac, reducing the sugar in the salad dressing, serving Evian water and beer, and offering a wider range of desserts. But nothing essential about the menu, the presentation of food, or restaurant operation was changed; the McDonald's "system" prevailed. To accommodate French sociability seats were movable so that patrons could form ad hoc gatherings. Owners also had to make adjustments because French customers tended to eat at conventional mealtime hours and spend a longer time in the restaurant than Americans.[74] McDonald's was willing to make such adjustments to attract the French, but it assumed they, like others in Europe and around the world, wanted what Americans wanted. They wanted the basic McDonald's menu; the bright, informal atmosphere; the relatively low prices, the gift toys and play areas for children.

McDonald's, much like Disney and Coca-Cola, exploited or traded on its identification with America. All these businesses associated their products with the stereotypical image of Americans: young, playful, informal, wholesome, and modern. McDonald's aimed at providing the French with an American eating experience. The appeal of the Golden Arches in the land of the Gauls—at least initially, as Rick Fantasia has argued—was less the food than it was the cultural association.[75] The appeal was the American ambiance—although fast service and price were also important. Young adults, who composed over 80 percent of McDonald's' paying customers in the late 1980s, patronized the restaurant because it was like eating in America.[76] What they liked was: the bright lights and noise, the colorful employee uniforms, the absence of adult mediators like waiters, the self-service, and the open seating. One first-time customer said it was like "visiting the United States," and adolescents found it "relaxing" or "cool" and "un-French." McDonald's traded on these associations in its advertisements: eating at the Golden Arches was fun and mildly rebellious. In one TV ad a child intoned proper table manners ("Don't eat with your fingers." "Don't make noise.") while pictures of customers showed them eating french fries with their fingers and joking. Eating at McDonald's, drinking Cokes, and visiting Euro Disney were what Americans did—and it was fun and hip. These corporations celebrated, and profited from, an intrinsic market advantage—offering others what Americans enjoyed. When asked by a polling agency in 1994 what products they most associated with the United States, *le hamburger* was number one (83 percent) for a cross-section of the populace.[77]

French food purists, however, refused to allow *le Big Mac* to have its way, especially with children. They mounted a counterattack. From the late 1980s on, schools held a Taste Week (*Semaine de goût*) featuring activities like bringing chefs into classrooms or taking children to farmers' markets.[78] The Ritz hotel participated by showing students from a neighborhood school how to a make a zabaglione sauce. In time Taste Week expanded to include adults and held its programs at sites like hospitals and museums. Jack Lang, then minister of culture, launched a more focused pedagogical campaign. Taste Classes for a few thousand ten- and eleven-year-olds began in 1991 and quickly grew to 25,000 students in four hundred public schools.[79] These classes aimed at weaning children off of fast food by making them discriminating consumers. For ten weeks volunteers, including chefs and nutritionists, taught classes helping the children "discover" the five senses and the four basic *saveurs* and learn about meal preparation, regional cuisines, and gastronomy. The Ministry of Education, the French Institute of Taste, and the National Council of Culinary Arts, which was inspired by Lang to protect the *patrimoine culinaire*, collaborated on the project and sponsors included the dairy industry and the Danone company. Whether or not such campaigns curbed children's appetites for *le Big Mac* is open to question.

Figure 7. "Taste Week" for a class of seven-year-old schoolchildren in Paris wearing paper toques. Courtesy Jean-Claude Coutausse/ *New York Times*/Redux.

When critics tried to tarnish the home of the Golden Arches as a heartless, American multinational, McDonald's emphasized its virtues and its French character. It established a Ronald McDonald House outside Paris for the families of children being treated at a nearby cancer center, and two others in Marseilles and Bordeaux. Like Disney, McDonald's reminded its hosts that it had helped relieve unemployment by hiring thousands of young French people. In large cities, more than a third of its employees were of recent immigrant origin.[80] When farmers picketed McDonald's in 1992 at the height of the imbroglio over the General Agreement on Tariffs and Trade (GATT), the Chicago firm counterattacked. McDonald's ran ads showing how half the regions of France provided supplies for the burger chain. A spokeswoman declared, "In France the only thing American at McDonald's is the name. Of our 18,000 employees only three are Americans."[81]

By the mid-to-late 1990s the American chain had won a dominant position in the market for hamburgers and for fast food in general. The bad days of Dayan were far behind: in 1997 the company had 550 outlets in France, over twice as many as its nearest rival, France Quick, and it controlled 60 percent of the entire fast food market.[82] McDonald's also broadened its appeal. Golden Arches were appearing outside city centers, in shopping malls, on major roadways, in small towns, and in even poorer suburbs. The company partnered with Galeries Lafayette, as well as Disney, and opened outlets that featured themes such as sports. Its clientele also matured: almost half its customers were not adolescents.[83] In total sales McDonald's was the top restaurant chain, lapping its French competitors like Buffalo Grill and Taverne de Maître Kanter. Unable to compete with McDonald's, Burger King shuttered its operations. By 1998 McDonald's was opening new stores at a pace of more than one unit per week, employing 25,000, earning €1.47 billion, and serving a million meals per day.[84] France had become the company's third largest overseas market in sales, trailing only Japan and Germany.[85] Fast food, however, occupied only a small fraction of the restaurant business, lagging far behind traditional restaurants and cafés.

The arrival of McDonald's remade the industry. Fast food was not new: long before the construction of the first McDonald's franchise one could buy crêpes and *gaufres* from sidewalk vendors. But fast food, defined as selling prepared food over the counter at relatively low prices to be consumed on the premises or taken away, boomed in the 1970s and '80s largely because of specialized American-style hamburger outlets—with McDonald's winning the biggest market share and forcing some competitors out of business, including many of the viennoiseries.[86] Some rivals closed shop, but others adapted to the competition from abroad. There was widespread copying of McDonald's operations within the French fast food business.[87] French chains—both burger outlets like France Quick, and viennoiseries—borrowed directly from the Americans. What was copied ranged from restaurant layout to standardized food preparation and computerized accounting (but not the franchise system). Many of these changes were adopted while McDonald's was paralyzed by its legal troubles in the 1970s. Large French hotel and restaurant chains invested and helped consolidate local fast food operators. Some even acquired expensive urban real estate, as McDonald's had done, for their prime sites. McDonald's also induced innovations in food processing and the manufacture of restaurant equipment. French and European food suppliers in general were not accustomed to high-volume, standardized output and could not produce everything needed for a McDonald's menu.[88] For example, when McDonald's arrived in Europe in the 1970s farmers did not cultivate Russet potatoes; suppliers were unable to provide frozen french fries; and bakeries could not produce uniform, soft buns. McDonald's intervened and through a combination of lucrative contracts, technical and financial aid, and threats to build its own facilities, transformed food processing. But farmers could only become suppliers if they "McDonaldized" their crops. In time European suppliers provided everything McDonald's needed and in so doing improved their own production techniques. The firm also changed labor practice in the fast food business by hiring young part-time help—especially students. Firms like France Quick followed suit.

Part-time employees, who could be trained in hours and viewed their job as temporary, challenged the pattern of work in traditional restaurants where cooks and waiters regarded their positions as careers.

Besides such deskilling, McDonald's exported its opposition to trade unions. Its strong antiunion stance, like that of the Walt Disney Company, caused continuous legal troubles, vandalism, and serious labor protests. Employees charged the company with paying a minimum wage, forcing employees to be available for surges of customers, and failing to grant them the rights guaranteed by the labor code like mandated breaks and bonuses for night shifts. And what McDonald's lauded as job flexibility—that is, irregular hours and seasonal work—would become synonymous with *précarité*—the opposite of job security. Unions and the political Left worried that "McWork," the exemplar of précarité and American-style deregulation, would spread to other service sector jobs.[89]

Beyond business and labor practices, what effect did McDonald's and fast food in general have on French eating habits? We have studies of McDonald's impact on other cultures, but little for France.[90] There are data indicating a slight decline of the traditional midday meal at home and other data showing the closing of cafés. Eating a quick lunch or buying take-out food became more common in these decades.[91] But causation is complicated here, and these changes cannot simply be attributed to hamburger chains. There were other reasons, such as the increased role of women in the workforce, intensified urbanization, traffic congestion, greater leisure, higher incomes among adolescents, and shorter midday breaks. But the proliferation of fast food outlets, led by McDonald's, also contributed. Similarly, as fast food boomed, the number of cafés declined: in the mid-1980s, compared to the 1960s, there were less than half of these neighborhood haunts for eating, drinking, and *bavardage*. An alternative to the café, especially for the young and for families, was the Golden Arches.

One should not exaggerate—hamburgers did not transform how the French ate. A mere 3.2 percent of all meals outside the home were consumed at McDonald's in the late 1990s.[92] Statistical studies for the period 1988–97 showed a firm attachment to traditional ways, to *bien manger* at home at regular hours. Researchers found that four of five continued to eat their midday meal at home and nine of ten did so for their dinner.[93] Eating outside the home was much less frequent in France than in the United States. Among the reasons for maintaining this tradition were the pleasures, including the conviviality and relaxation, that accompanied the family meal; the esteem awarded traditional and creative cuisine; and the growing interests in natural and wholesome products, as well as a diverse menu.

Among those who frequented hamburger outlets in the early 1990s, the most numerous were fifteen- to twenty-four-year-olds and frequency declined with age: only a tiny fraction of those between thirty-five and forty-nine ate burgers, and virtually none of those over age fifty.[94] Even among teenagers hamburgers occupied a small fraction of the diet. For those who did elect to eat outside the home at midday, most continued to devour other fare like sandwiches or eat at viennoiseries. McDonald's, the leader in fast food, had to compete with a host of nonhamburger fast-service restaurants, from grills, theme restaurants, and highway stops to trendy cafés, sandwich shops, and sidewalk quiche and pizza stands, not to mention school or company cafeterias and home delivery.[95] In fact, upscale French-style sandwich chains like Cosi outnumbered McDonald's and its counterparts in the late 1990s.[96] Eating in either the traditional or alternative fast food mode was one form of implicit resistance to the American way of food; but there was one episode that spoke to a more intense and direct confrontation.

In 1999 McDonald's inadvertently became the target of popular resistance to American–led globalization. This is the story of José Bové, the political radical turned sheep farmer who directed an assault against the Golden Arches. The background for his protest was the competition over trade, especially agriculture, between France and the United States in the 1990s. There was also the growing alarm over food safety including fears about hormone-treated beef from the United States, the outbreak of mad cow disease in Britain, a simmering debate over genetically modified American crops like soybeans, and contaminated Coca-Cola removed from stores in France and Belgium in the spring of 1999. And there was deepening anxiety about the alleged deterioration of French cuisine caused by the spread of fast food associated with McDonald's. The European Union (EU), with French support, had banned the import of hormone-treated beef on the grounds of safety, and this eventually provoked the U.S. government, as a reprisal, to raise duties on certain French luxury imports, including Roquefort cheese—which happened to be both Bové's crop and a specialty associated with *le terroir*. In August 1999 Bové and other activists vandalized a McDonald's construction site in the small southern town of Millau using a tractor, pick axes, and power saws.

Bové's brief jailing did not prevent him from leading the charge against "industrial food" and globalization. He said his action was "symbolic dismantling," in the name of "the battle against globalization and the right of the people to feed themselves as they choose."[97] Bové attacked Americans for forcing *la malbouffe*—meaning standardized, yet unsafe, food—on the French. He insisted that *l'agriculture paysanne* was essential to national culture, and thus the United States via McDonald's was threatening both food and small farmers—two markers of French national identity. The mayor of a town near Millau imposed a 100 percent tax on Coca-Cola, proclaiming, "Here we cannot make plastic cheeses and hormone beef. Roquefort is unique, a symbol of our battle against the globalization of taste."[98] These charges were informed by the trope about Americans who ate badly and treated everything, including food, as merchandise. Even though Bové denied he was anti-American, pointing out he had spent part of his youth in California, the American challenge was essential to the uproar. As one political analyst wrote, "Behind all this lies a rejection of cultural and culinary dispossession. There is a certain allergy in Europe to the extent of American power accumulated since the cold war's end, and the most virulent expression of that allergy today seems to be food."[99]

The incident at Millau catapulted Bové to national and international fame. The radical with his pipe, walrus moustache, jovial persona, and earthy demeanor became an instant folk hero, but this was a "peasant" who knew how to exploit the media. When he appeared for his trial the following summer he arrived in a farmer's wagon pulled by a tractor—reminding some of the tumbrels that carried victims to the guillotine during the French Revolution—surrounded by 20,000 colorful supporters, some wearing T–shirts saying "The World Is Not Merchandise and I'm Not Either," and a full retinue of television crews.[100] He later traveled to Seattle for a meeting of the World Trade Organization carrying a huge piece of Roquefort. After Millau, McDonald's franchises suffered from a rash of "incidents" throughout France, including the dumping of rotting apples and manure on their premises and the "kidnapping" of effigies of Ronald McDonald by so-called ecowarriors, one of whom identified the clown as "the subliminal ambassador of mercantile empires of standardization and conformism."[101] José Bové touched a national nerve. It was a battle between Roquefort and the hamburger, between true cuisine and la malbouffe, between the small farmer and the multinational, between the peasant and the *seigneur*, between France and American-led globalization.[102] Or, as a journalist for *Le Monde* exclaimed, "[Bové] was right. Resistance to the hegemonic pretentions of the hamburger is, above all, a cultural imperative."[103] Protestors of every sort joined in, including antiglobalization organizations, ecologists, small farmers, consumer groups, communists, labor unions, and a host of other specialized interests like housing activists and backers of the movement to revive the Occitan language. One radio broadcaster called Bové "the spirit of France"; the daily press praised him, and, to be sure, politicians joined hands. President Jacques Chirac said that wrecking McDonald's was not an acceptable way of protest, yet "[i]t would be in nobody's interest to allow one single power, a respectable and friendly one, to rule undivided over the planet's food markets."[104] Prime Minister Lionel Jospin said, "I am personally not very pro-McDo" and then invited Bové to dine with him.

Figure 8. A jubilant José Bové at his trial, as pictured on the cover of his book. Courtesy Éditions La Découverte.

Bové's antics shocked McDonald's, and the chain retaliated. The company had always prided itself on conveying both an American and a local image, but after the trashing at Millau it intensified its efforts at appearing French. It took out full-page newspaper ads mocking anti-Americanism and proclaiming the business was indigenous. In one ad an overweight American in a cowboy hat complained, "What I don't like about McDonald's in France is that it doesn't buy American beef."[105] The text of the spoof spelled out, in reference to the European ban on hormone treated beef, that only French beef was guaranteed to be safe. The message was that McDonald's may have been "born in the United States," but it was "made in France." Everything in the Big Mac was French except the cheese (because France did not produce cheddar). A manager of McDonald's-France proclaimed that 80 percent of all its food materials were French in origin and the rest were predominantly European. French farmers were McDonald's "partners": 45,000 livestock breeders supplied 27,000 tons of beef per year. He added that 90 percent of its franchises were owned by French entrepreneurs and its employees were virtually all French.[106] The CEO in Oak Brook, Illinois, Jack Greenberg, called Bové's crew "terrorists," pointing out that they had the wrong target since McDonald's was creating jobs for thousands of French adolescents and work for French business such as construction companies.[107]

An important element of the "made in France" campaign, which was led by the CEO of McDonald's-France, Denis Hennequin, after 1996, was the modifications made in menus and restaurants. Management admitted that the initial strategy emphasizing "external visibility"—that is, the standard Golden Arches look and ambiance of red and yellow plastic, fluorescent lighting, and white tiles, was outmoded: now the accent was on the quality of each restaurant's interior and the harmony of its exterior with its surroundings.[108] Refurbishing outlets that appeared shabby and dated became a priority.[109] On the Champs-Elysées the unit received new soft lighting and brick interior walls, while other branches were made more comfortable and more upmarket with fireplaces and leather furniture. For afternoon tea in the Galeries Lafayette, McCafé used porcelain tea services. Some Alpine restaurants were redecorated with wood and stone interiors, giving them the aura of chalets. And, as if to prove the circulation of culture, the classier look of French sites inspired the redesign of some American franchises, like the theater-style outlet in New York's Times Square. Not only was the decor improved but the menu became more varied, offering a version of a Croque Monsieur called a "Croque McDo," Danone yogurts, premium salads, and Carte Noire coffee as well as dainty macarons served at the McCafé–and, to the dismay of Coca-Cola, one would imagine, customers could now order Orangina.[110] The restaurants also served healthier dishes like a variety of salads and they became "transparent," meaning customers could consult a detailed guide specifying nutritional content such as calories, fats, and sugar for all of the food served. By clicking on *poulet* at the website one could find detailed information about the birds used for Chicken McNuggets, such as their age and feed.[111]

Hennequin fought back in other ways against the company's image as a globalized, computerized, tacky, supplier of la malbouffe. He retaliated with a booklet disputing the charges made by its critics and elaborating the company's contributions to employment, food hygiene, customer service, and philanthropy, as well as diversity.[112] McDonald's-France, to the chagrin of the home office in Illinois, even ran an "advertorial" about childhood obesity in a woman's magazine recommending a "slow down" in the consumption of junk food, stating there was "no reason to go more than once a week to McDonald's."[113] As the capstone to this remaking of McDonald's post-Bové image, the company retired Ronald McDonald and replaced him with Astérix as its icon.[114] The irony was obvious: José Bové, who with his grand moustache and sturdy stature resembled the comic-strip Gaul, had appropriated Astérix as his symbol of resistance to McDonald's. And now McDonald's had appropriated Astérix and, by extension, Bové.

One should not exaggerate the localization of product or the much touted autonomy of franchises. McDonald's, like Disney and Coca-Cola, was notorious for running a "tight ship" and monitoring standards. McDonald's claim that its outlets were operated by local retailers seems dubious since the company trained its top managers at Hamburger University in Illinois, provided suppliers, picked sites, and rigorously enforced its highly detailed operating procedures—specifying the placement of hamburgers on the grill and the dimensions of the french fry (9/32 of an inch thick). In fact, most of the outlets in Paris (as opposed to France) were owned and operated by the Chicago firm rather than by French franchisees. Parading one's local credentials was an important tactic, but in the end the essence of McDonald's appeal did not change. As Hennequin explained, the French liked McDon-

ald's because it was fast, convenient, affordable, and child-friendly, unlike traditional restaurants, and because the French were "fascinated
with America."[115] This fascination made France the most profitable
market in Europe—second only to that of the United States. And Hennequin's success in France made him CEO for Europe in 2004 where
he replicated his strategy of remodeling restaurants and introducing
healthier, more local, and more "transparent" menus.[116]

The incident at Millau did not interrupt McDonald's march to
dominate the fast food industry. It opened its 1,000th outlet in 2003;
its nearest competitor, France Quick, had only 316 units. The Golden
Arches could be seen in more than 700 French cities and towns. France
had more franchises per capita than its neighbors, including Germany,
Italy, Spain and the Netherlands—but not the United Kingdom.[117]
Twenty years after it had relaunched its expansion in France it had transformed fast food in the sense of how food was supplied, prepared, and
sold; what was consumed; and who was employed. It had pushed aside
some rivals and changed how others did business. McDonald's had also
adapted to its setting while retaining its identity. But the Golden Arches
had not transformed how the French ate or thought about food. The
U.S.-based chain did not control fast food, much less the traditional sector of the restaurant business or home preparation. McDonald's still had
to compete with other burger chains, as well as cafés, trendy sandwich
shops, theme restaurants, grills, viennoiseries, gas stations on the highways, and home delivery of pizza––and, increasingly, with simple take-
out service from the neighborhood *boulangerie* or *charcuterie*. In 1997
the French spent $30 billion eating out, $24 billion of it in independent
restaurants; of the remainder only $1.9 billion went to American-style
fast food places like McDonald's, and the rest was scattered among viennoiseries, takeout, and the like.[118] McDonald's found its niche within the
larger world of restaurants. At the same time its own menu had become
far more varied than one of just hamburgers and fries.

The coming of McDonald's added variety to a palate that was becoming more cosmopolitan and global.[119] The range of food available

in markets and restaurants was wider than ever before. Within the food industry itself, restaurateurs and "fast fooders" acted more like colleagues than rivals because they were serving different clienteles—even if they might quarrel over issues like the tax on restaurants. There were entrepreneurs who owned and operated both classic restaurants and fast food outlets.[120] And some of the finest French chefs admitted that their own children patronized McDonald's.[121] As one commentator noted, "Between the Chinese restaurants and the great chefs, between the shelves of his supermarket and the regional specialties brought home from vacation, the French consumer has never had more varied nutrition. He can, from time to time, spend his evening at the corner McDonald's without feeling guilty. His culture will survive."[122]

■ Coca-Cola

Of the three protagonists in this story Coca-Cola has the longest history in France; it made its debut in the era of the First World War. Then, in 1949–50, it crossed the Atlantic in force, expecting an easy entry into an allied country but running into fierce resistance. This episode has been analyzed in depth elsewhere and need only be sketched here.[123] Atlanta's marketing strategy for France, which featured an advertising blitz, heightened suspicions of a brash American takeover. The company inadvertently created a veritable anti–Coca-Cola coalition that featured the Communist Party, left-wing intellectuals, and much of the beverage industry, like fruit juice and wine interests. If this were not sufficient trouble, several government agencies including the Ministry of Finance joined the attack. Objections to the soft drink ranged from concern about national health, the corruption of taste, and a loss of scarce dollars, to fear of "Coca-colonization"—a new term for American imperialism. Coca-Cola was forced to wage a long, hard battle to overcome opponents who brought law suits and even managed to persuade the National Assembly to pass legislation that, if enforced, would have banned the drink on the grounds that it was injurious to public health.

The company had misjudged how the ideological struggles of the Cold War, French insecurity, and the dominating presence of the United States in the postwar era might affect the arrival of its soft drink. And it ignored the Gallic habit of magnifying the cultural meaning of American products. *Le Monde*, for example, asserted that what was at stake with Coca-Cola, and other recent American imports like the *Reader's Digest*, was "the moral landscape of France."[124] Some said the national beverage was the essence of national identity and that if Coke replaced wine France itself was at risk. In the end the Coca-Cola Company had to rely on its contacts in high places, including the U.S. State Department; its deep pockets and legal skills; and French vulnerability—that is, its need for economic aid—to overcome the opposition. By the early 1950s litigation subsided, the government surrendered, and the French could slake their thirst with the sweet import from the United States.

But this was only the beginning of Coke's adventures. It licensed most of its bottling and distribution to the subsidiary of a prominent French beverage firm, Pernod-Ricard. In the long run this proved to be a poor business decision. Pernod-Ricard's performance was listless, and French per-capita consumption lagged far behind what Atlanta expected.

Woven into the narrative of Coca-Cola in France was an orange-colored rival. Orangina, born during the 1930s in Algeria, crossed the Mediterranean in the early 1950s just as the American multinational was crossing the Atlantic. Family-owned and diminutive in scale, the Compagnie Française des Produits Orangina offered a lightly carbonated drink flavored with citrus juice and pulp. In some ways it mimicked the American import: Orangina also featured a distinctive bottle, a textured bulb shape rather than the classic Coke ribbed "hobble-skirt"; high-profile advertising; its own color scheme (orange rather than red); and a catchy motto, "Secouez-moi" ("Shake me," in order to mix the pulp). It promoted itself as a healthy alternative to Coke—given the rumors about Coca-Cola's secret and possibly harmful additives—and it capitalized on being homegrown given its origins in a French department of Algeria. Orangina found a niche within the carbonated drink market and in time occupied second place, although a distant second, to the American cola giant.

Our tale, however, begins in the 1980s rather than the 1950s. It was then, under the direction of CEO Roberto Goizueta, that the Coca-Cola Company decided to relaunch Coke in Europe, and in France in particular.[125] Since the home market was almost saturated, Goizueta reasoned the greatest potential for growth lay outside the United States. The European Community beckoned because the adoption of the Single European Act meant that Europe would, by removing trade barriers, create enormous opportunities for investment. France could serve as a production and supply center for all of Europe. Boosting global sales, however, required restructuring—above all, regaining control of concessionaires like bottlers who resisted expansion. The French situation was especially troublesome. Ever since 1949 Pernod-Ricard had been the primary bottler and distributor of Coca-Cola, but managers at the home office in Atlanta came to believe they were being short-changed, that the French firm was reluctant to invest, and that it promoted its own soft drinks like Orangina, which it had acquired, over Coca-Cola. What also piqued the Americans was the fact that the French were such slack consumers. On the basis of per-capita consumption, the British and Italians drank twice as many eight-ounce servings of Coke per year as the French; the Belgians, Spanish, and Germans three times as much. Of course, none of the Europeans drank as much the Americans. France had been a tough market for Coke for forty years.[126]

Goizueta picked the hard-charging Douglas Ivester to take European operations in hand. Ivester used a bare knuckles approach to business. He took aim at Pernod-Ricard, whose subsidiary, the Société Parisienne de Boissons Gazeuses (SPBG), acted as bottler not only for the

Paris area but also for the regions served by the Lille, Lyons, Marseilles, Nancy, and Rennes bottling facilities. When Pernod-Ricard balked at selling out, Ivester outflanked it by buying other regional bottlers like the one in Bordeaux and then filed a law suit in 1988 to terminate its contract. After eighteen months of bitter litigation Pernod-Ricard relented and Coca-Cola Beverages, a new company, replaced SPBG, gaining control of 80 percent of the production and distribution of Coca-Cola products in France by the U.S.-based company.[127]

Ousting Pernod-Ricard in 1989 was only the beginning of over-hauling the French market. In 1990 Ivester called on William Hoffman, the Atlanta bottler who had no familiarity with either France or Europe but was notorious for his aggressive tactics. He would sell Coke the way it was done in the United States: via huge promotional displays in su-permarkets, deals with food retailers that assured prime shelf space for Coca-Cola products, unorthodox advertising including racy ads, and partnerships with most everyone from oil companies to Club Med. Hoffman stunned the locals by presenting them with "Georgia Week," featuring American football, screenings of *Gone with the Wind*, and grits.[128] But what proved most offensive was selling Coke through vend-ing machines, including one placed at the base of the Eiffel Tower. The introduction of curbside vending machines in Bordeaux, sometimes just outside local cafés, spelled trouble. When customers began buying their Cokes more cheaply from the machines, café owners balked and staged a three-month boycott, forcing Hoffman to remove the offending ma-chines. An official of the café owners' association said, "In France we are not used to this sort of very forward and impersonal type of distribu-tion, and we were a bit shocked by it."[129] After only eighteen months Hoffman was recalled to Atlanta, but not before he had spurred sales increasing annual per-capita consumption from thirty-nine to forty-nine small (eight-ounce) bottles.[130] Atlanta officials admitted Hoffman's tactics had been provocative. The company also realigned its theme park alliances at this point. It terminated its contract with Parc Astérix in 1992 and shifted its loyalty to the new Disney park at Marne-la-Vallée.

Retaking Europe included constructing new plants in France in order to supply the continent. Signes, in the south, was the site of a new factory producing concentrate. But the heaviest investment was the $52 million spent on opening the biggest canning plant for soft drinks in Europe near Dunkirk in 1989 that would supply containers for Coca-Cola's products—for example, Fanta—to all of northern Europe.[131] No sooner did Dunkirk begin production when the Berlin Wall fell and it became the chief supplier not only for the north but also for the former communist states in Eastern Europe, helping Coke overtake Pepsi in countries like Hungary and Poland.

The Coca-Cola Company could be pleased with its early efforts. By 1990 Coke outsold every soft drink, like the rival brands of Cadbury Schweppes, in Europe as well as individual bottled waters like Perrier, Volvic, and Evian. In volume it held almost half the carbonated market.[132] Per-capita consumption in France rose steadily in the early 1990s, even if the French continued to trail far behind other Europeans. Pepsi was closing in, however, and this was a concern. But Coca-Cola was confident of, if not arrogant about, its global appeal. The former head of its international division named Coca-Cola, along with blue jeans and American popular music, as one of the "threads running through the modern world's cultural matrix," concluding that almost everyone seemed to want Coke and the American lifestyle.[133]

Hoffman's recall did not tame Coca-Cola's forceful tactics. It continued offering discounts and rebates to wholesalers in exchange for most of their cola sales and it installed vending machines without charge in cafeterias and in public institutions like hospitals in exchange for exclusive sales at these sites. Such sharp practices did not sit well with Coke's competitors. The rival soft drink Orangina, which by then was a unit of Pernod-Ricard, the slighted suitor who harbored a grudge against Coca-Cola, initiated legal action against Coca-Cola in 1991. Orangina was also the partner of PepsiCo France after 1992, taking over distribution for Pepsi. In 1997 after years of litigation, the Competition Council, the antitrust authority, fined Coca-Cola $1.8 million for abusing its dominant position in the soft drink market.[134] Coca-Cola trimmed the rebates, but persisted using other techniques like providing free vending machines. Michel Fontanes, the president of Orangina, applauded the decision, saying, "From now on Coca-Cola won't be able to do whatever it wants to in the French market."[135] But Fontanes wanted more: he pressed for an end to Coca-Cola's exclusive marketing agreements with businesses like Euro Disney.

Coca-Cola became the target not only for its competitors and government regulators but also for farmers. In this case it was less how the Atlanta firm behaved than what it represented. The GATT negotiations, especially the bargaining over farm subsidies between the United States and the EU in 1992, provoked demonstrations against Coca-Cola in several communities. Hundreds of farmers occupied a Coca-Cola factory outside Paris, while others in the Sarthe raided local supermarkets, emptied the shelves of Coke cans and bottles, and built a wall with their loot in front of the local prefecture and finished by hurling their fizzy contents at the building. Standing atop an overturned Coke vending machine, the head of the local farmers union complained about Coca-Cola as the symbol of "American hegemony."[136] Irate farmers simultaneously targeted McDonald's and Euro Disney. And just like the other American companies, Coca-Cola counterattacked by pointing out how French they were. A company spokesman stressed that Coca-Cola was one of the country's biggest purchaser of beet sugar from French farmers: "Coca-Cola today is a 100 percent French product."[137]

Perhaps the most discussed aspect of Coca-Cola was the question of its impact on the wine industry. Wine drinking was declining, especially among the young, and the consumption of soft drinks, including Coke, was on the rise. But what was the relationship? The average French person drank about half as much wine in 1995 as he or she did in 1965, and the number of daily drinkers plummeted from 47 percent to a mere 28 percent.[138] Was the head of a French winery right when he charged, "Our real enemy is Coca-Cola"?[139] Such an assertion is too simplistic. The reasons for the diminished interest in wine were complex, and Coca-Cola was not a prominent one: they include the shrinking numbers of farmers and factory workers who relied on wine as a cheap energy source; the fast-moving urban work culture and the decline of the leisurely meal; a wider choice of beverages; the shift to more expensive, higher-quality wines; concerns about health and safe driving; and the image of wine as old-fashioned and elitist. Consumption of soft drinks at mealtime did double between 1980 and 1995, but this only represented 11 percent of all mealtime beverages. The culprit was not Coca-Cola. The issue is better framed if it is asked more narrowly of young people. Among those ages twenty to twenty-four, those who said they never drank wine increased from 30 percent to 53 percent between 1981 and 1995 and within this cohort less than 5 percent reported they drank wine every day. And it was those between the ages of fifteen and twenty-four who consumed the most soft drinks.[140] According to one sociologist, the problem was image: for young people wine was associated with traditional bourgeois society rather than with dynamic modern life—so they turned to alternatives; or, as he concluded, "the young drink Coca-Cola."[141] To be more precise they drank mineral water, soda water, beer, and—to be sure—soft drinks, including Coke, with meals. Coca-Cola was related to the decline of wine consumption in the limited sense of offering itself as one among several alternatives to the youth of the fin de siècle who were abandoning old ways of drinking.

The cola wars came to France in the early and mid-1990s when Pepsi-Cola launched a major restructuring and marketing program. It stole a page from the Coca-Cola manual by reclaiming control over its brand: it bought out its contract with Perrier in 1993 and took charge of its own marketing, found a new bottler, and entered into a partnership with Orangina for distribution. In quick order the French encountered thousands of Pepsi vending machines, new Pepsi bottles, innovative drinks like caffeine-free Pepsi, and fresh ads including a slogan designed especially for them: "Pensez différent, pensez Pepsi."[142] The two cola companies went head-to-head in selling to hotels, restaurants, cinemas, cafés, service stations, and leisure parks. Pepsi claimed Parc Astérix, Futuroscope, and Relais H as its own while Coke made McDonald's, France Quick, and Euro Disney its private domain. According to one business review, it was "total war in the Hexagon."[143] From a tiny 6.3 percent of the cola market in 1992 Pepsi captured 14 percent by 1996 and then set its sight on doubling its share again within two or three years.

The Coca-Cola Company retaliated by accelerating the restructuring begun in the late 1980s. In 1996 Coca-Cola Enterprises, the world's largest bottler of Coke, purchased its French and Belgian subsidiaries with an eye to becoming the principal bottler in northwestern Europe. In the next two years Coca-Cola quadrupled its advertising budget. To promote itself as the official soft drink of the 1998 World Cup it set up regulation-size soccer goals in Parisian grocery stores to catch shoppers' attention and it distributed 30,000 café tables and chairs bearing soccer logos and Coca-Cola decorated umbrellas. Coca-Cola was everywhere—in movie theaters, cafés, service stations, and bakeries; in large retailers like Carrefour; and, certainly, in fast food outlets like McDonald's.[144] The head of Coca-Cola Enterprises in Europe, noting that Coke was made with French water and packaged in French bottles, crowed, "[I]t's almost as French as a bottle of Bordeaux."[145] And Ivester continued his rough-and-tumble marketing. In 1997 EU regulators, spurred by complaints from Pepsi-Cola in Italy, began investigating Coca-Cola's merchandising in several European countries, including France: there were the familiar charges of special rebates, bonuses, and discounts to retailers. Coca-Cola, it was alleged, not only abused its dominant market position but was trying "to oust Pepsi" altogether from Italy.[146] By this time Ivester had moved up in Atlanta and succeeded Goizueta as CEO; Ivester was the manager who had once upset a beverage industry conference by comparing Coke to a wolf hunting its prey and its rivals to sheep. Coke held its own in this war, raising its French per-capita consumption from seventy-one to eighty-seven small bottles between 1995 and 1997. Still, France and Italy remained in the bottom tier of European countries by this standard: Germany, Norway, Belgium, Luxembourg, Spain and Austria led the way.

The cola wars of the mid-1990s became the "uncola war" at the end of the decade. The challenge from "uncola" beverages like lemon-lime drinks broadened the Pepsi-versus-Coke competition. By this time Orangina was the top selling orange soda in France, second only to Coca-Cola among all carbonated soft drinks. Pernod-Ricard had purchased Orangina from its original owners in 1984 and gradually extended its reach to Europe and beyond.[147] But Pernod-Ricard, true to form, invested cautiously, so tentatively that it sometimes cost Orangina.[148]

Orangina was ripe for the picking. Pernod-Ricard looked to unload its soft drink holdings, but Pepsi turned down the opportunity in late 1997. Pernod-Ricard had been the Coca-Cola Company's French nemesis—recall that its favoritism toward Orangina had prompted Coca-Cola's buyout of its bottler in 1989 and Pernod-Ricard had later filed the law suit against Coke's marketing practices. But business was business, and Ivester wanted a new weapon, a "natural" orange drink to compete in the contest for the global "uncola" market. By acquiring Orangina, which had become the distributor for Pepsi's "off premises" or nonhome customers—such as cafés, hotels, and restaurants—Ivester would trump its rival. He tendered a bid for Orangina, knowing it was a gamble given Coca-Cola's dominant market position in France, the company's reputation for bending rules, and the determined opposition of Pepsi.

With almost half the market for carbonated drinks and three quarters of cola sales, Ivester's company was vulnerable to the charge of overplaying its hand. Pepsi asked the government to block Coke's $800 million bid for Orangina in the name of maintaining a competitive market. The case came before the Ministry of Finance's competition board in early 1998 and the key issue, in what turned out to be marathon deliberations, was whether or not the acquisition of Orangina's sales network, which distributed Pepsi's products for nonhome sales, would give Coca-Cola a stranglehold over the entire soft drink industry. Lawyers quarreled over the definition of nonhome sales and unions expressed concern over the multinational's willingness to honor Orangina's labor contracts. The head of PepsiCo France argued the deal would result in the "immediate eviction of Pepsi-Cola" from the restaurant and hotel market.[149] Pepsi's lawyers also contended Coke's market position would allow it to raise prices at will—as it had allegedly already done in Italy.[150] The principle of free competition was at risk. Orangina lobbied in favor of the buyout, arguing Coca-Cola's dynamism would energize its global operations. "Is it better to be a village of Gauls and continue to struggle against the Romans," its CEO asked, "or is it necessary to reach an agreement that will assure the development of our families within the Roman Empire?"[151]

The decision was in the hands of the competition board. Revelations that the company might move some of its plants to Ireland fueled fears about Coke's monopoly.[152] Minister of Finance Dominique Strauss-Kahn put his foot down in September 1998 and, in the name of a free market, suspended talks with Ivester's team.[153] The minister's decision did not end litigation: it dragged on for another year.[154] Finally, in November 1999 the board ruled in favor of Pepsi, concluding that "the takeover project does not present enough economic contributions to outweigh the risk of hurting competition." Strauss-Kahn complied. And in one of the most startling statements about French economic practice by an American company, Pepsi praised the French government as "one of the world's foremost defenders of competition."[155]

Before the bad news from France arrived, Ivester's reputation as CEO was damaged even further by events in northern Europe. In early June 1999 dozens of Belgian schoolchildren fell ill, and some were hospitalized, from drinking Coca-Cola and the incident quickly erupted into the biggest contamination problem the company had ever faced in Europe.[156] Within a week of the initial incident forty more Belgian children felt sick from drinking Coke or Fanta and scores of people in France also complained of nausea, fever, and headaches from drinking Coca-Cola. Ivester's team was slow to react, first handing off responsibility to local bottlers, then treating it as a psychosomatic—rather than a health—problem, arguing the nature of the contamination, according to company tests, could have made someone feel sick but it was "not harmful." The corporate offices in Atlanta seemed unaware of the anxiety among the Belgians and the French over food safety: only a few weeks earlier there had been a scare over dioxin entering the food chain. Panic spread: Belgium, the Netherlands, France, and Luxembourg banned Coke products for days; Spanish and German stores pulled Coke from their shelves and French health authorities closed the canning plant at Dunkirk because it was implicated as a possible source of contamination. Belgian and French officials complained that Coca-Cola could not tell them what had gone wrong. Managers in the Atlanta offices dallied, convinced that their quality control could not have been breached and that its products might taste or smell strange, but that they were not unhealthy. It took ten days before Ivester flew to Brussels, issued an apology, reassured customers about quality control, and in front of TV cameras drank from one of the contaminated bottles. The culprits turned out to be defective carbon dioxide (which produces the bubbles in carbonated drinks) used by an Antwerp bottler and a fungicide found on cans at Dunkirk that gave off an offensive odor. At the end of June the Belgian government lifted its ban after the company agreed to tighter quality controls. But this was not before millions of bottles and cans had been removed from vending machines and store shelves and Coca-Cola's reputation for purity had been called into question. The recall, the largest in the company's history, cost over $100 million. One beverage analyst called the affair "a public relations nightmare."[157] The irony was that the Belgians had been among Europe's thirstiest consumers of Coke.

By then Ivester was on the ropes. In the two years following his appointment as CEO in 1997 the company had been fined for market abuses, defeated in its effort at buying Orangina, forced by EU regulators to scale back plans for acquiring brands from Cadbury Schweppes, and bungled its response to the health scare in Belgium and France. In addition, Italian authorities were investigating Coca-Cola and EU regulators had raided company offices in Germany, Denmark, and Austria searching for evidence of possible violations of community rules on competition. After more than a decade of stunning growth in volume and profits under Roberto Goizueta, the Coca-Cola Company seemed to have run out of fizz. In 1999 global profits slumped, shareholder returns were paltry, and sales of its concentrate fell. Global economic conditions were not Ivester's fault, but his abrasive and arrogant ways, compared to the more genteel Goizueta, antagonized associates, regulators, and consumers.[158] In December 1999 he was forced out of office and his successor promised to pay more attention to local conditions and to "play by the rules" in marketing.

In France, Coca-Cola's spending, restructuring, and rough tactics boosted per-capita consumption to ninety or more servings by the end of the 1990s, gave it a 55 percent share of the market for carbonated drinks, and prevented Pepsi from winning even a 15 percent share. But the French still drank less Coke than most Europeans; the Germans, for example, gulped twice as much.[159] And in France bottled water still trumped Coca-Cola, forcing the company to concede to national taste and introduce Chaudfontaine, its own line of mineral water. Coca-Cola, like McDonald's and Disney in the 1990s, inched toward adapting to local taste and loudly proclaimed the local identity of its products rather than extolling its American or transnational character. But for its successes the Americans paid a price in fines, boycotts, law suits, adverse government rulings, and a damaged reputation. Coke's adventure in the land of the Gauls had brought it treasure, but its journey had been fraught with misfortunes.

It seems appropriate, after these three company narratives, to revisit the questions raised at the outset of this chapter: Did these Americans adapt to their environment? How did their host's culture affect their reception? And what impact did they have on France?

Together these questions address a fundamental debate about Americanization or American-led globalization. A benign interpretation of the phenomenon would assume that these American businesses adapted to local tastes and traditions and that their wares and ways blended with that of their hosts, merely adding options to consumers, without either unsettling markets or tastes, or bringing globalized uniformity.[160] A more aggressive view would expect these intruders to impose themselves on the locals, disrupt local economies, societies, and cultures, and Americanize them. These narratives tend to confirm the latter interpretation.

The conceptual issue here is not whether these Americans adapted to French ways—of course they did, to an extent. The real question is, Were these modifications significant? Contrary to some other scholars who have gone a long way in stressing the appropriation thesis—that local cultures have prevailed in transforming American imports—I am more skeptical. In the case of this American trio historical evidence runs against the appropriation thesis.

These companies directly exported across the Atlantic the techniques and products that had brought them success at home, and they did so with little modification. Moreover, they turned their associations with America to their commercial advantage and they even converted many domestic firms to American ways. Their basic strategy was, what worked for Americans would work for the French and the Europeans. Whatever alterations were made—in, say, the attractions at Euro Disney, the menu at McDonald's, or the advertising for Coca-Cola—were largely cosmetic. The essence—and the appeal—remained unaltered, remained American.

Direct transatlantic exports, however, do not mean that these American adventurers were inattentive to the natives. They tried to take into their calculations the presumed tastes, habits, and rules of the French. There was some adaptation. All three corporations, for example, allowed some measure of local control and made small adjustments in their products and their presentation. And when the natives became restless, these intruders knew how to defend themselves: they attempted to conceal their foreignness and emphasize that, in many respects, they were French enterprises. They would parry attacks by stressing they were really local companies and by parading the benefits they brought to France: innovation, jobs, and tourists. A manager of McDonald's in Europe said the hamburger chain was not a multinational company: "It's a multi-domestic company. The goal is to localize it as much as possible."[161]

But this defense rang false to French ears since these corporations routinely played the "Star Spangled Banner" so loudly, wielded their corporate power so blatantly, and made so few concessions to the locals. These American interlopers did not "go native." The Walt Disney Company's deference to the Europeans in its Magic Kingdom was slight: the park was intended to be a fantasized version of America. McDonald's diversified its menu and remodeled restaurants to blend with the locale, but the food, the setting, the operations, and the basic appeal of the Golden Arches were copied from the U.S. version; eating at McDonald's was an American experience. Nor did Coca-Cola do much to adapt to France. A café on the Avenue de l'Opéra might serve the soft drink in a small glass with lemon as an aperitif and the company might sponsor national sporting events like the Tour de France, but nothing was altered by this—neither the product nor its meaning.

Even the much touted autonomy of the French subsidiaries seems exaggerated. All three companies were notorious for running a "tight ship" and strict monitoring standards. McDonald's claim that its outlets were controlled by local retailers seems dubious since the company picked sites and franchisees, provided suppliers, managed advertising, and rigorously enforced its highly detailed operating procedures. Coca-Cola also claimed its bottlers were independent, but the corporate offices monitored foreign operations to make sure its beverage was absolutely uniform. And in 1989 the Coca-Cola Company bought out most of its French bottlers and assumed control of them from across the Atlantic. Similarly, the WDC ran Euro Disney from California.

According to the founding contract the company put up a small fraction of equity yet it secured total managerial control.[162] The U.S. offices of these giants closely supervised their subsidiaries, making sure they stayed true to the original.

All three companies also played by the American, rather than the French, rule book. McDonald's tried its best to avoid the French labor code. Coca-Cola's violations of French rules for marketing and competition earned it fines and official censure. Disney ignored norms of business behavior, dictated to its fellow French investors, imposed its dress code, and skirted customary labor standards. It ran the Paris park the way it did its parks in Orlando, Florida and Anaheim, California. All three companies imported the rough-and-ready ways of American free enterprise rather than submitting meekly to French rules. They acted in ways that confirmed Gallic stereotypes about the sharp competitive habits of American business. At one point the banks, who were Disney's partners, accused the Californians of "fraud and theft."[163] And the way McDonald's cornered the fast food market honored Ray Kroc's reputation for wanting not just to outsell his rivals but to destroy them. Such behavior only heightened French apprehension about the ruthless ways of Yankee capitalism.

There was neither much adaptation nor much autonomy. As McDonald's boldly expressed it, the natives would learn to like its hamburgers. These corporations repeated what they had learned in the United States and they celebrated, and profited from, an intrinsic market advantage—offering others what Americans enjoyed. They were intruders.

A second question posed in this chapter asks whether or not culture was important in determining how the French responded to these businesses and thus to how they performed. These three narratives demonstrate that the Americans ignored culture at their peril. But the story also shows how an open, diverse, and changing culture allowed the Americans eventually to have their way.

Insensitive is a fair description of how these three companies acted toward French cultural anxieties. All were widely regarded as cultural invaders and this reputation harmed them in their setup stage and hampered them afterward.

American managers underestimated both the cultural meaning of their products and Gallic conventions about merchandising; they then compounded their troubles with obtuseness. In the early 1950s Coca-Cola flaunted its challenge to traditional drinking habits with a marketing blitz that used the Tour de France as an advertising venue. When the French objected, a company spokesperson recalled America's role in the liberation and reconstruction of the country and denounced the French for their ingratitude. Four decades later William Hoffman thought Southern grits would sell Cokes in Bordeaux. In 1993, McDonald's made the mistake of planning to float the Golden Arches on a barge at the base of the Eiffel Tower after they had already been made conspicuous on the Champs-Elysées. An outcry in the press and intervention from the office of the mayor of Paris scuttled the barge. Similarly, Michael Eisner's management team misperceived how Europeans might react to an American-style theme park twenty miles from Paris and to Disney's appropriation of French national cultural icons like Cinderella (Cendrillon). One executive who arrived after the park opened acknowledged massive, if unintended, cultural insensitivity during the setup phase on the part of "older Disney people."[164] Disney managers became defensive, and sometimes truculent, when attacked. One spokeswoman said, "Who are these Frenchmen anyway? We offer them the dream of a lifetime and lots of jobs. They treat us like invaders."[165] Instead of defusing the cultural war, Disney waged it. When the new park had trouble training employees to act like "cast members," one official ungraciously observed that "the French are not known for their hospitality."[166]

These companies unintentionally raised phobias about Coca-Colonization and McDonaldization because they misjudged how the French infused commercial products with cultural meaning. Intellectual gatekeepers, political activists, the media, and certain interest groups escalated the Franco-American competition over food, drink,

and entertainment into grand cultural issues such as endangered national identity. McDonald's was accused of crowding out traditional
restaurants, disrupting the family meal, undermining cuisine, and ru-
ining *bon goût*. Coca-Cola supposedly threatened a revered marker of
French identity, wine. Walt Disney, according to Marc Fumaroli, was
a "cultural engineer" who threatened to "industrialize" leisure.[167] Such
attacks provoked sarcastic responses in the American press about the
French. The transatlantic cultural wars from time to time engulfed
these companies.

Culture was an obstacle to this trio, especially during their setup
stages. But in all three cases the setbacks were minor or temporary
and French culture proved to be malleable, or so diverse, that it was
a marginal problem for the Americans. Millions of French consumers learned to love the Big Mac, Disneyland Paris, and Coca-Cola. All
three firms managed in time to thwart, or at least weaken, Gallic cultural opposition. *French culture*, whether the term refers to the taste
for wine, bon goût, reflective leisure, refined sensibility, or stereotypes
about national identity, did not matter much. It may have ignited intellectual fireworks, inspired some popular grumbling, and provoked a
small measure of political resistance but, at most, it only slowed down
the Americans. Moreover, resistance faded. For example, the Communist Party, which had tried to stop the entrance of the sugary invader during the early days of the Cold War, was by the 1980s serving
Coke at its annual outdoor Fête de l'Humanité. And if the guardians
of tradition once condemned the drink's merchandizing tactics, the
shopping center at the Louvre in 1996 hosted an exhibition titled *Art
ou publicité?* (Art or Advertising?) featuring a vintage Coca-Cola ad.
Another museum in Paris, a decade later, hosted an exhibition of Walt
Disney's early designs and the European art that inspired him and his
animators. When in the late 1990s the most visited tourist attraction
in the Paris region turned out to be Disneyland Paris rather than Notre
Dame or the Louvre, these Americans icons seem to have become part
of French popular culture.

Figure 9. Poster for an exhibition at the Carrousel du Louvre,
Art or Advertising? Courtesy Carrousel du Louvre.

Finally, the experience of these companies raises the question of what effect American business had on French behavior—especially on patterns of consumption and French business practice.

The benign version of the globalization thesis holds that American products will have rather little impact and serve only to broaden options without diminishing prevailing ways of consumption and leisure. The coming of Coca-Cola, from this perspective, merely added to the repertoire of drinks without displacing other beverages, just as Euro Disney changed little except to add to French and European choices for leisure. Similarly, food supposedly did not become Americanized, it merely became more cosmopolitan, eclectic, and varied.[168] This perspective has some validity, but it is probably much too sanguine and uncritical. The Yanks changed the competitive environment, gained market shares at the expense of the natives, and modified patterns of consumption and leisure.

In general these Americans heightened competitive pressures and energized their French rivals. And there was also some loss of market shares for French business in all three sectors. Euro Disney attracted five times as many visitors as its nearest rivals and forced some French leisure parks into bankruptcy. But it also stimulated others to enter the market and to imitate its ways. Parc Astérix, for one, was founded because of Euro Disney and it borrowed from its practices. Coca-Cola transformed how soft drink companies conducted business, advertised products, and sought international markets; and Orangina learned from Coke. Fast food was not the same once McDonald's entered the business; its rivals competed by imitating how the Americans hired and trained employees, operated their outlets, and prepared, presented, and advertised their products. McDonald's enhanced the restaurant business by encouraging conviviality and raising hygiene, according to some of the country's finest chefs.[169] In the end all three won the lion's share of their markets: Disney, Coke, and McDonald's were the largest enterprises in their respective sectors and some of their growth came at the expense of local competitors.

The impact on consumers was equally formidable. The Americans did far more than add options for French consumers—they changed them and their habits. There is no doubt that the French proved to be eager customers. In 1949 the French consumed virtually no Coca-Cola, no Big Macs (admittedly, the company did not yet exist), and their only exposure to Disney was *Le Journal de Mickey* and some animated feature films. In 1999 five million French men, women, and children visited Disneyland Paris; McDonald's had almost a thousand outlets and the French consumed a million meals per day under the Golden Arches; and per-capita consumption of Coca-Cola doubled after 1989 so that the average French person drank about ninety eight-ounce bottles per year.

These market positions at the end of the 1990s may not have been all that the newcomers had hoped for. The French still lagged behind most Europeans and, of course, far behind Latin Americans and Americans in their per-capita consumption of Coke. And as a drink, bottled water still outsold cola. Fast food held only a small portion of the restaurant trade and the consumption of hamburgers, even among the young, was minuscule. And attendance at Disney's park fell short of expectations. But none of these shortfalls diminish the fact that the French became ardent consumers of what the Americans sold—often at the expense of traditional tastes and local business. The consumption of fast food grew spectacularly from the 1970s on and traditional fast food—that of the cafés, viennoiseries, boulangeries, and charcuteries—lost market share to hamburger sales. While fast food outlets grew, the number of cafés fell from 220,000 in 1960 to less than 65,000 by the 1994.[170] The consumption of wine among young adults fell dramatically in the 1980s and '90s and the willingness among this cohort, and even among some older groups, to drink a sweet beverage like Coca-Cola with meals increased. Causation here is complex, but the beneficiary, and to a lesser extent a cause, of these changes was the American product. This American trio helped change consumer habits of eating, drinking, and leisure.

The adventurers from the New World succeeded—they found the treasure, meaning they won customers, brand recognition, profits, and market shares. To achieve this, they had to adapt and make modifications to suit the locals, but they did so without changing anything essential about their operations, products, or appeal. Rather, they capitalized on their associations with America and imposed their ways.

The French response to these intruders varied. Most simply ignored what they were selling and remained indifferent to them. But
millions of others liked what the Americans offered. Among these fans
the younger generation was overrepresented. Within the economic
sectors targeted by these companies, some businesses became victims;
but most survived, and many learned from the Americans and pros-
pered. Politicians tended to welcome these newcomers because of the
benefits they offered, such as job creation. Then there were those, like
farmers and antiglobalization militants, who attacked the companies
as symbols of American imperialism. For these opponents the stakes
of the game soared to the level of national identity. But French culture
and habits adjusted—there was room for the Americans. In the end
Americanization occurred: there was displacement and loss of tradition—the French were changing how they ate, drank, and enjoyed
themselves. They gained diversity by adding an American menu, but
they also lost uniqueness by becoming more like Americans.

5.

Taming the Hyperpower: The 1990s

Jacques Chirac once observed that relations between France and the United States "have been, are, and will always be conflictive and excellent. It's in the nature of things. . . . The U.S. finds France unbearably pretentious. And we find the U.S. unbearably hegemonic. There will always be sparks, but not fire. . . ."[1] The president of France thus tidily enunciated the essence of the friendly, yet testy, relations between the two countries during the 1990s. Understanding French perceptions of America must begin with their basis in international affairs.

The end of the Cold War made the United States even more important than it had been earlier. Gone were the days when France could enhance its independence by maneuvering between Washington and Moscow. America was the lone superpower and the hegemon in Europe. To be sure, relations with Washington were not the only international concern of Paris: there were other serious issues like binding the newly united Germany to the European Union (EU); stabilizing Eastern Europe, including Russia and the Balkan states; and advancing European integration. But the United States mattered more than any other nation in accomplishing France's agenda and in determining its status. Thus in international relations, as in cultural and socioeconomic affairs, fin-de-siècle France measured itself against the United States: contests over major issues, and even minor ones, became indices of French diplomatic influence, global rank, and self-image.[2]

America, in the post–Cold War era, posed a dilemma because France wanted an ally but faced a hegemon. On the one hand France valued the United States because it needed the superpower to stabilize Europe, to keep Germany under control, to provide insurance against a resurgent Russia, and to accomplish many of its goals like peacekeeping in the Balkans or the Middle East; this made Paris wary of alienating Washington, especially when the Americans seemed tempted to retreat into domestic affairs under President Bill Clinton and lighten their commitment to Europe. France also esteemed its transatlantic ally because the two countries shared many common aims and values as well as a dense network of economic and trade relations. If France may have preferred less American presence in Europe, it did not want the Americans to go home and leave Europeans alone with each other. On the other hand, the United States, after its Cold War "victory," was tempted to act unilaterally. It was even more assertive during the 1990s than it had been in the 1980s: President George H. W. Bush hailed the arrival of a "new world order" and President Clinton extolled "the indispensable nation." By the end of the decade the United States was tagged as "the hyperpower." The dilemma was, how to live with Uncle Sam? How to be his partner yet not be overpowered by him? This was a problem, as we have seen, that François Mitterrand had failed to solve during the 1980s.

Taming the hyperpower became an index of a successful foreign policy. The principal issue was, how could France either direct or restrain the seemingly omnipotent, headstrong, and sometimes impetuous, transatlantic ally? Gulliver had to be domesticated so that his strength could be used for good ends. For a historian the question is, How did France go about this task, with what success, and with what consequences? In order to curb the unilateralist instincts of the hyperpower, as we shall see, France employed multiple tactics: it engaged in bilateral diplomacy; relied on international organizations; formed rival coalitions; constructed a European security capacity; acted without, and even against, the United States; and ultimately designed an alternative to the unipolar international system around the notions of multipolarity and multilateralism.

It may be useful to note that in French politics the first post–Cold War decade divided midway. François Mitterrand finished his second term at the Elysée in 1995: his socialist governments were those of Michel Rocard (1988–91), Edith Cresson (1991–92), and Pierre Bérégovoy (1992–93), and the foreign minister was Roland Dumas (1988–93). But for the final two years of his presidency (1993–95) Mitterrand again faced cohabitation and had to work with a conservative government whose prime minister and foreign minister were, respectively, Édouard Balladur and Alain Juppé. The Mitterrand era ended in 1995 with the election of Jacques Chirac as president: his first prime minister was Alain Juppé (1995–97), accompanied by Hervé de Charette as foreign minister. But the 1997 legislative election brought a left-wing majority forcing cohabitation on Chirac: from 1997 to 2002 he cooperated with a socialist government whose prime minister and foreign minister were, respectively, Lionel Jospin and Hubert Védrine.

A confluence of rather dramatic events during the early 1990s engaged France and the United States. My exposition separates these activities, but in real time they occurred almost simultaneously. Thus, the war in the Persian Gulf had barely subsided when a downward spiral into ethnic strife seized the inhabitants of Yugoslavia. At the same time the United States and France engaged in diplomatic brinkmanship over trade and waged a contest over reform of the Atlantic Alliance. Transatlantic sparring often occurred on many fronts and one struggle tended to complicate the other. This exposition will be thematic rather than chronological, beginning with war, and then security, followed by trade, the "indispensable nation," and more war, and concluding with the topic of the hyperpower.

■ Wars: The Gulf War and Bosnia

Iraq raised the question of American ambitions in the "new world order" when in August 1990 Saddam Hussein invaded Kuwait and threatened oil fields in Saudi Arabia. The administration of President George H. W. Bush organized an international coalition to eject Iraq and invited France to join, not only to broaden the ranks but also to secure its assistance on the UN Security Council, whose mandate the U.S. government sought. France, as it turned out, stood with the United States: it voted for UN resolutions and French forces fought under U.S. command in the Desert Storm campaign of January–February 1991. Nevertheless, there was friction and distrust: President Bush and Secretary of State James Baker harbored doubts until the fighting started that France was entirely on board because Mitterrand tried his best to avoid war by finding a diplomatic solution to the crisis and seemed reluctant to escalate his military commitment. The French meanwhile suspected that the United States sought not just to liberate Kuwait but to overthrow Saddam Hussein and remake the entire oil-rich Middle East.

Why did the Mitterrand administration (the prime minister was then Michel Rocard) pursue negotiations with Iraq that made it appear overly conciliatory to the United States? First, there was uneasiness about Washington's motives and ambitions in the Middle East. And there was the usual need to avoid the appearance of servility. France also sought to avoid damaging its reputation in the Arab world: moderate Arab countries, or so it seemed, required the French government to do its best to find a diplomatic solution. There were also considerable economic interests to be protected in Iraq. Finally, the two governments, from the French perspective, approached the issue differently: as Mitterrand's senior military adviser explained, Bush saw the invasion as a moral issue—Iraq must be punished for its faults—while Mitterrand believed it was a crisis that needed a solution; thus, war was only the last resort.[3] These and other concerns flared up in cabinet meetings, fracturing the Rocard government and leaving Mitterrand, who proved to be a strong advocate of supporting the Americans, surrounded by hesitant ministers.[4] Jean-Pierre Chevènement, the defense minister who eventually resigned over the war, ardently opposed joining the coalition and he had considerable sympathy within the Socialist Party. Outside the government prominent left-wing politicians like Georges Marchais, speaking for the communists; the ecologist Antoine Waechter; and major right-wing figures like Michel Jobert, Charles Pasqua, and Jean-Marie Le Pen, representing the Front National, all objected to fighting with the Americans.[5]

Then there was the usual sniping by the intellectual scolds: from Régis Debray, Jean Baudrillard, Claude Julien, and Max Gallo on the left as well as from Alain de Benoist and others on the extreme right. U.S. motives were suspect in these antiwar circles: besides wanting to control the oil-rich Persian Gulf or secretly providing protection to Israel, the United States was allegedly a global gendarme implementing President Bush's "new world order." France's joining the coalition, they argued, would only help Yankee imperialists in their drive to dominate the Middle East and would ruin French relations with the Arab world. A public opinion survey in November 1990 showed a majority of the French people opposed participation in the war.[6] And television news, especially TF1, appeared so sympathetic to Saddam Hussein that Michel Rocard reprimanded it for bias.

Despite their doubts about the war and despite some open opposition, the Mitterrand-Rocard team proved to be a reliable, if difficult, ally. In August 1990 Mitterrand committed French forces to defend Saudi Arabia, insisting before his cabinet that there were times when the French must show solidarity with the Americans, that they could not be false friends, and that they must, since forced to choose, fight against Saddam Hussein regardless of the consequences.[7] Saddam, he believed, had embarked on a "Hitlerian scheme" to control the oil deposits of the Middle East.[8] Or, as he told Secretary of State Baker, Saddam was "a brute," a dangerous dictator who had to be contained.[9]

Mitterrand reasoned that France could not stand aside and be left out of the remaking of the Middle East that was bound to follow the war. There was, moreover, the need to demonstrate that France deserved its permanent seat on the UN Security Council as the representative of Europe; or as Mitterrand told his ministers, "Germany is still a political dwarf. . . . The British are too submissive to the Americans," leaving only France to negotiate with Iraq—and, in the event that Saddam conceded, it would appear to have saved the peace.[10] Still, this did not mean, he instructed his ministers, that France needed to be "servile" to the Americans.[11]

As the march to war gathered momentum in the fall of 1990 Paris tried simultaneously to meditate between the United States and Iraq while preparing for Operation Desert Storm. Mitterrand hoped to demonstrate to both his own people and the Arab world that France was trying to avoid war. In a speech to the UN in September he angered the Bush administration by not only appearing to open space between France and the UN resolution that required the immediate evacuation of Kuwait, but also asking for an international conference to resolve disputes over Kuwait, Lebanon, and the Occupied Territories in Palestine. Such linkage was what Saddam advocated and what Washington was trying to avoid. Mitterrand told Bush that the United States and Israel were mistaken in opposing a UN conference on peace in the Middle East. French efforts at finding an alternative to war even as the January 1991 deadline approached and their reticence about clarifying their military commitment upset the U.S. government. Days before Desert Storm began, Baker visited Paris and "shocked" Mitterrand by asking him if French ground troops were ready to fight under U.S. command. The French president shot back, "Ten days ago I said that I was in agreement. Are the American military deaf?"[12] Afterward Baker cabled Bush, "The French will be with us when it counts. It just may be bumpy for the next week or so."[13] Baker was right: once ground operations began in February Mitterrand told Bush that the French were totally engaged with the Americans.[14] Much of Washington's suspicions about the firmness of Paris's military commitment can be attributed to Chevènement's holding back at the ministry of defense. Bush later acknowledged there had been differences between American and French officials, but not between the presidents, that "at our level . . . François was always there, and we always stood together."[15]

Mitterrand carried his country into war. The Rocard government won overwhelming parliamentary support for the fight in January 1991, including the backing of most of the Socialist Party and all the major right-wing parties. Thanks to Mitterrand's efforts, which demonstrated that all avenues for peaceful resolution had been exhausted, and thanks to the way the media presented Saddam's brutality and his contempt for international law, public opinion shed its initial reservations about the war. Once Operation Desert Storm began, roughly three of four supported allied military intervention and almost as many backed French participation.[16] Partisans on all sides, from the Socialist Party to the Gaullists and even the Front National (which in this case spurned its own leader), massively backed the war while expressing confidence in the United States; only the communists stood apart. And the intellectuals who had dissented months before were shoved aside by others like Alain Minc, Guy Konopnicki, and André Glucksmann, who rallied to the side of the government. As Jean Daniel from *Le Nouvel Observateur* argued, even if the United States was acting in its own interest, that did not transform Saddam from a criminal to an innocent.[17]

When hostilities finally began in January 1991 there were over 11,000 French troops in the coalition, along with fighter-bombers and an aircraft carrier. But this was a tiny force compared to the almost half million Americans, the large contingents from Arab countries, or even the 30,000 British troops. Moreover, the French military discovered, to its chagrin, how far behind the Americans it was in high-tech combat. Its Jaguar fighters, for example, lacked the capacity to navigate at night and its intelligence capability was so out-of-date that U.S. intelligence forces had to provide most of the data.[18] As images from CNN transmitted the coalition's rapid success, public opinion remained skeptical about American aims: more believed the goal of the United States was to control oil than it was to liberate Kuwait.[19] And CNN's monopoly of reporting from the Persian Gulf antagonized many who thought they were receiving only the sanitized American version of the fighting; or as one of Mitterrand's advisers observed, the Europeans were absent from coverage: "everything happens as if the American Superman confronts the Iraqi Evil alone."[20] If the Gulf War exposed anxieties about President Bush's new world order the French, in the end, sided with their American cousins and confidence in the United States remained high. While fighting subsided in the Gulf it erupted in Yugoslavia.

The collapse of Yugoslavia into civil war during 1991–92 seemed an opportunity for the Europeans to tend to troubles in their own backyard without recourse to NATO. France, in particular, obstructed NATO involvement in the hope of deterring the alliance from engaging in out-of-area activities and allowing the Europeans to develop their operational capabilities. Yet the Europeans were not eager to enter the conflict directly. The French and the British, among others, sought to avoid using military force and preferred to try to mediate a political settlement among the various factions. They assumed that they could guarantee humanitarian assistance and end the hostilities through diplomacy. Mitterrand commented that "adding war to war will solve nothing."[21] France preferred what it called a noncoercive approach and sought to work through the UN and the EU. These organizations were deemed more suitable frameworks for multilateral intervention than NATO, which, it was feared, would further militarize the chaos and might also antagonize the Russians. By relying on the UN, France would also legitimate its seat on the Security Council and avoid being overshadowed by the Americans.[22] Paris justified intervention in the Balkans by invoking what Foreign Minister Juppé said were "essential" if not "vital" interests, referring to "the risks of contagion" and the danger posed to the expansion of the EU.[23] The Europeans got off to a discordant start when, to the dismay of France, Germany recognized the independence of Croatia and Slovenia, which, it seemed, would only hasten the disintegration of Yugoslavia.

For its part Washington had barely terminated combat operations in the Persian Gulf and was not eager to enter another conflict, especially one in which it was not evident that vital national interests were at stake. The Bush administration, wary of being drawn into another Vietnam-like quagmire, preferred to step aside and let the Europeans take charge. It also realized that the Russians opposed NATO's intervention, which had no authority in the Balkans, in the region.[24] At first the Clinton White House continued its predecessor's passivity. Clinton's team, divided internally over intervening and facing strong opposition from both the U.S. Congress and the public against military action, was satisfied with passing UN resolutions and letting its European allies enforce them. Both sides misjudged the situation or, as Richard Holbrooke, assistant secretary of state for European affairs in 1994–95, would later observe, "Europe and the United States proved to be equally misguided. Europe believed it could solve Yugoslavia without the United States; Washington believed that, with the Cold War over, it could leave Yugoslavia to Europe. . . . It would take four years to undo these mistakes."[25]

The Europeans took the lead in making the UN the principal international actor: it adopted resolutions aimed at promoting peace and dialog in Yugoslavia and in 1992 it also created the United Nations Protection Force, or UNPROFOR, which provided security for both those supplying relief and for specified safe areas, but otherwise engaged only in self-defense. UNPROFOR, whose mandate divided Europeans, was a small, lightly armed, multinational force that ultimately proved unable either to provide security to enclaves under its protection or to prevent an escalation of fighting. Until 1993 NATO, except for enforcing a no-fly zone, watched from the sidelines.

France assumed a prominent role in implementing UN resolutions: it supplied the largest number of peacekeeping troops, helped enforce an arms embargo on Yugoslavia as well as the no-fly zone, and provided overall command of the UN's Blue Helmet troops. But the French and the Americans did not agree on how to pacify the region. Whereas France counted on a robust performance from UNPROFOR, the arms embargo, and diplomacy, Clinton's foreign policy team, led by Secretary of State Warren Christopher, advised the Europeans to adopt a "lift and strike" option as an alternative to UNPROFOR—meaning they should lift the embargo that prevented the arming of the Muslims in Bosnia and use air power selectively against Bosnian Serb positions. Such advice antagonized the French and the British, who had troops on the ground and feared the American approach would not only be ineffective but would also endanger their soldiers by inciting the Serbs to seek revenge and escalate the fighting between Bosnian Muslims and Bosnian Serbs. They rebuffed Christopher during his visit to Europe in 1993 and opposed the American plan in the UN Security Council. Mitterrand grumbled that "the Americans are always at an altitude of 12,000 meters and we are in the valleys." In private Clinton spoke of the "hypocrisy" of the French and the British, using "their troops on the ground as a shield to preside over the slow dismemberment of Bosnia,"[26] but he accepted their veto over "lift and strike."

Yet the escalation of violence, which included Bosnian Serbs shelling cities like Sarajevo and harassing UN aid convoys, convinced the Europeans that their efforts at mediating a peace were failing and that UNPROFOR needed help from NATO. Washington, London, and Paris argued about how to introduce air power and at one marathon meeting of the North Atlantic Council in 1993 agreement was reached, but, according to one American official, only after "as bitter and rancorous a discussion as has ever taken place in the alliance."[27] France and the United Kingdom acceded to limited NATO air strikes for specific targets in, for example, the support of humanitarian aid or lifting the siege of Sarajevo, but they insisted on prior approval by the Security Council, which meant they retained control over targeting. This "dual key" arrangement that required UN authorization hampered the delivery of NATO air power, and the intermittent air attacks that followed did nothing to interrupt the fighting.

A major issue, besides air strikes and the arms embargo, was boots on the ground. The Clinton administration was unwilling to send American combat units: it insisted that an end to military operations and a peace agreement come first. The Americans, from a French perspective, meddled from the outside while the Europeans put their military at risk as peacekeepers. Elisabeth Guigou, the French minister for Europe, compared President Mitterrand's visit to embattled Sarajevo in 1992 to the do-nothing rhetoric of Washington: "We in France prefer to remain sober and act."[28] When in 1993 the Europeans attempted to broker a peace initiative, the Vance-Owen Peace Plan, which divided Bosnia along ethnic lines, Washington objected, arguing that it would be impossible to enforce and that it ratified gains made by the Bosnian Serbs through ethnic cleansing.[29] The French suggested the Americans could be of more use by sending troops than by trying to show up the Europeans and UNPROFOR. American sniping riled the French, who had by then lost over twenty soldiers and had hundreds wounded. In the National Assembly Juppé attacked "governments that want to give us lessons when they have not lifted a little finger to put even one man on the ground."[30]

The alliance was at an impasse in 1993–94. While the U.S. Congress lobbied the White House to force the "lift and strike" strategy on unwilling Europeans, the latter in turn threatened to remove their peacekeeping units if the embargo was suspended.[31] The Clinton administration announced in November 1994 that it could no longer enforce the UN embargo and turned a blind eye on arms transfers by third parties to the Bosnian Muslims. The Quai d'Orsay rebuked the U.S. government for tampering with the embargo, asserting that the Americans would be responsible if the fighting spread.[32] Washington tried to deal with Bosnia from afar, hoping to broker an agreement among the warring factions without serious military engagement. Otherwise it drifted. Védrine told Mitterrand that the Americans had no idea of how to help the unfortunate people coexist peacefully; they were interested only in the "good Bosnian Muslims" as a way of fighting "the communist and fascist Serbs. . . . Compared to the fury of the political and military leaders of the three parties in conflict, the American attitude is undoubtedly the second cause for the continuation of the war."[33] Washington's recommendations that NATO expand air attacks to stop the Bosnian Serbs from escalating the violence were not welcome by the Europeans. Recriminations crisscrossed the Atlantic over who was at fault for failing to stop the bloodshed. The quarreling over strategies, "lift and strike" as opposed to UNPROFOR, and the arms embargo became so nasty that some believe the alliance came closer to imploding during 1994 than it had at any time since the Suez Crisis of 1956.[34]

Presidential elections in April–May 1995 brought Jacques Chirac to the Elysée and ended the fourteen-year presidency of François Mitterrand. Not only had the conservatives gained power, but "the bulldozer," as he was nicknamed, had arrived and with him came a major shift in transatlantic affairs. Chirac named Alain Juppé as his prime minister and Hervé de Charette as foreign minister. The new president, unlike his predecessor, immediately began urging Clinton to intervene more actively in Bosnia: his forcefulness and his candor impressed Washington and transformed relations between the White House and the Elysée.

In May 1995, after a NATO air attack, the Bosnian Serbs took hundreds of Blue Helmet troops hostage, among whom were a hundred French soldiers, and threatened other safe havens like Goražde and Srebrenica. The passivity and humiliation of French peacekeepers at the hands of the Serbs infuriated Chirac, who had been a trooper in the Algeria War. In July Serb units overran Srebrenica and massacred thousands of men and boys. In the midst of these events Chirac visited Washington, lobbying the U.S. Congress and pressing the hesitant White House to become more assertive, including mounting massive air attacks to protect UN safe havens like Goražde. He also succeeded in convincing the Americans, other allies, and the Security Council to accept the deployment of a new military unit, the Rapid

Reaction Force, composed of heavily armed European troops, to protect UNPROFOR. The Clinton administration now had a European ally, one with troops on the ground, as it moved toward taking a more aggressive stance. Chirac's boldness stirred Washington.[35] In August 1995 the Bosnian Serbs enraged international opinion by shelling a Sarajevo market crowded with civilians. Washington was convinced it had to act more forcefully. Several considerations weighed on the Clinton administration in the summer of 1995 including the possible collapse of UNPROFOR following the hostage crisis and the unwelcome prospect of deploying U.S. troops to rescue UN forces. Equally important was the credibility of the alliance in the post–Cold War era: American leadership was at risk.[36] After his visit Chirac had shamed Washington by calling the leadership of the free world "vacant" and likened Western leaders to the appeasers at Munich. Clinton also worried, in a presidential election year, about appearing indecisive. The White House decided to engage through intensive air strikes. Once again London, Washington, and Paris were at odds over how to proceed, but the Clinton administration prevailed and imposed its plan for a vigorous air campaign to protect Sarajevo and Goražde. NATO, finally unleashed from close supervision by the UN, intervened. Weeks of bombing sorties by NATO, mainly by American but also by French, British, and other European war planes, convinced the Bosnian Serbs and their backers in Belgrade that it was time for a settlement. The Serbs meanwhile had been chastened by the success of joint counterattacks by Croat ground forces and those of the newly armed Bosnian Muslims.

Alliance air power, which marked its first military action since its inception, proved instrumental in bringing about the cease-fire. But NATO's intrusion marked the marginalization of both France and the UN in running operations in Bosnia. Absence from the alliance's command structure, for example, meant that the French were excluded from participating in military decisions like selecting targets. More broadly, Bosnia buried French aspirations, at least in the short run, for developing a European defense alternative to NATO. War in the former Yugoslavia exposed differences among the Europeans, their inability at projecting force without NATO, and the value of integrated command for multinational operations. Above all, Bosnia had proved that American military assistance could only be assured by working with NATO.[37] One of Mitterrand's advisers admitted that ceding control to NATO had been a setback for the hopes of Europeans to develop their own means of defense.[38]

For the new president of France the first problem that claimed his attention was assisting in the resolution of the conflict in Bosnia. But the Americans took charge and Richard Holbrooke and his team of negotiators dictated the Dayton Peace Accord of November 1995, showing little concern for the allies attending the talks. At one point the Europeans threatened to walk out. Holbrooke later admitted he had been heavy-handed: "The French say that they were humiliated at Dayton and they were right."[39] Clinton was gracious and thanked Chirac for his "leadership" in organizing the talks, and Holbrooke spoke of Chirac as rendering "enormous service in forcing us to act."[40] At least the agreement reflected some French goals, like establishing a federal structure for an independent Bosnia and distributing territory equitably between a Croatian–Bosnian Muslim and a Serbian political entity. The Dayton Accord also created the Implementation Force led by NATO, to which France contributed the second largest contingent, and a civilian apparatus under EU direction. The Dayton Accord represented a reassertion of NATO supremacy because American officers would dominate the military occupation and the Europeans were relegated to economic reconstruction. Washington also initiated a program to equip and train the Bosnian Muslims. France, along with strong European support, stoutly opposed this move out of fear it would encourage a resumption of fighting, but it was ignored.[41] American unilateralism had been on view in Dayton, Ohio, if more blatant than usual in the hands of Holbrooke. Chirac was discreet and voiced no grievances in public. He had been shut out except for protocol that awarded Paris the venue for the final signing. France, which for over three years had contributed the most of any European nation to pacifying Bosnia, when it came to reconstruction was relegated to the role of a "backup mediator."[42]

After the Dayton meetings observers noticed a "new swagger" in the White House. Clinton, who had been tentative in foreign affairs, especially in the use of military force, was now more confident in exercising global leadership. Warren Christopher noted that his European counterparts were relieved that determination and unity had replaced impotence and division: "They grumble that we dominated Dayton, but they really know that it would not have gotten done otherwise."[43]

■ The Atlantic Alliance and the European Pillar

The end of the Cold War and Europe's feeble contribution to the victory in the Persian Gulf emboldened some Europeans to propose a common defense capability as a rival to NATO. The Americans, as it turned out, had other ideas. Reform of the Atlantic Alliance would put Mitterrand's France and Bush's America at cross purposes in the early 1990s.

The first premise of French security policy as the Cold War ended was that NATO, as constituted, represented American domination, or at least a restraint, on French freedom to act. A second premise was that the United States would relax its commitment to the Atlantic Alliance because without the Soviet danger Europe would no longer be the focus of U.S. attention. Another assumption was that a united Germany needed to be tied more closely to the European Union, and a common defense policy would be a means to this end.

This analysis meant France should resist any expansion of NATO's scope or functions and it need not seek a rapprochement with the alliance. The 1966 arrangement, which absented France from the alliance's integrated command, would continue as long as Mitterrand was president. Nevertheless, since NATO remained the basis of security, it required rebalancing with a European partner. Given the inevitable retreat of America, France had the need and the opportunity to lead the way toward equipping Europe with its own defense capacity outside NATO so that the EU could act by itself when the alliance was unwilling. After the Maastricht Treaty was signed the Mitterrand administration wanted to add a common foreign and defense policy to the EU as well as monetary integration: it was bent on making the union a counterweight to the American-run Atlantic Alliance.

Washington had its own project for European security: it sought to extend the reach of the Atlantic Alliance without sacrificing control. A renovated alliance would remain the instrument for assuring America's necessary and rightful leadership of the European continent. Neither the Bush nor the Clinton administrations had any intention of diluting, much less surrendering, U.S. direction of the alliance and they proved intransigent in their opposition to any new European security arrangement that might rival NATO or undermine American domination.

As we saw in chapter 3, alliance reform had been raised in the midst of German reunification. When Presidents Bush and Mitterrand met at Key Largo, Florida, in April 1990 their differences over the future of NATO emerged: Mitterrand figuratively winced when Bush stated that in order to maintain America's commitment to the Old World the alliance needed to widen its "field of competence" to all of Europe's problems, including politics. U.S. National Security Adviser Brent Scowcroft noted that if NATO were confined to its traditional role of defense, as Mitterrand wanted, the alliance would atrophy.[44] The Bush administration intended not only to add political and peacekeeping responsibilities to a post–Cold War alliance but also sought to extend it geographically to embrace at least some of the former Soviet bloc countries in Eastern Europe and also to expand its activities outside Europe. The French maintained a minimalist position.[45] They wanted no "out of area" activities; the alliance should remain confined to the defense of the continent. French foreign minister Roland Dumas said the alliance should not "extend its zone of competence and transform itself into a grand directory for world affairs."[46] When French officials spoke about renovating the alliance they thought about shrinking it or keeping it as is and constructing a European defense; the Americans suspected that the French saw reform as a way to diminish American leadership in Europe. In a top staff meeting on security, Bush worried that the French wanted U.S. troops out of Europe, but James Baker surmised they would prefer the Americans became "mercenaries," available for hire only when needed.[47]

At the London NATO summit in July 1990 the Bush administration imposed its plan for restructuring the alliance on the Europeans. The Americans knew that their approach would, in all likelihood, be emasculated if the allies were allowed to debate and amend it, so they curtailed discussion. The summit's declaration called for adding political options, like assigning NATO the task of mediating with the new democracies in Eastern Europe. In addition to stabilizing that region, the alliance was also to assume general responsibility for crisis management (the so-called non–Article 5 tasks). The French, in contrast, thought openings to the former Warsaw Pact countries as well as crisis management and "out-of-area" tasks belonged to the Europeans, not NATO. Both the negotiations themselves as well as the substance of the London declaration offended the French, who took exception to what they called "politicizing" the alliance. The French pique, according to American officials, revealed their frustration with the whole process of reordering the continent; one called French attitudes "a form of existential pessimism."[48] But the Americans had to admit they had been heavy-handed.[49]

In 1990–91, France, with German support, pressed for alliance reform aimed at a gradual shift of responsibility from the United States to the Europeans.[50] Mitterrand argued that Europeans had to develop their own means of defense because the United States was bound to disengage. He told German chancellor Helmut Kohl that even though the Soviet Union was withering away the Americans wanted to make the continent completely dependent and smother any impulse for a European defense, but this contradiction would not endure and within a few years "Europe will not exist and the United States will be less present."[51] France's defense minister Pierre Joxe observed that Europe had to provide for its own security because the United States "is unsure as to the role and responsibilities it wishes to shoulder."[52] The French were not alone in their contrariness: the Belgians, the Spanish, and in softer tones even the Germans wanted a greater place for the Europeans within the alliance. The Belgian foreign minister Mark Eyskens put it rather crudely: "Europe is an economic giant, a political dwarf, and a military worm."[53]

France proposed giving the European community a defense capacity as a "pillar" of the EU by reinforcing the Western European Union (WEU), the vestigial security organization from the 1940s, and linking it to the EU. A WEU/EU defense organization, separable from NATO, would possess European forces that could be used without NATO's approval in places like the Balkans or even outside the continent. Jacques Delors, president of the European Commission was upset by the community's ineffectiveness in the Gulf War and boldly proclaimed that Europe needed "a common defense policy" built on the WEU as "a melting pot for a European defense" forming "the second pillar of the Atlantic Alliance." The U.S. should not fear the creation of "an internal bloc" that, after proper consultations, would determine "its own course of action outside . . . the North Atlantic Treaty."[54] Not all EU members were pleased with this project; the British, in particular, opposed any departure that might diminish NATO or weaken the American commitment to Europe.

A second step was a joint proposal, formally advanced in October 1991, by President Mitterrand and Chancellor Kohl for the formation of a Eurocorps. This Franco-German military unit, beginning with a nucleus of 25,000 troops, could be expanded to other Europeans, but not to Americans: it would act on mission from either the WEU or NATO in Europe. France stipulated that in a crisis the Eurocorps would retain its identity as a European unit and any member state could veto the links to NATO.[55]

This Franco-German defense initiative encountered hostility in Washington and London and a cool reception from most Europeans who feared undermining American protection. Invigorating the WEU, it seemed, was fraught with problems and the Eurocorps might remove the German military from the alliance. Meanwhile the Americans opposed any plan that might conceivably become a rival to NATO or undermine their authority over the alliance. Washington, like London, did not want the WEU incorporated into the EU, thus raising the possibility of a "European caucus" that might interfere with the decision-making apparatus of NATO.[56] A defense planning document prepared by the Pentagon in 1992 was explicit about such fears: it called for "a substantial American presence in Europe," but noted that to avoid a competitive relationship developing the United States "must seek to prevent the emergence of European-only security arrangements which would undermine NATO."[57] Officially the U.S. government approved the construction of a "European pillar," but as one official candidly stated, it would not accept any independent structure that risked "emptying NATO of its substance . . . therefore losing the justification for the American presence in Europe."[58] The French government correctly attributed American opposition to the WEU/Eurocorps scheme as evidence of disingenuous posturing about the European pillar. The Americans, it seemed, were attempting the impossible: they wanted a greater contribution to defense from the Europeans while maintaining their traditional level of domination.

The Anglo-Americans actively subverted the WEU/Eurocorps plan. Bush wrote to Mitterrand, warning him that the Franco-German corps undermined the integrated command of the alliance and encouraged American isolationism.[59] Washington and London proposed connecting the WEU with NATO rather than with the EU and they also initiated a NATO-based Rapid Reaction Force as an alternative to the Eurocorps. Paris objected to the former and reluctantly accepted the latter as a way of maintaining French armed forces in Germany after unification.

A compromise was finally worked out at the Rome (NATO) Summit and the Maastricht (EU) Conference at the end of 1991, but not before disputes over renovating the alliance became public. In Rome Bush was so incensed with the French and Germans that during a public session he warned, "[W]e do not see the WEU as a European alternative to the alliance," and then, behind closed doors, vented, "If Western Europe intends to create a security organization outside the alliance, tell me now."[60] Mitterrand, in turn, was so infuriated by Baker's effort at adding political missions to the alliance that he complained, "The alliance is good, but it is not the Holy Alliance."[61] In Rome the Americans, collaborating with allies like the British, the Dutch, the Danes, and the Portuguese, made certain the WEU project would not be independent of the Atlantic Alliance.

The Maastricht Conference gave Paris some satisfaction by assigning the newly minted European Union a Common Foreign and Security Policy as one of its structural "pillars" and pledging itself to constructing a European defense entity around the WEU. But the Americans and their supporters sabotaged the autonomy of this new defense entity (named the European Security and Defense Identity) with the obfuscation that it would function simultaneously as "the defense component of the European Union" and as "the European pillar of the Atlantic Alliance." Similarly, the WEU was to act "in conformity with the positions adopted in the Atlantic Alliance."[62] These meetings thus affirmed NATO's role as the essential forum for defense policy. Most Europeans clearly preferred NATO as their protector rather than the promise of the WEU, which everyone knew was beset with structural and political problems. Six months later yet another conference settled whatever uncertainties lingered after the Maastricht Conference about the WEU/NATO rivalry. The Petersberg Declaration extended the WEU's tasks to humanitarian assistance, peacekeeping, and peacemaking functions, but subordinated the organization to NATO. NATO, moreover, could now act "out-of-area" in certain cases. The Europeans had opted for the Atlantic Alliance and rejected the French-led alternative. A frustrated Mitterrand told the German chancellor that the Americans wanted to make NATO a structure "completely dependent on a Washington that would stifle any notion of European defense."[63] One American diplomat admitted, "We wanted Europeans to do more for themselves as long as they did exactly what we wanted. We supported WEU but not if it went off on its own."[64]

The transition from the Cold War, even after these American diplomatic victories, continued to stir up transatlantic storms. The two foreign ministers, James Baker and Roland Dumas, were not on the best of terms. Talks between them so exasperated Secretary Baker that he challenged his counterpart: "Are you with us or against us?"[65] Underlying this outburst was the fundamental rift over America's role in post–Cold War Europe. Paris believed that Washington, despite its rhetoric about burden sharing with Europeans, did not want to share its authority over security. Bush-Baker policies led French—and some other European—officials to conclude that "the U.S. desires a perpetually weakened community unable to act on the continent or in the world except under the banner of U.S. leadership."[66] One senior American official reflecting on these events admitted, "In the whole U.S. approach to the new Europe, we had no adequate sensitivity for the need to develop a dialogue on the future of European political union and security activities with the French. This was a significant mistake."[67]

By 1992 it was obvious to Paris that Washington was having its way with NATO reform and stalling the alternative French initiative. The Americans had added political duties to the alliance, opened it to Eastern Europe, gained "out-of-area" competence, and retained their control. The WEU/Eurocorps remained a plan without much support among Europeans and one that was operationally dependent on NATO. Instead of building an autonomous defense capacity, Europeans were reducing military spending. And France's principal ally, Germany, seemed less than fully committed to the project. Above all, the premise of French reform had proved faulty. The Americans had reduced their force levels on the continent, but they were not departing: rather, as the Bush team demonstrated, they were committed to remaining a European power. And as Yugoslavia disintegrated into violence and European and UN peacekeeping missions faltered, an American commitment to continental stability seemed more vital. Indeed, the reticence of Washington to become involved in the Balkans spoke to a contrary concern: Might the Americans disengage when they were needed?

French diplomacy quietly reversed course. At first slowly in 1992–94, under Mitterrand, and then rapidly afterward, France launched a rapprochement with NATO.[68] It abandoned constructing a rival to the alliance and tried to work from within to build a European pillar. In July 1992, against the background of ethnic violence in the Balkans, Michel Rocard as prime minister spoke of "a long time misunderstanding" that marred relations with the alliance, hailed NATO as a "solid reference point in a world in turmoil," and recommended "France's "intensifying its cooperation with NATO."[69] Later that year an agreement among France, Germany, and NATO placed the Eurocorps under NATO's "operational command" with the clear understanding that the Europeans could only act if NATO stood aside; and small steps followed toward raising French participation in the alliance.

The rapprochement initiated by the socialists gained momentum when legislative elections in 1993 brought a massive conservative majority and another round of cohabitation with a government dominated by the Rassemblement pour la République (RPR): Édouard Balladur became prime minister and Alain Juppé foreign minister, and they would move France even closer toward the alliance. The master of the RPR, Jacques Chirac, sanctioned this strategy. He reasoned that because France's partners were uninterested in creating a European defense identity, "the necessary rebalancing of relations within the Atlantic Alliance, relying on existing European institutions such as the WEU, can only take place from the inside, not against the United

States, but in agreement with it."[70] And Juppé reaffirmed the presence of American forces in Europe as "indispensable for our security," noting, "The time has passed for haughty reserve with respect to the Atlantic Alliance as well as for a shameful presence which would be unworthy of our country. . . . It must be clear that France wishes for a solid alliance and that it will engage without reticence in its necessary renovation." Still Juppé admonished Washington: the U.S. must accept Europe as "a real partner" especially in cases where it did not want to be militarily involved: "We need a strong alliance and 'more Europe.'"[71] For the first time since the 1960s French defense ministers began attending meetings of NATO's Military Committee, and France hosted NATO exercises on its territory. It became imperative when the French military began to conduct joint operations with NATO in the Balkans that it gain some say in alliance decision making. Once Chirac became president, in 1995, the move toward working within NATO begun under Mitterrand reached a climax.

Far more than Mitterrand, the new incumbent at the Elysée tried to cultivate close personal rapport with his opposite in the White House. Jacques Chirac had the advantage of speaking English well, and he had visited the United States as a young man beginning in 1953 with a summer session at the Harvard Business School and a job at a Howard Johnson's diner. Touring America took him from San Francisco to New Orleans; then there was a "fiancée" from South Carolina who drove a white Cadillac convertible and called him "Honey Child."[72] As president, Chirac at first worried about Clinton's lack of experience in international life, compared to that of his predecessor, but the two presidents quickly warmed to one another. Clinton spoke of "the good chemistry" between them.[73] They were both affable extroverts who impressed others with their enthusiasm, familiarity, and chatter. Compared to Mitterrand, according to Ambassador Pamela Harriman, the new president was, in Clinton's estimation, "a breath of fresh air."[74] They communicated routinely by phone and letter, and when the

Clintons visited France in 1996 for a G7 meeting they dined with the Chiracs at a chic Parisian restaurant.

Washington welcomed President Chirac with a formal state visit that featured an address to the U.S. Congress on February 1, 1996.[75] Members of Congress, however, were most inhospitable: hundreds of them boycotted the speech in protest against France's resumption of nuclear testing. Pages and other staffers had to be rushed in to fill the empty seats. Ignoring the only partially filled chamber, the president of France declared his personal affinity with his hosts by recalling how as a boy he had watched American troops land in Provence in 1944. Anxious that the country might retreat into domestic concerns, Chirac exhorted his audience to remain engaged in international affairs, noting that "the world needs the United States." Chirac, who was known for chiding Congress for its isolationist ways, praised the United Nations as the source of international legitimacy, mildly rebuking Congress for refusing to pay its dues to the organization. After saluting the United States for its role in reconstructing Bosnia, the speaker affirmed that France regarded America's political and military commitment to Europe as "an essential factor of the continent's stability and security." The only dramatic moment of the address came when he confirmed France's intention of seeking a rapprochement with the military structure of NATO, which he connected with renovation of the alliance, referring to building a strong "European pillar" that was capable of sharing the burden of security. Chirac thus linked the promise of rapprochement with NATO reform. Not only Congress was absent that day; so were most Americans. The speech was rarely mentioned in television news that evening.[76]

By 1995–96 France was ready to resume its quest for NATO reform.[77] Four years of combat in the former Yugoslavia had demonstrated that the Europeans could not pacify the region by themselves. Bosnia revealed that France, among other deficiencies, lacked the air- and sealift capacity to project a sizable military force, and budgetary constraints kept it from spending what was necessary to make up for its shortcomings. NATO alone had the necessary logistical means. Officials in Paris became convinced that since a functioning European security capacity was years in the future, the American military was the only reliable force for the continent's stability.[78] Moreover, the French recognized that the WEU scheme had stalled because of the opposition from Washington and most European capitals. The only way to create a European security entity was to avoid the appearance of pursuing a course that would weaken the alliance. In addition, the high hopes once held for the EU constructing its own security capacity—aspirations that had peaked at the Maastricht Conference—had been dashed by the strong opposition to the Maastricht Treaty's ratification recorded in France and Denmark as well as by Franco-German quarrels over Yugoslavia. Perhaps most important for changing course, the Gaullist posture—that of standing outside the integrated military structure—no longer made any sense; not when France would, in all likelihood, engage in future combat with NATO forces as it had in the Balkans. Absence from NATO decision making denied France leverage in framing strategy and tactics. Thus Chirac complained he was unable to select targets for air strikes in Bosnia. This sober reappraisal led France to seek an accommodation by building the European pillar inside the alliance. Or, as one French expert observed, "in order to be more European tomorrow, it is necessary to be more Atlanticist today."[79] Happily the Clinton administration signaled it was open to such reform as part of a package that featured NATO enlargement to include Poland, Hungary, and the Czech Republic.

Once again France recalibrated the delicate diplomatic balance with the United States. If the presumption had been that there was less need for American presence in Europe at the end of the Cold War, after 1992 the premise was that the United States needed to be coaxed back. The Clinton administration was paying more attention to domestic than foreign affairs and, given its reluctance to intervene in the Balkans, seemed inclined to distance itself from Europe—at a time when ethnic and nationalist disorder had erupted and NATO was essential for peacekeeping. It was time, to a much greater extent than even Mitterrand's *démarche* of the early 1980s, to tilt the balance back toward the alliance.

The Elysée, especially the president and his advisers like Jean-David Levitte, backed by the defense ministry, took the lead in trying to construct a "new NATO" from within. Officials at the Quai d'Orsay, the guardians of Gaullist principles, were less enthusiastic. What was needed was a European chain of command that could take charge of the new peacekeeping—that is non–Article 5 and out-of-area missions—in cases where the United States did not want to participate. To be credible peacekeeping required access to NATO assets. Such missions might also involve non-NATO actors and thus would benefit from a more flexible and more Europeanized command apparatus than the old American-run, integrated structure—a hierarchy that was best reserved for Europe's defense or Article 5 crises. A new chain of command would begin at the top with European personnel. American officers, it should be recalled, not only staffed the key commands, including Supreme Allied Commander Europe (SACEUR) itself, but were also "double-hatted," meaning they received orders from both NATO and the Pentagon. This may have been tolerable when the Soviet Union had seemed poised for attack, but now it was out-of-date, especially when the alliance was facing the new kinds of threats seen in the Balkans.

In December 1995, François Bujon de l'Etang, the French ambassador in Washington, alerted Deputy Secretary of State Strobe Talbott that France intended to rejoin the military structure of the alliance.[80] This, as it turned out, was a tactical error. The Clinton administration wrongly assumed that France had made up its mind to rejoin NATO when in fact such a move was dependent on overhauling the alliance.

In August 1996 Chirac took up the promise he had made during his recent state visit and wrote directly to Clinton recommending two options for renovating the command structure of the alliance: either elevating Europeans to the post of SACEUR (after creating a "super-SACEUR" for an American) or to the two regional (north and south) commands. The quid pro quo was that France would rejoin the integrated military structure. The French proposal enjoyed substantial, but not solid, support from other Europeans—more from the Spanish and the Germans, less from the British—and outright opposition from the Italians. France also recommended to the White House that if the United States wanted to enlarge the alliance it should include Romania (Italy want to add Slovenia), along with the other three former Soviet bloc nations.

The Clinton administration was amenable to the return of France. In the eyes of American officials France was one of the few nations that had the means and will to share the security burden in Europe and project military power in areas like Africa, the Persian Gulf, and the Middle East. But Chirac's "new NATO" encountered mistrust and opposition from American officials, especially from some in the Pentagon and the State Department who thought the French proposals were "thinly conceived devices for curtailing U.S. influence in Europe."[81] Or, as one State Department hand informed the French ambassador, he thought France wanted to "kick us out of Europe."[82] Moreover, Congress gave priority to limited enlargement rather than reform. The sticking point was awarding a European—in all likelihood a French officer—the command of NATO's southern forces (AFSOUTH), based in Naples, which included the U.S. Sixth Fleet in the Mediterranean. The Clinton administration might have entertained assigning some commands to Europeans, but not a key one like AFSOUTH. Congress, it was said, would never countenance the Sixth Fleet taking orders from a European officer. Nor would the United States surrender control over decision making in the alliance: Washington was willing to grant more visibility to the Europeans, but not actual authority—which was precisely what France sought. The French position was weakened by the lack of an endorsement from the Italians, who enjoyed having the U.S. Navy stationed in Naples. For his part Clinton, engaged in a presidential campaign, could not be seen as giving away the Mediterranean command to the French. He wrote back to Chirac in September, explaining why he could not concede the southern command to a European officer. Nor could he surrender U.S. control over the alliance. Nor, as it turned out, because of Congressional opposition among other reasons, would he add Romania and Slovenia to the list of new NATO countries.

Negotiations went awry when Chirac's August letter was leaked, stirring up a press campaign that distorted his proposal as a scheme for the French to take charge of the Sixth Fleet. In fact, France had offered alternatives. By the fall, journalists and politicians on both sides of the Atlantic embellished the debate, making it more difficult to find a compromise. According to one French daily the White House had been brutal with Chirac; allegedly, Clinton wrote, "Jacques, I must be frank about the southern command: it's no."[83] Meanwhile, the socialists, including prominent figures like Laurent Fabius and Jean-Pierre Chevènement, distanced themselves from Chirac's project while a few hard-line Gaullists directly criticized him; the old Gaullist baron, Pierre Messmer complained, "It is rather astonishing that the government enters NATO at the very moment that it has lost its *raison d'être*."[84] Members of the U.S. Congress took aim at the French proposal and the press vented at an alleged slight of Warren Christopher by Hervé de Charette. As the story goes Charette, at a NATO meeting in Brussels, dashed out of dinner at the very moment when the secretary-general of the organization was presenting a toast to the American secretary of state. The *Washington Post* headline read, "French Snub NATO Tribute to Christopher."[85] The Quai d'Orsay believed the anti-French faction in the State Department inspired the article and Charette was embarrassed and angry. According to NATO sources, relations between the allies had become "vitriolic." "Chirac cannot back down," it was reported, "because he would be seen as caving in to the Americans, and the U.S. will not back down because it's too important a command to give up and Congress would never approve."[86]

In fact, negotiations continued, because Washington believed there was room for compromise and Paris persisted. Levitte and Defense Minister Charles Millon arrived in Washington in early 1997 with suggestions about finding a way to Europeanize AFSOUTH without making the Sixth Fleet subordinate.[87] One such recommendation was to share the Naples command, leaving air and naval forces under an American and attaching only the land-based forces to a European. Levitte argued if Europe were to exist inside the military alliance it must benefit from an autonomous command and, he added, politically France could not rejoin without winning some concession. At home the government needed something to keep the Gaullists on board. Instead of a compromise, the Pentagon closed the door. In April General John Shalikashvili, chairman of the Joint Chiefs of Staff, addressing his French military opposites, rejected the proposed European command because, he argued, the Europeans did not speak with one voice and France, given its independent role, could not assume command itself.[88] By then Clinton's second term had begun and his new secretary of defense, William Cohen, declared to Congress that the southern command was nonnegotiable and the new secretary of state, Madeleine Albright, concurred: "Our position on AFSOUTH has not changed. We consider it essential for that to remain an American command. . . ."[89] The most the two sides could do was issue a statement of principles about restructuring AFSOUTH without addressing the hard issues; the American negotiators admitted they had postponed everything and made the European a "commander-in-waiting."

What was on the mind of the Clinton team was NATO enlargement rather than structural reform. They wanted to extend the alliance eastward to Poland, the Czech Republic, and Hungary; Chirac accepted this expansion as a quid pro quo for reform, but he wanted to include Romania. In fact, he was wary of the Clinton administration's rush to expand the alliance from fear of, among other reasons, antagonizing Russia.[90] The NATO conference in Madrid in July 1997 settled the issue—as usual, in Washington's favor. Three countries, not five, were added. One of Chirac's advisers complained, "What bugs (*emmerder*) me with the Americans is their tendency to say, 'I have decided, period.' Certainly one can discuss up to a point. Then they say 'no' and it's no." Once again the French found themselves isolated; one diplomat complained, "I have never seen such doormats as the Europeans at Madrid." Chirac had to accept the decision, blaming the short list on Congress, but he had been humiliated. He told journalists that Europeans had only a secondary role in the alliance: they had subcommands and formal duties like attending receptions but no real power. It may have been a tactical error, Chirac admitted, to have announced reintegration without first specifying conditions.[91] The return to government in 1997 of the socialists, who had no interest in the project, effectively killed it. But by then the affair had damaged French-American relations by reinforcing each side's suspicion that the other was inflexible and untrustworthy.[92] The Americans did not trust the French: their Atlanticism seemed false. They were still suspected of trying to diminish America's power in Europe and taking charge of NATO for their purposes. The French did not trust the Americans: they had misled them about their willingness to share power and construct a European pillar within the alliance and in the process embarrassed them.

French policy, after the "new NATO" debacle, drifted until it found a new way forward with the construction within the EU of what came to be called the European Security and Defense Policy (ESDP). A major step in this direction had been inspired by the Americans who, like the French, aimed at making the alliance a more flexible, ad hoc, coalition-building organization that could meet a wide range of crises without mobilizing the entire apparatus. The solution was to transfer NATO assets, like satellite intelligence and airlift, to special missions designated as Combined Joint Task Forces (CJTFs) for tasks, especially out-of-area ones, in which Washington did not want to participate. Paris endorsed this extension of alliance functions but haggled over who would control the transferred assets. In 1996 an agreement stipulated the alliance could lend assets for operations conducted by Europeans, but such WEU-led CJTFs would be "separable but not separate" from NATO. The Clinton administration insisted that

SACEUR remain in control, although France at least succeeded in limiting NATO's day-to-day oversight of loaned assets.[93] France had gained rather little. Chirac tried to put on a brave face by saying the CJTF compromise indicated "renovation" of the alliance was underway. Not all of his fellow compatriots accepted the president's posturing. A former defense minister, the socialist Paul Quilès, wrote that Chirac had ceded authority to Washington, making the United States "the sixteenth member of the European Union whenever it comes to decisions about defense." How, Quilès asked, could France maintain influence in the world if, instead of sharing control of its military with the EU, it "squandered" it in NATO where the Americans would not relinquish real power.[94] Pascal Boniface, an authority on strategic studies, likened the CJTFs borrowing alliance assets to an adolescent having use of the family car on a Saturday night: "That avoids the need for the head of the family to go out at night; nevertheless the latter retains the right to decide whether or not to lend the car, and monitors the destination, the time when the car should be returned, the conditions for its use, and so forth."[95]

Such an arrangement did not go far enough for the French government, so it continued to try to reinforce a common foreign policy and security agenda for the EU. But, as usual, the British and several Nordic countries, who insisted on preserving the primacy of NATO, resisted. In 1997 the EU nevertheless took some small steps that strengthened its ability to articulate and implement a common foreign policy and make the Petersburg tasks—such as peacekeeping and humanitarian rescue—its responsibility. The European defense entity was still in its infancy when the British had a change of heart.

London began to warm to the idea of European defense after the troubles in Bosnia; British and French armed forces had fought together and they had quarreled together with the Americans, and London had come around to the view that a powerless Europe would not be a good partner for the United States, that "the way to save the alliance was via Europe."[96] The British now turned to creating a military and defense capacity within the EU. In the French coastal town of Saint-Malo in December 1998, Prime Minister Tony Blair, along with President Chirac, orchestrated an Anglo-French declaration that spoke of giving the Union "the capacity for autonomous action, backed up by credible military forces, the means to decide to use them and a readiness to do so, in order to respond to international crises. . . ."[97]

The turning point for the EU occurred at its meetings at Cologne and Helsinki during the summer of 1999. Washington's reluctance to intervene in Kosovo worried Europeans about American commitment to stabilizing the continent's periphery and spurred efforts at constructing a common defense capability.[98] Europeans declared their intention of constructing an ESDP that would furnish the EU with an autonomous defense capacity. The EU adopted the Saint-Malo declaration, adding that the EU Council would assume responsibility for a range of conflict prevention and crisis management tasks. (At this point the earlier WEU/Eurocorps scheme was folded into the new EU project.) Europeans proceeded to provide some military muscle to the ESDP by creating military staff and planning committees, naming Javier Solana as high representative for the Common Foreign and Security Policy and announcing plans to create a Rapid Reaction Force of up to 60,000 troops that the EU could deploy. But they were careful to point out that the "autonomous capacity" of the EU to launch and conduct its own military operations in response to international crises would be taken "without prejudice to actions by NATO."[99] They also called for full consultation, cooperation, and transparency between the EU and NATO. In other words, the ESDP remained embedded within the alliance. Unlike earlier proposals, these had the backing of the British. The United States was, nevertheless, concerned that ESDP and the Rapid Reaction Force would compete with NATO. Secretary of State Madeleine Albright responded with her famous "3-Ds," saying ESDP had American support as long as there was no decoupling, duplication, or discrimination.[100] Washington delayed reaching a compromise with the Europeans until 2003 when an agreement specified that NATO and the EU would have separate, yet connected, planning staffs and that the EU would undertake operations "only if NATO as a whole . . . decided not to be engaged."[101] A bargain had been struck. The U.S. guaranteed lending NATO assets to future European-led operations in return for the ESDP submitting to prior NATO authorization. Thus the United States via NATO continued to preside over European security.

The project of creating a European defense capacity had crept forward a few steps at the very end of the decade, but even then the ESDP was more a promise of autonomy than a reality: any significant European military operation still depended on the loan of NATO assets and U.S. willingness to share responsibility. And for the ESDP to become a reality it required that Europeans increase their defense spending and halt their wrangling over security policy. After a decade of diplomatic maneuvering not much had been achieved from the perspective of France.

A frustrated Hubert Védrine, the socialist foreign minister, let loose on the occasion of NATO's fiftieth birthday when he complained of U.S. high-handedness. "Since President Kennedy, we've been hearing from people on the other side of the Atlantic about a European pillar for the alliance," the minister noted. "In reality, this pillar is never built" because the alliance itself was constructed on "a hierarchical foundation with a strict subordination of all participants" to the United States.[102] Yet he was confident that the alliance would change. A year later he said of European defense, "I think the Europeans will end up imposing themselves as partners on a United States that will initially be reticent, but at the end of the day will be realistic."[103] France had been checked, but it had not surrendered.

Among the sixteen nations that composed NATO until the end of the 1990s, the United States and France—when it came to designing alliance goals, structure, scope, and especially the relative roles of Europe and America—were polar opposites. This transatlantic rivalry generated much of the debate about how the alliance should operate in the post–Cold War era. And the postures of the two, as well as the issues, lived on into the new millennium. In 2008, as the analyst Frédéric Bozo observed, the United States still objected to a European "caucus" within the North Atlantic Council that would challenge its leadership, and France still resisted efforts at politicizing the alliance and expanding its geographic scope at "the risk of seeing NATO become the cornerstone of an international order controlled by the United States."[104] France wanted the alliance to remain a Euro-Atlantic club confined to military and peacekeeping functions. Looking back, the gap between France and NATO opened by Charles de Gaulle was, in fits and starts, gradually narrowed in spite of the rebuff of 1996; at the same time, in a similar discontinuous manner, the Europeans, pushed forward by France, began to develop an autonomous defense capacity outside the alliance. It was not until 2009 that France resumed full participation in the alliance, but, as the past might have suggested, President Nicolas Sarkozy insisted that joining NATO was fully compatible with the ESDP: "Our defense has two pillars, the European Union and the Atlantic Alliance."[105] If the 1990s anticipated the future, harmony would not come easily.

■ Trade Warriors

Trade, which in theory and practice bridged the Atlantic, also contributed, like security, to rancor in the United States and France. Trouble peaked in the early 1990s over the negotiations of the Uruguay Round of talks on the General Agreement on Tariffs and Trade (GATT).

President Bush, it has been said, spent more time during 1991 on the Uruguay Round than any other foreign policy problem except for the Gulf War and the Russians. Fear of a breakdown of trade negotiations overlapped with concerns about the European Community's effort at launching a unified market through the Single European Act as well as with transatlantic security issues especially building a new architecture around NATO. All of these projects interacted and seemed to focus on France. Bush officials, according to one insider, worried that the Europeans, led by the French, were ganging up on the Americans and wanted to shut them out, both economically and politically, forcing them to deal with "a Europe that was protectionist, exclusivist, inward-looking and difficult to deal with."[106]

In designing a new Europe, American links with NATO took priority for Washington, but the project of a single market complicated matters. At first the Bush team, despite lingering anxiety about a coming "Fortress Europe," supported, much more explicitly than had the Reagan White House, the advance of the European Community (EC). At Boston University's commencement in 1989, where both he and François Mitterrand received honorary degrees, President Bush endorsed the Single European Act, declaring that, despite the apprehension of some Americans, "a strong, united Europe means a strong America."[107] The White House was less worried about a "Fortress Europe" than were the U.S. Congress and the business community. Trade experts in the Bush administrations like Robert Zoellick believed that openly backing integration was the best way for the United States to retain some influence within a remodeled and strengthened EC.[108] And Jacques Delors, the European Commission's president, helped allay fears by visiting the United States and dismissing nervousness about a pending rivalry between the Americans and the EC. Yet uneasiness about "Fortress Europe" persisted. In 1990 Zoellick raised the question of whether the new Europe would be "insular, itinerant, or international"—that is, whether it would be protectionist, an independent force, or a true partner with the United States.[109] Then the brutal negotiations over the GATT, along with quarrels over NATO reform—in both cases Paris acted as the principal protagonist—intensified Washington's concern about an inward-looking Europe that would discriminate against American interests. In a speech in the Netherlands shortly before the EC summit at Maastricht in late 1991 President Bush warned that "we must guard against the danger that old cold war allies will become new economic adversaries, cold warriors to trade warriors. There are signs on both sides of the Atlantic frankly, that this could happen."[110]

In late 1992 French farmers torched the Stars and Stripes in front of the American embassy in Paris and stirred the ashes with pitch-forks. Others blocked highways with their trucks and burned tires on railroad tracks. Still others protested outside McDonald's restaurants and trashed Coca-Cola vending machines. One Norman farmer complained, "The Americans have us by the throat . . . if GATT goes through, things could turn very nasty here."[111] What had stirred the countryside into this eruption of anti-Americanism?

Ostensibly the issue was rather mundane: it was one of trade talks—the Uruguay Round of GATT negotiations—and specifically farm subsidies and crops like rapeseed. (Audiovisual products and cultural protection were also involved, but this topic will be treated in chapter 6.) There were, needless to say, huge global markets, especially in agricultural exports, at stake in these talks. But the transatlantic clash over trade joined even larger issues. American officials worried that the EU might be moving toward closing the European market and becoming an ever greater rival in international commerce, especially in agricultural commodities. And it was France that was pushing Europe in the wrong direction. From the French government's perspective, keeping its rural constituents happy—farmers were adept at paralyzing traffic and arousing sympathy among the urban populace—was the most important, but not the only, issue in the Uruguay Round. France was willing to tangle with the superpower over agriculture principally because of the financial value of farm exports; after all, France and the United States were the two biggest exporters of such products in the world. France was also the largest exporter of food, including oil seeds, within Europe. And since the Americans cloaked their interests by invoking the principle of free trade, the French played the game in an even higher register by claiming farm subsidies called into question national identity, social protection, and even the future of the EU. What was at risk, it was held, was a rural way of life closely associated with national identity. Such pleas evoked nostalgia about the farm and the village as the carriers of Frenchness. Beyond identity were the European model and the EU itself. Prime Minister Pierre Bérégovoy expressed his fear that the United States intended to use the GATT to weaken the social and economic systems of Western Europe that afforded a high level of social protection.[112] Elisabeth Guigou, the minister to Europe, accused Washington and London of trying to undercut the EU, declaring, "We do not want a Europe that is just a free trade zone, as certain Anglo-Saxon countries would like to see. . . . Our attitude is explained by the French concept of Europe: it is not a Europe that is bellicose toward its outside partners, but it is a Europe that is more than a big market open to any and all influences." The European community, Guigou concluded, "is the best way of preserving our social model."[113] Moreover, the Americans were less than pure when it came to open markets: the French complained they were denied access to certain sectors of the U.S. market, such as investment in, or purchase of, American high-tech companies. The issues of the Uruguay Round were both earthly and highly principled pitting free trade against national identity and the integrity of a united Europe.

The essentials of the story are these: Almost from the beginning of the Uruguay talks in 1986 France and the United States had been at odds over reducing farm subsidies. The U.S. government, in the name of free-market access, demanded reductions in the EC's Common Agricultural Policy (CAP), which provided such support payments. French farmers were among the primary beneficiaries of the CAP, receiving an estimated $7 billion in 1991. Talks approached a climax at the end of 1992 and the deep fissures between Washington and Paris over the issue of farm subsidies threatened to send the negotiators home without a final agreement. In face of French inflexibility, the Bush administration threatened to impose punitive tariffs on imports from the EC—for example, tripling the duty on French white wine. Then in November, at Blair House in Washington, representatives of the European Commission negotiated reductions in crop subsidies under the CAP. Leon

Brittan, who shortly afterward took charge of trade talks for the commission, thought the compromise avoided a looming trade war.

If the European Commission believed the Blair House Accord conformed to the agreed-upon reform of the CAP, France did not, arguing that negotiators had exceeded their mandate and accepted more drastic reductions in subsidies and acreage than allowed. The accord committed the community to sharp cuts in subsidized agricultural exports—for example, 21 percent for grain exports, and a reduction in the acreage of oilseed crops like rapeseed. Bérégovoy called the accord "unacceptable" and a danger to "national interests": he told the National Assembly that he would veto it in the EU Council and block the GATT entirely, if necessary.[114] President Mitterrand and other socialists denounced the Blair House Accord as "imperialist," and Jacques Chirac called it an "agricultural Munich."[115]

In trying to checkmate the superpower, the French utilized several tactics. There was ultimately brinksmanship, as seen in Bérégovoy's threat to scuttle the Uruguay Round. Paris, however, wanted to avoid this option and preferred to use the EU, which was the official negotiator, as a means of leveraging its resistance. Bérégovoy asked his EU partners to sympathize with the sacrifices demanded of French farmers and pressured Chancellor Kohl to help, but only a few of the Europeans were listening. The British and the Italians endorsed the Blair House Accord; the Germans equivocated, leaving France in a weak position.[116] At risk for everyone were the many gains from global trade liberalization that a successful GATT would bring. In order to intimidate other member states the socialist prime minister had to invoke the veto threat.[117] A combination of a plausible veto and EU decision-making rules over trade, along with some backing from Belgium, Spain, and Germany, forced the commission to "clarify"—that is, try to renegotiate—the Blair House Accord.[118]

Another tactic was to dramatize the issue and blame the Anglo-Americans in order to stir popular protest against what was essentially an internal EU reform of the CAP. Alain Juppé, the foreign minister, told TV viewers that "American ukases were not a method of international discussion."[119] The Blair House Accord, in his estimation, raised issues that were "important for culture and civilization."[120] Rural France responded, and farmers burned the Stars and Stripes while singing the Marseillaise. As the talks headed toward a crisis protesters built a pyramid of wheat in the courtyard of the Louvre imitating, I. M. Pei's glass structure. "It's a symbol of European prosperity that is now under attack," one farmer commented.[121] Farm lobbyists implored the government not to "kneel" to the Americans and betray Europe by acquiescing to the "American logic."[122] A survey in late 1992 found that over 80 percent of those polled expressed solidarity with farmers and their opposition to the GATT bargain.[123] Government officials also raised the bogey of an Anglo-American conspiracy. It was said that

Figure 10. "No to the American diktat": farmers in Paris protesting against the GATT, December 1992. Courtesy Peter Turnley/Corbis.

the British were the Americans' willing partner in trying to weaken the EU, even wreck it as an economic rival.[124] Some noted that it was a British official who had negotiated the Blair House Accord. The head of the union of young farmers denounced Britain and the United States: "Europe today faces a moment of truth: right now in Washington, the two Anglo-Saxons are preparing to sacrifice the ideal of a humanist and solidarist European construction to the globalized interest of capitalists and merchants. This repudiation would be the greatest diplomatic humiliation of Europe since its creation."[125]

The political heat generated by the Blair House Accord and the CAP reform that antagonized farmers enflamed the French legislative elections of March 1993 and played a part in the defeat of the socialists. The election brought the conservatives to power and the Balladur/Juppé team took charge of negotiations; at first they appeared as obstinate as their socialist predecessors, but in the end they had to retreat. Balladur bargained hard, threatening to block ratification while trying to avoid a showdown with the superpower. He had to work quickly because there was a December deadline. Unlike during the quarrel over the entertainment industry, in which much of the EU backed it, France had had to resort to threatening a veto to garner some support from other member states against the farm deal. Even the Germans became impatient with French stubbornness. Chancellor Kohl recognized Mitterrand's troubles with French farmers, but did not want to be caught between the transatlantic rivals: he counted on the French not to scuttle the talks.[126] Balladur had to choose between a million farmers and his European community partners—especially the Germans. In June 1993 he dropped his objection to the cut in acreage for oilseed crops called for in the Blair House Accord. The Germans seem to have prevailed on this point.[127] To ease the pain for French farmers Balladur increased certain subsidies and persuaded other members of the EU to help compensate oilseed producers for their possible losses. But the Americans played hardball. It has been said that the Clinton administration made a more forceful effort at opening international commerce than any previous U.S. government. It declared there would be no GATT round unless agricultural subsidies were addressed; pressured Kohl; threatened to impose duties on European imports; and refused to renegotiate the Blair House Accord, only allowing it to be "reinterpreted."

At the last minute, in December 1993, Washington made a minor concession over the timing of the reduction in grain subsidies that softened the blow for French farmers.[128] In the end Balladur had to accept the Blair House Accord. Compromise was in the interests of France and the EU: if France remained inflexible, it would have faced serious pressure from its European partners, especially the Germans and the British, and risked the opprobrium of destroying seven years of trade negotiations. Balladur backed down and tried to put a good face on the compromise. The government pretended it had killed the Blair House Accord and Juppé said serenely that "everyone is happy because everyone has won."[129]

When the National Assembly voted on the final package there was a broad consensus that the Balladur government had achieved all that could be realistically expected. The principal political actors, which included the political parties of the Right, the major farm lobby, and some trade unions, endorsed the GATT bill.[130] Industry was silent because it wanted the GATT to succeed. If the socialists voted against it, they did so for domestic political reasons and backed the consensus that the GATT bargain was essential for a globalizing France. Opposition came from the periphery including the communists, the hard left faction of the socialists, the Green Party, and the Front National. Each had their reasons for attacking the agreement, be it protecting small farmers, developing countries, or the environment. But what they had in common was resentment against the United States, typically voicing dislike for American cultural and economic domination as a threat to French identity. On this common ground stood both those on the extreme right and left.

Despite French pretenses about killing the beast, the Americans succeeded in achieving the reform of the CAP stipulated at Blair

House. Theatrics, manipulation of the EU, and brinkmanship earned France little in the way of concessions.[131] If there was a French victory in the Uruguay Round, it was, as we shall see, over "the cultural exception" in which France enjoyed support from other Europeans, but it lost the battle over farm subsidies.

Besides the major clash provoked by the Uruguay Round there were minor dustups over issues like investments, arms sales, and mergers; for example, the French, invoking restraint of trade, stood behind the EU to block a proposed merger of aerospace giants Boeing and McDonnell Douglas in 1997. But a more acute source of trouble was American efforts at imposing international trade sanctions against Cuba and Iran.

Washington's fixation on isolating and weakening the Castro regime led to the Helms-Burton Act of 1996 that threatened lawsuits against foreign companies investing in formerly owned American properties in Cuba. In this case France was not intimidated. Foreign Minister Hervé de Charette charged that the legislation was "directly contrary to the rules which govern international trade" and the trade minister added that France would join in any reprisals the EU might take against the United States and also take steps of its own if French firms were harmed.[132] Other Europeans rallied to France's side. French officials threatened to take the Clinton administration to task before the World Trade Organization (WTO) to test the legality of the Helms-Burton Act.[133] A year later France signed an agreement with Havana that protected French firms investing in the island. In the end France resisted American pressure, insisted on maintaining normal relations with Cuba, and the United States had to back down.

In 1996 President Clinton signed the Iran-Libya Sanctions Act, which imposed penalties on foreign companies investing more than $40 million in these countries' hydrocarbon industries. Iran and Libya had been singled out as sponsors of international terrorism. Here again the French were not intimidated. President Chirac pointedly told his ambassadors that "a great country's unilateralism is threatening the international rule of law."[134] At the G7 meeting in Lyon he warned Clinton that the trade sanctions were unacceptable and they were going to produce a cycle of action and reaction that might damage the unity of the alliance.[135] Charette snidely added that "behind the intentions and the moralizing often lie powerful economic interests."[136] One senior White House official dismissed the opposition of the French and other allies to the policy of tough trade sanctions, noting that "it breaks the rules, but it works and the President says, 'we're doing it. In the end, they'll get over it. We're America, and they'll get over it.'"[137] The American hegemon spoke. But the French oil company Total escalated the conflict by signing a $2 billion contract to develop natural gas in Iran. Secretary of State Albright declared that the deal was "beyond her understanding" and accused France of undermining U.S. efforts at isolating Iran.[138] The White House proposed to enact sanctions against the French multinational, but Europeans objected. A spokesman for the EU warned that retaliation against Total was "illegal and unacceptable" and would trigger the renewal of Europe's complaint to the WTO over sanctions.[139] Neither the United States nor the EU wanted to bring the issue before the WTO. In 1998 the Clinton administration conceded and waived sanctions against Total. With the help of the EU, France had scored a small victory over Gulliver.

The Indispensable Nation

"America stands alone as the world's indispensable nation," intoned Bill Clinton at his second inaugural address.[140] Or, as he had proclaimed months earlier, "We cannot become the world's policeman, but where our values and our interests are at stake, and where we can make a difference, we must act and we must lead."[141] Gone was the reticence in foreign affairs of his first administration replaced now by a sense of American triumphalism. This new assertiveness translated into a series of setbacks for France and a high level of transatlantic discord at the end of the decade in spite of Chirac's courtship of the White House.

Most of the bilateral problems emerged from basic policy differences that were acute enough to antagonize officials, engage the media, and, at times, arouse the public. The concerns besides NATO reform were the UN, Africa, the Middle East, and, at the end of the 1990s, war again over Iraq and the former Yugoslavia (Kosovo).

Reappointment of Boutros Boutros-Ghali, a graduate of the Sorbonne and a French favorite, as secretary-general of the United Nations should have been routine since every member of the UN Security Council, save one, recommended him. But that one was the United States, which vetoed his renewal in 1996. His critics, some in the White House, castigated Boutros-Ghali for involving the U.S. military in the violence in Somalia and for interfering with the operations of NATO in Bosnia; they also viewed him as aloof and arrogant, and as a lousy administrator. Madeleine Albright, then delegate to the UN, had had several altercations with the secretary-general. Republicans in the U.S. Senate blamed him for the shortcomings of the organization and the U.S. Congress withheld payment of its funding obligations unless he was removed. Jacques Chirac personally championed Boutros-Ghali's reappointment, pointing out his overwhelming support in the Security Council. But the indispensable nation had made up its mind. Reform of the UN was impossible under Boutros-Ghali, the White House argued, and Congress had dug in. Faced with American determination, the phalanx of the secretary-general's supporters collapsed and France had to submit. Boutros-Ghali withdrew his name and the U.S. choice, Kofi Annan, became the new secretary-general.

In Africa, the United States and France worked together in supporting human rights and democracy, as they did in Somalia in 1992. But they were also rivals. As the United States became more engaged on the continent, France became more defensive.[142] Francophone areas were the country's *domaine réservé*, and these African nations lent credence to its claim to global influence and legitimated its seat on the UN Security Council. As one French official boasted, "Thanks to this tie, France will never be a Liechtenstein or even a Germany."[143] In the mid-1990s the Clinton administration became more actively engaged in Africa, openly criticized France for its postcolonial habit of propping up repressive regimes, and advocated opening up of the continent's economy.[144] Officially speaking, the Quai d'Orsay denied that it ever considered Africa as a domaine réservé, saying it welcomed America on the continent if it meant an increase in foreign aid. Yet some French officials, especially among the military and those most closely associated with maintaining the notorious patron-client networks that Mitterrand had condoned, spoke of an "Anglo-Saxon conspiracy" aimed at replacing France in central Africa.[145] Washington and Paris were at loggerheads over Zaire and Rwanda, where they acted at cross-purposes in ending civil strife that eventually turned into genocide. In central Africa, France's influence "drastically declined" to the advantage of the United States and various local interests.[146] French forces were also withdrawn from Gabon, Chad, and the Central African Republic and the number of troops scaled down on the continent. In Africa, France and the United States both cooperated and contended, but where they competed, France lost ground.

In the Middle East, France saw its once formidable influence in places like Lebanon dwindle. It tried to become a player in the Israeli-Palestinian question without much success. In 1996 President Chirac toured several Arab capitals and Israel searching for a role for France in the ongoing peace negotiations. In Damascus he spoke about the reasons why France and the European Union should be part of the negotiations, noting that "people have to get used to a return to the presence of France, in particular in this part of the world. We have interests and ideas and are determined to be seen and heard."[147] The U.S. government was equally determined, and its interests and ideas were different. It did not want the French government to complicate its mediation of the crisis. Israel also suspected Chirac of bias, and his visit to Jerusalem was marked by some tense moments. In the end the United States prevailed in preventing France as well as the EU from inserting themselves in the Israeli-Palestinian dispute.[148]

The testy character of transatlantic relations took the form of a media uproar in late 1996. According to the *Washington Post*, Hervé de Charette's snub of Warren Christopher—that is, his inopportune departure at the NATO dinner—had been an "incredible display of petulant behavior."[149] The gesture was supposedly an act of Gallic retaliation for being spurned over NATO's southern command, for subverting French dominance in Africa, for vetoing Boutros-Ghali's reappointment, and for monopolizing the Middle East peace process. The *New York Post* chimed, in accusing the Chirac government with playing the anti-American card to bolster its political standing at home. In response the French Consul General in New York denounced the *Post's* insinuation about domestic politics, arguing that the issues were purely diplomatic and that a good alliance partner was not a sycophant.[150] The American media, according to *Le Point*, were not just expressing their irritability but showing the French who was in charge and telling them to fall in line. And *Le Nouvel Observateur* opined that Washington simply expected France to implement its decisions: "Paris is either the spokesperson for the losers, or the grain of sand that fouls things up, or, in the best of circumstances, initiates policies that are often effective, but that are ultimately credited to the United States as in the Middle East or Bosnia." The bad blood between Charette and Christopher continued, clouding a gracious effort by the French foreign minister at making amends by staging a sumptuous dinner party for the outgoing secretary of state.[151]

War Again: From Desert Fox to Kosovo

This media firefight served as a prelude to a far more substantial transatlantic skirmish over Iraq at the end of the decade. France and the United States had fought together in the Gulf War, but that did not mean they agreed on how to manage Saddam Hussein after the liberation of Kuwait. Earlier differences reemerged. For example, France sided with the United States in trying to use sanctions to force a chastised Baghdad to comply with UN resolutions controlling its nuclear, chemical, and biological weapons. But later when Paris sought to weaken sanctions Washington suspected it did so simply to protect its oil interests.

In general France sought a more conciliatory policy toward Iraq, much like it had in 1991–92. From a geopolitical perspective, Paris hoped to maintain its standing in the Arab world and did not want to see Baghdad so weakened that it would invite Iran to exploit its ties with the Shi'a population. There was, in addition, a major difference in opinion between Washington and Paris about how to treat rogue states like Iraq.[152] The French believed sanctions had been ineffective: the Iraqi people suffered, Saddam survived, and the West's standing with the Arab world deteriorated. They concluded that negotiation and trade were the best ways to bring Iraq back into the international fold. In contrast the Americans thought engaging, rather than containing, Saddam was either naive or cynical. It would assist the dictatorship economically and eventually fail, or at least it would not succeed before the rogue state had wreaked massive damage. Engagement was also considered a cover for gaining advantage in the competition for Iraqi oil. The best approach for the regime in Baghdad was isolation and punishment, if necessary using military might. Thus, while the French were eager to weaken or drop economic sanctions against Saddam, U.S. Secretary of State Albright insisted they remain in place as long as it took to bring the Iraqi dictator to heel.

A potential rift occurred in late 1997 and early 1998 after Saddam blocked UN weapons inspectors. France angered American officials by abstaining rather than voting for a tough UN Security Council resolution. Clinton then threatened massive air strikes, but Chirac warned him such action would turn the entire Arab world against the West and destabilize the region. In this case the two presidents found a way to work together in a kind of "good cop/bad cop" scenario, with Chirac negotiating and Clinton menacing. It worked, and Saddam gave way and allowed the inspectors back before American aircraft and missiles were scheduled to strike in February. The French public strongly backed their government's approach to Iraq. Chirac acknowledged that the threat of force played its part in curbing Saddam, but he also declared that the crisis "proves one can obtain the respect of the law, which was our goal, by diplomacy and not only by force."[153] But then came Operation Desert Fox.

When Saddam once again interfered with UN weapons inspections he triggered an Anglo-American attack in December 1998 by aircraft and missiles targeted mainly at his capacity for developing and delivering weapons of mass destruction. The Clinton administration did not consult the Security Council because it believed it had a mandate for enforcement under existing UN resolutions, which Saddam had blatantly defied, and it knew in advance that the Security Council—given Russian, Chinese, and possibly French opposition—would not endorse military action.[154]

France disapproved of Operation Desert Fox, as the U.S. plan was called, and withdrew from participating in the southern no-fly zone, ending any French role in the military containment of Iraq. Officials in Paris assumed (correctly) that Clinton sought regime change, which the UN had never sanctioned.[155] But Chirac and his prime minister Lionel Jospin refused explicitly to condemn the bombing. They hedged—expressing reservations about Desert Fox—that it would probably fail to bring the dictator to heel and certainly add to the suffering of the Iraqi people, yet they blamed Saddam for provoking the attack. The government's equivocation derived from, on the one hand, its insistence on buttressing the Security Council's authority over Iraq and its own reluctance to use force, and, on the other hand, its fears that an open break with the United States would be ineffective and would be interpreted as concealing base motives like serving French economic interests.[156] While the Jospin government demurred, its parliamentary majority, situated on the left, demanded an immediate end to the bombing and reproached the Anglo-Americans for bypassing the Security Council, and opposition parties on the right echoed the disapproval out of fear of setting a bad precedent. And public opinion became more suspicious of U.S. ambitions because, coupled with Desert Fox, NATO began massive bombing in Kosovo three months later. Operation Desert Fox demonstrated once again that trying to act as America's partner, yet appear nonaligned, won few friends either at home or in Washington.

Far more controversial than Desert Fox, from the French public's perspective, was stopping the further disintegration of Yugoslavia at the beginning of 1998 into ethnic conflict, this time between the Serbian and Albanian communities in Kosovo. It was in the interest of the United States and its European allies to extend stability to the Balkans and to prevent a humanitarian disaster. But to most Europeans, including the French, the alliance had no mandate to intervene since Kosovo was not a matter of self-defense. Military action could only be legitimated by the United Nations. Given a certain Russian veto, such authorization was unattainable, so the Clinton administration never pursued a formal resolution. The Chirac-Jospin tandem, and other European governments, found a way round the problem by arguing that the stalemate in the Security Council and the urgency of the humanitarian crisis justified making an exception. In the end the Security Council never explicitly authorized the use of force though the secretary-general implicitly endorsed it.[157]

The use of force again divided the allies. They tentatively agreed on threatening air strikes in the event that Slobodan Milošević, the Serb president, refused to concede autonomy to the Kosovars and halt the carnage inflicted by his police and military units. But they disagreed on actually bombing because the U.S. government refused to commit ground forces to a follow-up NATO peacekeeping operation. The Clinton administration was wary of sending American troops under any circumstances. Only after negotiations between the Albanians and Serbs at the Rambouillet Conference failed in early 1999 did the White House reluctantly agree to the possibility of inserting a small number of ground troops to implement a future political settlement. The Americans mistakenly assumed the threat, or at most the demonstration, of air strikes would bring the Serbs back to the table. The British and the French, in contrast, from early on leaned toward using ground forces to enforce a political settlement and in January 1999 Tony Blair and Jacques Chirac jointly endorsed military action, including the dispatch of ground forces.[158] The Serbs refused to be intimidated by such threats and intensified their harassment and brutalization of the Albanian Kosovars, trying to force as many of the native populace as they could out of Kosovo. The Atlantic Alliance, led by a cautious White House, finally launched an air campaign in March.

Attacks by cruise missiles and allied aircraft, mostly American but some French and British, dragged on through the spring while the Serbs continued expelling Albanians from their homes. Domestic support among some of the Europeans began to waver when the bombing campaign failed to stop Milošević. There was disagreement among the allies about stronger tactics: Tony Blair aggressively pushed for a ground invasion, Chirac objected, the Germans and the Italians favored other options, and the Clinton administration slowly came around to the British position.[159] A land attack, however, proved unnecessary. By the end of May Milošević wanted to stop the bombing and NATO, with the diplomatic assistance of the Russians and the EU, won his agreement to withdraw his forces from Kosovo with the UN, providing diplomatic cover for a NATO takeover of peacekeeping. More than 30,000 troops, including 7,000 from France, formed the Kosovo Force for peacekeeping. In the end the alliance hung together and did not falter.[160]

The war in Kosovo did not damage relations between France and the United States to the extent that the events in Bosnia did; it may have even marked a high point in cooperation. But there were strains. The Americans felt confined by NATO's cumbersome apparatus; selecting bombing targets required the agreement of more than a dozen allies. The French wrestled with the U.S. military over limiting targets

Figure 11. Presidents Jacques Chirac and Bill Clinton at the Elysée celebrating French-U.S. cooperation in Kosovo, June 1999. Courtesy French Embassy Press and Information Division, Washington, D.C.

in Belgrade, seeking both to preserve their long-standing relations with the Serb people and to constrain the superpower's ability to act alone in Europe. But the French found themselves subordinate to an erratic and dominating ally. They observed, for example, how many American aircraft operated independently outside the NATO battle plan. This second Balkan crisis thus underscored, according to Chirac, the need for an autonomous European defense capacity.[161] In retrospect the initial reluctance of the United States to help stabilize Kosovo and its overbearing conduct of the bombing prompted Europeans to intensify their efforts at constructing the ESDP.

Despite relative alliance harmony, Kosovo ignited the loudest protest among French elites compared to any similar event in the 1990s. Politicians and intellectuals questioned the legitimacy, purpose, and consequences of NATO's intervention and they writhed under what appeared to be European submission to the almighty superpower.[162] Among the political class the extremes, as usual, joined hands: on the far left were the communists and the Citizen's Movement of Jean-Pierre Chevènement, and on the far right were Jean-Marie Le Pen's Front National, and senior Gaullists like Philippe Séguin, Alain Peyrefitte, and Charles Pasqua. According to these critics Chirac and Jospin had pandered to the Yankee overlords, who dragged Europeans into "NATO's war." NATO aggression had trumped the United Nations, international law, and national sovereignty. Peyrefitte called the war "illegal and immoral"; Le Pen complained that Kosovo proved Europe was "under America's heel"; and Chevènement's friends warned intervention would exacerbate ethnic and nationalist tensions in the region. The front page of the Communist Party newspaper, *L'Humanité,* resurrected a Cold War slogan: "NATO Go Home." Among the intellectuals who feasted on Kosovo were familiar names like Régis Debray, Pierre Bourdieu, Jean Baudrillard, Max Gallo, and Pierre Vidal-Naquet; they regretted Europe's powerlessness and asked for an alternative to either bombing or ethnic cleansing. The editor of the magazine *Marianne*, Jean-François Kahn, amazingly saw a kind of moral equivalence between Euro-American air strikes and Serbian forced deportations. Kahn went on to make the ludicrous prediction that one day Alsace would ask for its independence and 30,000 NATO troops would arrive to assure it. Régis Debray visited the region: he found no evidence to validate the charge of Serbian genocide and saw numerous mosques intact and Albanian pizzerias open for business while noting the damage done to Serb schools and factories. As a media expert Debray thought the French had been so "mesmerized" by CNN's coverage of the war that they accepted the State Department's account of "moral idealism and technical superiority—let's say Wilsonianism plus the tomahawk [missile]."[163] And Baudrillard opined that the United States projected its power in the Balkans as a way of preventing a united Europe from becoming a rival.[164]

The taunts of these left-wing intellectuals did not go unanswered. The anti-anti-Americans faced them down. Bernard-Henri Lévy assailed Debray while André Glucksmann proclaimed, "We have to be ready to die for Pristina [the capital of Kosovo] because to die for Pristina is to die for the future of Europe. Americans have died for Europe twice. Now we have to make sacrifices to show this continent will no longer tolerate policies that recall Stalin."[165] And scholars at a colloquium on anti-Americanism held at the Sorbonne in June joined . Sociologist Michel Wieviorka labeled such posturing as "one of the most outdated expressions of the classic figure of the French intellectual."[166] Pascal Bruckner lost his temper with the "idiocies" of Kahn, Debray, and the other anti-Americans, pointing out that it was the Europeans, not the Americans, who sought NATO's intervention. Bruckner added he much preferred the values of freedom, law, and pluralism associated with the West than those like ethnic purity that were championed by the Serbs.[167]

The French government and its defenders refuted accusations of being America's lapdog. France was a leader, not a follower. *Le Monde* claimed that the French, along with the British and the Germans, initiated the diplomatic offensive against Milošević, won the blessing of the secretary-general of the United Nations, and persuaded Clinton to both risk military intervention and engage the Russians in the diplomacy that ended the conflict.[168] Moreover, France, it was pointed out, was a major military partner whose air sorties were second in number only to those flown by the Americans. Chirac and the defense minister stressed their country's participation in the alliance's decision making, with the president asserting that France approved the targets for all 22,000 air sorties and the survival of most of the bridges in Belgrade was the doing of France.[169] Paris, at least officially, overlooked alliance tensions and argued that Kosovo proved that NATO as a transatlantic partnership could be effective.

The public largely accepted the rationale for bombing.[170] Polls suggested that between one-half and two-thirds of the French people

backed the campaign. Nevertheless, the Kosovo crisis exposed deepening mistrust of the United States. In a survey conducted as NATO
bombs fell in Yugoslavia, two of three said they were worried about "the
unique superpower status of the U.S."[171] And two-thirds also thought
Washington's motives for intervening in the Balkans were to serve its
political and military interests rather than to defend human rights and
democracy. These motives were attributed to the Clinton administration despite the fact that both President Chirac and Prime Minister
Jospin had endorsed the bombing. The same survey also showed that
almost as many of the French preferred a common European defense
without the United States as those who backed the alliance.

■ The Hyperpower

The Gulf War, Bosnia, the European pillar, the Uruguay Round, Africa, the Middle East, Cuba, Iran, Operation Desert Fox, Kosovo—it
was a long list of confrontations with the "indispensable nation." Few,
if any, of these skirmishes, which focused on international security,
geopolitics, humanitarian crises, and trade, went well for France. In the
unipolar world American power prevailed. And if one looked beyond
these kinds of encounters to rivalries over technology and popular
culture, America loomed equally large. The French foreign minister,
Hubert Védrine, added up this list and coined the term *hyperpower* for
the United States. In 1997 he declared, in a celebrated speech, that "in
this liberal and globalized world, there is today only one great power:
the United States of America. It's particularly obvious in the domain
of strategy. It's equally true in economic affairs. . . . The United States
benefits from assets denied every other power including Europe: political weight; the supremacy of the dollar; the control of communications
networks; the dream factories; new technologies, the Pentagon, Boeing, Coca-Cola, Microsoft, Hollywood, CNN, the Internet, English.
This situation is almost without precedent."[172]

The term *hyperpower* rapidly entered the lexicon of international relations and just as quickly antagonized the U.S. government. President Chirac, later noting how the term incensed Americans, sent them "into overdrive," told an American journalist he would not use it, but explained it was not pejorative: French children used the prefix *hyper-* as they did *super-*.[173]

After the Kosovo and Desert Fox skirmishes the Clinton administration became concerned about how the world, especially Europeans, viewed its power and unilateralism: the State Department referred to it as the "hegemony problem."[174] Officials in Washington read reports showing that two-thirds of the globe's populace saw the United States as the single greatest external threat and Sandy Berger, the national security adviser, worried about America being perceived as "the biggest rogue state in the world." The president warned his staff against triumphalism and addressed the issue in Aachen, Germany, on the occasion of receiving the Charlemagne Prize, which honored him for his leadership in promoting European integration. "There is a perception in Europe that America's power—military, economic, cultural—is at times too overbearing," Clinton stated. But in their heart of hearts U.S. officials took pride in their hyperpower, or as Berger, speaking of Kosovo, confided, "I never have bought the 'indispensable nation' thing; it has always bothered me because it sounds a little too triumphalist, but when it comes to something like this, America has to lead."

The French response to the full-blown emergence of America as the hyperpower was articulated at the end of the 1990s primarily by the Gaullist president Jacques Chirac and by the socialist prime minister and foreign minister Lionel Jospin and Hubert Védrine. These officials, and other sympathetic foreign policy experts, spelled out their grievances, focusing on the general deportment of the United States toward France, the construction of a European defense, and the authority of international organizations.

"Imperious" was the common charge against the indispensable one. In a long interview intended for an American audience Védrine acknowledged cooperation with the Clinton administration; dialogue, he noted, "has never been more intense or consistent" and "in Kosovo we worked together in the spirit of true partnership." But then the foreign minister retracted much of what he had just said. "America as a whole can see itself only as the leader," he complained, and "when the United States works with others, it always has a hard time resisting the temptation to tell them what to do."[175] Jacques Andréani, the former ambassador to Washington, was even more candid. America's success in the post–Cold War era, Andréani wrote, led it toward condescension and unilateralism. It tended to ignore its European allies when disagreements arose and acted without consultation, as if its views had universal validity. The French, he added, resented the way the Americans classified others as good or evil, and championed principles like "open markets" that were in fact self-serving. Andréani scolded Bush and Clinton for confusing their "benevolent hegemony" with the general interest.[176]

Bypassing international organizations was a second major grievance. After Operation Desert Fox, Jospin assailed American and British air strikes for moving relations between Baghdad and the United Nations backward—away from negotiation and toward confrontation. "The United States often acts in a unilateral way and has trouble achieving its ambition of mobilizing the international community," he observed.[177] In general, French officials considered the Clinton administration's willingness to intervene militarily in Kosovo without explicit UN authorization a dangerous precedent. The Republicans on Capitol Hill were singled out for their isolationist tendencies—for example, the Senate's rejection of the Test Ban Treaty—and blatant disdain for the United Nations. Washington, in the eyes of French foreign policy makers, had retreated from its early postwar multilateralism and its former respect for international agencies like the WTO. Presidents Bush and Clinton, unlike their predecessors in the era of President Harry S. Truman, had not lived up to their promises of multilateral diplomacy and respect for the consent of the international community.

The reality of the "new world order," according to Andréani, has been "NATO [acting] in the role of gendarme armed permanently with a blank check."[178]

Washington's apparent hypocrisy about European defense was another major irritant. Years of struggling with Americans over constructing the European pillar left Paris deeply suspicious of Washington's professed interest in sharing responsibility. The Americans, according to Védrine, "have always been for sharing the burden. They've never been much for sharing the decision making."[179] Or, as Chirac exclaimed in an interview in the *New York Times*, Washington's criticism of the European Rapid Reaction Force almost caused him to fall off his chair: "The Americans kept saying Europe had to do more for its own defense, so we finally said, all right, we will. Now you shouldn't criticize us for doing what you wanted us to do."[180]

These appraisals led the French foreign policy establishment to revise the way they addressed the hyperpower in the last few years of the twentieth century. They dubbed this approach the new realism.[181]

Realism began with the premise that France was still a global power. France may be overshadowed, but, according to Védrine, it still numbered among the elite nations. Of the nearly two hundred nations of the world, he reasoned, France was one of the five or six with global influence. He referred to assets like France's seat on the UN Security Council; its military forces, alliances, and diplomatic stature; its place in the G7; and its business and economic resources. "And we also possess our soft power," he noted; "our language, our intellectuals, our culture, our writers, our nonstate actors, our artists, our music, our cuisine, the beauty of our country, our image."[182] Yet the disparity in power with the United States convinced Védrine that his compariots needed to be realistic. If France had "good cards" to play in international affairs, it needed to stop "acting like the Great Nation" whose voice everyone was supposed to heed.[183] It was "unhealthy" to insist upon the universality of French civilization and believe France occupied "a position close to the center of the world." He scolded the French for their arrogance, which deceived themselves and provoked others. "We are a country that has trouble facing up to the reality of the world," he admitted.[184]

In dealing with the Americans Védrine rebuked the French for "routine and vain aggressiveness that led to nothing" and only compromised efforts to convince "other essential partners" from working with France.[185] "Let us try to have relations with the United States that are normal, calm, dispassionate and useful," he suggested.[186] The proper way for France to deal with the hyperpower was to "perform a delicate but indispensable balancing act." France should say yes when it was in its interest to do so and to say no when it was not, he explained; "That's what it means to be friends that are allied but not aligned."[187]

The new realism in transatlantic relations formed one element of a grander vision that looked beyond the unipolar world. The antidote to the hyperpower was multipolarity and multilateralism—a formula that some American officials saw as merely a device to check the United States. A multipolar world, according to Chirac, described a global equilibrium based on several centers of power such as India, China, Japan, and Russia, as well as the EU and the United States; the latter two occupied a certain privileged status. In 1998 the French president observed, "It's in everyone's interest that we are heading toward a multipolar world. The United States, to be sure, is at the top. Europe, in spite of its problems, is growing stronger." And so were others. "All this is leading us toward a world composed of several poles of political, economic, and cultural power."[188] The unipolar world, according to the French president, was giving way inevitably to a multipolar system and the only question was whether or not this transition could be accomplished peacefully. And in a multipolar order not even the hyperpower could act alone; it needed Europe. Security in the unipolar world was precarious, Chirac warned, especially when the American Congress "too often gives in to the temptations of unilateralism and isolationism."[189] In other words, Gulliver could be either too rambunctious or too reticent for the French to feel safe.

President Chirac was explicit about Europe's future: "My ambition is for the [European] Union gradually to assert itself as an active and powerful pole, as an equal with the United States, in the world of the twenty-first century, which . . . will be multipolar."[190] The European Union should equip itself "with all the instruments of a real power," alluding to the creation of the Euro and "a Europe with a credible defense, capable of acting either within the Atlantic alliance or autonomously according to the nature of the crises."[191]

Multilateralism was the twin of *multipolarity*. It was a term Americans once used to describe a virtuous approach to world trade, but in the Gallic vocabulary of the 1990s it referred to locating decision making and legitimacy in a multilateral institutional setting like the United Nations, the International Monetary Fund, the World Trade Organization, or the European Union. These institutions represented progress in international relations as nations moved from national sovereignty and confrontation toward shared sovereignty and international cooperation. Strengthening multilateral bodies would offset American dominance. The French president hammered away at the pretentions of the United States and NATO: "France cannot, and will not, accept an organization of regional defense arrogating to itself the role of world policeman, [a] role entrusted by the charter of the UN to the Security Council and to it alone."[192] Tying down Gulliver with international institutions and rules was the aim.[193]

■ Looking back, one might ask: How, and how well, did fin-de-siècle France cope with the U.S. hyperpower? What would a report card on French transatlantic diplomacy show?

Negotiating alone with the U.S. government usually turned out badly. Mitterrand's project at "rebalancing the alliance" by building a European defense capacity outside NATO, which had only tepid support from the Germans, was checked by the Americans and other Europeans who preferred the status quo. Similarly, Chirac, acting in virtual isolation on the question of NATO enlargement, had to surrender his agenda and concede to Clinton. And without backing from its EU partners in the GATT negotiations, France could not restrain the Americans. To be sure, the U.S. government's modus operandi for treating the cantankerous Gauls was to isolate them, but the tactic did not necessarily persuade the French to surrender. As Jacques Andréani noted, "The certainty of being on the right path and in the right leads Americans to treat our critiques with disdain and our country's advantages with condescension. Their major argument is that France is often alone in its critiques and its objections. It is the only argument that, by its very nature, does not impress the French. For them, it is possible to be right all alone, which does not mean that one is right because one is alone."[194]

Negotiating with European support or through international organizations as an alternative, however, did not achieve much better results. Even though Chirac enjoyed considerable backing from other Europeans for his project of constructing a European pillar within NATO, he failed to convince the Clinton administration. The United States simply refused to share command with the Europeans. And in the case of the reappointment of Boutros Boutros-Ghali as secretary-general of the UN, France lined up the entire Security Council against the United States, but the latter ignored the august body and named its own candidate. Or when France and the United Kingdom tried to use the UN to control NATO, as they did during the final stages of the conflict in Bosnia, they only frustrated the United States without deterring it. France had more success utilizing international bodies and rules on trade issues, especially when it enjoyed EU support and invoked the WTO, as it did in blocking the United States on sanctions against Cuba, Iran, and Libya.

Another option was playing the role of the hyperpower's partner—either prudently or unreservedly. But when France behaved as a cautious ally it forfeited its leverage with the United States. In the Gulf War, Mitterrand's hesitancy and search for a diplomatic alternative aroused Washington's suspicions and did not slow the march to

Desert Storm. In the end Washington led and Paris followed. In trying to control Saddam Hussein after the Gulf War, Chirac also oscillated between acting as loyal lieutenant and critic to the White House
and achieved little in influencing Clinton's decisions. The alternative
to caution—adopting the role of a loyal, fully committed partner—
brought only slightly better results because this posture ran the risk
of being taken for granted. During the Dayton Accord talks France
was ignored and humiliated. In the Kosovo crisis the loyalty strategy
earned a measure of cooperation and some consultation in military operations. But Chirac's courtship of Clinton and his offer of rejoining
the Atlantic Alliance did not pay off. Bill said no to Jacques.

What remained as alternatives were acting without the hyperpower or engaging in brinksmanship. In Bosnia, at least until 1994,
France, along with other Europeans, tried to pacify a combat zone
without the United States. They had no success. In the end the Europeans and the UN had to call on NATO for help and, once engaged, the
U.S. government ran military operations and dictated the settlement
in Dayton to the dismay of many Europeans. The most extreme form
of defiance, brinksmanship, occurred only once at the climax of negotiations over agricultural subsidies in the Uruguay Round of GATT
negotiations. Paris encouraged rural protest and threatened to scuttle
the entire round of trade talks. Such theatrics did not convince Washington, and Paris ended up conceding.

What was the lesson? Appearing as either the eternal Grinch or
behaving as a loyal subordinate failed. Mobilizing other Europeans,
especially through the EU, helped, but it was an uncertain and difficult route. The same was true for international institutions. In essence,
when the hyperpower said "no," it was "no" and France had to retreat.
Uncle Sam was unreceptive to the entreaties, advice, blandishments,
and threats of Marianne. So what was left was acting as a wise consultant to the hyperpower, avoiding confrontation, and, at the same time,
building a multipolar/multilateral international system to supersede
the unipolar order. But this "realism" would still have to face transat-

lantic differences over such fundamentals as building a European pillar, dealing with the Russians, controlling rogue states, employing trade sanctions, and engaging international institutions. And realism would still have to overcome the mistrust that was common to governments on both sides of the Atlantic and remained firmly anchored in public perceptions—a mistrust that impaired cooperation.[195]

In international affairs, as in so much else, France measured itself against the United States during the final decade of the twentieth century. The compliment was not returned by the United States, which passed off the French with indifference and mistrust. For the French government and the French people, however, it was the United States, the overbearing, unreliable, and impetuous ally, that blocked their ambitions and denied them their rightful place and prestige in world affairs. Responding to the hyperpower defined French foreign policy: constraining America and attaining self-reliance was the standard of measurement for the country's success and identity.

6.

The French Way: Economy, Society, and Culture in the 1990s

When the G7 gathered in Denver, Colorado, in June 1997, President Bill Clinton, in an exuberant mood, invited Jacques Chirac, Helmut Kohl and other world leaders to don cowboy outfits. But the French president and the German chancellor declined the invitation; they refused to wear Western hats and boots. The Europeans held back in both dress and spirit. They were mildly offended at the way Clinton's economic advisers extolled America's success and lectured them about how they could profit from the new global economy. When reporters asked Chirac whether or not Europeans should adopt American recipes, he shot back, "Naturally not. Each has his own model, our structures are different. We have the greatest respect for others, but we have our traditions, our model, and we wish to hold on to it."[1] On board his return flight Chirac complained that he found the Americans "*un peu* too much."[2]

In domestic affairs America served as a foil to fin-de-siècle France in two ways, as a challenge and as a warning. On the one hand the example of American dynamism and its intrusion within the Hexagon made the French take notice of a worrisome gap between the two countries. The gap had economic, technological, and cultural dimensions and it commanded a response. In this sense America acted as an incentive for change. On the other hand America functioned as an example to be shunned. If the New World's successes—for example, in economic growth—were admired, the ways Americans employed to attain such prosperity were to be avoided. America was simultaneously a model and an antimodel. France had to catch up without necessarily emulating the transatlantic giant. What the French accomplished in the 1990s was to adapt features of the American way, without admitting it, in an effort to find their own way forward. This chapter addresses policies of the Fifth Republic that were explicitly, or in some instances only implicitly, inspired by the American model. Americans, or Anglo-Americans, may not have been invoked when discussing reforms, but they were often present. The French used a coded vocabulary. Everyone knew that the economic doctrine of "ultraliberalism" or words like *précarité* or *flexibilité* when used in the context of employment meant *Beware, the Anglo-Saxons are coming.*

A comprehensive examination of the American challenge is an impossible task in a single chapter, and I shall leave topics like immigration or gender, where America was at least indirectly involved, to others.[3] The dimensions I have chosen to present are economic and social policy, business practice, and cultural affairs. Even here I have been selective. Economic and social policy, for our purposes, will encompass issues like economic and technological competitiveness, unemployment, and the welfare state. In cultural affairs my focus will be on language—that is, the spread of American English—and on the audiovisual sector.

Economy and Society

The dilemma France faced in the 1990s was that it trailed the Anglo-Americans yet was unwilling, at least openly, to follow their lead. France lagged behind the "Anglo-Saxons" in several respects including adding jobs, developing an information technology sector, and attaining international competitiveness. It was distressing to hear the Americans boast about creating millions of new jobs, to read about talented young French men and women, perhaps as many as 50,000, emigrating to Silicon Valley, and to learn of the purchase of equity in French companies by American investors. When the president of the huge California public employee pension fund arrived in Paris, his visit was likened to the arrival of the new masters of globalization—those awe-inspiring CEOs who forced companies to give priority to short-term profits and retrench employees to raise productivity.[4] Even the nation's architectural symbols were seemingly in play: at a stormy meeting of the Paris City Council in 1998 the mayor had to reassure his colleagues that a bid by a subsidiary of General Motors to buy a controlling interest in the Eiffel Tower would not be accepted. The British were almost as threatening as their American cousins. It was upsetting to learn that the United Kingdom seemed to have surpassed France in gross domestic product (GDP). But it was downright embarrassing to watch young French workers and businesspeople cross the English Channel to labor in what they deemed a more favorable business climate. In the English town of Ashford, located on the Euro star rail line that linked the two countries, French entrepreneurs registered over three hundred French-owned companies, one of which was a bakery that imported dough and supplied the local Gallic population with baguettes. Even worse, famous *couturiers* like Givenchy and Christian Dior hired British designers.

At the same time that the Anglo-Americans were forging ahead France was encountering troubles caused by both the EU and globalization. On the one hand there were the adjustments forced by the pace of European integration, especially in readying for the coming of the Euro. After the Maastricht Treaty of 1992, which initiated the process that would lead to the creation of a single currency system for the EU, pressure mounted on France to meet the various "Maastricht criteria" for adopting the Euro, including keeping domestic inflation and budget deficits in check. On the other hand France faced problems stemming from widening foreign trade and globalization. The economy had become more thoroughly immersed in trade than at any time in its past. National economic frontiers counted less and less and international competitiveness more and more. Meanwhile anxiety grew about the effects of globalization. Fears that foreign competition contributed to unemployment prompted a government investigation in 1993 that warned three to five million jobs in France were threatened by low-wage countries.[5]

Anglo-American performance made certain domestic troubles seem worse. Unemployment was the number one problem. It had reappeared in earnest following the oil crisis of the 1970s. First one million *chômeurs*, then two million, and by 1993 over three million. During the 1990s French unemployment hovered around 11 percent in comparison to the United States, where it was half that. At the end of the decade the relative jobless rates were: France, 10.5 percent; the United Kingdom, 6 percent; and the United States, 4.2 percent. Despite economic growth in the late 1980s the private sector had created few jobs and then growth decelerated in the early 1990s. Double-digit unemployment rates became the rule after 1985, and for the young they reached as high as 25 percent by 1997. Whereas the United States between 1970 and 1995 had more than doubled the hours of work created in the private-sector services, a major employer of youth, in France they declined. And the French who were unemployed needed five times as long to find new work as their American counterparts.[6] Critics complained that the rigidities of the labor market and the high social payments for employers kept unemployment high by discouraging employers from hiring. Payroll taxes for health, retirement, unemployment insurance, and other charges paid by both employer and employee, were more than double those in the United Kingdom in 1990.[7]

Unemployment was not the only domestic trouble. The welfare state had become expensive, and in some ways inadequate and inequitable. France was an outlier in the trends of the 1980s and '90s: instead of wholesale retrenchment, as in other advanced states, it increased social spending, even adding new programs. In social expenditures it moved near the top of the countries in the Organisation for

Economic Co-operation and Development by the late 1990s. Deficits in the social security system, most of which came from pensions and health care, increased rapidly in the 1980s and mushroomed in the 1990s, reaching 62 billion francs in 1995.[8] At the same time the system seemed to reward the haves and exclude the have-nots. Life in many of the grim suburbs or *banlieues* that surrounded major cities, marked by unemployment, drugs, crime, and desperation, testified to the failure of social policy. A closely related problem was the elephantine dimensions of the state and its budget. French total tax revenue as a percentage of GDP was much greater than that of the United States, and larger than that of almost every other Western European country. And French public expenditures as percent of GDP ranked among the highest in the EU.[9] Spending was inflated by the large number of employees on the state payroll, a good number of whom had been added under socialist governance in the early 1980s. It was estimated that over half the French population were civil servants or the parents, children, or spouses of one.[10] Some public enterprises, notably the national railways, ran huge deficits, and the practice of bailing out poor performers was often hugely expensive.

This ominous list of problems should not obscure the progress made on other fronts. Most notably, the adoption by President François Mitterrand after 1988 of the *franc fort,* requiring restrictive fiscal and monetary policies—which were scrupulously followed by his successors—had wrung most inflation out of the system.[11] Equally important, the economy looked increasingly to the world. Since the 1960s, expanding trade, especially with other countries in the European Union; the entry of multinationals; and massive foreign investment, much of it from the United States, all opened the economy. France had become far more dependent on imports and exports than ever before. For example, when the Fifth Republic began, the part imports and exports played in GDP were 9.7 and 8.9 percent, respectively. By 1980 these shares had climbed to 26.5 and 24.2 percent.[12] By 1990 France had, on the basis of the percentage of production exported and the fraction of consumption accounted for by imports, a far more open economy than either that of the United States or Japan (if somewhat less open than either that of the United Kingdom or Germany).[13] And for the first time in over a decade, after 1991 France began to run a trade surplus. Rates of growth in GDP, which had been miserable at the beginning of the 1990s and modest in the middle of the decade, accelerated from 1998 to 2000. Meanwhile, a succession of governments, both conservative and socialist, from the early 1980s on tried to reform the social security system by such means as controlling costs and reducing benefits—even while they added programs.

In fact, the French had much to brag about. They enjoyed the benefits of excellent and extensive public services like a splendid transportation network; the job protection afforded by a rigorous labor code; generous social rewards, including lavish unemployment benefits, hefty family allowances, virtually free education, high-quality medical care for which patients paid only a small share of costs, and substantial pensions for workers, both public and private, after forty years of service. Far more French workers could afford to take early retirement than Americans. And there was generous paid leave: whereas Americans had the stingiest vacation time in the industrialized West, averaging only two weeks after three years on the job, the French enjoyed five weeks of annual paid vacation—the longest in Europe—plus a guaranteed minimum annual income. The French benefited from one of the most comprehensive systems of social protection in the world. Moreover, economic sectors that were deemed either "strategic" or "prestigious" or formed part of the national patrimony benefited from state protection and often from subsidies. Farming and the cinema were examples. And when prominent firms including banks faced bankruptcy or hostile takeovers, the state frequently intervened, sometimes in defiance of EU rules on competition. For France the question became, Was there a way to close the gap with the Anglo-Americans without sacrificing this comfortable arrangement? Or, as a former minister of economics expressed the question, "How can we catch up with the United States, without losing our souls, that is without sacrificing the solidarity that lies at the heart of the European model?"[14]

Domestic problems like stubborn unemployment rates, the rigidities and costs of a paternalistic state, and lagging international competitiveness, especially vis-à-vis the Anglo-Americans, provoked introspection among public officials not unlike what France experienced during and after the Second World War. In 1990 the government planning commission summoned experts to answer the question, What would it mean to be French in the year 2000? The planners focused on the country's ability to meet challenges to practices like state *dirigisme* and to national identity. The disarray of national identity, as they phrased it, came in part from the loss of a universal political and cultural mission. The French voluntarist model of democracy, which featured the revolutionary process and the Republican state as guide and emancipator, had lost its pride of place to other political traditions, especially to Anglo-American liberalism: "It is no longer the French tradition of centralization and the revolutionary overhaul of society that appears at the heart of Western history; it is rather the less lyrical and less flamboyant Anglo-Saxon tradition of monitoring power and protecting against arbitrariness."[15] Meanwhile the French state faced challenges from without by such forces as globalized markets and from within by those who believed democracy derived from civil society rather than from the state as liberator. Jobs and the standard of living, according to the planners, in a globalized world could not be guaranteed by the state but had to be earned through international competitiveness. The answer to economic catch-up was not less state but a different kind of state, one that would collaborate with and negotiate among economic actors: "It's the end of a certain historical role embodied after the Liberation in the form of French *dirigisme*."[16] The planners advised moving toward a freer economy without, however, imitating the Anglo-Saxons. These forecasters proved prescient.

How to redirect and energize the French economic and social system without importing the American model was the dilemma. Pursuing the path of what was termed "ultraliberalism," which itself was a nasty euphemism for what went on across the Channel first under Margaret Thatcher and later across the Atlantic beginning with Ronald Reagan, might jeopardize the benefits and traditions embedded in the Gallic order. Social solidarity and state paternalism seemed at risk. One journal on the left framed the issue this way: the Americans had created more than 11 million new jobs, reduced unemployment to less than 5 percent, effected 3.5 percent growth in GDP without inflation, and advanced so far with twenty-first-century industries like information technology that the Europeans and the Japanese feared they would never catch up. But U.S. methods like downsizing, retrenchment, income inequality, and temporary work had unbearable social costs. The question became, "How can we obtain the same results as the United States without adopting their methods?"[17]

American Ultraliberalism versus Republican Solidarity

Both "liberalism," and more emphatically "ultraliberalism," was coded language in the political discourse of the 1990s—avatars for the Anglo-American market approach to economic and social problems. The debate over liberalism demands close attention because it reveals how American practices divided the political elite, figured prominently in an election, and informed the making of policy.

In general the French held a low opinion of American market liberalism. As we have seen, three out of four of those interviewed in the 1990s routinely castigated the U.S. economic system. It was commonly described as "savage" and "brutal" and marked by job insecurity, insufficient welfare protection, a low minimum wage, and inadequate public services. American "hard capitalism," it was said, exhibited little concern for the environment and even less concern for those who couldn't compete. Americans, referring to their deference to the rich, actually approved egregious income inequality, the French asserted. *Le*

Monde was typical: it acknowledged the magnitude of American economic achievements but ruefully pointed out the "pauperization" of many American workers and the précarité of employment.[18]

Claims by the euphoric Americans that they had found the way to perpetual prosperity did not impress French experts.[19] They admired the American "job machine" but doubted that it created well-paid and secure types of employment. They pointed out the high level of indebtedness of companies and households, the stock market bubble, and the rising deficit in current accounts. One day, it seemed, the United States would have to face the constraints that limited other nations. America was dynamic but, they contended, it had not transcended the business cycle.

French reservations about America in the 1990s extended to a society that seemed violent and fractured by inequalities of race and wealth. Three out of four of those polled said American and French values were different with respect to the family, morality, law and order, work, and lifestyle. The French complained about Americans' mania for political correctness, their fixation with work, the unassimilated immigrants, the crime rate, the gun culture, treatment of the homeless, and reliance on capital punishment. The French ambassador to the United States wrote that the "harshness" of Americans was reflected in the way they fought crime and in their competitive ethos.[20] A prominent journalist on the left described the social costs of "American methods" as "the poverty of twenty million whites and ten million blacks, the largest prison population in the world, the weakest social protection, the implosion of the educational system, crime and drugs in the urban ghetto."[21] Correcting French weaknesses by imitating American liberalism did not seem like the answer.

If the good economy could not be achieved solely through market forces, neither could the good society. The better route, most French people assumed, was through a commitment to social solidarity, or, more accurately, to republican solidarity. *Republican* precedes this notion of solidarity because it derives from the founding principles of republicanism that date back to the French Revolution. The French believed they took the goals of equality and fraternity, as the basis of a national community, more seriously than did Anglo-Americans. They attacked, rather than exalted, inequalities of income and wealth, and they preached the responsibility of all for the poor.

The editor of *Le Nouvel Observateur* contrasted Franco-American approaches to social policy. Citing conversations with President Clinton's economic team, Jean Daniel reported that these advisers, despite the spectacular achievements of their methods, admitted they had impoverished and marginalized many of their compatriots. As Daniel observed, "Modernity, happily, is no longer in any case a matter of renovating the economy by allowing an invisible hand, that of the market, to assure the happiness of everyone while prohibiting the state from imposing the slightest regulation. Now that communism has collapsed, it's not liberalism that has triumphed. On the contrary, it's the constructive critique of capitalism—its moralization—that has been rehabilitated. We see this flourishing in ten European countries (France could be the eleventh) that have rewarded themselves with a left-wing government and have declared their support for a social Europe. . . ."[22] A social Europe, in contrast with an Anglo-American liberal Europe, for Daniel meant, at a minimum, placing social objectives—like helping the disinherited and the insecure—at the same level as economic, monetary, and political goals.[23]

Any reflection on this virtuous presentation of republican solidarity and the reality of social life in France at the fin de siècle would have exposed discrepancies.

Solidarity both masked a defense of the status quo by vested interests and failed to reach all the disenfranchised, especially those living in the dismal banlieues. Much of the resistance to ultraliberalism and the pose of solidarity was little more than protecting entitlements or so-called *droits acquis* or *acquis sociaux*. Some scholars have denigrated republican solidarity as a fraud.[24] All was not perfect with the French model and some, especially on the far right, wanted it overhauled.[25] Nevertheless, the republican social contract remained the intellectual and political bulwark against adopting Anglo-American social policy.

Historically, free-market liberals had a difficult time getting a fair hearing in France. Neither before nor during the fin de siècle did the French embrace laissez-faire fundamentalism to the extent of either the British or the Americans. Raymond Aron once spoke of liberals in France as "the eternal vanquished, the internal exiles, admired outside of France but without visible influence inside the country."[26] Liberal economics had few champions in the 1990s; more common were rants against it, such as the antimarket polemic titled *The Economic Horror,* which sold some 350,000 copies.[27] Gallic aversion for the market was both striking and resilient. In a 2005 survey of twenty nations the French led everyone, including other Europeans, in disagreeing with the proposition that "the free enterprise system and free-market economy is the best system on which to base the future of the world."[28] (Americans, of course, largely approved.) The market was, and is, not popular in the land of the Gauls.

"Ultraliberalism," with its Anglo-American associations, was not an acceptable option for either the Right or the Left in the 1990s. Plain vanilla "liberalism," however, was tolerable on the mainstream right— though it was usually spoken sotto voce. On the left even "liberal" was offensive. Among the political class there was virtual unanimity that America was not a model for reform. Liberalization would come, but only *à la française.* As Alain Duhamel wrote in 1993 about attitudes toward the market, "The Socialists are still reticent, the communists remain stoutly opposed, the Jacobins are allergic, the ecologists are ignorant, and the vested interests have an insatiable appetite for exemptions."[29] This remained the case throughout the 1990s.

The Left in this decade updated its critique and reified free-market liberalism into an economic vocabulary conflating it with economic inequality; rampant profit making; the disruptive forces of globalization, including the outsourcing of jobs; and, to be sure, the Anglo-Saxons.[30] In the era of globalization *les gros,* the trope that market economies are run by a wealthy oligarchy, became the "masters of the universe" (*maîtres de monde*)—that is, the CEOs of American investment funds who reputedly acted as the pitiless agents of the new share-holder capitalism. *Liberalism* was equated with the market and all its unwelcome consequences at the expense of acknowledging its more appealing political dimension, which spoke to individual rights and civil society. To express their distaste the term was usually preceded by prefixes like *hyper-* or *ultra-*.

One should not, however, exaggerate French aversion for market forces. Strictly speaking, France was a market economy and became more so at the end of the century. If virtually no one invoked Reaganomics as they did in the 1980s, at least "liberalism," in the sense of recognizing the benefits of allocating resources via the market, gained adherents among conservative politicians, some economists, and business managers—especially those with global ties. It became legitimate among mainstream parties on the right such as the Union pour la Démocratie Française (UDF) and the Rassemblement pour la République, and had its spokesman in the person of Prime Minister Édouard Balladur. And in the late 1990s, in a grudging way, moderate socialists like Lionel Jospin and Dominique Strauss-Kahn came to endorse a "managed" market economy. The market gained disciples among policy makers across the political spectrum—even if few celebrated it openly. Among the public at large, polls suggested that despite a continued attachment to a powerful state acting in the general interest, there was a growing acceptance of the market economy—at least in principle. By the end of the decade, two-thirds of voters on the moderate right and almost as many on the left endorsed the market economy.[31]

■ Liberalization by Stealth

In the 1990s the Fifth Republic opened the economy to such an extent that it resembled what it looked like in the halcyon days before the First World War. It deregulated, privatized, and encouraged international competitiveness, including foreign investment, and it tried to streamline the welfare state by trimming the costs of pensions and health care. But none of this, or so it was claimed, was in imitation of the Americans. To paraphrase Philip Gordon and Sophie Meunier, who explained the process of "globalization by stealth," one might speak, in this case, of "liberalization by stealth."[32]

What was driving fin-de-siècle France toward market remedies was less the gap with America than it was the need to reform an unsustainable welfare state, reduce unemployment, and gain international competitiveness, especially in light of European integration and globalization. Politicians on both the right and the left improvised: they tried, sometimes simultaneously, a dose of competition as well as what they hoped was more enlightened dirigisme. But they masked their turn toward the market by claiming their reforms did not subvert the French model and were not inspired by the Anglo-Americans. The elite of the Fifth Republic had to be wary and employ subterfuge if they were to introduce competitive policies as remedies for social and economic problems: they had to liberalize, yet sustain, republican solidarity and some measure of dirigisme.

Both socialist and conservative governments tacked away from the protectionist and statist policies of the past. They deregulated financial markets by opening them to foreigners, giving the central bank autonomy, initiating a NASDAQ-like stock market, and freeing investment from the control of the Ministry of Finance. Public monopolies like Electricité de France and France Télécom were exposed to private competition. The labor code was circumvented. In spite of rigid rules on employment contracts, loopholes allowed millions of new jobs as temporary work. Privatization accompanied deregulation. In 1993 Édouard Balladur specified a score of companies, starting with such giants as Elf Aquitaine (petroleum) and Rhône-Poulenc (chemicals and pharmaceuticals), and by the end of the decade virtually all these targeted firms had been returned to private ownership. All of the banking and insurance sectors were gradually privatized, as were most state-run manufacturing industries. Minority private shareholding was permitted in such flagship nationalized firms as Air France. In fact, more privatization occurred under the socialists between 1997 and 2002 than under any of their conservative predecessors. Governments, both conservative and socialist, reduced taxes, worked to open the economy to EU competition, and adopted restrictive fiscal and monetary policies to prepare for the coming of the Euro at the end of the decade. And they blessed foreign trade and foreign investment and encouraged small business start-ups.

"Le capitalisme zinzin" is the way the editor of *Le Monde* typed the French economy that emerged in the fin de siècle.[33] "Zinzin" meant "nutty," but it had also come to refer to "institutional investors" like foreign pension funds. This Gallic version of the "Anglo-Saxon economy" featured dependence on foreign investors, a market unimpeded by government regulation, a shrinking public sector, a potent stock market, and almighty shareholders. Its elite were the managers of recently privatized firms who courted stockholders and spiced their speech with imported terms like *les startups*. In his book this prominent journalist urged the French people to face this new capitalism but also to gain control over it.

By the late 1990s France had the same level of openness to trade as Germany, almost as much as the United Kingdom, and twice that of the United States.[34] Entrepreneurship became fashionable: at the end of the decade a survey found that thirteen million people over the age of eighteen wanted to create their own company; only three million had had such an aim in 1992.[35] In 1999 one of the sharpest detractors of French economic policy, the *Economist*, admitted that it had "liberalized beyond recognition."[36] Looking back at the period, Peter Hall has written, "Within Europe, France stands out, not only because it has liberalized some domains more fully than its neighbors, but because, in so doing, it has dismantled the most forceful system of *dirigisme* in Europe."[37]

What did America have to do with this liberalizing trend of public policy? If the grander forces of European integration and globalization and pressing domestic problems like a rigid labor market and costly welfare state forced the issue, America served as a foil that both inspired and disguised adaptation and shaped political discourse. Given Gallic reticence to invoke America as a positive reference, it is possible to identify only a few examples of direct influence on social and economic policies. Such a strategy was, to say the least, not politically wise. If America, in only a few instances, served as a disguised model for Gallic innovation, it certainly framed the general political debate on reform.

The principal, but not the exclusive, impetus for American-style reform came from the Right. Among self-proclaimed party loyalists, those who backed right-wing parties expressed more sympathy for America than those on the left. A major reason for this preference was a modicum of respect for the American economy. Where over one-third of right-wing partisans found merit in the American model, only 19 percent on the left did.[38] The Right, more than the Left, associated American economic prowess with innovation and social mobility.

On the mainstream right there was advocacy for free-market liberalism, but not for the Anglo-American version. Édouard Balladur, the Gaullist prime minister from 1993 to 1995, accepted the label of liberal, but denied he was ultraliberal and distanced himself from "the unbridled liberalism of the 1980s"—that is, the liberalism of Ronald Reagan and Margaret Thatcher. Liberalism needed rules, he insisted.[39] Rhetorically he asked, "What is the market? It is the law of the jungle, the law of nature. And what is civilization? It is the struggle against nature."[40] "What France needs is to invent a model that balances liberty and solidarity," he explained, adding that he dismissed both "outmoded ideologies: the one based on unbridled and heartless liberalism and the other based on *dirigisme* and protectionism."[41] Responding to the protectionist wing in his party, Balladur said the French economy was too open to the world to contemplate closing it to globalization. He blamed relative French decline on the accumulation of restrictions on economic life and sought greater freedom for producers and labor, noting, "we have still not emerged from social democracy, neither in fact nor, more seriously, in spirit."[42] The UDF, the other conservative party, held positions close to that of Balladur. As prime minister, he advanced privatization and deregulation; he also introduced a new private pension scheme, eased certain social taxes, and simplified the labor code—all aimed at strengthening market forces and improving French competitiveness. But there were strict limits. As premier he refused any "American-style deregulation of the labor code" that might endanger the minimum wage, claiming "it's not necessary, under the pretext of fighting unemployment, to destroy all our social protections."[43]

Jacques Chirac, like Balladur, tried to bend Gaullism away from its past without abandoning *dirigisme* altogether, noting, "Every society has as much need for stability as it does for flexibility. Because the economy has no sense of serving man, it needs markers, fixed points, as well as continuity. The state must play its role in clarifying the future, in building confidence, in explaining the reforms that accompany change; and it must also avoid ruptures. The state must make the pace of markets and that of men compatible in order to build for the long term beyond the fluctuations of the economy."[44] Yet if the state's role was to create the conditions for economic growth, its function was not "to monitor, frame, or hinder the activities of the country's vital forces. It is not there to play the role of business in the competitive sector of the economy."[45] Addressing the G7 meeting at Lille on employment in 1996 Chirac endorsed a "third way" that was, in theory, equally distant from the Anglo-Saxons and the policies of continental Europeans, which were "a little too social."[46] Such a median course would avoid choosing between the précarité of American jobs and the chronic unemployment of Europeans. But the president of the republic did not specify his alternative: both his notion of supple dirigisme and a "third way" remained vague.

Chirac was curious about American innovation. At the Elysée he welcomed a young French software multimillionaire, a graduate of Stanford University, who instructed the president in the ways of Silicon Valley and he met with Microsoft's CEO Bill Gates as well as Jean-Marie Messier, the head of the transatlantic telecommunications and entertainment giant Vivendi Universal.[47] But advice about the new world of information technology did not lead to action. In fact, Chirac was slow to embrace contemporary telecommunications. He apparently encountered his first computer "mouse" at the opening of the new Bibliothèque Nationale de France in 1996 and did not get his own e-mail address until two years later. The president spoke resentfully of the Internet as "an Anglo-Saxon network."[48]

The resident of the Elysée harbored reservations about the American way. When members of President Clinton's economic team lectured him at the G7 meeting in Denver, as we have seen, Chirac insisted on maintaining the European model. And when the U.S. government tried to pry open the EU for free trade, Chirac stubbornly defended agricultural protection. He had once observed, rather poetically, "Farmers are the gardeners of our country and the guardians of our memory."[49] The market, in his estimation, should not hold French identity hostage. At the end of his second term as president he confessed his apprehensions about liberalism and called it as "equally dangerous" as communism: "I am convinced that liberalism is doomed to the same failure and will lead to the same excesses. One and the other are perversions of human thought"—which was, he thought, why an "intermediate solution" was needed.[50] Chirac might try to charm Americans with nostalgia for his student days in New England and express interest in Yankee know-how, but American economic liberalism had to be kept at bay.

On the far right the American model was even less popular than it was among the Gaullists and the UDF. The Front National, which had adhered to Reaganomics in the mid-1980s, moved toward protectionism and away from America a decade later. The deteriorating place of France in the world economy, the flight of jobs abroad, the effects of the Maastricht Treaty and the Uruguay Round all called into question the principle of open borders. In order to defend the national economy and national identity as well as please its electorate of farmers, fishermen, and small business owners, Jean-Marie Le Pen's party inveighed against globalization, the EU, and the US—even if it retained its commitment to programs like privatizations and a leaner welfare state. Globalization, according to a party spokesman, forced France to "accept humiliating conditions (*les fourches caudines*) of American egoism which threatens indiscriminately our steel, our peasantry, not to mention our culture."[51] Le Pen proclaimed, "France is at war with the United States."[52]

Bashing the Americans could be politically useful for French conservatives. In February 1995 *Le Monde* carried a sensational front-page story about American economic espionage.[53] Five CIA operatives, attached to the U.S. embassy in Paris or working undercover, had been using cash bribes (and sex) since 1992 to gain information from high officials about the government's negotiating strategy during the General Agreement on Tariffs and Trade (GATT) talks, domestic politics, and the French telecommunications network. Instead of letting the wrongdoers slip out of the country according to diplomatic protocol, the affair was leaked to *Le Monde* after Charles Pasqua, the minister of the interior, had summoned U.S. Ambassador Pamela Harriman and confronted her with the spying charges. Why the affair was made public is a bit mysterious. A possible motive was that Pasqua, who backed Balladur's candidacy for the presidency against Chirac and Jospin, sought to cover up a wiretapping scandal of his own doing and to energize the flagging campaign of Balladur. But it is just as likely that the affair was part of a wider, and increasingly nasty, transatlantic espionage war. France was a prime target of the Clinton administration because of competition in sectors like defense, space, aeronautics, and telecommunications. Balladur was so alarmed by American efforts at gathering economic secrets that he created a special advisory committee to protect French companies.

A second Gaullist prime minister, Alain Juppé, who succeeded Balladur from 1995 to 1997, also flirted with liberalism, but he refused to go as far as his own finance minister, Alain Madelin, in endorsing the market. Madelin, the head of a small party, was something of a maverick who fervently embraced free enterprise, small government, and the American model. The division within the Right over the market surfaced when in early 1995 the outspoken Madelin boldly proposed to trim the welfare state, reduce taxes, and rely on the market to put the three million unemployed back to work. His specific proposals, which featured cuts in the pension privileges of public-sector workers and reductions in welfare benefits, antagonized the more pragmatic Juppé and the rest of the government who preferred to advance in a more cautious and consensual way.[54] Trade unions and the political opposition erupted in protest against what they perceived as an attempt at damaging their droits acquis. Rather than risk a confrontation Juppé forced his minister out, explaining his ouster as necessary in the name of republican solidarity to "restore the country's social cohesion."[55] In fact, Madelin's departure represented how little political space existed for a free-market, supply-side minister who celebrated the Anglo-American way, even on the right.

Juppé faced the limits of liberalization himself in late 1995 when he proposed a broad range of reforms aimed at drastically cutting the government deficit so that France could meet the Maastricht Treaty's criteria to qualify for the European currency in 2000.[56] The "Plan Juppé" wisely refrained from mentioning Anglo-American efforts at trimming welfare expenses, but the intent was similar. Juppé proposed new controls on health care expenditures along with cuts in benefits for certain state employees, including the early retirement age of railway and subway conductors, weakening union control over social security spending, and lengthening the years public sector workers paid into the pension system while also advancing their retirement age to sixty-five years. President Chirac announced, "France is at a crossroads. This is the path of reform that has been put off too long."[57]

The trade unions took to the streets. Huge strikes, estimated at two million demonstrators, paralyzed rail and subway transportation from

late November until almost Christmas.[58] The militants argued that the
social contract was at risk because the austerity program would begin
stripping away the various subsidies and protections afforded families
by republican solidarity. In fact, the strikers projected a bunker mentality: their bywords were "maintain," "reassert," and "defend." They
simply opposed the Plan Juppé without offering any alternative.[59] Despite the inconvenience caused by the paralysis of transportation, the
public displayed at least patience with, if not support for, the strikers.
While the American and British press tended to praise Juppé for his
courage, the titular leader of the strikes Marc Blondel, the head of a
major union, scolded him: "The French do not want to live like Anglo-
Saxons and the government has to understand that."[60] In the end the
government, even if it held firm on some of its cutbacks and on extend-
ing parliamentary control over Social Security, had to back down, making important concessions to the railway workers who spearheaded the
strike and canceling the proposal to modify public sector pensions. The
conservatives' frontal assault had failed, and serious efforts at trimming
l'Etat-providence were not to be resumed until the early years of the
next century. There were many issues that generated the turmoil over
the Plan Juppé, including the EU, union rights, acquis sociaux, broken
promises, government arrogance, and a general sense of insecurity. But
the Anglo-Americans were also present in framing the dispute. Juppé's
attempt at liberalization raised the threat among its opponents of turning the republic toward "hard capitalism."

■ The Left

On the left politicians were more outspoken about their disdain for
America's "new economy." Some socialist parliamentarians attributed
most of France's troubles to its "progressive Americanization," which
they described as "growing individualism, the impoverishment of the
state, the omnipotence of television, intemperate consumer spending

and the emerging power of lobbies."[61] Pierre Bérégovoy, the socialist prime minister from 1992 to 1993, contrasted the mixed economy of France, which he described as combining economic competitiveness and social protection, with the American system that "dissolved solidarity."[62] To the left of the Socialist Party, the Mouvement des Citoyens (Citizens Movement) led by Jean-Pierre Chevènement, was adamant about preserving the Jacobin alternative with its powerful state and nationalist agenda, and scorned its socialist allies like Michel Rocard, who expressed admiration for America. And some of the members of the Green Party were even harder on the Americans than were the socialists. They attacked the United States for its indifference to the environment and its advocacy of market-driven globalization. Noël Mamère, who would become the Green Party nominee for president, described American society in the harshest possible light, damning it for its bigotry, ignorance, and violence and outrageously asserting, for example, that the United States had more gun shops than it did gas stations. Mamère concluded his polemic titled *Non merci, Oncle Sam!* with the remark, "[R]eally, perhaps it's not so unseemly to declare oneself for the time being as . . . simply anti-American."[63]

American ways were ostensibly unacceptable to the socialists and their leader at the fin de siècle, Lionel Jospin. In the 1997 legislative campaign that brought them to power the socialists and their allies, the communists, the Green Party, the Citizens Movement, and others, gave their conservative opponents the tag of "hyperliberalism." Since this phrase was a code for Anglo-American economic practices, America, the foil, figured in the election. Jospin accused his opponents of preparing "a liberal purge" featuring cuts in public sector jobs, accelerated privatizations, dismantled public services, and loss of social protection. The choice, as he phrased it, was between liberalism, which inevitably brought the "uncontrolled reign of money" (America) or a more humane society in which the general interest ruled (France).[64]

Jospin endorsed economic reform during the campaign but warned against those who would submit to the market: "Market forces are now working with such violence, with such harshness, with such political support, that I fear if we don't take notice the country will tip completely over to one side. . . . I want open socialism, not unbridled liberalism."[65] While he called for an "evolution from statism and old-fashioned centralism toward initiative, decentralization and forms of *autogestion*" (self-management), he cautioned against a "rupture with public service, with the values that founded the republic." Jospin pledged he would create 700,000 jobs in the public sector, introduce the thirty-five-hour workweek, and fight for a "social Europe," which meant maintaining existing benefits and labor protection. He advised against trying to mimic the market practices of Americans because French capitalism was much weaker and lacked the means; in doing so the French might jeopardize their major industrial achievements like those in aviation, space, and nuclear power. "That might please the Americans, but where is our interest [in doing this]?" he added.

Édouard Balladur and Alain Juppé, the former and the incumbent prime minister in 1997, had to respond to Jospin's campaign in the legislative elections. Of the two the former was more explicit. Balladur defended liberalism, but called for "inventing a French liberalism" that did not copy "the Anglo-Saxon model," one that helped create jobs and made France competitive in the international arena yet would not harm "a society of justice and equity."[66] Balladur's call for "a liberal turn" was rather too explicit for Juppé, who offered a similar program without the liberal vocabulary. When the votes were counted the conservatives and free-market liberalism had lost the election and the socialists and their allies took charge.

As head of government after 1997 Jospin clarified his position by distinguishing the market economy from the market society: "We accept the market economy because it is the most effective means—provided it is regulated and managed—of allocating resources, stimulating initiative, and rewarding effort and work. But we reject 'the market society.' For although the market produces wealth, in itself it generates neither solidarity nor values, neither objectives nor meaning. Because society is far more than an exchange of goods, the market cannot be its only driving force. So we are not 'left-wing liberals.' We are socialists. And to be a socialist is to affirm that the political should take precedence over the economic."[67] Jospin refused to "give in to the fatalistic idea that the neo-liberal capitalist model is the only one available,"[68] for "capitalism is a force that moves, but it does not know where it is going."[69] Rather, Jospin asserted, "we can shape the world according to our values," meaning constructing an economy and society that conformed to French national traditions and institutions such as that of social solidarity. To this end he continued to extol dirigisme, though he preferred to call it *volontarisme*, referring to an active state that "can clear away or navigate around the archaic forces standing in the way of changes that society wants."[70] The state, Jospin felt, should lead the way in combatting unemployment, promoting innovation, directing investment, and assuring a fair distribution of economic wealth. *L'Etat-providence* was the term he preferred for the welfare state because it suggested activism.

In this vein socialist officials made the case that globalization represented the unbridled force of the market and benefited Americans more than others. "Managed globalization" (*mondialisation maîtrisée*) became the slogan of the late 1990s. It evoked the notion of tying the American hyperpower down with international rules and organizations, such as making it honor treaties like the Kyoto Protocol and taxing international financial transactions to mitigate their volatility. Socialists championed the WTO as a replacement for the GATT because it could better bind the "world company," as French satirists labeled the United States. Speaking in Brazil, Jospin—after noting the beneficial effects of globalization—emphasized how it increased inequalities among peoples and threatened cultural diversity; he called for governments to take charge and "humanize" the process rather than leaving it to the fate of "so-called natural economic laws."[71]

Despite these criticisms of the market, Jospin broke with socialist orthodoxy by endorsing the market economy. His declared aim was constructing a new balance between state and market that would advance "a collectively constructed modernity"—one that addressed issues of production as well as those of redistribution.[72] Thus he endorsed the privatization of capital in order to create jobs and improve economic competitiveness and in fact carried out large-scale privatizations as well as cutting taxes and placing caps on health spending. To be sure, the socialists refused to label selling off public companies as "privatization"; instead they called it "involving the private sector" and they secured it against foreign—that is, Anglo-American—takeovers.

His move toward the market economy forced Jospin to pay some attention to America. In the summer of 1998, accompanied by three of his ministers, Dominique Strauss-Kahn, Claude Allègre, and Hubert Védrine, the prime minister made his first official visit to the United States, after which he confessed that he was impressed with America. Jospin admitted that job creation in the United States produced skilled positions in the service and high-tech sectors rather than only low-paid, dead-end jobs. France, he acknowledged, had much to learn from American economic dynamism, its competitive spirit, and the vitality of its research and innovation.[73]

Yet back home he distanced himself from America, distinguishing "capitalism" (America) from a "market economy" (France) and, in order to camouflage domestic reform, declared priority must be given to republican solidarity. The pay-as-you go pension system based on the principle of *répartition* (sharing out) was in crisis, but Jospin refused to do more than tamper with it: he called répartition "the symbol of the solidarity that links the generations. It is one of the most important terms of the nation's social compact." There would be no pension reform "on the model of certain Anglo-Saxon countries—that is not our approach."[74] He introduced a voluntary long-term saving scheme for workers, which was heavily subsidized by tax breaks, that served as a de facto form of private pensions, yet he rejected any notion that they were either pensions or that he was following the Americans. Instead of labeling them "pensions" Jospin insisted they be called *épargne re-*

traite, or retirement savings. President Chirac disagreed with his prime minister and dared to speak of these as "pension funds *à la française*."[75]

Private-sector initiatives aimed at curbing unemployment that seemed like Anglo-American practices failed to win commendations from the Jospin administration. The government winked at short-term, flexible contracts that skirted the labor code and accounted for the vast majority of jobs created in the private sector by the late 1990s. But officially ministers in the Jospin government distanced themselves from such practices; they complained that these kinds of jobs were too "precarious" and unfortunately resembled what the Americans were doing.[76] Similarly, when young French men and women flocked to London to take service-sector jobs, the Jospin government seemed to suggest unemployment was preferable to such unskilled "McJobs." "We want quality jobs, not low-paid ones," explained an adviser to the labor minister Martine Aubry. "Our model is certainly very heavy and costly, but it guarantees our solidarity."[77]

Meanwhile the government continued to rely on subsidies or direct handouts to relieve unemployment. Jospin's ministers were unapologetic. "When the private sector does not do the job, I would like the public sector to do it," explained finance minister Strauss-Kahn in 1999. "The goal is economic and social inclusion: there are now 179,000 youngsters who are not on the streets, who are integrated into society."[78] Most emphatically the Jospin government confronted the Anglo-Americans and satisfied the left wing of the Socialist Party by adopting the thirty-five-hour workweek in 1998. This attempt to create jobs by legislating a shorter workweek seemed like dirigisme at its worst and made no sense to President Clinton's economic advisers in the United States.

Jospin refused to embrace America even after his 1998 transatlantic trip. During his second visit, a year later, while addressing the financial press in New York, he dismissed the concerns of American business about the thirty-five-hour workweek and, speaking of globalization, scoffed, "One doesn't replace the dictatorship of the proletariat with that of shareholders."[79] Even the socialist-liberal Strauss-Kahn ridiculed the panacea of relaxing the labor code preached by the Americans: "We have no interest in Anglo-Saxon flexibility that entails for us the risk of a social implosion."[80] Attacking America, or at least distancing his policies from the Anglo-Saxons, made it easier for Jospin to liberalize quietly. "Flexibility" advanced in the field of employment in the 1990s with increasing part-time and temporary jobs, irregular work schedules, and firm-level contracts.[81] Baiting America served as an effective political screen.

At the end of the decade Jospin's government tried its hand at one type of American-inspired reform. There was rising concern about the gap between the French and the Americans, as well as others, in the development of new technologies and about the drain of technical talent to the United States and Britain. France wanted to reach the cutting edge of biotechnology, information technology, and similar sectors of the so-called "new economy."

The lag with the Americans in developing the information technology (IT) sector was especially distressing. When Jospin became prime minister in 1997 no one in his office was using e-mail; only 2 percent of the French population could access the Internet; and only one in four, mainly large-scale, businesses had Internet connections. Far fewer French households had Internet access than in the United States or in many other European countries like Sweden and the Netherlands. Even La Villette, the national showcase for science and technology, banned the Internet from its displays. In the early 1980s the French had adopted their own, digital, text-based system called Minitel that, using the national telephone network, performed tasks like offering train schedules and making online purchases. Minitel acted as a brake on the Internet, because users, service providers and France Télécom, which operated the service, were reluctant to abandon a popular and profitable technology, but it was also a catalyst because it provided experience in using an interactive network.[82] Despite objections about introducing what some derided as an "Anglo-Saxon network," Jospin acted.

In 1998 he unveiled an expensive plan to push the country into "the Information Society." The plan targeted sectors like electronic commerce, public services, and schools. State intervention, eager global IT companies including firms like America Online, and a cooperative populace closed the gap quickly. Within a few years almost every large enterprise used the Web. Within a decade the French public enjoyed access to the Internet that was comparable to that in the United States, and they logged on for more hours than other Europeans. And French firms like Thomson and France Télécom had become dominant players in Europe's IT sector. Anxious about America and others speeding ahead, France used the state and global private enterprise to catch up.

France also needed to find ways to commercialize the inventiveness of its science and technology labs. New high-tech companies would offer an opportunity to reduce unemployment through job creation afforded by small firms. But the government effort, headed by the dynamic and pragmatic ministers Strauss-Kahn and Allègre, did not want to upset the nation's social contract that depended on wage equality, risk-sharing, and job security.

The answer, according to Gunnar Trumbull, was to construct a "homegrown analog to Silicon Valley."[83] To develop this sector France needed to imitate the Americans by providing venture capital for start-ups, incentives for entrepreneurs, encouragement to engineers and scientists from research labs to assist the private sector, and more relaxed regulation of investment. Strauss-Kahn, who had made frequent trips to California and consulted with Americans, turned away from traditional means of technological innovation—through state-sponsored research channeled to large-scale industrial corporations—toward promoting private venture capital that would in turn finance small start-up companies in leading technologies.

Even though the French were inspired by Silicon Valley, they fostered technological innovation differently. The state continued to play a guiding role. The government created a new institutional framework by creating special funds and offering tax incentives to induce investment in innovative companies, sponsoring technological "incubators" and industrial parks, and introducing new legal arrangements to assist start-ups. Allègre created networks of research institutes and private firms that identified technology spinoffs that could be funded. A special state agency monitored innovation and certified which companies were suitable for investment, thus alleviating risk. At the same time, policy makers adopted measures to ensure that these private enterprises would not damage social solidarity. For example, stock options were designed to reward technological innovation rather than stockholder interests—in contrast to American usage. And schemes for promoting private investment and venture capital were created in ways that did not endanger the nation's welfare system. In other words, France relied on state activism and found ways to encourage high-tech innovation without turning to deregulation or upsetting the social contract.

Such efforts brought some success. By the end of 2000 France had some eighty high-tech incubators or *pépinières*, though these were small in number compared to those in the United States and the United Kingdom. The most glamorous of these installations was the science park of Sophia Antipolis near Antibes, where science and art mingled and over a thousand companies, some American, pursued research in fields like biotechnology and telecommunications. The republic advanced toward the high-tech economy, employing techniques pioneered in Silicon Valley, but it adapted them to more traditional ways of promoting innovation and guarding social solidarity.

The political record of the 1990s demonstrates that policy makers, socialist or conservative, used a trope about America to cover their reforms and avoid the appearance of embracing the New World. Those like Michel Rocard on the left and Alain Madelin on the right, who were associated with transatlantic connections, suffered politically. Orthodox members of the Socialist Party denounced Rocard and his followers as *la Gauche américaine* and Gaullist regulars hounded Madelin out of office. Given such resistance, politicians in France had to pretend Anglo-American practice had little to do with their taking up more market-driven policies. Such reforms had to be masked—in fact, America served as a foil, as the "un-French" way.

America and the Private Sector

Business managers, or at least those who were most closely tied to global networks, proved far more willing to embrace openly American ways than were politicians. It was in the private sector that America was most appreciated. For example, Ernest-Antoine Seillière, who led the Mouvement des Entreprises de France (MEDEF), the refounded employers association after 1997, pursued a free-market agenda with flair and furor. [84] Seillière fought for reforms that liberals on the political right sought but could not readily acknowledge. He had taught at Harvard University and was not shy about invoking the American model or criticizing his own people for their anticapitalist attitudes. Seillière wanted the state to withdraw altogether from economic and social affairs. His message was, let the market create jobs and adapt the economy to globalization and the Euro. One journalist concluded that France had finally found its answer to Reagan and Thatcher.[85] In 1999 the forceful Seillière organized employers to take to the streets against the government's adoption of the thirty-five-hour workweek. A second example is Alain Minc, the head of a major consulting firm, who applauded the efforts of the MEDEF; he disputed the notion that competition was a kind of tyranny by arguing that the modern market faced such counterweights as the media and public opinion, which brought more pressure on economic actors than the state had exercised in the past.[86] Minc boldly insisted that competition was even beneficial as a force for reform of education or health services. Versions of Minc's free-market views were shared by other globally minded CEOs like Claude Bébéar of the insurance giant AXA; Jacques Maillot, founder of the travel business Nouvelles Frontières; and Paul Dubrule, copresident of the international hotel group Accor. But these managers cannot be made representative of the diverse world of business: they were more an exception than the rule.[87]

French business was Americanizing and globalizing. As two experts observed, "Whereas as recently as 1985 foreign ownership of French firms was only around 10 percent, it is estimated that more than 40 percent of French shares are now held by foreigners—mostly large U.S. and British pension funds."[88] Between 1988 and 2000 American institutional investors raised their share of equity from $128.7 billion to $1.787 trillion.[89] Keen on job creation, France surrendered its past reticence about receiving foreign capital: subsidiaries of American corporations provided employment for 400,000 by the early 1990s, concentrated in sectors like IT, automobiles, petroleum, pharmaceuticals, telecommunications, electronics, chemicals, agro-food, leisure (Disney), and retailers with the arrival of chains like Toys R Us and Gap.[90] France became a favored location for foreign investment. Toyota, for example, in 1998 selected Valenciennes in northern France to build a new factory; this was the largest Japanese investment in Europe since the Japanese began making cars in Britain in the 1980s. At the same time, moving capital across the Atlantic had made France a major investor in the United States so that its direct investments trailed those of the United Kingdom but virtually equaled those of countries like Japan, the Netherlands, and Germany.[91] The French had arrived stateside. In 1991 AXA Insurance, directed by Claude Bébéar, bought the Equitable Life Insurance Company for one billion dollars while the Michelin tire company built plants in several states and came to employ 25,000 workers in America. French companies won bids for high-tech contracts with the Pentagon; Sodexho, the institutional food company, employed over 100,000 workers in the United States and, during the war in Iraq, fed U.S. Marines.[92] Alcatel bought two up-and-coming California data networking firms. And in 1999 Vivendi, the water utility turned media empire, managed the biggest purchase ever of an American company in acquiring U.S. Filter, America's principal water-treatment firm, for $6.2 billion.

The 1990s saw French business move toward certain American-ized practices, like raising capital through the equity market or paying executives with stock options, but they did so sparingly and without embracing them fully.[93] Even among those who were most receptive there were reservations and disputes.

Some French corporations adopted a more American operating style, including the requirement that English be spoken in the board-room. The board of directors of cable TV channel Canal Plus, for ex-ample, held its Monday meetings in English to "blend cultures" with its American managers. Marc Lassus, chairman of Gemplus, the world's largest manufacturer of smart cards (cards containing computer chips that can be used to store information) illustrated an extreme case of transplanting Yankee ways. Lassus ordered his employees to speak En-glish at work, hired American executives, adopted the informality of Silicon Valley, declared war on French unions and the welfare state, and hounded his workers to become more service-minded. "The model we have to copy is American, not French," he declared, and, in the ultimate act of Americanization announced it was inevitable that the company move to the United States.[94] The need to sell smart cards in the Ameri-can market was crucial in his adopting American techniques, but even Lassus did not dare import other American tactics, like shipping jobs overseas or cutting benefits, for fear of being vilified. And some of his employees objected to his unrestrained imitation of Americans.

The transatlantic merger and transatlantic CEOs made their appear-ance at the end of the century. Vivendi Universal, which had begun as a water company during the 1850s, became one of the world's media giants when it acquired Universal Studios in 2000 as well as American properties in music, television, and publishing, and its chairman Jean-Marie Messier became the superstar of Americanized French managers. Messier, who en-joyed enormous power in the French movie and television industries by operating Canal Plus, the first pay-TV channel, took up residence in New York City where *Paris-Match* photographed him ice skating in Central Park. He viewed his highly publicized buyout of Seagram's, the owner of

Universal Studios, as a French rejoinder to American domination of tele-communications. *Fortune* magazine dubbed him France's "first rock-star CEO" but, as we shall see, he was not popular with all of his peers.

Financial institutions were also involved in adopting American-style techniques. In early 1999 Société Générale (SG) and Paribas took steps toward a friendly merger, but the Banque Nationale de Paris (BNP), managed by Michel Pébereau, thwarted this effort by initiating a hostile takeover of the other two.[95] By the summer a three-way battle for control of the banking sector had developed. BNP merged success-fully with Paribas, but the takeover of SG became an American-style donnybrook. Even if the purpose of the merger was conventional—building a large French bank that could better compete globally—the manner of the takeover came straight from Wall Street. BNP failed to first win the approval of the Ministry of Finance, as was common prac-tice. SG's tactics were also reminiscent of Wall Street: its head, Daniel Bouton, objecting to the takeover on grounds that BNP's bid was too low, insisted that winning value for his shareholders took precedence over national interest.[96] Meanwhile SG's employees took to the streets trying to intimidate government regulators into stopping the takeover. The government, caught between two warring commercial banks, was reluctant to act in the now discredited *dirigiste* manner: it tried to mediate by calling an unprecedented hearing before the Credit Insti-tutions Committee. To complicate matters further it became evident during the controversy that outsiders also coveted SG.

As negotiations developed, officials became anxious that blocking BNP would risk allowing SG to fall into the hands of foreign finan-cial institutions, but they had to face the fact that BNP's bid did not meet minimum requirements for a legal takeover. In the end regula-tors prevented BNP's bid for SG. Critics like Jospin's interior minister, Jean-Pierre Chevènement, commented that the national interest had been ignored and warned that foreign predators would step in.[97] In the end the affair exposed both how Americanized and how globalized the financial sector became by the late 1990s.

At the level of internal structure there was also change imported from abroad. Some of the largest French corporate groups were, in the words of one management expert, "directly inspired by the American 'shareholder model.'" "The extent to which U.S. and British norms have penetrated the system is impressive and total," François Morin wrote.[98] Morin was referring to the way companies like the merged AXA-UAP insurance group abandoned cross-shareholding, a system of interlocking and concentrated ownership structures, and veritable networks of tight corporate financial alliances, and instead adopted market-oriented structures closer to U.S. and British models. Instead of companies holding financial stakes with one another, forming interlocking circuits of ownership and management, they turned to capital markets and accepted massive investment from North Americans, especially from pension funds like Calpers and TIAA-CREF. The old system provided mutual protection and close managerial control, but it tended to immobilize capital; the new arrangement opened companies to capital markets, both foreign and domestic, and made management yield to the demand of shareholder values. Morin observed that "the largest French firms are subject to Anglo-Saxon management and return on capital norms" and French managers admitted that it was "impossible to escape the demands made by the United States and British investors."[99] In short, the norms of top corporate management were becoming more like those of the Anglo-Americans.

Yet crossing the Atlantic did not mean completely embracing American ways. Jean-Luc Lagardère, director of the Lagardère arms group, evoked republican ideals of social cohesion and equality to distinguish French employers: "French business leaders in general," he said, "have a much greater sense of their social responsibility than their Anglo-Saxon counterparts."[100] Serge Tchuruk, the head of Alcatel, which manufactured telephones and high-tech telecommunications equipment, acknowledged that he ran a multinational whose language was English, but he insisted the company's "culture" continued to be French.[101] The owner of a small construction firm concurred. He admitted circumventing the labor code by taking on temporary labor, but said he regretted the practice: "If charges were lower and sacking was easier, I'd gladly take on more regular staff. But we don't want to get like America. It is right that workers should have some protection."[102]

French companies increasingly adopted performance incentives for managers like those in America, but they borrowed without imitation. Large French firms like the food giant Danone and AXA began rewarding their managers with stock options. They did so for several reasons: in order to catch up with the performance of their American competitors; to respond to demands of their Anglo-American investors; to ward-off unwanted acquisitions; and to retain highly qualified staff.[103] According to one expert, "A little over half of the total remuneration of French CEOs and top managers now comes in the form of variable pay based on some performance measure as opposed to fixed salary. As a result, large French firms now pay out the biggest stock options packages among continental European companies."[104] Managers whose income now came from stock options were more inclined to link their operating decisions to shareholder returns. But such change did not mean French enterprises followed American and British practices of corporate governance. On the contrary, they fiercely resisted greater accounting transparency and they effectively disenfranchised minority shareholders.[105]

The plunge into stock options as managerial compensation had its limits. In 1999, when Philippe Jaffré, the former CEO of Elf-Acquitaine, received a severance package in stock options estimated at €24 million, it sparked a political counterattack and a public backlash because it called attention to the hazards of American practices and, in principle, challenged republican notions of equality and solidarity. To opponents, mainly on the parliamentary left, the generosity of his severance package was both shocking—an affront to solidarity—and underhanded: it appeared as a device to avoid income taxes. Jaffré was also accused of being compensated not for his merit in operating Elf-

Acquitaine but for selling out his company in a merger with the petroleum giant Total, which suggested the Anglo-American practice of catering to shareholders. The Jaffré affair forced Minister of Finance Strauss-Kahn to retreat from plans to enhance the appeal of stock options. In the end the socialists, supported by the Right, created a complicated tax structure that distinguished between stock options as compensation from those that aided entrepreneurial risk-taking; the latter became known as *stock options à la française*.[106]

Given the vogue of American entrepreneurial practices one might have expected that young, English-speaking, managers of French Internet companies would have been the most likely candidates to embrace the ways of their Yankee cousins. In fact such dynamic managers said they admired the United States for its entrepreneurship and easy access to capital; and they expressed the conventional criticism of the French system—it was too highly regulated and taxed, and the thirty-five-hour workweek was a constraint.[107] But at the same time these IT workers in their thirties and forties were highly critical of the American socioeconomic model—they said it was "ultraliberal," dominated by the profit motive, and "immoral" in its treatment of those left behind. Their self-image was not one of imitators of American Internet business; they were "French" or "European." They endorsed the French system of social protection and accepted the state as the best guardian of the general interest; they thought they were adapting, not adopting, American business methods in France.

The exit of one transatlantic manager suggests the tolerable limits of business flirting with American ways: this is the story of the stunning collapse of Jean-Marie Messier's empire. Within two years of his acquisition of Universal Studios in 2000 the shareholders of Vivendi Universal, including American investors, ousted him as CEO. His fall came principally because of business mistakes like overpaying in a spree of acquisitions, withholding information from his shareholders, and failing to convince his investors that he had a sound overall strategy, but there was also a certain measure of retribution engineered by more conservative managers who disapproved of his fascination with America and his distancing himself from France—which he once disparaged as "an exotic little country." Messier told American journalists that he liked New York more than any city in the world and wanted to raise his children as Americans, adding "I am the most un-French Frenchman you will ever meet."[108] Rumors spread that he intended to move the headquarters of Vivendi Universal to New York. And he sneered at those of his own people who disapproved his venture into the American market: "France has much less a culture of risk than the U.S.," he wrote.[109] His attempt to sell the former core business of the company, Vivendi Environnement, to outsiders earned him a rebuke from President Chirac.

Messier also seemed ready to sell out the French cinema to the Americans. He provoked an uproar in the French entertainment world by proclaiming, appropriately in English to journalists in New York, that "the Franco-French cultural exception is dead."[110] He was referring to the exemption of the audiovisual from the WTO and the web of government subsidies that supported the cinema. His remark was more than a gaffe because Canal Plus, owned by Vivendi Universal, contributed financially to the production of 70 percent of French films and Messier had criticized both film subsidies and the narcissistic ways of Parisian filmmakers. Minister of Culture Catherine Tasca scolded Messier for his provocative declaration. By acquiring Universal Pictures Messier had also purchased the studio responsible for the movie *Jaws*. Daniel Toscan du Plantier, a spokesman for the film industry, said, "It was a mistake to make a marriage between Canal Plus and Universal. They are two opposing cultures. America is great, France is great, but they make a bad couple."[111] In the end anxious investors who distrusted Messier forced his resignation. As the *Economist* summarized it, Messier "was too French for the Americans and too American for the French."[112]

■ Language

The struggle with America in the final decade of the century extended to cultural questions, including how one spoke. Language has been the single most important marker of French culture. No other expression of Frenchness—be it food, or fashion, or fine art—has occupied such a preeminent position. And it was American English that mounted the principal challenge not only to the purity of French but also to its global status.

The issue had already reached the highest levels of the republic during the presidency of Charles de Gaulle. During the 1960s words like *le weekend, le parking,* or *le pressing* (for dry cleaning) had become commonplace while advertisers borrowed Anglicisms to suggest modernity and style and business managers and officials sprinkled their speech with Anglo-Saxon borrowings. It seemed to some that the language was collapsing into "Franglais," the bastard spawn of two tongues. In 1966 Prime Minister Georges Pompidou created the High Committee for the Defense of the French Language and President Charles de Gaulle castigated "Franglais." This struggle to keep the Yankee linguistic intruder at bay escalated in the last decades of the century.

It is difficult to exaggerate the esteem the French attached to their language at the fin de siècle. The spread of Anglicisms and the abuse of grammar and orthography were an affront to a country where sales of a book titled *La Grammaire est une chanson douce* (Grammar Is a Sweet Song) were in the hundreds of thousands; where the national spelling bee was conducted on prime time television; and where "defending or reforming spelling [was] a national psychodrama."[113] "The language of a people is its soul," declared Maurice Druon, the secretary-general of the Académie Française, the hoary institution whose role since the days of Cardinal Richelieu has been to guard the language.[114] "The French language . . . quite obviously and for some decades, has deteriorated, loosened," Druon warned, and in some cases it had "purely and simply been

abandoned."¹¹⁵ Prime Minister Balladur solemnly intoned the defense
of the tongue as "an act of faith in the future of our country."¹¹⁶ According to the premier the entire world was menaced by "the domination
of a primitive English unsuitable for nuance or intellectual sophistication."¹¹⁷ Balladur's socialist successors were only slightly less vehement.
Prime Minister Jospin connected language to republican institutions,
proclaiming that French was the "cement of the Republic and the values it is founded on."¹¹⁸ And his foreign minister Hubert Védrine, while
admitting that English had become the language of global communication, and that the French needed to learn foreign languages, insisted,
"I don't accept the idea that it would be 'old-fashioned' to defend our
language . . . (because) it remains vital to our identity."¹¹⁹

Since linguistic defense was a matter of national identity, global
status, and republican integrity, politicians had to act. In 1975 the
Bas-Lauriol Law made it obligatory to use French in commerce—in
advertising and instructions on packaging, for example—as well as in
workplace agreements. Penalties were in order. Evian, for example, was
fined for marketing its product as "le fast drink des Alpes."¹²⁰ This legislation was not strictly enforced, and borrowing from American English
continued, especially in areas like science, computers, music, and business. The legislature decided to take further action in defense of what
was called linguistic patrimony. In 1992, at a joint session held in the
Palace at Versailles, it amended the constitution to read, "The language
of the Republic is French." But even this initiative did not satisfy everyone. Several hundred intellectuals, including luminaries like Alain
Finkielkraut and Régis Debray, protested that French should also be
declared the language of business and education and awarded special
status in the international community. They blamed multinationals
that conducted international commerce in English as the principal villain and asked, if Europe is to have one language, "[W]hy should it be
that of the United States?"¹²¹

Jacques Toubon, Balladur's minister of culture, brought the issue to a boil in 1994 by convincing the National Assembly to remedy

the Bas-Lauriol Act with new legislation affirming the right of French speakers to use French and specifying ways to curb adulteration of the native tongue. Sanctions, including fines, would be imposed on those who used foreign expressions, unless there was no French equivalent, in official announcements and documents, work contracts, advertising, teaching, and radio and television programs —with exceptions, such as for foreign-language broadcasts. Scientific meetings risked losing public subsidies if they failed to provide translations or summaries in French of papers presented in a foreign language. The undeclared enemy was, of course, American English; as Toubon later acknowledged, he aimed at saving Francophony from the "unique Anglo-mercantile model."[122] The Toubon Law formed one element of a wider campaign. Public authorities had been enjoined to find French substitutes for Anglicisms in specific fields like finance, computers, and the media and they published a directory of synonyms in 1994. At the same time separate legislation set quotas for foreign music in radio broadcasting.

The Toubon Law won an endorsement from some, but it also aroused skepticism and derision in many quarters and stirred Americans to mirth and mockery. Those who encouraged Toubon cited the lament of the philosopher Michel Serres about Paris streets displaying fewer expressions in German during the Occupation than they currently did in English. The publisher-writer Yves Berger applauded Toubon, expressing concern that the national culture would become so *franglaicisés* that in twenty years the French wouldn't know how to read Montesquieu or Chateaubriand. *Le Monde diplomatique*, true to form, applauded Toubon's "modest" effort, blamed linguistic debasement on multinationals, and rejected speaking the "language of the masters." A member of the Académie Française and columnist for *Le Monde*, Bertrand Poirot-Delpech worried that "American jargon" was becoming the talk of everyone who thought of themselves as "modern." There was no need to import terms, he contended, that added nothing to what existed. For example, Poirot-Delpech suggested, *romans d'anticipation*, a phrase coined by Jules Verne, was prettier and more appropriate than "science fiction."[123] Yet even this academician who backed the Toubon Law noted that one could not legislate or police usage; power and inventiveness determined parlance and when the French displayed sufficient creativity, then *logiciel* would naturally supplant "software."

For Toubon's detractors it was easy to make fun of the effort to find French equivalents of English words. Exchanging *le coussin gonflable de protection* for "airbag," or *maïs soufflé* for "popcorn," or *la puce* (flea) for "microchip," or *restauration rapide* for "fast food" made the French flinch and Americans guffaw. The effort seemed doomed to fail because it was impossible to police language and the pressure for adopting American phrases was unstoppable. How could one persuade teenagers immersed in American pop culture from using slang like *cool* or stop the media from referring to *high tech* or *le marketing* or praising the multicultural composition of the French World Cup champions as *Black, Blanc, Beur*? Researchers who relied on communicating in English were baffled about what to do. Requiring summaries or translations of papers at conferences would close France as a site for international meetings. Opponents sneered at such cultural protectionism, arguing that French had always been enriched by importing foreign words such as *opéra, pantalon*, or *valse*. One tabloid scoffed, "All proposals designed to legislate the use of language give off a stale smell."[124] Another paper satirized Jacques Toubon ("toubon" = "all good") as "Jack Goodall, the *chargé d'affaires* from the British Embassy" and ran a hilarious column in English laced with French words.[125] And a *disque-jockey* from a popular radio station complained the law was "pas très cool."

The Constitutional Council intervened and in the name of freedom of speech struck down much of the law without overturning it. But conservatives led by Toubon were not to be deterred. Fines were levied. For example, government inspectors visiting an outlet of The Body Shop in an Alpine town found several products like bubble bath labeled in English. The local court fined the British cosmetic company 1,000 francs. The Disney store on the Champs-Elysées was called out for its labeling. In one year diligent officials carried out almost 8,000 inspections, issued over 600 warnings, and brought more than 200 cases before public prosecutors, of which half were successful.[126]

Transatlantic attacks on his efforts prompted Toubon to answer his critics directly in the American press. He insisted, "A foreign language . . . often becomes a tool of domination, uniformization, a factor of social exclusion, and, when used snobbishly, a language of contempt."[127] Reminding Americans that many of their states had also legislated the use of English he then condescended:

> Admittedly, Americans may have some difficulty in understanding that a problem exists. Europeans would not assume that Americans, who are known for not being too open to foreign cultures and for pursuing their own cultural protectionism, understand foreign languages. Many Americans, on the contrary, often forget that one has the right in other countries not to understand their language and to speak another one. . . . What France does still generates interest in the entire world. It is probably because France defends a certain concept of freedom and diversity that some people are troubled. France remains, to paraphrase General Charles de Gaulle, the country that sometimes feels compelled to say "no," not out of egotism but a sense of what is right.[128]

Once the socialists returned to power in 1997 the policing campaign relaxed somewhat. The party had abstained from voting for the Toubon Law, but declared support for its aims. Lionel Jospin continued the fight at the rhetorical level, making the link between language and foreign policy by stating, "French is no longer the language of a power (but) it could be a language of a counter power"[129] While the Ministry of Finance banned many words imported from America, like "e-mail," and insisted its officials employ French equivalents like *courrier électronique*, at the same time the core of the ministry, the Treasury Department, circulated drafts of new regulations in English because "they will be discussed in English in Brussels."[130] Jack Lang, who had recently served as minister of education and culture, though he disapproved of Franglais thought the Toubon ban was absurd. Pragmatic administrators like Claude Allègre, who was a scientist and the minister of education, tried to tamp down the furor. He argued that protectionism in this case was ineffective and it would make more sense to encourage schoolchildren to learn English as their foreign language because this was eminently practical and would also help preserve the purity of French.[131]

In the end the protectionist strategy could not stem the linguistic tide that surged across both the Atlantic Ocean and the English Channel. The reasons either to learn English or to incorporate American English words overwhelmed official efforts. Trying to find French equivalents for the flow of technical and scientific language and then force the French to use them was hopeless. Requiring French translations of every ad on the Paris metro was comical. Blocking the influence of American television was impossible: watching American detective shows prompted a number of adolescents appearing in court to address the judge as "Your Honor" rather than "Monsieur le Juge." Policing language worked only fitfully in narrow realms like the bureaucracy, but not in wider venues like international conferences; thus the Institut Pasteur in 1996 held half its meetings in French and half in English. Despite the law, almost one-third of television commercials continued to feature some form of English.[132]

Linguistic traditionalists did not enjoy strong support for their actions. The socialists were unenthusiastic about the Toubon Law, dissenters outnumbered supporters, and the public took a more utilitarian stance than policy makers and cultural/media elites. A majority approved the use of Americanisms, calling it modern, useful, or amusing.[133] Furthermore, France had to act alone on this issue; it could not strengthen the cause of "linguistic diversity" through the EU because other members like the United Kingdom and Germany worried that national linguistic rules would impede commerce.

The status of French continued to sag as an international language. French, among the number of speakers worldwide, ranked only eleventh as a first language, behind even German in 2005.[134] In the global arena one study estimated that 85 percent of international organizations were using English as one of their working languages, as opposed to less than half for French.[135] By the end of the decade virtually every child chose English as either his or her first or second foreign language; only one in ten elected German as a first choice.[136] And despite what officials proclaimed about the soul of France residing in its language, almost two-thirds agreed with the proposition "Everyone should be able to speak English."[137] One should not, however, despair about the language since French remains the only other truly global language and it is spoken in more countries than any other language except English. Nevertheless, it was apparent that the French had to come on board the global transporter where the passengers spoke American English or risked being left behind.

◼ The Cultural Exception

If halting the linguistic intrusion of America succeeded in only a few specific areas and otherwise failed, the Republic fared better in the culture wars over audiovisual products.

Defiance has been a historic feature of the Gallic response to Hollywood. Leading the resistance has been the cinema industry, its praetorian guard of intellectuals, and republican officials. Apprehension about an American takeover of the French screen dates back to the days of the silent movie and persisted after the Second World War. But concern intensified in the 1980s. Box office for American films ballooned from 35 percent to 54 percent between 1980 and 1993, with the sharpest rise coming after 1985, while the share of the domestic market for French films fell in almost the same proportion.[138] During the 1990s the American share of the market oscillated between 54 and 63 percent.[139] Films like *Basic Instinct* and *Terminator 2* were runaway hits, outdistancing any French competition. The crowning blow came in October

1993 when Steven Spielberg's *Jurassic Park* sold two million tickets in its first week, leaving Claude Berri's film version of Emile Zola's classic novel *Germinal* far behind. Minister of Culture Jacques Toubon declared the dinosaur film a threat to national identity and set off a wild debate.[140] The reasons for this loss of market were complex; they involved a younger audience, the appeal of Hollywood blockbusters, the advent of the multiplex, and fewer ticket sales. Some argued the cinema had also lost its creativity. So many French film professionals moved to California seeking a better place to make films that they formed an informal Hollywood circle.[141] Or as some grumbled, French taste in films had descended to the infantile level of Hollywood productions. One prominent film producer observed, "What works in Chattanooga now works in the sixth arrondissement of Paris. It's a little sad."[142] Whatever the cause, the industry was once again in trouble.

Hollywood movies, as well as other kinds of American programming, also came to dominate French television screens. By 1993 American TV shows accounted for about half of French broadcast time.[143] And in the fall of that year the Turner Broadcasting Company launched a new European satellite channel combining programs from Turner Network Television and the Cartoon Network that threatened to subvert the prevailing quota system. Among the reasons for this saturation of American images were deregulation, which came in the 1980s; the proliferation of private stations, many of which depended on cheap imports of American programs and films; and the sale of videocassettes. In the audio world American music outsold local recordings and Michael Jackson sold more CDs than Jacques Brel.

The European Community, as we saw in chapter 2, adopted a directive in 1989 to curb foreign (that is, American) television imports largely at the behest of France.[144] The misnamed Television without Frontiers ruling required Europeans to reserve a minimum of 50 percent of TV programming, including broadcast of films, for European productions. Individual nations could, if they wanted, raise the ante— and France did. It reserved 60 percent of broadcast time, including

Figure 12. Theaters on the Champs-Elysées showing Hollywood movies, including *Jurassic Park*; Wednesday, December 8, 1993. Courtesy AP Photo/Remy de la Mauviniere.

prime time, for European works and 40 percent for French programming. Music, meanwhile, broadcast by radio stations fell under quotas set by French legislation in 1993. There was flexibility in the television quota system to the extent that the directive stipulated application was limited to where it was "practicable." In fact the EC directive changed little since most programming was already below the limit. The Americans protested, but the French managed to get most of the EC to rally to its side. The row over the 1989 directive was only a prelude to even stormier negotiations over the audiovisual sector.

Washington and Hollywood objected strongly to quotas and other barriers sheltering the rich European entertainment market. Together politicians and lobbyists attempted to use the Uruguay Round of the GATT negotiations, which aimed at a broad reduction of trade restrictions, as a way of gaining access to the continent. The Americans wanted free entry to the audiovisual market, which meant reducing subsidies to film producers, lifting fees on movie tickets and videocassettes, and easing limits on television programming especially quotas that might apply to new technologies like satellite transmission and cable. But the French refused. They, with some support from their fellow Europeans, insisted on a "cultural exception." Unless culture was exempt, the French argued, European cinema and television would not survive. They warned of the danger of standardizing the world's taste for entertainment at the level of *Jurassic Park*. Subjecting the audiovisual sector to free trade would mean the end of the subsidy system that had sustained the cinema and would turn television programming over to the Americans. The French government levied an 11 percent tax on all film tickets and it collected fees from the profits of television networks and the sale of blank video- and audiocassettes. This revenue, which amounted to hundreds of millions of dollars, was used in turn to finance the production, distribution, and exhibition of French films.

The Fifth Republic was willing to put the Uruguay Round at risk in the name of the cultural exception. French resistance, it seems, had less to do with the survival of a profitable economic sector—though that was how the Americans attributed motives—than it had with defending France and Europe from the Americanization of culture. In 1993 Prime Minister Balladur, continuing the tough stance of his socialist predecessors, instructed his negotiators to make no concessions. At home Balladur won wide political endorsement for facing down the United States, and he also gained the open backing of Spain and the tacit support of Germany. On the other side of the Atlantic, President Bill Clinton, who had close ties with Hollywood, took personal interest in the negotiations. Tough bargainers like Mickey Kantor, U.S. trade representative, and Jack Valenti, head of the Motion Picture Association of America, represented the United States at the GATT talks.

The controversy over the cultural exception raised tempers in both Paris and Washington. When President Clinton rejected the principle of excluding culture, Jack Lang, who had been culture minister when the GATT talks began, warned that the time had come to declare "war" in order to safeguard the nation's traditions, art of living, and culture.[145] French officials insisted the cultural exception defended not just their national audiovisual industry but that of all Europeans as well as the cause of global diversity.[146] President Mitterrand, speaking in Poland, linked national identity to the freedom to create images and asserted that a nation that abandoned its means of representation to others was "a slave society."[147] There were echoes in this campaign of Jack Lang's Mexico City tirade in 1982 against American cultural imperialism (see chapter 2). European movie directors including celebrities like Pedro Almodóvar and Bernardo Bertolucci as well as French professionals like actors Gérard Depardieu and Catherine Deneuve and directors Bertrand Tavernier and Alain Corneau demanded protection. Tavernier vented that "the Americans want to treat us the way they treated the Redskins," and Corneau warned against an American monopoly: "Think of a world in which there is only one image."[148] The prospect of a "world culture" saturated by American movies, television, leisure parks, music, fashion, and food prompted Nicolas Seydoux, the head of Gaumont, the oldest French producer and distributor, to ask whether or not "our children will resemble us[.]"[149]

Hollywood celebrities like Steven Spielberg and Martin Scorsese, who supported a free market for entertainment, squared off against their French colleagues while the former chairman of Columbia Pictures complained, "This is simple protectionism, it's arrogant, as anti-American as you can get. What they don't like is that audiences find American entertainment desirable."[150] What particularly galled American negotiators was that revenue from the tax on box office receipts, over half of which was generated by American films, was diverted to the French cinema industry. Valenti groused about Europeans invoking national identity: "The negotiation has nothing to do with culture unless European soap operas and game shows are the equivalent of Molière. This is all about the hard business of money."[151] He made the case for open markets: "I think the people of Europe . . . should have the right to choose their own television. The audience is king. I want more competition in the market place, less man-made barriers. Let the market forces collide and something better will come out of it."[152]

French opponents of the free-trade approach responded: because Hollywood now insisted on some measure of international income from all its productions, the inevitable outcome was formulaic movies depending on special effects and minimal dialogue that would sell in the global market. They thus complained not so much at the takeover of an "American cinema" as they did about the proliferation of a kind of global, standardized image—which they were quick to add was either vulgar or barbaric.[153] The result would be that nations like France would be unable to "tell their own story." The celebrated Greek moviemaker who worked in France, Costa-Gavras, warned that without the cultural exception big Hollywood studios would overrun small independent European producers who, in his eyes, were the most creative sector of the industry.[154] *Le Monde* added, "In the era of globalized exchange, images . . . export a style of life, a 'model' of society. On the terrain of the imagination whoever captures minds also wins at commerce: 'standard' images, 'standard' aspirations."[155]

Citing commercial gain was a vulgar appeal that the French tried to avoid. Jack Lang asserted, "Cinema is a national art by which one expresses the history and imagination of a country. . . . Cinema is not merchandise."[156] Yet French negotiators like Toscan du Plantier, the head of Unifrance, the cinema's export marketing office, also stressed that tens of thousand of jobs and large revenues were at risk. And the inability of French films to penetrate the American market only fortified the determination of French officials to secure the exemption of the audiovisual sector from the GATT talks. They complained about the unwillingness of American distributors to exhibit French films—a kind of de facto Yankee protectionism. Explaining the apathy of American audiences, Toscan du Plantier grumbled, "Americans don't even know what the world 'cultural' means. Hardly ten percent of them are educated in the sense that we use the term in Europe. A film like *The Visitors* is just too complicated for them. It contains references to the Middle Ages that the average American would absolutely not understand: he doesn't imagine a past that existed before him. . . . In fact their cinema has become a kind of giant video game where the family amuses itself."[157]

Once again, as in the 1980s when the socialists campaigned against cultural imperialism, the American threat to cultural identity provoked open debate among intellectuals. And many of the earlier discussants stepped forward again, including such stars as Bernard-Henri Lévy, Max Gallo, Régis Debray, Mario Vargas-Llosa, and André Glucksmann. What set up the debate was a warning by Lévy, Glucksmann, and others against letting the GATT dispute revive the old nationalistic demons of anti-Americanism: the poor quality of French films was not the fault of the Americans.[158] And the Peruvian-Spanish writer Vargas-Llosa triggered the reaction by charging that the dinosaurs of *Jurassic Park* "do not in any way threaten the cultural honor of the land that gave birth to Flaubert, the Lumière brothers, Debussy and Cézanne, Rodin and Marcel Carné. They threaten only the band of little chauvinistic demagogues who talk about French culture as if it were a question of a mummy that any contact with the outside world would quickly reduce to ashes." The denationalization of culture was irreversible, the Latin American author contended; even the French were trying to create films for the world market. Creativity would not be served by bureaucrats, politicians, and intellectuals who arrogated to themselves what was to be viewed or heard; such an approach only served "state parasites," as one could see in the mountain of inferior movies sheltered as "national culture."[159]

Régis Debray, vexed by being labeled a chauvinistic demagogue, answered that there would soon be one vision of the world in circulation, that of the Americans. "The guarantor of pluralism is Europe," because, he deemed, the Americans force their vision on the world while they effectively close their movie screens and their broadcasting companies to outsiders: "What's good for Columbia and Warner Brothers is good for the United States, so the question now is whether it's good for humanity." Debray argued that the application of free trade to the audiovisual hurt weaker producers, citing the Italian movie industry, which produced less than twenty films a year. The stakes were high because "the image governs our dreams and dreams our actions." He warned that "the monoculture that colorizes imaginations into monochrome" would ignite a global cultural rebellion: "Do you want to convert the planet into a supermarket leaving people the choice between the local ayatollah and Coca-Cola?" Watch out, he warned, because cultural minorities who cannot express themselves will regress into the worst forms of essentialist identities and xenophobia. Debray advised saying no to America since its empire would fade like all the others: "[L]et's at least make sure that it does not leave behind irreparable damage to our reservoirs of creativity."[160] Max Gallo, historian and former socialist deputy, joined Debray, insisting that defending national culture was not tantamount to acting as a chauvinistic demagogue or subscribing to anti-Americanism; it represented a rejection of the United States as the global cultural model. Gallo argued singular national cultures composed European culture, unlike the United States, where culture was supposedly divorced from history, locale, and memory—thus *Jurassic Park* was a world film whereas *Germinal* belonged to a nation. The cultural exception would save culture from being treated as merchandise for a global supermarket. "Is this anti-Americanism," he asked, "or defense of pluralism?"[161]

"Dear Régis," Vargas-Llosa replied in turn, adding that it was Debray's fantasy that a conspiracy of Hollywood multinationals could corrupt French tastes when in fact television audiences everywhere preferred soap operas and reality shows to high culture. Market capitalism had integrated the world, not socialism, and this process could not be reversed by a return to the "tribal era." As a former backer of Fidel Castro turned liberal, Vargas-Llosa warned the strategy of the cultural exception led straight to state control. "Dear Mario," Debray responded, dismissing the accusation of anti-Americanism as the latest way to excommunicate an opponent. "I refuse America as a model and I feed off its culture. Euro Disney bores me and California enchants me." Of course, conspiracy was not responsible for America's cultural imperium, he held; it followed the natural momentum of empire. The market was no solution because competition between Hollywood and, say, the African cinema would asphyxiate the latter. The one-time adviser to François Mitterrand concluded that nations are not prehistoric tribes but contemporary collectives of memory and belonging that the market would like to eradicate. If we didn't build a dike against American culture we would all end up with the same perspective, heading down "the same asphalt road toward the future."[162]

While the likes of Vargas-Llosa and Debray debated the merits of the cultural exception, French negotiators nearly blocked the Uruguay Round as it neared completion in late 1993. It was a game of high-stakes poker that pitted the United States against France over a hugely profitable entertainment business. The American negotiator, Mickey Kantor, was unable to persuade the Europeans that they should ease their quotas on American movies and television programs or to lift levies on movie tickets and videocassettes. What strengthened the hand of the French negotiators was a domestic political consensus. From socialists like President Mitterrand to Gaullists like Prime Minister Balladur and, on the far right, Jean-Marie Le Pen, the political community united behind the cultural exception. On this aspect of cultural policy the Left and the Right stood together. Or as Jacques Toubon boasted, "Culture transcends political divisions here. It is part of the national consensus of our country."[163] The European Community, at least tacitly, backed France against the United States. At times the Germans became impatient with French stubbornness, but they nonetheless sided with their friends. In the end the French had their way and the audio-visual sector was excluded from the final agreement. The issue was thus not settled; it was put off to the future. President Clinton expressed his disappointment over what was an agreement to disagree, while Valenti complained that the Europeans had turned their back on the future and Kantor declared that the United States would continue the fight. Lang lauded the exclusion of the audiovisual sector as "a victory for art and artists over the commercialization of culture."[164]

Audiovisual issues remained a standoff for the rest of the 1990s. French officials sought stricter enforcement of quotas and removal of the "where practicable" clause, a strategy that garnered support from some other European countries like Belgium, Spain, and Portugal. But in 1995, when the EU reviewed the Television without Frontiers directive, France could not overcome the opposition of the United Kingdom, the Netherlands, Denmark, and others to strengthening restrictions. Lang, who had orchestrated the 1989 directive, complained that this setback showed that "the majority of Europeans will lie down as soon as the United States gives the order."[165] Meanwhile, the United States was confident that new technologies like satellite broadcasting, video-on-demand, digitized compression, Internet streaming, and other new forms of information communication would eventually render whatever quotas imposed by the cultural exception obsolete.[166] They would simply bypass such barriers. Valenti admitted after the GATT talks that the real issue had not been film subsidies but the free entry of new technologies like pay-per-view and revenue sharing from levies on sales of blank videocassettes.[167] The two sides continued to agree to disagree.

The issue resurfaced at the end of the decade during negotiations of an international agreement designed to end discrimination against foreign investment, the Multilateral Agreement on Investment (MAI). Once again France led the Europeans against the accord, fearing weaker rules would limit the state's ability to protect areas like the environment and culture.[168] And once again there was a mobilization of the interested parties, like celebrities from the arts including movie directors as well as various nongovernmental organizations concerned with antiglobalization. There were representations to the government, and in 1998 the Jospin administration withdrew from the talks in order to defend the cultural exception and the system of domestic subsidies. Philip Gordon and Sophie Meunier concluded, "The catalytic role played by protestors in the failure of the MAI was perceived as the first major success for France's anti-globalization movement."[169] It was not until the Inter-Governmental Conference at Nice in 2000, however, that the principle of the cultural exception was officially recognized by the EU.[170] The French paid a heavy political price for this victory, but they had finally secured its triumph.

During the 1990s the Fifth Republic acting under this exception protected the audiovisual sector, limiting American television programming and aiding the cinema. The industry continued to produce about 140 films per year and to retain a third or more share of domestic ticket sales, as opposed to a half share for Hollywood, and to enjoy a certain global status as the producer of high-quality cinema.[171] Relative to that of other European countries, French cinema was more successful in retaining its domestic market. By 1999 the figures for share of ticket sales were 38 percent for France compared to 24 percent for Italy and much less for the United Kingdom, Germany, and Spain.[172] The celebrated Italian film industry, for example, became, to a considerable extent, an offshore facility for Hollywood productions. French policy, despite its national preference, also lent substantial support to transnational films, to the European cinema, and to the exhibition of movies from all over the world.[173] And France performed better in retaining its share of television audiences than did other Western European countries. In 1995 American films occupied only 35–39 percent of programming on the principal broadcast stations in France, like TF1, and this was far less than in Germany, Spain, the United Kingdom, or Italy.[174] Similarly, quotas on radio broadcasts cut Anglo-American popular music in half by 1996 so that the French heard slightly more of their own music than did other Europeans.[175]

Should one conclude then that French policy worked? Yes, the 1990s are an example of successful cultural protection. Among the principal reasons for the performance of the audiovisual sector, according to many authorities, was the system of quotas and subsidies (actually, transfers, since the state budget was not the source of funding) that the cultural exception sheltered.[176] Financial support, which was massive but also complex and opaque, made a difference. Requiring subventions for the cinema from private television stations probably saved the industry from disaster. Protectionism, contrary to liberal market orthodoxy, also worked in many countries other than France to preserve domestic film industries, including those of Korea and Australia.[177] It must be noted that survival was not due entirely to state policy, because the industry proved to be inventive. As much as a third of its output in the 1990s was of international coproductions, and it tried its hand at producing entertaining films for both domestic and foreign audiences: action films like *La Femme Nikita*, comedies like *Les Visiteurs*, science fiction movies like *Le Cinquième Elément* (The Fifth Element), costume dramas like *Valmont*, and grand spectacles like *Indochine*. Much of this imitated Hollywood.[178] The government, beginning with Jack Lang in the late 1980s, authorized subsidies for big-budget, English-language movies that competed for global audiences. Lavish coproductions like *The Lover* (based on the novel by Marguerite Duras) and *1492: Conquest of Paradise* starring Gérard Depardieu emulated Hollywood and minimized elements traditionally associated with French cinema, including the language. One director, Luc Besson, trumped the Americans, making costly blockbusters in English that displayed pyrotechnic special effects and graphic violence and featured American actors like Bruce Willis. Besson's *Fifth Element* proved a smash success as the top-grossing film at the French box office in 1997, outdrawing Disney's *The Hunchback of Notre Dame* and earning an unprecedented 65 million dollars in export income—much of it from American audiences. Besson, to be sure, was denigrated by French critics for being "too American." Hollywood was so impressed with some French productions that it bought and remade them; for example, *La Femme Nikita* reappeared as *Point of No Return*. But this strategy raised the question, Could one win this contest by Americanizing French cinema?

Not everyone was impressed with the system. One economist claimed the French exaggerated their success. He pointed out if one were rigorous about what constitutes the nationality of a film, then French output diminished to a level similar to that of the Germans and Italians by the early 1990s.[179] Skeptics contended that the intricate web of support harmed the industry by nurturing a kind of dependence and unwillingness to face the demands of the market. One such study concludes that state subsides created an elitist, inbred network that rewarded auteur films at the expense of more commercial films that would have a global appeal.[180] Subsidies were wasted on films that had no audience; in fact, large numbers of what the industry produced were utter failures at the box office. Or as one critic complained, young French directors were satisfied if they reached an audience of three hundred and received a review in *Le Monde*.[181] From an opposing perspective, aiding mainstream, historical, or literary films like *Cyrano de Bergerac* or *Germinal* was an aesthetic and creative mistake.[182] Then there were the perverse effects of the system, like restricted entry for new filmmakers and benefits awarded Hollywood clones. Did it make sense to subsidize the production of quasi-American films? Contrary to intentions, handouts often went to films that were essentially made by foreign (sometimes American) companies that exploited the official criteria for what defined a film as French. Thus the British-French coproduction *Valmont* from Czech director Milos Forman was made in English using nine American or British actors and actresses. But because the film included one French actress, some scenes shot in France, and was based on a French text, it qualified as French.

Despite such objections, it seems clear that the elaborate system of state subsidies for cinema and foreign film quotas for television helped the French industry retain its position vis-à-vis American cinema better than other European cinemas did. It consistently produced more films per year than any other European country and retained a relatively large share of its domestic audience. Comparatively, the French preferred their local productions over American films more than the Germans and the Italians did.[183] France also curbed American television programming more than did other European countries. In short, the audiovisual sector was one area where French policy succeeded in at least limiting the American invasion. In this case governments on both the left and the right had to resort to brinksmanship with the U.S. government in order to win the argument. But, unlike the controversy over language, the cultural exception commanded some European support and wide and active domestic political backing.

In 1999, American, or Anglo-American, films like *Star Wars Episode I: The Phantom Menace, The Matrix,* and *Notting Hill* occupied seven of the top ten money-making slots while the French had only three—but the number one movie was *Astérix et Obélix versus Caesar,* an expensive Hollywood-like production that seemed like a parody of the transatlantic rivalry in which the indomitable, wily Gauls outwit the mighty Roman/American invaders. Astérix, *Le Monde* proclaimed, was "the image of resistance to American cinematographic imperialism."[184] Less haughtily one might simply say that in the realm of the audiovisual Astérix held his own against Caesar in the 1990s.

■ French policy makers overtly resisted the American example, attacked it as an antimodel, and defended the mixed economy, the social contract, and national culture. What they selectively borrowed from abroad they altered and disguised as a French innovation or alternative. Using America as a foil during the fin de siècle the Fifth Republic adapted. It may have disdained *capitalisme dur* yet it deregulated, privatized, and opened the economy and made heroes out of entrepreneurs. It may have assailed "flexibility" in employment, but many new jobs were temporary or part-time. It may have ridiculed America's welfare practices, but it transformed its system by increments until it, in the eyes of one authority, had adapted to the "new global economic paradigm"—referring, for example, to lowering costs in order to make social assistance compatible with international competition.[185] It may have championed the cultural exception, but it also subsidized the production of films that were Hollywood clones. If the political class tacked toward the Anglo-American model, it did so without admitting it, and the means employed were as much French as they were American. That was the case with the new high-tech incubator at Sophia Antipolis. Whether it was stock options à la française, épargne retraite (pensions), "involving the private sector" (privatization), or cinematic coproductions, the answer was to create hybrids. Bashing America did not obstruct reform, and served as a useful camouflage for making the necessary accommodation to market liberalism and globalization.

Adaptation also percolated from below. In many instances adjustments came from the private sector rather than the state: it was business managers working in a globalized environment who innovated most by borrowing from abroad. The cinema industry also remade itself in part by following Hollywood's example. And the public, while yielding to a darkened image of America, pragmatically accepted a measure of liberalization, globalization, and Americanization–including learning American English.

Extremism about the American model, however, was not a winning strategy. Overt and wholesale imitation of the Americans could spell trouble. It cost Alain Madelin his ministry and Jean-Marie Messier his job. Even association with American ways could be a handicap, as it was for the Right, because of its alignment with market liberalism, in the 1997 elections. And it could stir popular protest. In the name of resistance to American-led globalization there were manifestos and demonstrations over agricultural subsidies, *la malbouffe*, the "cultural exception," the Plan Juppé, and the MAI. Yet overt and wholesale rejection of America could be equally perilous. Jacques Toubon's language purge seemed excessive and out of touch with the globalized world. One had to engage in transatlantic transfers without acknowledgment and add a Gallic twist.

7.

The Paradox of the Fin de Siècle:

Anti-Americanism and Americanization

As the twentieth century drew to a close, Americanization was transforming how the French ate, entertained themselves, conducted business, and even communicated. Yet the fin de siècle also witnessed the strongest expression of anti-Americanism since the 1960s. It was visible in opinion polls, newspapers, books, television, and politicians' pronouncements. It is this paradox, this tension between a society seemingly immersed in America and one that posed America as "the other," that merits attention.

A decade after the war in the Persian Gulf, Uncle Sam had fallen off his pedestal. Parisians hunting for books on America could find titles like *Le Cauchemar américain* (The American Nightmare) or *Non merci, Oncle Sam!*—the latter written by a member of parliament—describing American society in the most lurid terms.[1] A large majority of the French elite thought the United States and France were at odds over a wide range of issues. A former head of the Foreign Ministry's policy planning staff attacked American elected officials for their ignorance of international affairs and labeled the U.S. government's untutored guidance to others as "imperialism."[2] At an international conference in Warsaw more than a hundred nations issued a manifesto, sponsored by the United States, advancing worldwide democracy. Only France refused to sign the manifesto, provoking the *New York Times* to run an article titled, "At Democracy's Picnic, Paris Supplies (the) Ants."[3] Then there was José Bové, the radical turned sheep farmer, who won international attention for vandalizing the site of a new McDonald's outlet in 1999 and later traveled to Seattle for a meeting of the World Trade Organization to attack American-led globalization.

But there is another story, one that makes this surge of anti-Americanism seem contradictory. In 1999 France sent more military aircraft to bomb Serbia than any European nation, and it placed them under American command. Trade between the countries had doubled since 1985, and French direct investment in the United States also doubled in the 1990s, making France the fourth largest investor—ahead of countries like Japan and Canada.[4] Meanwhile Americanization swept across the French landscape. In the summer of 2000, Hollywood movies attracted almost two of three paid admissions in French theaters and there were almost 800 McDonald's restaurants in France.[5] In a nation that celebrates its language as the prime marker of national identity, almost two-thirds had come to agree with the proposition "Everyone should be able to speak English."[6]

These two contrasting sets of behavior suggest a paradox. Despite the fact that the United States and France became more closely linked than ever before; despite the apparent cordiality between Washington, D.C., and Paris; and despite the fact that France was more Americanized than ever before, anti-Americanism during the 1990s reached its highest intensity in over thirty years. Not since Charles de Gaulle's presidency was such animosity expressed—in political speeches, in the media, in polls, and even in public demonstrations.

What happened, in brief, was once the Cold War ended, the transatlantic superpower, from a French perspective, became more overbearing. The French in turn became more critical of domestic trends in the United States and less comfortable with the inroads of American culture. As a result they intensified their efforts at both asserting their independence and defining themselves differently from their American cousins.

There is no need to engage in a tedious definitional debate about what constitutes "anti-Americanism." This issue has already been addressed (see "A Note on Anti-Americanism" at the beginning of this volume). As the term has been used throughout this study it refers to both the dystopian version, labeled *anti-américanisme primaire*, that reflexive hate of all things associated with America that was confined to a small minority, as well as to surges in more popular criticism of important aspects of American foreign and domestic policies that could extend to American institutions, Americans as a people, and the American "way of life." In this chapter the subject is the second version, the more volatile manifestation of criticism associated with perceptions of American policies. There were statements and responses to pollsters, and sometimes actions, by the French people, often powerful and knowing, that explicitly criticized American policies, institutions, and values. I term these attitudes and behavior "anti-American"—acknowledging that it means only criticism of something important about America. Unfortunately for transatlantic relations this grumpy mood became increasingly common in the 1990s.

Yet if this was so, if anti-Americanism attracted popular support, then there is a paradox: Why did an "Americanized society" like France endorse or at least acquiesce under such criticism? Wasn't it hypocritical for the French, for example, to consume a million meals per day under the Golden Arches yet condone attacks on McDonald's? It is best to postpone addressing this paradox until later in this chapter; first we need to examine the evidence for growing anti-Americanism.

How can the historian know what the French thought about Americans and the United States? Transatlantic troubles stirred interest in ascertaining the state of public opinion. The result was an extraordinary number of comprehensive surveys conducted by various French and American polling agencies. These surveys, some done systematically over this period, were conducted for newspapers, foundations, and other institutions like the U.S. Department of State. Over twenty thousand Frenchmen and women recorded their opinion in such polls. This evidence, supplemented by other conventional historical sources like the press, books, the statements of public officials, and

TV news give a researcher a good idea of how persons in the street viewed the United States. If the chronological focus for these surveys is the 1990s, they stretch from the middle years of Ronald Reagan's presidency to the end of Bill Clinton's second term.

Treating these data from a comparative perspective establishes the distinctiveness of French perceptions. Whenever the sources permit, I shall contrast the French voice with that of other Europeans. The most common frame of reference utilized in these surveys was Western Europe. In this analysis "West Europeans" usually meant the French, the British, the Germans, and the Italians. When others, like the Spanish or the Dutch, were polled, it will be noted. If in certain aspects the French took the lead in expressing unease about America, in other respects they were no different, and even trailed behind, other West Europeans in their critical attitudes.

A fastidious researcher might contend that polls are not a reliable source for public opinion. The wording or order of questions can shape responses, and it is difficult to distinguish between casual answers and deeply held attitudes. Moreover, respondents often select from a prepared menu of choices and rarely have the opportunity to offer alternatives or explain their selections. Nevertheless, these surveys do provide a large number of responses to skillfully phrased questions posed by pollsters in specific contexts. To those who are skeptical of polls in principle, one can argue that they are as accurate an index of opinion as other sources like newspapers, best-sellers, Internet chat rooms, interviews, or debates among media intellectuals. Thousands of people who were systematically interrogated by numerous professional polling agencies offer solid evidence of attitudes.

Polling responses were, to be sure, heavily shaped by the respondent's sources of information. There is no mystery concerning how the French learned about America at the end of the century. The answer is: television. The French relied heavily on the little screen for their information about America. Newspapers, films, radio, music, books, visits, friends, schooling, and the Internet contributed something, but rather little.[7] Television influenced perception more than any other type of media.

The Image of Americans and the United States

When asked about their transatlantic friends the French usually distinguished between "Americans" and the "United States" or "America." The category "Americans" was the most specific, and conveyed a personal or human dimension to the collectivity; it usually evoked a kinder response than the other two terms. "United States" and "America" seemed interchangeable to respondents. But "United States" often carried a strong connotation of international policy and was associated with Washington. The French said they liked Americans. Large majorities consistently expressed a favorable attitude toward us. In fact the French (71 percent) were as friendly as the Germans and the Italians.[8] But this sunny disposition was marked by distance. In some surveys almost half of those consulted voiced indifference toward Americans. In 1999 nearly two-thirds of those polled said they did "not feel close to the American people."[9] This was a friendship of distant cousins. (If it is any satisfaction for Americans, the British came off worse in one poll.[10]) And there was a small minority, about 10 percent, who were predictably hostile.

Opinions about the "United States" or "America" were more detached from the connotation of people and linked to notions of policy, power, society, and culture. They tended to evoke more volatile responses.

In general, during these years, when faced with the simple choice between favorable or unfavorable attitudes about the United States/America, the populace tended to display a rather genial disposition. About two-thirds of French people surveyed held a favorable opinion of the United States. Such attitudes closely resembled those held by the Germans.[11] But this crude choice concealed shifts, distinctions, and reservations. The overall trend in the 1990s was for a hardening of attitudes. Sympathy for the United States declined sharply between 1988 and 1996 (from 54 percent to 35 percent), and both antipathy and indifference toward the United States increased (from 6 percent to 12 percent and from 38 percent to 47 percent, respectively).[12] On the eve of the Al Gore–George W. Bush presidential election, another poll found more dark clouds than sunshine. Selecting from a list of five options about how they felt about the United States, almost half selected either "critical" or "anxious," while only a quarter chose either "admiring" or "kindly" and another quarter opted for the adjective "indifferent."[13] Indifference about the United States, as well as about Americans, was consistently voiced by many of the French, who dissented from those who were either fascinated or repulsed. According to a poll taken in May 2000, 41 percent said they were "sympathetic" toward the United States and 10 percent said "antipathetic." The rest who answered (48 percent) said neither one nor the other.[14] The "favorable" reputation that polls regularly recorded proved fickle when international affairs interfered as the scuffles over Operation Desert Storm and the events in Kosovo showed. The image of "the United States" was less complimentary than that of "Americans" and, being intimately connected to international affairs, fluctuated wildly.

If a majority of the French displayed a favorable opinion of the United States/America during these years, their views were detached, checkered, and unstable—and they were becoming darker.

What is striking about public opinion in the period 1984 to 2002 was the persistent fear of American domination. Anxiety about Yankee domination of French domestic affairs oscillated at a high level—around 60–65 percent. It dipped to less than 50 percent in the middle years of the Clinton administration, but returned to 62 percent at the end of his tenure.[15] Fifty to sixty percent also expressed concern about the U.S. government's domination of international affairs.[16] In general the French found the United States overbearing. Ninety percent of the French in 1995 —far more than the Germans (60 percent)—said

Figure 13. "I thought they were in Central America!" U.S. military and financial power invading France. Courtesy Plantu, "Je les croyais en Amérique centrale!" In *C'est la goulag!* Paris: Éditions la Découverte/Le Monde, 1983, 140.

the United States was "domineering."[17] In 1999 close to 60 percent of the French said the United States was too influential in Europe with respect to culture, economics, the military, and politics.[18] A year later over two-thirds, when asked if they wished for "more or less American influence," opted for less of America in the categories of: international affairs, culture, economic life, globalization, and the development of the European Union (EU).[19] Doubts about the U.S. government's altruism were common. Four out of five of the French polled in 2001—more than the British, Italians or Germans—believed that the United States did not generally consider the views of other countries and acted only in its own interest.[20] Asked to explain their dislike for American influence respondents in one poll mentioned "seizing control of other countries," "acting as world policemen," "imposing their lifestyle," "American imperialism," and/or "economic hegemony."[21]

The French shared with other West Europeans a growing apprehension that the United States had too much influence in their affairs.[22] If nine out of ten French people accused America of being domineering, so did the same proportion of Italians and the British. The Germans were far more restrained in attributing domination.[23] In comparison to other West European elites, however, the French proved the most nervous about U.S. hegemony. In general, French perceptions of America closely resembled those held by other West Europeans: they all characterized America as having a will to dominate.

French concern about transatlantic domination extended beyond international politics. More than other West Europeans the French believed that the United States practiced unfair trade.[24] The irritant here was probably the host of disputes like trade sanctions against the Soviet Union, Iran, and Cuba; the quarrels over agricultural subsidies; and later troubles over the export of fruits, vegetables, and seeds grown via the use of genetically modified organisms (GMOs). Among French elites there was a noticeable increase in anxiety during the early Clinton years about excessive U.S. interference. A surge occurred in 1993 at the peak of the General Agreement on Tariffs and Trade (GATT) controversy when those who complained jumped from about 50 percent to 70 percent; it remained at this elevated level for the rest of the 1990s.[25] Globalization framed many of these trade problems. If a majority of the French approved of globalization, as did other West Europeans, they also accounted for the largest negative minority opinion of any wealthy nation.[26] In general less than one of ten respondents in Western Europe linked globalization with American domination, but in France one in five made this connection and one in four thought globalization mainly benefited the United States.[27] Thus the French proved more likely than their West European counterparts to see the greedy hand of Uncle Sam lurking behind globalization.

Closely related to the perception of American domination was the question of confidence in U.S. global leadership. The French were never satisfied with the U.S. government, particularly not during either the Reagan or the Clinton eras. The polls showed volatility on this question rather than long-term trends. There were ups and downs related to events, policies, and leadership. Confidence soared under the presidency of George H. W. Bush. This peak coincided with the reunification of Germany and the first war in the Persian Gulf. But this episode was fleeting. Generally polls show that confidence in the United States fluctuated around a rather tepid 50 percent for most of these two decades.[28] There was little change in this level after President Clinton succeeded his two Republican predecessors.

In the last two years of the Clinton administration, Washington's approval rating faded. At the end of the decade polls revealed acute anxiety about the U.S. superpower and widespread cynicism about what motivated policy makers. Doubts about Washington's altruism became commonplace. French elites singled out transatlantic trade as a major reason to distrust the U.S. government.[29] The crisis over Kosovo exposed this deepening mistrust among the public. In a survey conducted during the bombing of Yugoslavia, two of three expressed concern about the superpower and also questioned its motives.[30] Moreover, in this same 1999 survey 61 percent said the United States exercised too much influence over Europe and an even higher number expressed their distance from the American people.[31] By the end of the Clinton administration few believed the United States was acting to promote peace or democracy. More common was the perception that the superpower's aims were principally to "protect and extend American interests and investments in the world" and to "impose the will of the U.S. on the rest of the world."[32]

Even though perceptions of the United States had become much gloomier by 2000, once George W. Bush took office, and especially when the military campaign in Iraq seemed imminent, America's standing collapsed. Once the war began, favorable opinion of Americans plunged precipitously, but the president, not "America" or "Americans," was the primary target of Gallic reproach. Given French cynicism about U.S. motives in world affairs, it was no surprise that the French, far more than the Germans or the British, believed that the U.S. government attacked out of self-interest, such as a desire for Iraqi oil.[33]

In general the French did not see the Americans cooperating with them in international affairs. On only a few issues did the majority think that the two nations were working in the same direction; and in some cases substantial majorities perceived them working at cross-purposes—for example, in trade, the environment, and aid for developing nations.[34] It follows that the French were not eager to endorse strong U.S. leadership in world affairs. Compared to the Germans, the British, the Italians, the Dutch, and the Poles, they were the least willing to do so—even if they were deeply divided.[35] Indeed, a majority of the French at the end of the decade admitted that their country did not always act as a "faithful ally" toward the United States.[36] But what was most distinctive about the French was that by 2002 they openly and in overwhelming numbers (91 percent) said they wanted the EU to become a "superpower like the U.S." In this respect the Italians, the Germans, the Dutch, the British, and the Poles trailed far behind.[37] At the end of the Clinton years almost half the French said they wanted a European defense policy without American involvement.[38] And if slim majorities in Germany, Great Britain, Italy, the Netherlands, and Poland accepted the "cook-dishwasher" division of labor—that is, that the United States specialized in fighting wars and the Europeans reconstituted societies afterward—a majority of the French rejected the lowly role of acting as America's dishwasher.[39]

The French, from the late 1980s to the first years of the new century, came to think of the United States as a domineering, self-interested nation that used its inordinate power to seek global hegemony. In this respect they may have surpassed other West Europeans, but their views were widely shared across the continent.

■ American Culture

If American hard power aroused Gallic apprehension, so did its soft power. Given the heated controversies that American mass culture generated and the efforts by the French government to curb American imports like television programs and censor use of the English language, a casual observer might have concluded that France was an unwelcome site. Despite growing concern about Yankee popular culture, however, ambivalence and selectivity, rather than total rejection characterized French opinion.

Between 1984 and 2000 the number of those who found American mass culture excessive increased substantially. Television programming, the cinema, and food were the principal targets. Objections also rose, but less sharply, to the English language and American fashion. Concern about American-style advertising remained high, but unchanged, while pop music gained in approval.[40] On a comparative basis the French generally recorded more unfavorable views of American popular culture than did the British, the Germans, or the Italians.[41] In 1999, 33 percent called American culture a "very serious" or "serious" threat and another 44 percent labeled it a "minor" threat (and 22 percent "no threat at all"). The British, Germans, and Italians were less anxious.[42] Fear of American domination via soft power rose from the 1980s on. At the political level France was notorious in the 1990s for taking state action to curb American imports like regulating radio programming or protecting the French language as a response to this presumed threat.

Which products, one might ask, most evoked America for the French in the mid-1990s? In descending order they were: hamburgers/ McDonald's, chewing gum, and blue jeans, followed at a distance by soda/Coca-Cola, video games, "light" cigarettes, and (Hollywood) cinema. Imports of mass consumption led the way in framing America's image. Yet in describing American products from a menu of adjectives the French gave a mixed assessment. In descending order these imports were assessed as *intrusive, modern, standardized, trivial, effective (performants),* and *expensive*; only a handful thought they were *high-end, sturdy, aesthetic,* or *delicate* (i.e., stereotypical French attributes).[43]

Despite growing concern, a majority of the French consistently expressed a favorable opinion of American movies, television series, and popular music.[44] The huge appetite displayed by French customers for these three imports as well as American fashions and fast food corrob-

Figure 14. Shady French businessman. "It's true: I have Swiss bank accounts; I've sold armaments; I've swindled the state; I've dined with Tapie [a convicted wheeler-dealer]. . . . But I've never drunk Coca-Cola!" Courtesy Plantu, "Mais jamais je n'ai bu de Coca!" In *L'Année Plantu: 1999*. Paris: Éditions le Seuil, 1999, 129.

orates such surveys. A positive reading of the data cited above would conclude that 66 percent of the French said American imports posed a minor threat or no threat at all.

There is a conundrum in these contradictory responses. A huge majority said the spread of something vaguely called "American ideas and customs" was bad.[45] But this did not prevent almost the same number of those consulted from also declaring, in answer to other questions, that they liked American products, such as movies, that transmitted these ideas.[46] Similarly, although majorities among the French and other West Europeans condemned fast food as a change for the worse, in these same countries, the Golden Arches were an enormous commercial success.[47] Of course, such data may describe different segments of the population, and people may say one thing and do another. What is clear is that at most a minority of the French objected strongly to American products like Hollywood films, and perhaps a majority, given the specific wording of a question, said that they disapproved of them. But substantial majorities regularly expressed their approval of most American cultural imports and whatever reservations they may have harbored did not hamper the mass consumption of these products. Compared to the issues posed by foreign policy or the American social model, the French were more ambivalent about popular culture. Nevertheless, they were, in the 1990s, increasingly bothered by American movies, television, and fast food (read: McDonald's) and, to a lesser extent, by the spread of American English.

■ American Society, Economy, and Values

More indicative than popular culture of deteriorating perceptions was the sagging appreciation of American society.

In 1988 the words most frequently selected to describe America from a menu of choices were: *power, dynamism, wealth,* and *liberty.* If *power* is at least ambivalent in the sense of approbation, all the choices were positive. By 1996 the top choices changed dramatically to *violence, power, inequality,* and *racism. Liberty* fell and *imperialism* rose.[48] Reviewing these results *Le Monde* observed that "the image of the United States has not stopped deteriorating."[49] Four years later the picture was more forbidding. The number of those selecting words like *violence, power, inequality,* and *racism* had all increased; they were checked by as many as two-thirds of those polled.[50] Asked to elaborate on these descriptive terms, respondents explained that *violence* referred to a general perception of a violent society and specifically to crime, drugs, guns, and the death penalty.[51] The most popular descriptions (in descending order) from another survey conducted the same year, which also provided a menu of choices, were: *violence, the death penalty, social inequality, innovation, racism, permissiveness (tout est permis)*, and *economic opportunity*.[52] In yet a third set of surveys respondents also selected from a list of words to describe the United States. In 1995 those most frequently deemed accurate, in descending order, were *domineering, materialistic, democratic, violent, trustworthy, racist, cultured, religious, cooperative, isolationist*, and *hypocritical*. Five years later virtually all the negative choices (e.g. *domineering* or *violent*) increased, and all the positive ones (e.g. *democratic* or *trustworthy*) fell.[53] The popular image of American society had become rather ugly.

American social policy also did not find many fans in France. In the 1980s rather few of the French embraced *Reaganisme*. In the early Clinton years a substantial majority said the United States failed in taking care of its sick and elderly.[54] In 1996, two-thirds of one sample disapproved of the American social system because it offered "little social protection."[55] At the end of the Clinton administration the French cited alleged American failures in providing social protection, fighting crime, and integrating immigrants.[56] The death penalty was singled out as a typical example of American barbarism. In 2001, after surveying how West Europeans assessed U.S. performance on social issues, the U.S. Department of State concluded that "the French are most critical, followed by the Germans."[57] The French dunned Clinton's America for doing a poor job of protecting the environment, safeguarding minority rights, providing quality health services, caring for the sick and elderly, and providing access to higher education. At the same time the French, as well as other West Europeans, awarded high marks to the United States for maintaining law and order, religious freedom, and economic opportunity.[58] The apparent contradiction between approving the maintenance of law and order and criticizing Americans for violence and failing to combat crime is obvious.

Appraisals of the American economy matched those of social policy. The French people, much like their political leaders, opined that the market worked best when it was strongly regulated. At the end of the century only 30 percent of the public considered the New World a good economic model. Almost two-thirds found, much like the Germans and to a lesser extent the British and the Italians, that the United States neglected many problems like job insecurity and unemployment benefits.[59] But they found reason to praise it for creating jobs and developing new technologies.[60] What was distinctive about the French, in comparison to other West Europeans, was their strong antipathy for "American ways of doing business."[61]

What seemed to inform these views of American society and economy were different personal and social values. Paraphrasing an American ambassador, for the French a good society offered equality and social protection and for Americans it provided opportunity and risk.[62] Americans, unlike West Europeans, strongly believed individual success lay largely within one's control. In contrast, one continent-wide survey concluded that in most European countries majorities believed that forces outside an individual's personal control determined success.[63] The French, like other West Europeans, were more likely to assign some responsibility to society for personal failure rather than blaming the individual. Americans were much less likely do so.[64] It follows then that the French believed more strongly than Americans that government had a responsibility for the "very poor who can't take care of themselves."[65] Or, as the European-wide survey concluded, "Americans—alone among the populations of wealthy nations—care more about personal freedom than about government assurances of an economic safety net."[66]

What is apparent is that the French, like many other West Europeans at the end of the century, did not think they shared much with Americans with respect to certain basic values. The French asserted that they and the Americans did not have the same conception of democracy (49 percent), family (58 percent), morality and ethics (69 percent), law and order (73 percent), work (76 percent), and lifestyle (81 percent). The French found greater difference in every one of these comparisons than did the Germans or the British.[67] Such distancing did not mean that there were no positive feelings registered. America was awarded high marks for traits like dynamism, wealth, economic opportunity, and democracy. But the perception of social difference was unmistakable. What is less certain was why the French believed they differed from Americans. The polls were silent on this question. One can only guess, for example, that the selection of *work* as a contrasting activity meant that the French assumed Americans valued work as an end in itself rather than as a means to an end—that is, Americans were "workaholics" while the French knew how to live. Such inferences require sources other than survey data.

If there was one value that came to most separate Americans from the French, it was religion. One poll queried: Is it necessary to believe in God in order to be moral? Over half of Americans answered yes. But only 13 percent of the French did.[68] Similarly, when asked, "Is the U.S. too religious a country or not religious enough?" the French were unique among West Europeans. Almost twice as many French as Germans or British said that Americans were "too religious."[69] Another survey conducted systematically since the 1980s corroborates these findings; it shows that the United States became more patriotic and more religious than most European countries.[70] By the end of the century the three thousand miles across the Atlantic corresponded to a perceived chasm in values.

Whose Opinion?

Up to this point, the opinion of the French has been treated as a unit, but one would like to know if attitudes varied according to criteria like age or gender. The survey data available tend to omit such distinctions. Fortunately there are some exceptions and these provide some hints about how attitudes were distributed among the population.

The best evidence for at least the elementary distinction between elites and the public derives from several surveys conducted by the U.S.

Department of State during 1999–2001. In these surveys "elite" samples were composed of the political elite (e.g., national party leaders; second-tier politicians and officials (e.g., mayors, ministerial staff); private businesspeople from large- and medium-size firms; public sector managers; educators from secondary schools and universities; media and cultural elites; and religious leaders. For each category an effort was made to assure a distribution between Paris and the provinces. The gender of the typical sample, which contained some five hundred respondents, was 80 percent men and 20 percent women.[71]

Elites, more than the public (63 percent vs. 43 percent in January 2001), thought strong leadership in world affairs from the United States was desirable for the interests of France.[72] But such approval did not disguise the fact that elites also expressed stronger reservations than the ordinary person on several issues and perceived Franco-American rivalry differently. One poll showed that if the two strata agreed that the United States and France were moving in opposite directions on several issues, elites adopted a much harsher stance. Topics on which elites saw transatlantic differences more sharply than nonelites were addressing trade and economic questions, protecting the global environment, reducing poverty in developing nations, and promoting democracy in Cuba.[73] When elites were asked to volunteer in an unstructured interview what they thought were the major points of contention between the two nations, they gave priority by a wide margin to economics and trade, followed at a distance by U.S. foreign policy and hegemony.[74]

Elites were also more critical than the public of the performance of the United States on social issues. The two strata agreed that their American cousins were not performing well on several fronts, but elites were, as in international affairs, more severe. Compared to the public, elites more often dunned the United States for not providing health care; not taking care of the elderly; not protecting the environment; and not assuring quality education to all.[75] On the only two issues for which the two social groups thought the United States was performing well, which were offering economic opportunity and maintaining law and order, elites were more positive than the public. Elites were more extreme: they were more negative on what they disapproved, and more positive on what they approved, than the public.

Most notable was elite versus public difference over social values as opposed to social policy. Elites targeted lackluster American performance on meeting social problems. For the public the transatlantic gap seemed even more basic: it stemmed from supposedly dissimilar conceptions of social institutions and values.[76] The public, for example, more so than the elite, concluded that the French and the Americans did not share a common lifestyle. An analyst, however, is left guessing what exactly the French thought was different in lifestyles.

With respect to American popular culture, conventional wisdom has held that elites have been less receptive than the public. This stems from the loud and strident voices emanating from St. Germain des Prés in contrast to the eager consumption by the masses of imports like Hollywood movies. But these surveys do not corroborate this thesis for the fin de siècle. Or, at least, the two social groups seemed to agree if the question asked was simply, "In general what is your opinion of American popular culture such as music, television, and films?" Faced with a favorable/unfavorable binary, favorable answers were given by the public and elites at almost the same levels (52 percent and 49 percent, respectively) in 2000.[77] Nevertheless, almost half of both these strata also registered "unfavorable" opinions so that American popular culture did not receive a standing ovation.

The data afford a small opportunity at refining elite responses further. Party affiliation mattered among political elites. When given the chance to select extreme—either "very positive" or "very negative"— opinions of the United States, the "nays" gathered on the left of the political spectrum. The most censorious choices came from communists and members of the Green Party.[78] Even though the Cold War had ended, the communists continued to form the hard core of those expressing anti-American sentiments. As for the socialists, some 18 percent awarded the United States with the "very negative" assessment, but that was not much different from the Gaullist Rassemblement pour la République, or RPR (15 percent). (In 2002 the RPR was renamed the Union pour un Mouvement Populaire, or UMP.) The fewest negatives came from the centrist Union pour la Démocratie Française and the far right Front National. Significantly "very positive" views were negligible among political elites on both the left and the right. For example, only 14 percent of the supposedly pro-American RPR was willing to give a high rating to the United States.

These surveys permit some interrogation of the various elite subcategories, when given the choice between the extremes of "very positive" and "very negative" opinion of the United States.[79] It mattered rather little what kind of an elite you were with respect to the "very positive" attitude. Such enthusiasm was rare. Affirmative attitudes clustered at the bottom of the scale and ranged from 4 to 16 percent, but the variations in the sample seem too small to reach any conclusion about preference among these elite subgroups. In contrast there was a large range among those asserting "very negative" views. Virtually no businesspeople, public sector managers, or second-level political leaders expressed such hostility. But there was a rising chorus of shrill voices beginning with educators and increasing with media elites, and cultural and religious leaders, and peaking with elite politicians.[80] What is clear is that the top strata of the political class spoke most harshly of the United States; they were among those least willing to admit to any positive attitudes and they were the most vehement in expressing very negative attitudes. It should be no surprise that the loudest critiques of the United States often came from the most prominent national political figures in these years.

Data for disaggregating the general population according to other variables are scarce. But what exist give some tantalizing numbers. In general, age and gender made some difference, but political affiliation counted most in determining attitudes. Evidence for occupation, religion, and region is too rare to reach any conclusions.

On the question of whether the respondent had more sympathy or antipathy for the United States (from a poll taken in 2000), women were less likely than men (34 percent to 49 percent) to opt for sympa-thy.[81] Another poll taken in the same year showed that women were slightly more likely than men to associate negative terms like *violence*, *racism*, or *the death penalty* with the United States.[82] But women were no different from men in voicing anxiety about the status of the United States as the sole superpower.[83] In general, evidence for gender is too thin to generalize about its role as a variable.

Data were somewhat more plentiful for age, but they were, at best, suggestive for two cohorts, the oldest and the youngest. The U.S. State Department categorically concluded that, when compared to Britain and Italy, "in France age has no effect."[84] A private survey agreed, at least in one respect, finding almost no generational difference among the French as regarding approval of American cultural imports.[85] But these assessments overlooked the data that indicated there were some subtle distinctions for those over sixty-five and for those in their late teens or twenties. Two surveys found that those sixty-five and older were the most sympathetic audience for the United States, though the margins were small.[86] The most senior generation, another poll found, less often than others employed uncomplimentary terms like *social inequality* or *racism* to describe the United States.[87] And another poll demonstrated that far more of those over sixty-five than those under that age said they felt close to the American people.[88] The common notion that the generation who experienced the Second World War harbored kind feelings toward the United States seems to have some validity. At the opposite extreme of age, evidence for the young was not what one might have expected. Some surveys reported that French youth were more disillusioned with their American cousins than other age groups.[89] Almost three-fourths of those between the ages of eigh-teen and twenty-four said in 1999 that they did not feel close to the American people.[90] Three years later, compared to the national average, more young people expressed unfavorable impressions of the Ameri-can people.[91] Other polls found nothing unusual for those eighteen to twenty-four.[92] But it is somewhat disconcerting that the fascination among the young with American music, fashion, and film did not translate into enthusiasm for Americans. Neither gender nor age seems to have determined much about attitudes toward the United States.

The only variable that clearly differentiated among the general public was political affiliation.[93] Without exception surveys all reported that there was more sympathy for the United States on the right than on the left. Choosing between sympathy and antipathy in 2000, far more respondents who identified as leaning to the right (51 percent) expressed sympathy than those leaning to the left (34 percent).[94] Judgments of Americans as people were also much more favorable among those who declared themselves as supporting the right rather than the left.[95] In the same year when selecting from a menu of words describing feelings toward the United States, respondents from the right selected *admiring* or *kindly* much more often than those on the left.[96] One reason for the Right's relative warmth stems from its respect for the American economy. There was a marked right/left split among those who found merit in the American economic model.[97] From a menu of terms that supposedly described the United States, those on the right selected complimentary categories associated with economic prowess like *innovation* or *everyone can make his or her fortune*. Those on the left were less attracted to these attributes.[98]

The right/left polarity is rather crude and can be subjected to further analysis according to party loyalty. Respondents aligned with the Socialist Party and the Greens (i.e., supporters but not necessarily party members) followed closely the norms for those affiliated with the Left.[99] To describe the United States, approximately half of those on the left chose *violence*, *the death penalty*, and *strong social inequality*; over a third picked *innovation* and *racism*; and a quarter selected *permissiveness* (*tout est permis*) and *everyone can make his or her fortune*. Those who identified with the communists made similar choices, except that they ranked *violence* even higher and *innovation* very low.

The only right-wing parties for which sufficient data permit generalization are the RPR/UMP, whose adherents closely followed the norms of the Right, and the extremist Front National, whose adherents did not. Backers of the Front National were both attracted and repelled by America—even though the party itself in the late 1990s became passionately anti-American, attacking the United States as the enemy of national identity and the stalking horse for globalization.[100] Compared to others who identified with the Right, Front National supporters were less willing to criticize American society for violence; they were more forgiving of the death penalty; and they were more inclined to approve of what they perceived was America's priority of jobs over social promotion. But they also were harsher in their condemnation of American moral permissiveness and they believed that France and the United States increasingly disagreed on "the world's important political, economic, and cultural debates."[101]

If partisans on the right expressed relatively more sympathetic opinions, they could not be dubbed enthusiasts or "pro-American." Among backers of the RPR/UDF, near majorities scored the United States poorly on social conditions and practices like the death penalty. Criticism of the United States may have been heavier from partisans on the left, but the separation between left and right was not great. When the issue was U.S. hegemony in particular, they were not far apart.[102] Nevertheless, political affiliation was a potent determinant of attitudes.

The United States in the recent past, according to this survey data, functioned more as a source of consensus than it did as a basis for division within French society. The shades of difference among partisans on the left or the right, as well as among age cohorts, or between men and women, were insufficient for America to be a cause of controversy— although intellectuals sparred over it. The unflattering image of the United States was so widely shared among the French that it tended to bring them together. Thus, opposing the United States served as a way for politicians to rally support for their own agenda.

At the end of the 1990s the French were, according to the polls, more worried and more suspicious of the United States than at any time since the tense days of the early Cold War. The warmth of the mid-1980s had cooled markedly. These trends raise questions of historical causation: Why were the French so pessimistic, so concerned, about the American threat? Why, more than for other Europeans, was America such a problem for the French? These questions require some close analysis.

■ Analysis

Any global explanation of such a complex phenomenon as fin-de-siècle anti-Americanism would be unsatisfactory. Pundits asserted that the French were simply jealous of their transatlantic cousins and displayed their envy by belittling Americans and their achievements. Such a simplistic and condescending answer fails to take into account the distinctions among those who disapproved, the spectrum of motives, or the array of opinions that were voiced about America. Some objected to American mass culture, others to the U.S. government's international practices, and a few said they were unimpressed with Americans as a people. Variables like political affiliation or elite status distinguished how one disapproved. And individuals often harbored complicated, even contradictory, views. One might, for example, have praised the United States for law and order yet scorned Americans for capital punishment. Moreover, attitudes in general evolved over time: they darkened—a shift that any static analysis misses.

The paradox that pairs the simultaneous rise of anti-Americanism with the immersion of France in Americanization can be partly resolved with the application of common sense. We should expect neither consistency nor logic from human beings. People compartmentalize attitudes and behavior; someone might approve of one form of American culture, like popular music, but criticize Hollywood movies; another might admire American business yet deplore materialism. Take the example of the young woman who joined the rally at the trial of José Bové. She told a reporter that she had nothing against Americans, but she disliked "the American system"—"all the bad food makes for bad thinking." But when asked if she ever ate at McDonald's, she said, "Well, sometimes. I have no choice. And I get a stomach-ache every time."[103] Or, maybe the explanation is not one of human inconsistency, but a reasonable reaction to an overdose of America. Some of the French seem to have had enough of America, and they were reacting to the very scope and intensity of Americanization. It was not hypocrisy; it was drawing a line and trying to limit the intrusion of American products like television programs. Or maybe it was guilt. Having overindulged in American mass culture, the French felt embarrassed and condemned it.

None of these reasons fully resolve the paradox. There is more to the story than human foibles. Explaining the resurgence of anti-Americanism in the last decade of the twentieth century requires a different approach.

Answering why there was growing resentment toward America in the 1990s depends on making some distinctions, the first of which is the difference between constants and contingencies, between historical givens and historical circumstances. There was a latent Gallic apprehension about America and there were events, leaders, and policies that aroused this anxiety. Analytically one must distinguish between the two. A second distinction should be made among the different issues—economic, political, social, and cultural—that excited distrust and dismay. Each contributed in different ways and intensities to the sour mix of resentments. And allowance must be made for human ambivalence—most French people harbored ambiguous and even contradictory feelings toward America. Mindful of these distinctions, I shall argue, nevertheless, that there was a paramount reason for anti-Americanism. Mounting American assertiveness in international affairs along with the accompanying celebration of the American way encountered French insecurity and defensiveness. The Gallic reaction was to chide and belittle the Americans as well as defend indigenous French traditions.

The French image of America in the 1990s had many parents and a long pedigree. Among its ancestors were those of a perennial nature—

the constants. First, there was the composite stereotype of Americans marked by multiple binaries, such as religious versus materialist, whose origin can be found in the eighteenth century; this was well honed by 1900 and seemingly impervious to any contrary experience or information that might modify it.[104] As far as the public was concerned, it was sure it knew what Americans were like. In the early 1950s polls showed the French believed Americans were youthful, optimistic, wealthy, and dynamic. But they were also less favorably stereotyped as materialistic, vulgar, violent, racist, and puritanical. By the century's end little changed except that Americans no longer appeared youthful and seemed arrogant and given to excesses of all sorts. This latter characteristic supposedly informed Americans' opulent lifestyle, exuberant religiosity, and zealousness in pursuit of evil in international affairs. A second constant was Gallic pride and the refusal to act as subordinates in the transatlantic alliance. French prickliness about being treated as a lesser ally disturbed every occupant of the White House from Franklin D. Roosevelt to Bill Clinton. The French were determined that the United States should treat them as equal partners, and they could be manipulative and obstreperous if they were slighted or relegated to the status of passive followers. A third constant was twin universalism or narcissism. Rooted in history and lodged in the people's collective psychology was the conviction that the French, like the Americans, had a special global mission. For Americans it was the spread of democracy and free enterprise; for the French it was the *mission civilisatrice*. Such presuppositions were bound to clash. Or, put in another way, the Americans and the French are the only two people who believe everyone else in the world would like to be them. Such a coupling was bound to cause the two to see each other as rivals. What intensified this rivalry was yet another constant, that of a French sense of cultural superiority. In the late 1770s and '80s the French nobility combined admiration with condescension in their behavior toward Benjamin Franklin when he resided in Paris; 150 years later came the writer Georges Duhamel, who, after touring the country in 1929 claimed he could associate no cultural achievements with the New World (e.g., no great artists or composers). Americans, he wrote, preferred movies, sports, and cars. By the interwar period intellectuals sounded an early alert about the American menace.[105] During the early years of the Cold War when Louis Aragon, Emmanuel Mounier, and Jean-Paul Sartre ruled St. Germain des Prés, the same haughty posture toward their rude American cousins characterized Parisian mandarins. And the sentiment persisted in some quarters to the end of the century.[106] The conviction that France was the guardian of high culture and America the peddler of mass culture was stoutly defended by intellectual gatekeepers. A final constant was the way traditional culture configured the sense of national identity. French identity, for hundreds of years, has been defined by literature, the arts, humanism, food, *bon goût*, and the French language itself. As the twentieth century developed, Americanization seemed to mount a direct threat to this conception of identity.

One begins an explanation of the 1990s by recalling these perennial sources of transatlantic friction. But they are insufficient because anti-American attitudes were complex and they evolved: this requires paying attention to the contingencies that brought these latent causes into the open. Perceptions of America in the 1990s drew from sources other than stereotypes, historical rivalries, and self-images of mission and identity.

The essential perception that structured the French view of America was that of Uncle Sam as a domineering ally. The reputation of the United States lost luster because it appeared increasingly to act as a hegemonic superpower concerned with its own national interests, forcing itself on others, and unabashedly celebrating its triumphs. America became unbearable.

Does anxiety about the United States as a hegemonic friend simply confirm then what is called a realist's approach to international affairs? Is there little more to add after pointing out that once the Soviet danger passed, transatlantic differences—which had been dampened during the Cold War—reemerged? A realist stance in international relations, which stresses the preeminence of national interest and power, would have expected as much. But the data suggest that a more complicated account is necessary. Confidence in U.S. leadership actually rose after 1989; it peaked in 1991 at the time of the first war in the Persian Gulf and it did not ebb until the middle years of the Clinton administration. There was a lag rather than an abrupt about-face. The republic's leaders may have detected trouble early on, but it took years of growing friction between Washington and Paris over a wide range of issues, some of which were not political, before the public's trust in the United States eroded and they came to recognize that the post–Cold War, unipolar world posed a problem.

If there was a lag, it was not long after the end of the Cold War that the image of the New World began to turn threatening and transatlantic relations became testy. By the early 1990s there was squabbling over reform of NATO, a European defense capacity, the United Nations, trade, environmental policy, the Balkan states, the Middle East, and Africa. Such disputes were hardly new, but the post–Cold War context was. The United States seemed to be acting more and more as an unrestrained superpower. It was halfway through the Clinton presidency that the United States became more openly assertive, recognizing its growing military power and its unique global responsibilities. Whatever the issue, during the mid- to late 1990s, Washington always seemed to impose its will on Paris.

France was not passive and did more than respond to its ally's policies: under Presidents François Mitterrand and Jacques Chirac it sought European parity within NATO, worked to strengthen the EU as a counterweight to the United States, raised the goal of multipolarity, and tried to contain the superpower through international bodies and rules. Yet whatever initiatives France took, it seemed to encounter formidable resistance from the United States. Meanwhile, fighting alongside the Americans proved to be an embarrassment. First the Gulf War and then the interventions in Bosnia and Kosovo underlined the shortcomings of the French military in comparison with how the Pentagon had remodeled its armed forces.

The "hyperpower" had arrived. In 1997, the French foreign minister, Hubert Védrine, introduced this term to describe the United States,
alluding to its vast range of powers. Along with concern about the new
imperious America came mistrust of its policies. U.S. intervention in
the Balkans, for example, made the French suspicious of Washington's
goals. The Senate's rejection of the Comprehensive Nuclear Test Ban
treaty suggested to many, including President Chirac, that the United
States preferred a unilateral course. Paris and Washington were also at
odds over Iraq. By 1998 the two allies were in public disagreement over
U.S. commitment to regime change in Baghdad as well as a strategy
to control Saddam Hussein. The reach of American power seemed to
extend to within the Hexagon itself. When the Michelin company laid
off workers, Chirac blamed the decision, at least in part, on California
retiree stakeholders who, supposedly, were insisting on higher returns
from their investments.[107] By the end of the decade the hyperpower
seemed omnipotent in world affairs and possibly within the Hexagon.

Trade disputes deepened the French people's distrust of their
American partners: the two allies went head-to-head over many commercial issues, topped by wrangling over agriculture and culture. U.S.
officials openly stated that they used trade negotiations to "open up"
other societies.[108] This was precisely the strategy pursued by Hollywood and Washington in the GATT negotiations that tried to force
open the French audiovisual market and prompted Paris to retaliate
with the defense of "the cultural exception." French determination to
defend its audiovisual industries as well as its program of agricultural
subsidies almost scuttled the talks in 1993.

The GATT debacle ushered in a rancorous decade as the two countries continued to bicker over agricultural subsidies, civilian aircraft,
and armaments sales. Even food caused trouble. The dispute began
with EU restrictions on imports from the United States of hormone-
treated beef; escalated with U.S. retaliation on import duties; and
erupted when José Bové trashed a McDonald's site in 1999. The most
flagrant use of political power may have been the U.S. government's

willingness to interfere with others doing business with countries like Iran and Cuba.

This transatlantic trade rivalry fed the perception that the two countries were at odds and that in this competition France was usually the loser. The aspect of American behavior that most infuriated French elites was their alleged unscrupulousness in the conduct of trade and business. This feature of the American image, based in part on a persistent French stereotype of the ruthless Yankee businessman, emerged because American trade officials were rough competitors who wielded their economic and political advantages at the expense of French interests and because of the behavior of American multinationals. Coca-Cola's hard-nosed merchandising practices in France confirmed Gallic suspicions about the cold-blooded ways of Americans. Paris even publicly indicted its ally of economic espionage; American officials were, it seems, using sex and money to discover the French negotiating position in global trade talks. To be sure, the French engaged in similar stratagems, but that seems beside the point. This transatlantic rancor over business accounts for much of the deteriorating image of the United States in the 1990s.

▪ Perceptions of Social Difference

Perceptions of growing social difference, like international rivalry, contributed to anti-Americanism. Polling data, as we have seen, recorded rising Gallic concern about violence, inequality, and callousness in America in the 1990s. It seems unlikely, however, that French and American societies actually grew farther apart in a single decade or so. More likely the change in attitudes was caused by shifts in policy as presented to the public by officials and the media.

An inherited anti-American discourse formed the basis of such views. Stereotypes about Americans and American ways, including tropes about racism and obsession with work, provided a fertile field for opponents to harvest. Stereotypes aside, there were real contrasts between these societies—such as the ubiquity of the homeless, visible to even the casual observer. More important, in addressing domestic problems the New World seemed to move on a tangent away from Europe. Awareness of difference was most likely caused by the direction of U.S. socioeconomic policy under Presidents Ronald Reagan, George H. W. Bush, and Bill Clinton. The United States embraced market solutions to problems like providing for the needy that ran counter to French notions of social solidarity. Reagan fired recalcitrant federal employees (e.g. air traffic controllers) and called government "the problem"; Bush hollowed out regulatory rules; and Clinton toughened the federal welfare program. In contrast, Mitterrand increased the minimum wage, reduced the number of hours in the workweek, banned the death penalty, raised taxes on the wealthy, and in general made aid to the poorest members of society a priority. Under his successor, Jacques Chirac, the government adopted the thirty-five-hour workweek to help distribute jobs and enhance leisure. While Washington, especially under Republican administrations, trimmed federal programs including funds for agencies like the National Endowment for the Arts, Paris continued to tax and spend at a far higher pace and tried to raise spending on culture to 1 percent of the national budget. If France followed the United States in some respects (e.g., toward deregulation), it combined such measures with high outlays especially on social programs.

The source of French dismay at their hard-hearted Yankee cousins derived from a historical commitment to, and pride in, social solidarity as embodied in the second and third values of the republican triad: liberty, equality and fraternity. It prompted most to believe that they adhered to a more advanced conception of the social contract. Both the Left and the Right, both Mitterrand and Chirac, paraded their devotion to solidarity and cited it as a way to distinguish the two societies. Despite the shortcomings of their policies—for example, in the blight around French cities or the decaying educational structure—the French could legitimately claim they tried to honor these priorities.

Given these transatlantic divergences America became more of a target than it was a model for the French. Most insisted that American and French values were different with respect to the family, morality, law and order, work, and lifestyle. The French charged Americans with lacking a sense of social solidarity—pointing, as we have seen, to how Americans shredded their safety net or failed, from their perspective, to integrate immigrants. They reproached American business for its ruthlessness, for its indifference to the unemployed, and for wrecking the environment. They complained about political correctness, multiculturalism, income inequality, crime, the gun culture, the homeless population, and capital punishment—*especially* capital punishment. The U.S. embassy in Paris received a petition against the death penalty signed by 500,000 people.[109] And American multiculturalism seemed like the pursuit of individual rights gone mad.[110] The French also chided Americans for their excessive religiosity. Some of this America-bashing was a stretch. In his polemic Noël Mamère, a prominent leader of the Green Party, warned that the Religious Right in the United States was poised to take the offensive against French secularism (*laïcité*).[111] What intensified these complaints was the perception that the American model, flawed as it was, put an idealized formulation of France at risk. The French, according to this self-image, unlike Americans, prized solidarity over self-interest; promoted toleration rather than political correctness; refused to commercialize culture; assimilated immigrants rather than accepting ethnic fragmentation. They were, in short, civilized—and Americans, as always, were less civilized.

French politicians ranging from left to right opportunistically exploited these perceptions. Baiting America was a consensual rather than a divisive political strategy. And intellectuals and the media brought the message to the person in the street. This gambit of arousing public concern can be illustrated by an example from Texas.

Violence was the word the French most commonly associated with American society in the 1990s and this was, in a comparative sense, a reasonable attribution. Homicide rates were at least four times higher in the United States than in France. Americans also owned far more guns and incarcerated far more of their population in prison. Whereas France had banned the death penalty, some states, like Texas, continued to practice it, allowing the French to seize what they believed was the moral high ground. High-profile criminal mayhem made headlines and French politicians and the media publicized these social troubles. Television paraded images of random U.S. school shootings and urban drug wars and it relentlessly reported executions. Media intellectuals discussed the stories of death-row inmates and, the former minister Jack Lang flew to Texas in an attempt to influence the Board of Pardons to stay a pending execution. Lang failed, but Bernard Pivot, the prominent television host, responded to Lang's mission by saying "I'm proud to be French."[112] Is it any wonder that the French believed American society was violent?

In general the French at the fin de siècle distanced themselves from what they believed was the harsh way Americans approached social security and the callousness of their economic practices. The two nations seemed pointed in opposite directions.

■ Americanization and French Identity

There is yet another aspect, besides Washington's unilateralism and divergent social and economic policies, that accounts for the more threatening posture of America in the 1990s. American domination extended beyond its military, economic, and technological prowess to encompass mass culture including the cinema, television, fashion, fast food, music, and language itself. There was a growing sense that France was being overrun by America, whether it was the mounting number of McDonald's franchises, the long lines at Disneyland Paris, the sale of American clothes and music, the saturation of TV with American programs, or the triumph of Hollywood blockbusters. In 1998 Hollywood movies earned almost 70 percent of ticket sales in France. Of the top twenty films only three were French—the rest were American. As if this were insufficient, Microsoft and the Internet also arrived as the newest carriers of America. Worst of all, this surge of Americanization arrived when the French already thought of themselves as under siege by the bureaucrats in Brussels, by immigrants, and by globalization in general.

Americanization may have concerned all Europeans, but it antagonized the French more than it did others. It seemed to target many of the markers of French identity—more so than it did in Germany, Britain, or Italy. That is, to the extent that French national identity was defined by food, wine, agriculture, fashion, and a certain conception of high culture—one that featured literature, the fine arts, language, and the cinema—then America seemed to trample on these signifiers. In a country whose identity was heavily attached to *haute cuisine, la gastronomie, le terroir, haute couture, les beaux arts,* and *la langue française*—then McDonald's, Tex-Mex food, GMOs, Ralph Lauren, Coca-Cola, movies like *American Pie,* rap music, television ads in American English, and television shows like *Baywatch* seemed aimed at the essence of Frenchness. American English in particular not only eclipsed French as the language of cultural and international communication but also corrupted the native tongue at home. While other Europeans passively accepted this linguistic invasion, Jacques Toubon as minister of culture in 1994—to the mirth of many Americans—tried to police the language. Food in particular caused trouble. José Bové responded to such worries by playing on the need to safeguard the small farmer, healthy food, *bon goût,* tradition, and diversity against (American) multinationals, *la malbouffe,* and GMOs. In other words, as the polls showed, many of the French wanted to draw a line against an Americanized, globalized, and homogenized culture. They may have waited in line to see *Titanic* and even eaten at the Golden Arches, but they refused to be overrun. Thus they told pollsters that they found much of American popular culture "excessive." Americanization in the 1990s struck at the heart of French identity—and it stirred resistance.

■ The French Malaise and American Triumphalism

An adequate explanation of negative French perceptions should look not just to transatlantic rivalries but to life within the Hexagon. It was commonly said in the early 1990s that the French were in a "funk"; they were, according to the experts, nostalgic about the past, worried about the present, and pessimistic about the future. The prestigious journal *Le Débat* featured essays about the "French malaise," and bookstores carried titles like *French Fears, French Blues*, and *Is France Going to Disappear?* Stanley Hoffmann wrote an article titled "France, Keeping the Demons at Bay"; and government planners worried about the disarray of French identity.[113]

The French were in a defensive crouch and this defensiveness had its roots in what was often described at the time as the "French malaise," referring to a loss of confidence, a feeling of decline, a sense of waning independence, and concern about a vanishing national identity. The causes of this malaise were numerous and some date back, as we have seen, to the 1970s or earlier with the exhaustion of two postwar identity narratives, Gaullism and communism, and the disintegrative effects of long-term socioeconomic change—especially consumer society—that generated nostalgia for a vanishing rural life and for much else, like Catholicism, that had traditionally defined Frenchness. The disappearance, or what some called the *désertification*, of the traditional countryside provoked a warning from one senator: "We are spoiling France, we are undermining its identity."[114] The enthusiastic reception of Pierre Nora's multivolume, national history titled *Les Lieux de mémoire* (Realms of Memory) suggested that in a time of uncertainty the French sought refuge in the memories of the nation as they searched for anchors in the new fluid and diverse society that lacked the old defining institutions, social classes, habits, and elite culture that once gave it its character.[115]

The more immediate causes for national melancholy included concern about an immigrant Muslim population that seemed to resist assimilation; intolerance exposed by the presence of these same immigrants; a faltering economy, especially double digit unemployment; a loss of control to Brussels and the EU; looming crises in social programs like social security; doubts about the quality of the educational system; the retreat of French influence in world affairs; frustration with a political class that seemed closed and corrupt; and rising urban pathologies, especially crime. Urban disorder and the state's ineffectiveness prompted a distressed socialist deputy to exclaim that "postwar society is falling apart."[116]

Given the multiple sources for the national malaise, America could only be one contributing—though surely not the primary—factor in the psychodrama. None of three major challenges—immigration, globalization, or European integration—were principally about America, but they were frequently connected to it in an indirect way. Muslim immigrants and their alleged resistance to assimilation raised the possibility that the French republic, especially its educational system, was failing. But Americans seemed to mock assimilation with their advocacy of multiculturalism as the preferred approach to immigration. Both extreme right and Jacobin Republicans in turn rebuked American multiculturalism. And globalization, abetted by Brussels—or so it was argued—seemed to drain away national identity through porous borders, outsourced jobs, businesses lost to developing countries, and the arrival of workers from Eastern Europe. Here, too, one could detect the hand of Uncle Sam. Globalization, which the French more than other Europeans attached to the United States, was allegedly an American plot that primarily benefited the Americans just as the EU pried open the Hexagon to Anglo-American interests.

French national pride is a given. But the irritability and pessimism of the 1990s were extraordinary. The social, economic, and cultural transformations of the postwar decades created a sense of national loss and vulnerability that accounts, at least in part, for the testiness. The vanishing peasant, immigration, open borders, and Americanization intersected, or clashed, with a collective memory of what France was and, many thought, should be. Rapid change struggled against a sentimental reluctance to accept it. As Pierre Birnbaum explained, "Our problem is that we have not found the way to modernize while preserving our imagined community."[117] The French became uneasy about their inherited sense of collective identity, purpose, and direction. The malaise was both mental and sentimental—it derived from a sense of *déracinement* or uprootedness that was both real and imagined and that was expressed in several ways, ranging from nostalgia to paranoia. An easy way out was to blame America. A number of socialist deputies attributed France's malaise to its "progressive Americanization."[118] Or, as it was said, "on s'anglo-saxonise de plus en plus." As one expert writing about the morose mood of his compatriots in 1998 observed, "Today France is torn more than ever between the desire to be a modern, normal country and the reflex to cling to the belief that France is not like other nations. The first choice presupposes openness, flexibility, and a secure sense of one's identity. The second opposes globalization, is wary of a more unified Europe, and embraces anti-Americanism."[119]

The malaise surfaced when the Maastricht Treaty, which aimed at advancing European integration, faced a referendum in 1992 and almost half the electorate voted against it. Although the reasons for this opposition were numerous, a principal one was that many voters blamed the European Union for expediting the erosion of national identity—for example, by supposedly fostering immigration, globalization, and Americanization (e.g., American television programs). Analysis of the Maastricht referendum suggests opposition came largely from farmers, workers, and the unemployed; from the countryside and depressed industrial cities; and from those who felt most threatened by recent changes, whereas the electorate that approved was more highly educated, held better jobs, had experience of international travel, and lived in major cities.[120] Almost two out of three Parisians, for example, favored the accord. *Le Monde* observed that the vote divided France in two: "a France of fear, of preserving vested interests, of rejecting the other, of indifference to the world, and a France, open to the exterior, convinced that responses of the past will not do for the twenty-first century. . . ."[121] The Maastricht referendum revealed the anxieties generated by the massive transformation of French economy, society, and culture since the war. The testy mood of the fin de siècle expressed the apprehension and defensiveness that came with recognition of the loss of an "Old France."

Expressed in socioeconomic terms, France had chosen modernization during the 1950s and '60s, but not everyone accepted the consequences of this transformation and many felt disoriented by the 1990s. As Alain Duhamel wrote, "French fears do not prefigure the future, they reflect the difficulty of purging the past."[122] It may be useful to examine in more depth one of these social changes or ruptures that informed the malaise—that of the countryside.

One of the most striking ruptures was the disappearance of peasant society. The family farm and the rural life associated with farming receded or were so transformed that the way of life that historically defined Frenchness virtually vanished.[123] The social class that still accounted for a third of the workforce at midcentury fell to less than 5 percent, and this social fragment bore no resemblance to the historic class called "peasants." Since the Second World War, over half the farms—many of which were cherished family units—disappeared and large farms came to provide the bulk of total output. The family farm and diversified agriculture all but vanished because of the need for concentration and specialization. *Le terroir* (or "soil/climate") was replaced by *le bassin* ("basin" or "field"), as in *bassin céréalier* ("grain field"). Those who remained in the rural setting were an aging population and many who did reside there were not farmers; they were retirees or farm wives who supplemented farm income by working outside agriculture. Even the link between land and agriculture was broken with crops grown *hors-sol*. Surviving farmers, as Bertrand Hervieu has pointed out, lost their historic mission of providing food for their compatriots. When markets became global, when the French spent less and less on food, when farm products lost their local character and were sold by brand name, when farm commodities became raw material for prepared food, then the connection between food and farm was less tangible and more remote. Hervieu concluded, "In the decade [1980s] when France became the second agricultural exporting power [in the world] it ceased to be an agrarian society."[124]

In this context Laurence Wylie's celebrated study *Village in the Vaucluse* is relevant. Wylie told how one Provencal village, the town of Roussillon, was transformed after his initial stay in 1950. Writing in 1987, Wylie explained how the old village, once marked by polyculture farms, isolation and fear of outsiders, a lack of amenities, and anxiety about the future had become a wealthy resort community with cosmopolitan residents, boutiques, and a sense of connection with the region, the nation, and the world.[125] In other communes like Roussillon that have become tourist attractions, professional organizers have tried to re-create traditional festivals at which farmers play at using old farm tools. When farming becomes entertainment, then a way of life has been abandoned.

For a society that for a millennium defined itself by its peasantry and in modern times kept a larger portion of its population on the land longer than other industrialized nations, the transformation of the countryside diminished a social stratum that anchored the French to their past. The French of the fin de siècle had difficulty locating their identity in a vanishing way of life. What had been possible in 1900, or even in 1950, was no longer possible in 1990. In itself this vanished world would not mean a loss of identity because the French, like every other community, have multiple references for defining themselves. But some of these fundamental references—such as language or Catholicism—in addition to the peasantry were being challenged and thus the waning of *la France profonde* was an important loss.

Why is this rural story relevant to anti-Americanism? Because long-term socioeconomic change in the countryside so diminished a traditional point of reference that Frenchmen and women had difficulty defining Frenchness—and someone or some force, like American-led globalization, had to be at fault. Or, as Dominique Moisi observed in 1993, "There is less and less of France abroad, and more and more that is foreign in France. . . . One minute it's dinosaurs [*Jurassic Park*], the next North African immigrants, but it's the same basic anxiety."[126] Into the midst of a nation engaged in self-doubt and introspection stepped the United States.

Once again, as in the early 1950s, Uncle Sam was in a proselytizing mood. American leaders unabashedly celebrated the market economy and globalization. The Clinton administration seemed to lecture, if not hector, the French about following American ways. The message from the New World was, if only you opened your economy and stopped subsidizing uncompetitive sectors like agriculture, you could create more jobs and enjoy our standard of living. This celebration of the market ran against a French sense of tradition and solidarity. It revived stereotypes about the ruthless ways of Americans and their willingness to submit all activity, including agriculture, to market criteria. The more Bill Clinton's America challenged the French over globalization and the primacy of the market, and the more the distance between present and past grew, the more the French tried to preserve traditions like rural life that defined identity.

In 1992 there was an expression of this sentiment when many urbanites rallied to the cause of farmers in their protest against American efforts at cutting agricultural subsidies during the GATT negotiations. The farmers' plight evoked nostalgia among a sentimental urban populace. When farmers presented their case to Paris by erecting stands serving wine, cheese, pâté, and other produce, according to the press, "a million Parisians turned out to welcome them as if they represented a threatened species."[127] This GATT affair evoked the aura of a desperate effort to reconnect the mass of urban society with a rural past—even though the contemporary farmer barely resembles this past.

As a way of illustrating this analysis of late-twentieth-century anti-Americanism it is helpful to recall the case of José Bové, who gained national and international notoriety by vandalizing a McDonald's construction site in 1999. The basis of Bové's protest was intensified Franco-American competition over trade—especially over food—and specifically the U.S. government raising duties on certain French luxury imports including his own crop, Roquefort cheese. Besides endangering small producers, in Bové's eyes there was the threat of American-led globalization because the United States was trying to force la malbouffe—represented by McDonald's—on the French. He argued that the Americans threatened two markers of national identity, the small farm and food. The Bové affair, moreover, expressed a third aspect of anti-Americanism, the stereotype of Americans who allegedly ate badly and treated everything, including food, as merchandise. A final familiar element was the way politicians, including the president and prime minister, exploited anti-Americanism and helped make Bové a national hero.

In 1990 the French asked themselves a question that was unimaginable in 1930 or even 1960: Was France any longer France? Did France exist if there were no peasants and only a few practicing Catholics? If immigrants refused assimilation? If the French language was bastardized by American phrases, McDonald's sold hamburgers on the Champs-Elysées, Hollywood films appeared on over half of French cinema screens, and Euro Disney attracted over three million French visitors in its first year of operation? If the government let the price of a baguette rise and Renault became a private company? If the state could not control the exchange rate of the franc and Brussels dictated agricultural policy? Such doubts reflected just how acutely self-conscious and defensive the French had become.

Why did America at the fin de siècle appear as the appropriate target for this sense of loss, powerlessness, and malaise? There are three reasons.

First, America was the target because the United States was the principal obstacle to French independence and influence in international affairs. The U.S. government tried to impose its laws on France, for example, against doing business with Iran and Cuba. It opposed the creation of an independent European defense capacity. It dragged France into war against Iraq. It excluded France from vital decisions like NATO expansion and the Middle East peace process. And it did all this out of self-interest rather than for its alleged desire to maintain peace or advance democracy. By the end of the century half of those polled, in a truly remarkable finding, said France and the United States were either adversaries or semiadversaries.[128]

Second, America was intrusive and its behavior seemed self-serving. The United States, given its vast array of privileges and its self-confidence, appeared to be willful and omnipotent. The "hyperpower" not only promoted policies like globalization and trade liberalization but, when necessary, inflicted them on the French. Uncle Sam forced changes, like the import of genetically modified seeds, feed, and food, which many thought were unsafe. And Americans did so to serve their interests, it was said, for example, to fatten the profits of multinationals like Monsanto. Globalization, in the eyes of 25 percent of the population, primarily benefited the United States.[129] Hubert Védrine observed that America profited most because of its economic scale, technological advantages, market-oriented economy, and mass culture, and because globalization spoke American English.[130]

Finally, America became the target because there were, from a French perspective, obvious shortcomings to the "American model" of society and its "unculture." The two countries seemed to have different conceptions of what defined a good society, leading the French to charge their transatlantic friends with lacking a sense of social solidarity—pointing to how Americans shredded their safety net or failed, under the guise of multiculturalism, to assimilate immigrants thus tolerating the Balkanization of their society. And resistance to Hollywood, fast food, and American English was necessary in order to preserve bon goût and elite culture.

Anti-Americanism in the 1990s was a form of retaliation—retaliation against an obstructionist, unreliable, and expendable American hegemony in international politics; retaliation against a seemingly omnipotent United States that tried to impose the self-serving process of globalization on France; and retaliation against American promotion of economic practices, a flawed social model, and mass culture that challenged a traditional construction of Frenchness and debased true culture.

■ Comparing Two Decades

An explanation of anti-Americanism during the 1990s invites some reflection on the more benign decade that preceded it. In the 1980s there were still two superpowers, which allowed France some space for maneuver; after 1989 there was only the old transatlantic ally/nemesis in Washington. The earlier decade was also marked by the relative absence of issues that provoked anti-Americanism later: there were no major wars that required France to fight as an ally with the United States and the contentious problem of remaking the Atlantic Alliance was not yet on the table. There were also no demonstrations, except possibly for Libya, of America's enormous lead in military power that would be apparent later in the Balkans and Iraq. What wrangling occurred between Washington and Paris was over less passionate issues, at least for the ordinary French man or woman, like trade sanctions against the Soviets, the exchange rate of the dollar, arms control, the Strategic Defense Initiative, or aid to the Sandinistas in Nicaragua. Unilateralism and triumphalism in the earlier decade were also less blatant despite Reagan's posturing and Bush's assertive management of German reunification. In the Reagan-Bush years triumphalism had not yet reached the stage of parading the "indispensable nation" or extolling the American economic model as displayed at the G7 summit in 1996. And imports of American popular culture seemed less intrusive.

Moreover, during the 1980s the French malaise—that is, the anxiety over problems like immigration, Brussels, and globalization— was only beginning to emerge. In brief, to the French the United States appeared less hegemonic: in the mid-1980s half of those surveyed expressed little or no concern about U.S. interference in French foreign policy and even fewer said they were anxious about interference in economic affairs.[131] Polls ten years later revealed far more worry about the hyperpower.

It would be misleading to draw too sharp a contrast between the decades, for in many respects the Reagan-Bush years anticipated the 1990s. Mistrust and rivalry marked international relations; positive attitudes toward America concealed anxieties and ambivalence; Americanization, or at least certain vectors of American popular culture, appeared as threats; and dystopian anti-Americanism still carried a certain cachet among intellectuals and those on the political margins. Looking back, the presidency of George H. W. Bush ushered in the testy new decade with the emergence of the controversial questions of restructuring the Atlantic Alliance and controlling Iraq. War in the Balkans roused French anxiety about American policy while quarrels over a new European security policy soured relations. In short, well before Bill Clinton took office the familiar rivalry and anti-Americanism were in the ascendancy.

■ The Novelty of Contemporary Anti-Americanism

Despite the striking continuities in the history of anti-Americanism what emerged at the fin de siècle was in certain respects different from its interwar, or even its early Cold War, predecessors.[132] The phenomenon under discussion here is principally the expansive, popular form of the phobia rather than its restrictive, dystopian variant.

Contemporary anti-Americanism is less about the horrors of the coming standardized, technology-driven modernity, or the suffocation of mass culture, or even the empty lifestyle of consumerism than it was in the interwar years, though some of these tropes persist. Americanization had advanced too far by the end of the century to sustain these phobias. Consumer society and American popular culture were so accepted, so ubiquitous, that it was difficult to denounce America as an outsider that had perpetrated a cultural crime. The anti-Americanism of the fin de siècle focused less on modernity itself and more on American policies—both domestic (principally socioeconomic) and foreign—as they impinged on France. What was driving contemporary anti-Americanism was mainly the policies and politics of the hyperpower.

Fin-de-siècle anti-Americanism was also different because it was inserted into the wider debate about globalization. The process of globalization had shaped Franco-American relations for a long time, but the flows of commerce, investment, technology, people, culture, and information across the Atlantic in recent decades expanded in magnitude and kind and accelerated in velocity. This new interconnectedness seemed to magnify the presence and power of America and fuel anti-Americanism. To the French, as to many others, globalization came with an American face. The Internet begot Microsoft, American websites, and American English while foreign investment brought the power of American investors. Fast food, soft drinks, and family entertainment increasingly bore the trademarks of McDonald's, Coca-Cola, and Disney. International organizations like the International Monetary Fund or the World Trade Organization, and even the European Union, in the eyes of the more paranoid were supposedly accomplices of the U.S. government. As popular opposition to globalization grew among the French, it generated new activist movements and created new fractures among political parties.[133] Those who actively resisted globalization tended to target the United States as the champion of "ultraliberal" capitalism and free trade, though they usually claimed they were not "anti-American." But protests against American-led globalization often seemed incoherent and confused; much of what these demonstrators denounced as globalization was only remotely linked to America. The rally for José Bové in 2000, for example, included not only adversaries of McDonald's but also housing activists, Greenpeace militants, proponents of the Occitan language, and opponents of the Lyon-to-Toulouse superhighway.

Yet another difference in contemporary anti-Americanism was the displacement of the "other." The space once monopolized by the Americans became rather crowded at the fin de siècle, and this had the effect of diffusing phobias about outsiders. The American menace became diluted by the emergence of alleged dangers mounted by new "others"—the domestic Muslim population, EU commissioners, East European workers, and cheap labor in developing countries. In the 1950s America offered a convenient, catchall target for critics like the communists, who could attack Uncle Sam as the scapegoat for everything from German rearmament and the loss of colonies to the adulteration of literature (i.e., comic books and the *Reader's Digest*) that ailed the Fourth Republic. But by the 1990s Americans, despite their hyperpower status, could not convincingly be blamed for all the country's troubles: there were other culprits.

A final end-of-the-century distinction was the retreat of the dystopians or partisans of *anti-américanisme primaire* and the corresponding advance of their rivals, the anti-anti-Americans. The former no longer represented the voice of St. Germain des Prés as they had during the early postwar decades. The fin-de-siècle polemics of the likes of Jean Baudrillard and Alain de Benoist met counterattacks from intellectuals like Jean-François Revel, André Glucksmann, Jacques Julliard, Bernard-Henri Lévy, Guy Sorman, and Pascal Bruckner, some of whom insisted that demonizing Uncle Sam only served to confirm the perception of national decline and blind the French to learn from the New World.[134] Nor did it seem that the dystopians had the same status they once enjoyed. If the anti-American monthly *Le Monde diplomatique* had a large circulation, it was less prestigious than either *Esprit* or *Les Temps modernes* were in the days of Jean-Marie Domenach and Jean-Paul Sartre.[135]

"Primary anti-Americanism," furthermore, lacked the bite of the Cold War because it was no longer informed by a coherent alternative. Once there was the Soviet dream, or the social democratic model, or Gaullist grandeur. By the end of the century it was not apparent what the alternative to American-led globalization was—other than nostalgia for tradition, or a revival of Republican solidarity, or a new European identity, or construction of French modernity that was not American.

■ This chapter began with a paradox: anti-Americanism seemed more illogical at the fin de siècle than it did in the postwar period because Americanization and globalization had transformed France. Transatlantic interdependence had advanced so far that complaints often seemed incongruous and anachronistic. When French investments poured into the United States in the 1990s and when Vivendi, the French communications and utilities giant, bought Universal Studios and the publisher Houghton-Mifflin and bid for control of the American water service industry, worrying about the investment of American pension funds in France seemed unreasonable. Legislating against American English seemed silly when it was commonly used by business leaders, scientists, academics, and others and permeated French popular culture. And certain actions aimed against American business were just amusing, such as when the government, in order to maintain a competitive market for soft drinks, blocked the expansion of Coca-Cola—at the request of Pepsi-Cola.

Yet the growth of anti-Americanism made sense if one looked behind the polls and the posturing for the reasons why the French displayed growing apprehension. Above all there was the *hyperpuissance*, American triumphalism, and intrusive American-led globalization—all of which challenged a society plagued with self-doubt about its identity and prone to defensiveness. In 1999, at the end of his tenure in Paris as U.S. ambassador, Felix Rohatyn spoke of the enormous weight of the United States in world affairs, mentioning the pressure of its financial institutions on the French stock market, for example; he warned that the United States must avoid appearing like a bully.[136] The Yankee bully aroused Gallic anxiety and prompted retaliation.

Anxiety generated a complicated reaction from the French. First, they directed criticism at the United States. The public reproached the United States for its domineering posture in world affairs, censured its socioeconomic policies, and expressed ambivalence about American popular culture. The self-congratulatory mood across the Atlantic provoked the French to expose the hollowness of American claims to social and economic progress. Second, there was self-defense: the French tried to protect what was deemed essential from the grasp of its friend. The French complained that they wanted fewer American movies and television programs. They rallied behind government efforts at maintaining "the cultural exception" and subsidizing the cinema and agriculture. They made José Bové a national hero and sent their children to special classes that instructed them about bon goût so that they would be less tempted by fast food. In short, the French rebuffed America and asserted that they could chart their own way to modernity—without imitating their transatlantic cousins.

France was facing disruptive change, and it was easy to indict the United States for it. But contemporary anti-Americanism was not mere scapegoating—in the sense of blaming America for some imagined threat. Rather, the transformation the French faced was distressing and America was one of its agents. Globalization, and its partner Americanization, challenged a traditional self-image of "Frenchness" and America promoted and benefited from it. Whether it was food, the national cinema, or language, America usurped these signifiers of identity. And Americans sometimes browbeat their friends. The tormenters were not just officials in Washington; corporate America often misbehaved. Take, for example, the imperious conduct of Disney in building its theme park or the Coca-Cola Company's marketing abuses that earned the company fines from the French government. America was in part responsible for the troubles associated with late-twentieth-century globalization.

To be sure, this fin-de-siècle anti-Americanism seemed unfair and misguided in some respects. It was unfair, for example, to pretend, as the dystopians believed, that American leadership in fields like global security, mass entertainment, or genetically modified seeds brought no benefits, only loss. It was misguided to blame what was wrought by various forces, including globalization, solely on the United States and to omit French complicity. A majority of the French wanted to globalize, modernize, Americanize, and expand European integration. Suburban sprawl made France look more and more like America, but this was not the fault of Americans. What seemed like duplicity to anti-French critics in the United States represented a nation trying to adapt to change and finding some solace in assailing the hegemonic power and champion of market-based globalization.

REFLECTIONS ■

Following an international conference sponsored by the United States advancing worldwide democracy, Madeleine Albright sparred with Hubert Védrine. Only France had refused to sign the manifesto. The U.S. secretary of state admonished the French foreign minister for failing to lead an effort at improving solidarity among democracies, reminding him that France had sent the Marquis de Lafayette to assist America's fight for freedom. Védrine supposedly smiled and replied, "Ah, but you see *chère* Madeleine, Lafayette did not go to help the Americans, he went to defeat the British."[1] Franco-American misunderstandings have a long history, and it is the purpose of this book to help Americans understand France—in particular, to clarify how the French, in recent decades, have viewed America and transatlantic relations.

To the French at the fin de siècle America appeared in two forms, real and imaginary. There was first the palpable, inescapable presence of the United States. Its military might guaranteed French and European security during and after the Cold War and its power proved essential to ending violence in the Balkans and defending Europeans from dangers generated outside the continent like Iraqi ambitions in the Persian Gulf. The United States doubled as the diplomatic hegemon, safely steering the potentially dangerous process of German reunification and forcing a settlement on the combatants in Bosnia. It was, at the same time, a financial, economic, and technological colossus that commanded the attention of the French. The dollar exchange rate; American investors like Calpers; trade in products like hormone-treated beef; companies like Microsoft and Proctor and Gamble; the science and technology represented by the Internet, the Strategic Defense Initiative , AIDS therapies, and Silicon Valley—all impinged on them. So did American mass culture in the form of Euro Disney, McDonald's outlets, films like *Titanic*, television series like *Baywatch*, the sounds and images of Michael Jackson and Mariah Carey, fashions by Ralph Lauren, and advertisements in American English. The character and magnitude of this outside presence gave the French reason to both welcome and worry about America—to be ambivalent.

Enveloping the reality of America and informing the French response to it was the image of the New World. This fantasized America was both a model and a threat, an "other" to be both emulated and rejected. Here was a second source of Gallic ambivalence constructed around binaries of perception. Americans were simultaneously viewed as individualists and conformists, craven materialists and religious zealots, humanitarians and racists. The United States was either isolationist or imperialist, an ally or a rival. And American prosperity represented either the coming globalized economy symbolized by Silicon Valley or "jungle capitalism" associated with urban homelessness. Accordingly, most discourse about the New World was mixed in a normative sense. Contradictory expressions were the rule so that perceptions were usually compounds combining philo- and anti-American attitudes—except at the political extremes where derision was uninhibited. This "America" of Gallic fantasies emerged from stereotypes, an inherited discourse, media images, and misinformation as well as collective hopes and anxieties. It was often a caricature that simplified complexities and omitted diversity. This imagined America had been created by elites; spread by the press, education, and the electronic media; manipulated by politicians, intellectuals, and interest groups; and stored in the psyche of the populace. This discourse of ambivalence served as a lens, a magnifier through which the French perceived developments and it intensified their response. A TV report of an incident of mayhem in Detroit could evoke the stereotype "More violence! Americans are like that."

Attitudes toward America were volatile even within the relatively short span of the last two decades of the twentieth century. Oscillation resulted from the interplay of the imagined and the real, from the constant and the variables. The fantasized America—which mixed promise with peril—was fixed, or at least slow to evolve. It could be awakened by events, developments, and policies that engaged France with the United States. The "real" America—that is, its domestic presence—was diverse and unstable. U.S. policies, for example, might alarm the French at one moment and comfort them the next while American investors might come and go. Thus, an adequate explanation for the shifting pattern of attitudes requires historians to focus on how policies and developments on both sides of the Atlantic interacted with the latent image,—the binaries—of America and Americans. For example, the celebrity of Henry Ford and the isolationist foreign policies of the U.S. government in the 1920s fed French assumptions about American conformity and parochialism, just as the late 1940s, the moment of the Marshall Plan and NATO, activated tropes of American fraternal concern about Europe. During the 1980s Ronald Reagan's maladroit handling of disarmament and Iran confirmed suspicions that amateurs once again ran the White House and his seemingly heartless social policies fueled latent anxieties about the New World's worship of "hard capitalism." Conversely, the success of George H. W. Bush in ending the Cold War, guiding the peaceful reunification of Germany, and the quick victory of the American-led coalition against Saddam Hussein in the first Gulf War confirmed widespread admiration for American power making both the president and the American people popular.

If anti-Americanism, the negative polarity of the love-hate binary, continued to filter French perceptions and responses, it also evolved during the fin de siècle. *Anti-américanisme primaire*, the dystopian version of the phobia—despite its persistence among those on the political extremes—receded. It lost its former status for the intelligentsia and disappeared among other elites like globalized business managers. The anti-anti-Americans became so aggressive that Régis Debray complained that the way to discredit an intellectual was to label him or her as "anti-American." At the same time the popular version of anti-Americanism adjusted its language and content. At midcentury the American menace had been external and it had assumed the form of a standardized, technologically driven modernity, a mass culture represented by movies and television, and a lifestyle dominated by consumerism and suburbia. Such a specter did not altogether disappear, but it altered its shape during the fin de siècle largely because what had been contingent and distant in 1930, or even 1950, was flourishing within the Hexagon by the 1970s. It was difficult to blame the Americans for what the French were doing to themselves. Even President Mitterrand watched the *Dallas* TV series. What began to replace the midcentury phobia about modernity was an anti-Americanism based on resistance to American international and domestic policies and its commercialized culture. Disagreements over security, like the architecture of the Atlantic Alliance; disputes over trade, like agriculture subsidies and the cultural exception; and differences over reform of the welfare state, like the programs of presidents Ronald Reagan, George H. W. Bush, and Bill Clinton provoked anti-Americanism. There was also the threat of "American-led globalization" that represented new practices like unimpeded foreign investment and global labor markets, as well as an escalation of the danger posed by the pseudoculture of America. Protecting national independence and identity remained at the heart of the phobia. If resisting modernity itself had once been the issue, the question at the fin de siècle was how to design an alternative French, or European, modernity that was not American.

While anti-Americanism evolved, it could still be exploited because it formed part of the Gallic national psyche. For the political class it functioned as a way to camouflage economic liberalization, disparage opponents, rally support for foreign policy, cover scandals, and pander to the extremes. Similarly, economic interests—in particular, those that feared American competition whether it be in the form of farmers or film directors—played the anti-American card to rouse the crowd and shape policy. Anti-Americanism lived on, if in a contemporary form, and could be excited for political, economic, and cultural advantage.

The fascination with America combined rejection with admiration. At its worst it translated into anti-Americanism, which not only survived, if modified in character, but in its popular form darkened during the 1990s. At its best it prompted respect for American achievements and selective imitation.

From a comparative perspective one might ask, Why were the French more eager to confront America than other Europeans? The answer is, to be sure, a matter of degree or intensity because, as we have seen, Germans, Italians, Spaniards, Greeks, and even the British also expressed strong reservations during these two decades. Yet the French often, though not in all instances, led the opposition. They did so for two reasons. First, more than other Europeans, the French aspired to, and had the means to exercise, international leadership. If they conceded that they lagged behind the hyperpower, they were still persuaded that they were an elite nation with the power, both hard and soft, as well as the experience and self-confidence, to merit a commanding position in Europe and beyond. More keenly than others the French also distrusted American hegemony, found it unreliable and self-serving, and linked the United States with the invasive process of globalization. The United States became the villain of the drama because its government punctured Gallic pretensions more emphatically than those of Europeans who aspired to less conspicuous roles on the international stage. Second, American practices and values targeted signifiers of identity more closely in France than they did those of its neighbors. Free-market liberalism and the harsh social policies associated with Ronald Reagan and his successors, for example, appeared as direct and unwanted challenges to *dirigisme* and a Gallic sense of social solidarity. And American social values—for example, esteem for work, ostentatious religiosity, and frenetic lifestyle—appeared more misguided to the French than to other Europeans. Similarly, Americanization seemed to collide with cultural ideals in France more noisily than it did elsewhere. French identity at the fin de siècle encompassed numerous elements, but among them were the small farm, food, wine, and, by extension, *bon goût*; culture defined as the fine arts, fashion, and the cinema; and, especially, *la langue française*. All of these signifiers seemed endangered by the advance of Americanization. Thus France mounted efforts at keeping America at bay, such as harassing Hollywood and American television networks with the "cultural exception"; educating children's tastes to inoculate them against fast food; and imposing official regulations to curb the use of American English. Compared to other Europeans the French contested the American model more aggressively. Germans, for example, may have also regretted the loss of their traditional landscape, expressed a certain pride in German *Kultur* and language, and preferred their movies, but they did not invest protection of these signifiers, except perhaps their forests, with the same existential meaning as the French. The French, more than other Europeans, thought of their identity as a potential victim of Americanization. They were distinctive, but not unique, in their resistance.

The premise of this study is that the French measured themselves against an American standard at the fin de siècle. Invoking the New World functioned as both an incentive to change and as an excuse to maintain the status quo. In the latter case, censuring America could conceal motives and interests and serve as a reason to avoid renovation and adaptation. Marc Bloch, in his account of the French military debacle of 1940, which he had witnessed, indicted his own people for, among other failings, denouncing Americanization or the age of machines and material progress in the name of the quiet pleasures of the countryside. Such thinking, this great historian observed, led to the defeat by a dynamic Germany that had adjusted to the new age. If France were to survive the national catastrophe of 1940, Bloch insisted, it too would have to adjust because "[t]he donkey cart may be a friendly and a charming means of transport, but if we refuse to replace it by the motor-car, where the motor-car is desirable, we shall find ourselves stripped of everything—including the donkey."[2] In other words, rejecting Americanization was a way of suffocating adaptation and a recipe for national disaster. In 2004 in the wake of another war and the "shocking" reelection of George W. Bush, Jean-Marie Colombani, the editor of *Le Monde*, reiterated Bloch's point: given America's dynamism—that is, its defense spending, assimilation of immigrants, research and development, and high-tech sector—if Europeans were to be able to conduct themselves on a more equal basis with the United States in world affairs, they could not crouch safely behind an insular "European model" but must learn to compete with their transatlantic ally.[3] During the 1980s and '90s the American example was often cited in order to evade change. Governments evoked it to dodge market-oriented reform: socialist officials, for example, condemned temporary work and modifications in the labor code as *précarité* or the way of Americans. And trade unions, instead of accommodating needed social reforms like reducing pensions, took to the streets in the name of combating an Anglo-Saxon way of life. But, in general, the French during these decades heeded Bloch's admonition and used America as a reference for change rather than as an alibi for avoiding it.

The question of meeting the American challenge was hardly new, but it became more pressing over the course of the century. In 1930, as Georges Duhamel in *America the Menace* graphically warned, the threat to French humanistic culture from across the Atlantic was potential. By the late 1950s Jean-Marie Domenach in *Esprit* lamented the arrival of Americanization and the flattening of French life. A decade later Jean-Jacques Servan-Schreiber in *The American Challenge* issued a grave, if specific, warning about a coming takeover of the European economy by American subsidiaries. By the 1980s and '90s the anxiety had mounted to the point that the French feared they were losing the contest with America in virtually every forum: diplomacy, the military, economics, finance, technology, medicine, science, language, and culture. Responding to America became mandatory. Admittedly, the Gallic infatuation was intermittent, capricious, and diluted with a dollop of indifference. Nevertheless, the question was, How could France match the Americans without copying them? How could it catch up without sacrificing its independence, traditions, and national identity? If France refused to follow the American way, it risked becoming a has-been, a picturesque, anachronistic, survivor from the belle époque that had once been a modern society and a great power. If France imitated the Americans, it risked a different death.

Given this dilemma, this study has examined how well, and with what consequences, the French measured up to their goals toward finding a French way toward modernity that did not simply imitate that of the Americans. America served as a foil to determine success at raising France's international status, defending and developing a vigorous national culture, advancing economic progress, and sustaining social solidarity—or attaining power and modernity the French way. In summation, this historian offers the following appraisal.

In international affairs France tried to balance between retaining the U.S. superpower as a close ally and asserting its independence. This desired equilibrium required continuous recalibration of transatlantic relations because the United States seemed to lurch from passivity to hyperactive interventionism. How well did France manage this balance during the fin de siècle, and at what price? If quarrels between Paris and Washington were frequent and sometimes serious, they never provoked a break in the alliance: the partnership survived. On many issues Washington and Paris were in general agreement and cooperated closely, as they did in the crisis over Euro missiles, the first Gulf War, and Kosovo. The search for independence and leverage within the Atlantic Alliance, however, rarely brought success when there were disagreements. The few triumphs came when the United States was at odds with its major allies or the international community as in the case of the Soviet pipeline, or when France was able to form a countervailing coalition, usually from within the European Union, as it did in the dispute over the cultural exception. But trying to change Washington's mind usually brought frustration and disappointment for Paris. Pursuing its own policies and standing up to Uncle Sam probably enhanced self-esteem, but earned few victories. When the hyperpower said "no," as it did in the dispute over NATO reform, Jacques Chirac was helpless. Then there were issues such as the Sandinistas in Nicaragua, or the bombing of Libya, or the dollar exchange rate, or German reunification, or the negotiations in Dayton, Ohio, over Bosnia where the United States exercised its diplomatic muscle, bypassed French objections, and went its own way. And France paid a price for its recalcitrance and obstructionism. It raised mistrust in certain circles in Washington and made France appear as arrogant, self-interested, and uncooperative. And some French sparring with the United States was for naught. After more than four decades of trying to stand within, yet apart from, the Atlantic Alliance, France rejoined an "unreformed" NATO.

Meeting the American cultural challenge achieved mixed results. My assessment is limited to the specific encounters addressed in this study. If France could not hold back the tidal wave of fin-de-siècle Americanization, in certain instances the dikes held. While French cinema lost some of its audience to Hollywood and accepted the need to adapt its productions, it did not succumb and remained a standout among the continental film industries. And French television, though inundated with American programs and films, was relatively better sheltered than other European networks. But survival of the audiovisual sector came at a price: quotas, costly and often misdirected subsidies, government regulations, quarrels with European partners, and open confrontations with the United States. Resisting American English, however, was a fiasco. Not only did government initiatives fail to stem the spread of the Anglo-Saxon linguistic intruder but the Ministry of Culture under Jacques Toubon earned almost universal ridicule. French students made American English their first choice of a foreign language, and French itself became populated with borrowed expressions. In the case of Disney, McDonald's, and Coca-Cola, the Americans scored some successes but only within limits. Euro Disney represented a dramatic advance for a new form of American entertainment and leisure: the park attracted more visitors than the Louvre, and nearly half its entrants were natives. Yet it also triggered the renovation and expansion of French theme parks that, by identifying niches and adapting, found that they could compete with Disney. McDonald's, like Disney, gained a substantial market share so that by the millennium there were a thousand outlets, and its methods of operations, from food preparation to part-time labor, transformed the French fast food industry. Nevertheless, hamburgers won only a tiny share of restaurant meals and McDonald's had to adjust to please the natives. Coca-Cola also captured a large of share of its market and it, too, spawned imitators in the soft drink industry. But the Atlanta-based company could not conduct business as it pleased: the French government intervened to chasten the company for its marketing methods and limit its expansion. The Americans arrived, be it in the form of Euro Disney at Marne-la-Vallée, the local *épicerie* selling liters of Coke, the neighborhood Golden Arches, *Star Wars* on the silver screen, *La Roue de la fortune* on the television set, or a vocabulary studded with anglicisms like "e-mail," but French ways survived. The cinema, television, restaurants, beverages, theme parks, and the language itself were not overwhelmed by Yankee imports. And one cannot measure the psychological comfort, the boost in self-esteem, gained by keeping America at bay, at keeping France French.

The record in competing with the Americans in economic performance while sustaining the French model of solidarity is commendable. France resisted the fad of Reaganomics as well as the Clinton administration's promotion of a globalized market, yet it shifted sufficiently toward the market and openness to stimulate economic growth while paying for the social charges of its generous welfare state. If American-style capitalism was rejected in principle, much of it was renamed and adapted (e.g., *stock options à la française*). There was extensive privatization and deregulation, expansion of financial and stock markets, openness to international trade, validation of entrepreneurship, acceptance of new forms of incentives for management, and promotion of strategic sectors including the construction of high-tech incubators like Sophia Antipolis. In social policy France maintained its commitment to solidarity while incrementally making adjustments—in pensions and health care, for example—to sustain its programs. When the government pushed too hard, however, as it did under Alain Juppé in 1995, resistance forced it to retreat. There were limits to the retrenchment of *l'état providential*, even though much more needed to be done.

Economic performance in these decades, with one glaring exception, virtually matched that of the United States. A few numbers are revealing. Inflation, which had reached 13 percent in 1980–81, was brought under control, falling to 1.6 percent in 2000—a level half that of the United States. Productivity rates increased in these two decades so that they were virtually the same (3.4 percent) as those in the United States in 2000. The bilateral trade balance with America improved, especially during the late 1990s, bringing a surplus for France of almost $10 billion at the end of the decade while French direct investment in the United States rose rapidly in the 1980s and then doubled in the 1990s. As the new millennium dawned France was second only to the United Kingdom as a leading investor in the U.S. economy. Growth in gross domestic product was comparable in the 1980s (averaging 2.4 percent) but France fell behind in the early Chirac-Clinton years. Recovery followed in the late 1990s so that the two economies reached near parity at the new millennium.[4] The obvious blemish in this record was unemployment. The U.S. rate of joblessness peaked in 1982 at 9.7 percent and then, with some volatility, declined. Under the Clinton administration it moved sharply down, reaching a low of 4 percent in 2000. In contrast, France had a miserable record for the entire period: unemployment hovered around 10 percent and was still at 9.1 percent, or twice that of the United States, in 2000.

Such economic achievements came without jeopardizing republican solidarity that featured a high degree of social protection and a relatively equitable distribution of income. Nor did the French sacri-fice the defense of sectors that contributed to national identity, like ag-riculture or the cinema, and they continued to promote such dynamic industries as aero-space, nuclear energy, high-speed rail, and informa-tion technology. The French achieved a better balance between indi-vidual initiative or free enterprise and social protection than did the United States. But there was a price—most obviously the congealed labor market that kept unemployment at double-digit levels. And maintenance of the republican social model entailed toleration of its shortcomings—that is, the sick *banlieues*, the "angry young men" left behind, the poor living conditions for many families from immigrant backgrounds, the abuses of the *droit acquis* like those enjoyed by union-ized and retired workers, the accompanying bloated state bureaucracy, and the high costs of the welfare state. Seemingly intractable problems remained. And if some of the economic disparities with the Anglo-Saxons had been addressed, the French in many respects remained behind their rivals in job creation, business start-ups, and the develop-ment of certain high-technology sectors.

In the 1980s and '90s France scored major successes in improving its economic performance and opening its economy to domestic and foreign competition while preserving social solidarity. Yet if one of the goals of reform was to catch up to the Anglo-Americans, along with adjusting to European integration and globalization, a gap remained after two decades.

The French simultaneously borrowed from the American model and shunned it. What they transferred was accomplished without ostensibly imitating their transatlantic cousins: they camouflaged market-inspired reforms, insisted on designing French alternatives, and, above all, defended the essentials of their socioeconomic order and their national culture. They bridged the ocean, but did so with a difference. In so doing they enunciated a French alternative within the transatlantic community at the fin de siècle. They could boast about making enormous progress toward adapting to a market economy and globalization while preserving the fundamentals of the French way. They had maintained the republican social contract, a mixed economy, a vigorous state, and a distinctive cultural identity. The American challenge had spurred the French to renovate their socioeconomic order so that by 2000 they had advanced a long way from 1981, when François Mitterrand had entered the Elysée seeking a rupture with capitalism. Yet the French way was intact.

The speculation that France and the United States are drifting apart remains a hypothesis. Two decades do not make a historical trend and much of the divergence and much of the anti-Americanism of the fin de siècle represented a persistent gap inherited from the past that circumstances aggravated, such as the French malaise and the U.S. government's triumphalism. Some of the perceived differences did express long-term shifts like the retreat of religion among the French while others are of more recent vintage and scarcely qualify as trends. For example, France waited until 1981 to ban capital punishment and came late to the environmental cause. Furthermore, the thesis of growing apart neglects growing similarities, for France and the United States are more alike today than they were fifty years ago: they are democracies that share market economies softened by redistributive social policies; they worry about common issues like immigration and urban blight, and face the same dangers like nuclear proliferation, international terrorism, and Islamic fundamentalism.

Rather than confirming a trend of continental drift, these decades represent the paradox of American-led globalization. The emergence and celebration of the French (or European) way can be explained as a reaction to the integrative and homogenizing effects of globalization and its partner, Americanization. The simultaneous progress of Americanization and expressions of anti-Americanism are an example of the dynamics of globalization, a process that intensifies interdependence and uniformity and in turn incites resistance, often in the form of assertions of identity, be it ethnic, religious, or national. As France and America became more alike, the French protested the process and defended an identity that rejected the American way. Time may, or may not, confirm the trend of transatlantic drift, but what happened in fin-de-siècle France was an example of the paradox of American-led globalization that fostered both resemblance and divergence.

The question remains for the new millennium: Will France have to embrace more fully a globalized, Americanized modernity? Or can it continue to adapt incrementally without sacrificing the essence of the French difference?

This history of the recent past leads to the conclusion that there is a viable French way. If this is true, it will be healthy for the French, for Americans, and for others.

NOTES ■

Note: All translations from the French are my own unless otherwise indicated.

Preface

1. Federico Romero, "The Twilight of American Cultural Hegemony: A Historical Perspective on Western Europe's Distancing from America," in *What They Think of Us: International Perspectives of the United States since 9/11*, ed. David Farber (Princeton, NJ: Princeton University Press, 2007), 172. The beginning of hostilities in Iraq spurred Jürgen Habermas and Jacques Derrida, two European intellectual celebrities, to issue a "manifesto" in May 2003 calling for the "rebirth of Europe" and for Europeans to redefine their common identity. The literature on the transatlantic drift is plentiful; some examples are Tony Judt, "Europe vs. America," *New York Review of Books*, 10 February 2005, 37–41; Tony Judt, "Europe as a Way of Life," in *Postwar: A History of Europe since 1945* (New York: Penguin, 2005); Charles Kupchan, *The End of the American Era: U.S. Foreign Policy and the Geopolitics of the Twenty-First Century* (New York: Knopf, 2002); Steven Hill, *Europe's Promise: Why the European Way is the Best Hope in an Insecure Age* (Berkeley and Los Angeles: University of California Press, 2010); T. R. Reid, *The United States of Europe* (New York: Penguin, 2004); Jeremy Rifkin, *The European Dream* (New York: Tarcher/Penguin, 2004); and Robert Kagan, *Of Paradise and Power: America and Europe in the New World Order* (New York: Knopf, 2003).

A Note on Anti-Americanism

1. The literature on anti-Americanism is vast and in most cases the definitional issue is skirted. But there are some recent, explicit, and instructive attempts at

definition. Pierre Rigoulot defines it as "a hostile predisposition to all aspects of American life" tinged with either "political disagreement or cultural revulsion"; it is irrational and touches the unconscious and emotions like fear and nostalgia. See Pierre Rigoulot, *L'Antiaméricanisme: critique d'un prêt-à-penser retrograde et chauvin* (Paris: Éditions Robert Laffont, 2004), 15, 259. Philippe Roger regards anti-Americanism as an obsessive, cumulative, self-replicating discourse created by generations of intellectuals, and likens it to geological sedimentation; see Philippe Roger, *The American Enemy: The History of French Anti-Americanism*, trans. Sharon Bowman (Chicago: University of Chicago Press, 2005). Seth Armus, like Roger, argues that anti-Americanism is basically a cultural and elitist response but he discerns a second strain that is political and popular; see Seth D. Armus, *French Anti-Americanism, 1930–1948: Critical Moments in a Complex History* (Lanham, MD: Lexington Books, 2007), 3–5. Jessica Gienow-Hecht goes too far in defining anti-Americanism in Europe as cultural revulsion and dismissing politics and transatlantic relations as mere "triggers" rather than "causes"; see Jessica Gienow-Hecht, "Always Blame the Americans: Anti-Americanism in Europe in the Twentieth Century," *American Historical Review* 111 (October 2006): 1067–91. Josef Joffe insists anti-Americanism is not criticism of American policies, but an obsessive denigration, demonization, and stereotyping of America and its culture; see Josef Joffe, *Überpower: The Imperial Temptation of America* (New York: Norton, 2006), 69–77. David Ellwood defines anti-Americanism as a catchall that combines attacks on the U.S. government and its policies; who or whatever is American (e.g., products); and American values in a normative sense; see David Ellwood, "Comparative Anti-Americanism in Western Europe," in *Transactions, Transgressions, Transformations: American Culture in Western Europe and Japan*, ed. Heide Fehrenbach and Uta Poiger (New York: Berghahn, 2000), 26–44. Ellwood develops his thesis in *America as a European Power: Modernity, Prosperity, Identity, 1898–2008* (Oxford: Oxford University Press, 2012). Assuming a global perspective. Peter Katzenstein and Robert Keohane advance a spacious definition—"a psychological tendency to hold negative views of the United States and American society in general"—which leads to a recognition of variety, or what they call "anti-Americanisms" in the plural; see Peter J. Katzenstein and Robert Keohane, "Varieties of Anti-Americanism: A Framework for Analysis," in *Anti-Americanisms in World Politics*, ed. Peter J. Katzenstein and Robert Keohane (Ithaca, NY: Cornell University Press, 2007), 12. The psychology that fuels anti-Americanism ranges from a mild predisposition to more systematic distrust to strong bias. Katzenstein and Keohane refine their definition to include a typology of anti-Americanisms—"liberal," "social," "sovereign-nationalist," and "radical"—and they add other varieties like "elitist" and "legacy." To these political scientists the subject is important as a political phenomenon. Sophie Meunier applies their approach to France and stresses politics arguing that, at least since the 1990s, French anti-Americanism can be explained more by the principles of French policy, be it wariness of the U.S. government's unilateralism or cultural defense; see Sophie Meunier, "The Distinctiveness of French Anti-Americanism," in Katzenstein and Keohane, eds., *Anti-Americanisms*, 129–56. She contends that anti-Americanism is based on distrust, which she ascribes to causes like the deep reservoir of attacks by elites and to the exploitation of these sentiments by politicians. A useful comparative treatment, but one that does not directly address the definitional issue, is Alexander Stephan, ed., *The Americanization of Europe: Culture, Diplomacy and Anti-Americanism after 1945* (New York: Berghahn, 2006).

2. The New Philosophers were among those who indicted *anti-américanisme primaire* to express their disgust with ideological dogmatism past and present. See, for example, Bernard-Henri Lévy, *L'Idéologie française* (Paris: Éditions Bernard Grasset, 1981), 288–89.

Chapter 1. America à la Mode: The 1980s

1. Jérôme Dumoulin and Yves Guihannec, "La France est-elle encore une grande puissance?" *L'Express*, 27 January–2 February 1984, 12–19.
2. Pierre Rosanvallon, *L'Etat en France de 1789 à nos jours* (Paris: Éditions du Seuil, 1990), 262.
3. Frank and Mary Ann, "France est devenue civilisée," *La Croix*, 6 May 1976.
4. Examples of commentary on the new society are Henri Mendras, *La Seconde Révolution française, 1965–1984* (Paris: Éditions Gallimard, 1988); Alain Touraine, "Existe-t-il encore une société française," *Tocqueville Review* 11 (1990): 143–71; John Ardagh, *France in the 1980s* (London: Secker and Warburg, 1982).
5. United States Information Agency (henceforth USIA), "American Image in France remains Positive," 28 January 1988, Regular and Special Reports of the Office of Research, 1988–89, National Archives, RG 306, box 4, 1988 Research Memoranda. In 1984 the ratio of pro- to anti-Americans was 43:18 and in 1987 it was 44:15.
6. Ibid. See also "What the World Thinks of America," *Newsweek*, 11 July 1983, 44–52; Steven Smith and Douglas Wertman, *U.S.–West European Relations during the Reagan Years* (New York: St. Martin's, 1992), 110.

7. Société française d'enquêtes par sondages, poll, October 1988, published as "Les Français aiment les Etats-Unis, mais . . . ," *Le Figaro*, 4 November 1988; henceforth cited as SOFRES/*Le Figaro*, October 1988. The percentage (multiple responses) were: power, 56; dynamism, 32; wealth, 31; freedom, 30; violence, 28; racism, 27; inequality, 25; relaxed morals, 15; imperialism, 12; youthfulness, 11; generosity, 7; naïveté, 4. Similar findings are reported in Gallup International for the French-American Foundation and *L'Express*, "France and the United States: A Study in Mutual Image," survey, April 1986, which appears in an abbreviated form in Sara Pais, "Plus ça change . . . ça change: A Survey of French-American Attitudes," *France Magazine* 6 (1986): 5–8; henceforth cited as Gallup/French American Foundation, 1986.

8. Smith and Wertman, *U.S.–West European Relations*, 108. While the French and the West Germans were quite similar in all categories of this assessment, the Italians and the British were more distinctive.

9. In a 1985 survey, some 60 percent of the French saw their values as different, compared to 43 percent of the West Germans, 38 percent of the British, and 42 percent of the Italians; see Smith and Wertman, *U.S.–West European Relations*, 105.

10. SOFRES poll, January 1983, reported in Elizabeth Hann Hastings and Philip Hastings, eds., *Index to International Public Opinion, 1983–1984* (New York: Survey Research Consultants International/Greenwood, 1985), 201–2.

11. For a comparison among Europeans who professed anti-Americanism, see Smith and Wertman, *U.S.–West European Relations*, 94–97, and 294, n. 7. In 1988, 22 percent of those who were backers of the socialists said they were anti-American, but so did 8 percent of the Union pour la Démocratie Française (henceforth UDF) and 4 percent of the Rassemblement pour la République (henceforth RPR). In comparison, for West Germany, 23 percent of members of the Social Democratic Party and 13 percent of the Christian Democrats identified themselves as anti-Americans.

12. If one adds those who thought American influence was insubstantial (*insuffisant*) to those who said it posed no problem, the percentages were: food, 77; clothes/fashion, 70; language, 58; advertising, 53; and cinema, 50. Music and TV programming were much more divisive, with the approval-to-disapproval ratio being 48:41 and 46:45, respectively; see SOFRES poll, cited in Daniel Vernet, "Les Français préfèrent M. Reagan au 'reaganisme,'" *Le Monde*, 6 November 1984, 1, 6; henceforth cited as SOFRES/*Le Monde*, November 1984. Another poll conducted in 1988 (SOFRES/*Le Figaro*, October 1988) found that the percentages of those who thought American cul-

ture was excessive as opposed to insubstantial or didn't pose a problem were: TV programming, 67, 2, 24; cinema, 53, 2, 36; music, 47, 2, 44; advertising, 42, 1, 47; language, 32, 4, 54; clothes, 19, 2, 71; cuisine, 10, 2, 79; and literature, 3, 4, 75. A *Newsweek* survey ("What the World Thinks") had similar results.

13. A USIA survey using a four-way ranking (very good; somewhat good; somewhat bad; very bad) reported the ratios as: music, 62/17/9/12; cinema, 66/19/9/18; sports, 71/8/5/16; television, 40/39/9/12, (USIA, "American Image," 1988).

14. USIA, "American Image," 1988.

15. SOFRES survey, June 1987, cited in Elizabeth Hann Hastings and Philip Hastings, eds., *Index to International Public Opinion, 1987–1988* (New York: Survey Research Consultants International/Greenwood, 1989), 208–9. The friendly votes along party lines were (in percentages): RPR, 76; UDF, 66; Front National, 67; Parti Socialiste, 55, Parti Communiste Français (henceforth PCF), 46.

16. As a child, Mitterrand's parents, who were Catholic, spoke to him more fervently about the American War of Independence than the French Revolution because the latter was anticlerical. See Jacques Attali, *Verbatim*, vol. 1, *Chronique des années 1981–86, première partie, 1981–83* (Paris: Éditions Fayard, 1995), 176. A rather positive assessment of Mitterrand's view of America is recorded in Hubert Védrine, *Les Mondes de François Mitterrand: à l'Elysée 1981–85* (Paris: Éditions Fayard, 1996), 163–65.

17. Jean Lacouture, *Mitterrand: une histoire de Français*, vol. 2, *Les Vertiges du sommet* (Paris: Éditions du Seuil, 1988), 124–25; Attali, *Verbatim*, 1:10.

18. Noël-Jean Bergeroux, "Le nouveau venu . . . ," *Le Monde*, 7 November 1980, 7, and Michel Tatu, "Déclin ou repli?" *Le Monde*, 4 November 1980, 5.

19. Louis Pauwels, "Lettre au futur président des Etats-Unis, quel qu'il soit," *Le Figaro Magazine*, 31 October 1980, n.p.

20. Jacques Rupnik and Muriel Humbertjean, "Images of the United States in Public Opinion," in *The Rise and Fall of Anti-Americanism*, ed. Denis Lacorne, Jacques Rupnik, and Marie-France Toinet (New York: St. Martin's, 1990), 86–87.

21. Gallup/French American Foundation, 1986. In April 1980 a majority said that, in the event of a world crisis, they lacked confidence in President Carter; SOFRES, *Opinion publique, 1985* (Paris: Éditions Gallimard, 1986), 255.

22. *Libération*, 6 November 1980, 1. See also Jean Lefebvre, "Chez Reagan, c'est beau comme un western," *Le Figaro Magazine*, 31 November 1980, 66.

23. Nina Sutton, "En attendant Zorro," *Libération*, 6 November 1980, 16.

24. Charles Lamborschini, "Un nouvel Eisenhower," *Le Figaro*, 6 November 1980, 1–2.

25. Jacques Chirac, quoted in "Giscard: des amis de toujours," *Le Figaro*, 6 November 1980, 4.

26. Laurent Fabius, cited in *Le Monde*, 7 November 1980, 7; Jean-Pierre Chevènement, cited in "Giscard: des amis de toujours," 4.

27. "Défi à l'Europe?" *Le Monde*, 7 November 1980, 1. See also Michel Tatu, "Deux conceptions," *Le Monde*, 30 October 1980, 1; and "Déclin ou repli?" *Le Monde*, 4 November 1980, 5.

28. Smith and Wertman, *U.S.–West European Relations*, 228–30. From 1982 to 1984 roughly half the French found Reagan's policies harmful to the French economy. From 1983 to 1988 the French were consistently—compared to the British, West Germans, and Italians—the most critical of the U.S. lack of cooperation in resolving economic problems with Western Europe.

29. SOFRES survey, November 1982, reported in Hastings and Hastings, *Index to International Public Opinion, 1983–1984*, 214.

30. Survey conducted by the Nouvelles littéraires publimétrie in October 1981, reported in Elizabeth Hann Hastings and Philip Hastings, eds., *Index to International Public Opinion, 1981–1982* (New York: Survey Research Consultants International/Greenwood, 1983), 345.

31. SOFRES/*Le Monde*, November 1984. Queried about whether they thought the United States "determined" French policies, 49 percent replied "in small part or not at all" for foreign policy, and 39 percent for economic policy.

32. See Guy Sorman, *La Solution libérale* (Paris: Éditions Fayard, 1984); Guy Sorman, *The Conservative Revolution in America*, trans. Jane Kaplan (Chicago: Regnery, 1985); and Guy Sorman, "La voie libérale," *Le Point*, 5 November 1984, 27–28.

33. Sorman, *Conservative Revolution*, 196.

34. Gilles Anquetil, "Reagan Yes, Reagan No!" *Le Nouvel Observateur*, 14 September 1984, 34.

35. Guy Sorman, "Le nouveau libéralisme est arrivé," *Le Monde*, 2 August 1983, 2.

36. Ronald Reagan, "Remarks at Eureka College," 6 February 1984, http://www .presidency.ucsb.edu/ws/index.php?pid=39377&st=remarks+at+eureka +college&st1=#axzz1GKW1Q400.

37. Philippe Lefournier, "Pourquoi Reagan a réussi," *L'Expansion*, 19 November 1984, 53–63.

38. Louis Pauwels, "La grande leçon que nous donnent Reagan et son équipe," *Le Figaro Magazine*, 26 January 1985, 56–61.

39. "Quatre ans de reaganisme," *Libération*, 6 November 1984, 2.

40. The bookstore tour and the Minc quote can be found in Gilles Anquetil, "La musette du parfait libéral," *Le Nouvel Observateur*, 5 October 1984, 44; and Alain Minc, "L'enfant de la crise et de la puce," *Le Nouvel Observateur*, 5 October 1984, 45.

41. See, for example, Jérôme Dumoulin and Yves Guihannec, "Reagan: l'incroyable destin," *L'Express*, 2–4 November 1984, 19–22.

42. Lefournier, "Pourquoi Reagan," 63.

43. Sorman, "Le nouveau libéralisme est arrivé," 2.

44. Léo Sauvage, *Les Américains* (Paris: Bibliothèque Mazarine, 1983), 723–45.

45. See, for example, Roger Priouret, "La petite différence," *Le Nouvel Observateur*, 14 September 1984, 33; and Serge Christophe Kolm, cited in Anquetil, "Reagan Yes, Reagan No!" 33–34.

46. Philippe Bloch, "Avoir 30 ans sous Reagan," *L'Expansion*, 19 October–1 November 1984, 291.

47. Dominik Barouch, "L'Etat de santé de l'économie américaine," *Le Monde*, 15 August 1985, 16; Alain Lebaube, "Les oubliés de l'emploi," *Le Monde*, 19 January 1988, 40.

48. Nicole Bernheim, *Les Années Reagan* (Paris: Éditions Stock, 1984), 115–37, 193–95, 208–12, 228–30.

49. Franz Olivier Giesbert and Jacques Mornand, "Pourriez-vous vivre à l'américaine?" *Le Nouvel Observateur*, 14 September 1984, 46–50.

50. Bloch, "Avoir 30 ans," 289; Barouch, "L'Etat de santé," 16.

51. SOFRES survey of November 1982, reported in Hastings and Hastings, eds., *Index to International Public Opinion, 1983–1984*, 201.

52. SOFRES polls, March 1984 and November 1985, reported in Elizabeth Hann Hastings and Philip Hastings, eds., *Index to International Public Opinion, 1984–1985* (New York: Survey Research Consultants International/Greenwood, 1986), 232, and reported in Elizabeth Hann Hastings and Philip Hastings, eds., *Index to International Public Opinion, 1985–1986* (New York: Survey Research Consultants International/Greenwood, 1987), 223. The trend in the ratio of good versus bad opinion versus no opinion of the United States' political role in the world was 30:51:19 in 1982; 40:30:22 in 1984; and 43:27:30 in 1985. This trend was confirmed in other polls: SOFRES/*Le Monde*, November 1984, and Gallup/French American Foundation, 1986. Ratings climbed

further when the question asked was for a favorable/unfavorable rather than a good/bad distinction. By the late 1980s the favorable/unfavorable ratio in France was 69:23 which was comparable to that in both West Germany (79:14) and the United Kingdom (72:24). See Smith and Wertman, *U.S.– West European Relations*, 99.

53. This perception had improved only marginally since Jimmy Carter, from 69 percent to 79 percent; see SOFRES/*Le Monde*, November 1984.

54. The question asked was for attitudes (good, bad, or no opinion) about U.S. policy in the world. In 1977 the responses were 46:24:30 and in 1984 they were 40:38:22. In the latter case it was RPR (65 percent) and UDF (51 percent) partisans who lent their approval. Data from SOFRES/*Le Monde*, November 1984.

55. The reactions to Reagan's stance toward the USSR were: positive (34 percent), negative (31 percent), no response (35 percent). Source: SOFRES/*Le Monde*, November 1984.

56. SOFRES/*Le Monde*, November 1984.

57. Results of a CBS/*New York Times* poll are reported in E. J. Dionne, "Poll Finds Europeans Divided on U.S. Presidential Candidates," *New York Times*, 31 October 1984, A21.

58. The percentages were: Britain, 50; West Germany, 38; France, 24; see Dionne, "Poll Finds Europeans."

59. "Un grand-père de rêve," *Le Monde*, 8 November 1984, 5.

60. Michel Colomès, "Le nouveau défi américain," *Le Point*, 5 November 1984, 26. Alain Besançon admired how Reagan had "put things in place" after the "tormented style of Jimmy Carter"; see Alain Besançon, "Reagan entre deux mandats," *L'Express*, 9–15 November 1984, 30.

61. Vernet, "Les Français préfèrent M. Reagan au 'reaganisme.'"

62. Only 28 percent wanted France to follow Reaganomics, as opposed to 41 percent who did not and 31 percent who offered no opinion. The minority who liked the American way came mainly from backers of the RPR (49 percent) and the UDF (35 percent). SOFRES, *Opinion publique, 1985* (Paris: Éditions Gallimard, 1986), 257, 262.

63. Smith and Wertman, *U.S.–West European Relations*, 106.

64. The percentages of "votes" Reagan received according to party supporters were: RPR, 62; UDF, 51; Socialist Party, 24; and Communist Party, 18. With respect to the desirability of his economic and social policies the distribution was: RPR, 49; UDF, 35; Socialists, 18; and Communists, 7. Favorable answers about the United States in the world were: RPR, 65; UDF,

51; Socialists, 28; and Communists, 18. Data from SOFRES/*Le Monde*, November 1984.

65. "Les réactions françaises au triomphe de Reagan," *Le Figaro*, 8 November 1984, 7.

66. Serge Maffert, "Un test pour l'Amérique," *Le Figaro*, 7 November 1984, 1.

67. Backers of the RPR (66 percent) and the UDF (56 percent) answered in the affirmative compared to those associated with the Socialist Party (36 percent) and the Communist Party (31 percent). Data from SOFRES/*Le Monde*, November 1984.

68. "Les réactions françaises au triomphe de Reagan."

69. Alain Berger, "Le Pen s'explique," *Le Figaro Magazine*, 23 June 1984, 82–84.

70. "Les réactions françaises au triomphe de Reagan."

71. Paul Fabra, "Les trois leçons de l'expérience Reagan," *Le Monde*, 1–3 November 1984, 1.

72. SOFRES, January 1984, reported in Hastings and Hastings, eds., *Index to International Public Opinion, 1984–1985*, 231–32.

73. Diana Pinto, "Le socialisme et les intellectuels: le conflit caché," *Le Débat*, January 1982, 5.

74. Vivien A. Schmidt, *From State to Market? The Transformation of French Business and Government* (Cambridge: Cambridge University Press, 1996), 106.

75. Jean-Jacques Salomon, *Le Gaulois, le cow-boy, et le samouraï: la politique française de la technologie* (Éditions Economica, 1986).

76. Laurent Fabius, quoted in Paul Lewis, "Man in the News: At 37, Captain of France: Laurent Fabius," *New York Times*, 18 July 1984, A6.

77. Schmidt, *From State to Market?* 104.

78. Giesbert and Mornand, "Pourriez-vous vivre à l'américaine?" 46.

79. Henri de Kergorlay, "Mitterrand au paradis américain de la libre enterprise," *Le Figaro*, 27 March 1984, 5; Michael Dobbs, "Mitterrand, Silicon Valley Figures Meet," *Washington Post*, 27 March 1984, 27.

80. Jean-Yves Lhomeau, "Le Président de la République a défendu sa politique économique devant les milieux d'affaires de New York," *Le Monde*, 30 March 1984, 3; Henri de Kergorlay and Denis Legras, "Mitterrand aux Etats-Unis: un bilan mitigé," *Le Figaro*, 29 March 1984, 3.

81. The quotes in this paragraph are from François Mitterrand, "Mitterrand parle," interview with Jean Boissonat, *L'Expansion*, 19 November 1984, 60–67.

82. Jacques Fontaine, "Les Français ont viré leur cuti," *L'Expansion*, 7–20 October 1983, 241–47; Jérôme Jaffré, "Le retournement de l'opinion," *Le Monde*, 1 January 1984, 2.

83. Fontaine, "Les Français," 241.

84. "M. Madelin," *Le Monde*, 5 November 1985, 7.

85. Édouard Balladur, quoted in Jean-Marie Colombani, "L'action avant la gestion," *Le Monde*, 25 March 1986, 7.

86. Suzanne Berger, "Liberalism Reborn: The New Liberal Synthesis in France," in *Contemporary France*, ed. Jolyon Howorth and George Ross (London: Pinter, 1987), 84–108. My account relies heavily on Berger's presentation. A rather different analysis of this topic is in Vivien Schmidt, *From State to Market?* 133–39. Examples of neoliberal treatises are Sorman, *La Solution libérale*; André Fourcans, *Pour un nouveau libéralisme* (Paris: Éditions Albin Michel, 1982); Henri Lepage, *Demain le libéralisme* (Paris: Librairie Générale Française, 1980).

87. Berger, "Liberalism Reborn," 100.

88. Ipsos survey, reported as "Les Français satisfaits de la cohabitation," *Le Monde*, 25 March 1986, 13.

89. Poll conducted by *Le Figaro*-SOFRES, reported in "Entreprises: la liberté avant toute chose," *Le Figaro*, 17 December 1985, 11.

90. Jacques Chirac, quoted in Marie Guichoux, "Le premier minister sort de la crise et rentre au parlement," *Libération*, 17 July 1986, 2; Jacques Chirac, quoted in Andrew Knapp, *Gaullism since de Gaulle* (Brookfield VT: Dartmouth Publishing, 1994), 228.

91. Édouard Balladur, *Le Pouvoir ne se partage pas: conversations avec François Mitterrand* (Paris: Éditions Fayard, 2009), 33.

92. Pierre Péan, *L'Inconnu de l'Elysée* (Paris: Éditions Fayard, 2007), 459.

93. Alain Lebaube, "Aux Etats-Unis, l'emploi mobilise la communauté toute entière," *Le Monde*, 23 January 1988, 23.

94. Schmidt, *From State to Market?* 157–63.

95. Stanley Hoffmann, "The Odd Couple," *New York Review of Books*, 25 September 1986, 71.

96. Gérard Grunberg and Etienne Schweisguth, "Libéralisme culturel et libéralisme économique," in *L'Electeur français en questions*, ed. Daniel Boy and Nonna Mayer (Paris: Presses de Sciences Po, 1990), 50.

97. Michel Rocard, "Ces 'libertés' qui affament le monde," *Le Nouvel Observateur*, 5 October 1984, 39–40.

98. Laurent Fabius, "Qui a peur de l'économie mixte?" *Le Monde*, 28 February 1989, 1–2.

99. Steve Bastow, "Front National Economic Policy: From Neo-Liberalism to Protectionism," *Modern and Contemporary France* 5, no. 1 (1997): 61–72.

100. On the superiority of the Rhineland model over the ultra-liberal American alternative see Michel Albert, *Capitalisme contre capitalism* (Paris: Éditions du Seuil, 1991), translated by Paul Haviland as *Capitalism vs. Capitalism* (New York: Four Walls Eight Windows, 1993).

101. Anne-Marie Casteret, *L'Affaire du sang* (Paris: Éditions la Découverte, 1992), 98. Casteret was a physician-journalist who led the way in exposing the blood scandal. Other highly critical guides to this affair are Jean Sanitas, *Le Sang et le SIDA: une enquête critique sur l'affaire du sang contaminé et le scandale des transfusions sanguine* (Paris: Éditions L'Harmattan, 1994); Caroline Bettati, *Responsables et coupables: une affaire de sang* (Paris: Éditions du Seuil, 1993); and Mark Hunter, "Blood Money," *Discover*, August 1993, http://discovermagazine.com/1993/aug/bloodmoney250. A more balanced account is Olivier Beaud, *Le Sang contaminé: essai critique sur la criminalisation de la responsabilité des gouvernants* (Paris: Presses universitaires de France, 1999). Beaud insists the cause of the affair was less individual misbehavior than it was organizational dysfunction.

102. Casteret, *L'Affaire*, 115; Beaud, *Le Sang contaminé*, 23ff.

103. Rone Tempest, "Transfusions AIDS-Tainted: Doctors on Trial," *Los Angeles Times*, 21 July 1992, 16.

104. Casteret, *L'Affaire*, 136.

105. Bettati, *Responsables*, 70.

106. Sanitas, *Le Sang et le SIDA*, 44–6; Bettati, *Responsables*, 69–70.

107. Casteret, *L'Affaire*, 167.

108. Bettati, *Responsables*, 75, estimates that if France required 60 million units in 1985, each of the six largest suppliers—of which Travenol was only one—could produce 250 million units.

109. Sanitas, *Le Sang et le SIDA*, 48–49.

110. Casteret, *L'Affaire*, 135; Hunter, "Blood Money."

111. Bettati, *Responsables*, 59; Casteret, *L'Affaire*, 138.

112. Beaud, *Le Sang contaminé*, 17.

113. Quoted by Beaud, *Le Sang contaminé*, 77.

114. Hunter, "Blood Money," notes that a report to the CNTS in 1992 calculated that there were "about 1000 victims," excluding those subsequently infected, like spouses. Casteret, *L'Affaire*, 192, cites 1,200 victims. Beaud, *Le Sang contaminé*, 10, gives a much lower figure.

115. Lawrence Altman, "French Sue U.S. over Aids Virus Discovery," *New York Times*, 14 December 1985, 1.

116. Lawrence Altman, "Discoverers of AIDS and Cancer Viruses Win Nobel," *New York Times*, 7 October 2008, A8.

117. The percentages were: John F. Kennedy, 78; Ronald Reagan, 33; Dwight D. Eisenhower, 30; Richard Nixon, 15; Jimmy Carter, 7; Harry S. Truman, 6; Lyndon Johnson, 1; and Gerald Ford, 1. All the survey data for this and the following paragraph come from SOFRES/*Le Figaro*, October 1988.

118. The distribution was: Mitterrand, 41 percent; Gorbachev, 40 percent; Thatcher, 32 percent; and Reagan, 26 percent. Helmut Kohl received only 3 percent.

119. The response to a question about which superpower was more sincere about limiting the arms race was almost identical to that about world peace. That is, those who saw no difference on this issue increased from 1985, from 33 percent to 39 percent, and among those who selected a superpower there was more balance: 28 percent chose the United States and 17 percent the USSR in 1988, compared to 36 percent and 9 percent, respectively, in 1985. In 1985 half the French found the United States more attached to world peace than the Soviet Union and only a quarter saw no difference between the superpowers. But by 1988, 40 percent saw no difference between Reagan and Gorbachev and those giving precedence to the United States had fallen to one-third.

120. Jan Krauze, "L'héritage en trompe-l'œil de Ronald Reagan," *Le Monde*, 3 November 1988, 1, 6.

121. François Hautier, "L'antirêve américain," *Le Figaro*, 9 November 1988, 6.

122. Philippe Lefournier, "Rajeunie mais ruinée," *L'Expansion*, 23 September–6 October 1988, 50–53.

123. Jacques Renard, "Les cactus du bureau ovale," *L'Express*, 11 November 1988, 44–45.

124. Marie-Claude Descamps, "Une morale à la carte," *Le Monde*, 3 November 1988, 6; Saul Landau, "L'administration la plus corrompue," *Le Monde diplomatique*, December 1988, 4–5.

125. Pierre Lellouche, "Le ligne de défense du Président Bush," *Le Point*, 14 November 1988, 34–35. Patrick Wajsman, "Bush ou Dukakis?" *Le Figaro*, 4 November 1988, 2. Christian Menanteau, "A la recherche du social-libéralisme," *L'Expansion*, 23 September–6 October 1988, 62–63, posited that Americans were attached to Reagan's gains but wanted a society less cynical about personal success and one that paid more attention to the problems of minorities and the poor. On the left François Sargent, "Un inconnu dans le fauteuil du Président," *Libération*, 10 November 1988, 4, disapproved of Bush's campaign, calling it "mean" and "demagogic," but found him decent and experienced, a perpetual

second in command who was difficult to assess as a future president. The article "La dernière victoire de Ronald Reagan," *Le Monde*, 10 November 1988, 1, optimistically viewed Bush as " less doctrinaire and messianic" than Reagan.

126. SOFRES/*Le Figaro*, October 1988.

127. The words most frequently selected to describe the United States were: *power* (56 percent), *dynamism* (32 percent), *wealth* (31 percent), and *liberty* (30 percent). More pejorative selections were: *violence* (28 percent), *racism* (27 percent), *inequality* (25 percent), *moral laxity* (15 percent), and *imperialism* (12 percent). See SOFRES/*Le Figaro,* October 1988.

128. Gallup/French American Foundation, 1986. Over half admitted, however, that they were poorly informed about the United States.

Chapter 2. Anti-Americanism in Retreat: Jack Lang, Cultural Imperialism, and the Anti-Anti-Americans

1. Philippe Urfalino, "De l'anti-impérialisme américain à la dissolution de la politique culturelle," *Revue française de science politique*, 5 October 1993, 834.

2. David Loosley, *The Politics of Fun: Cultural Policy and Debate in Contemporary France* (Oxford: Berg, 1995), 77. My account of Lang's policies relies heavily on Loosley's study. See also Laurent Martin, *Jack Lang: une vie entre culture et politique* (Brussels: Éditions Complexe, 2008).

3. Frédéric Edelmann and Colette Godard, "Un entretien avec M. Jack Lang," *Le Monde*, 5 September 1981, 8.

4. Mark Hunter, *Les Jours les plus Lang* (Paris: Éditions Odile Jacob, 1990), 116.

5. Jack Lang, quoted in "Le discours de Mexico: 'La culture peut être l'une des réponses à la crise,'" *Le Monde*, 7 August 1982, 2, and in Martin, *Jack Lang*, 243.

6. Lang, quoted in "Le discours de Mexico," 2.

7. Marcel Niedergang, "Les délégués du tiers-monde soutiennent la 'croisade' de M. Lang contre les Etats-Unis, *Le Monde*, 30 July 1981, 5.

8. Marcel Niedergang, "La France veut être un pont entre le Nord et le Sud," *Le Monde*, 23 July 1982, 5; Marcel Niedergang, "M. Fidel Castro compte sur l'aide de la France," *Le Monde*, 28 July 1982, 6.

9. Lang, quoted in "Le discours de Mexico," 2.

10. Tahar Ben Jelloun, quoted in A. Monnerie, *Le Nouvel Observateur. En France aujourd'hui, idées, arts, spectacles* (Paris: CLE International, 1987), 14.

11. Gérard Blain, "Le poison américain," *Le Monde*, 19 September 1981, 23.

12. "Comité pour l'Identité Nationale: cinéma français et cinéma américain," *Le Monde*, 17 September 1981, 10.

13. Hunter, *Les Jours*, 118.

14. Guy Konopnicki, "A des années-lumière," *Le Monde*, 7 August 1982, 2; Guy Konopnicki, "Le poison français," *Le Monde*, 10 October 1981, 2.

15. Alain Finkielkraut, quoted in Monnerie, *Nouvel Observateur*, 15.

16. André Glucksmann, quoted in Philippe Boggio, "Le silence des intellectuels de gauche," *Le Monde*, 27 July 1983, 6.

17. Michel Tournier, quoted in Monnerie, *Nouvel Observateur*, 15.

18. Georges Suffert, *Les Nouveaux Cow-boys: essai sur l'anti-américanisme primaire* (Paris: Éditions Olivier Orban, 1984), 9–11; Jean Daniel, "Les mythes américains de la gauche française," in *Le Reflux américain* (Paris: Éditions du Seuil, 1980), 115.

19. Claude-Jean Bertrand, "L'impérialisme culturel américain, un mythe?" *Esprit*, May 1985, 76.

20. Jacques Julliard, "Cette souris est-elle dangereuse?" *Le Nouvel Observateur*, 3–9 January 1986, 20–27.

21. Gilles Anquetil attacked Moati in "Les socialistes de 1981 . . . ," *Le Nouvel Observateur*, 3–9 January 1986, 21.

22. Julliard, "Cette souris est-elle dangereuse?" 21.

23. Pierre Daix, "Une démission de la France," *Le Nouvel Observateur*, 7 August 1982, 21.

24. Bernard-Henri Lévy, "Anti-américanisme primaire," *Le Matin de Paris*, 3 August 1982, 11.

25. On the silence of the intellectuals, see Max Gallo, "Les intellectuels, la politique et la modernité, *Le Monde*, 26 July 1983, 7; Philippe Boggio, "Le silence des intellectuels de gauche," *Le Monde*, 23 July 1983, 1, 6, and 28 July 1983, 6; and Jean-Denis Bredin, "Les intellectuels et le pouvoir socialiste," *Le Monde*, 22 December 1981, 1, 5, 12. For analysis see Diana Pinto, "The Left, the Intellectuals and Culture," in *The Mitterrand Experiment*, ed. George Ross, Stanley Hoffmann, and Sylvia Malzacher (Oxford: Polity Press, 1987), 217–28.

26. Quotes in this paragraph come from Lang, "Ne confondons pas les artistes et les multinationals," 7 August 1982, quoted in Monnerie, *Nouvel Observateur*, 13. See also Jack Lang, "Jack Lang, 'Je ne suis pas anti-américain,'" interview with Richard Liscia, Jean-Vincent Richard, and Jérôme Garcin, *Les Nouvelles littéraires*, 28 October 1982, 10–12.

27. Samuel Freedman, "French Minister Cites U.S. Cultural Influence," *New York Times*, 16 November 1984, C26.

28. Loosley, *Politics*, 90.

29. Urfalino, "De l'anti-impérialisme américain," 847.

30. Diana Pinto, "Mitterrand, Lang and the Intellectuals," *Conference Group on French Politics and Society Newsletter*, May 1983, 10–12.

31. Raymond Sokolov, "Junket of the Year: 'Les Intellos.'" *Wall Street Journal*, 15 February 1983, 32.

32. "Les intellectuels français répondent," *Le Matin*, 18 February 1983, 3–4.

33. Pinto, "Mitterrand," 12.

34. Loosley, *Politics*, 158.

35. My account of Lang and the audiovisual industry depends on Loosley, *Politics*, 197–21; Hunter, *Les Jours*, 158–162, 205–14, 290–97; and Kerry Segrave, *American Television Abroad: Hollywood's Attempt to Dominate World Television* (Jefferson, NC: McFarland, 1998), 175–211. Relevant general accounts are Shaun O'Connell, "Television without Frontiers: The European Union's Continuing Struggle for Cultural Survival," *Case Western Reserve Journal of International Law* 28 (1996): 501–31; C. Anthony Gifford, "Culture versus Commerce: Europe Strives to Keep Hollywood at Bay," in *Kazaaam! Splat! Ploof! The American Impact on European Popular Culture since 1945*, ed. Sabrina Ramet and Gordana Crnković (Lanham, MD: Rowman and Littlefield, 2003), 37–54.

36. Hunter, *Les Jours*, 159.

37. Wendy Pfeffer, "Intellectuals Are More Popular in France: The Case of French and American Game Shows," in *The Americanization of the Global Village*, ed. Roger Rollin (Bowling Green, Ohio: Bowling Green State University Press, 1989), 29.

38. Cartoon, *Le Monde*, 9–10 August 1987, 11.

39. Jacques Delors, quoted in Philip Schlesinger, "Europe's Contradictory Communicative Space," *Daedalus* 123 (1994): 31.

40. Jack Lang, quoted in Segrave, *American Television*, 208.

41. Max Gallo, quoted in Hunter, *Les Jours*, 292.

42. Peter Riddell, "Fears of 'Fortress Europe' Resurface in U.S.," *Financial Times*, 18 October 1989, 7.

43. Gifford, "Culture versus Commerce," 48.

44. O'Connell, "Television without Frontiers," 507.

45. Segrave, *American Television*, 200.

46. Data compiled by the Centre National de la Cinématographie, reported in Jacques Buob, "Culture: l'assaut américain," *L'Express*, 7–13 October 1993, 73.

47. For Lang's promotion of popular music, see Hunter, *Les Jours*, 173, 191–97, 201–4.

48. Sharon Waxman, "Allons Enfants! Le Jour de rock est arrivé!" *Washington Post*, 8 April 1990, G1, G5.

49. Régis Debray, Mitterrand's adviser, told this to an American reporter; see Hunter, *Les Jours*, 157. Lang admitted he had not sought authorization.

50. Freedman, "French Minister Cites U.S. Cultural Influence." See also Philippe Gavi, "New Deal audiovisual entre la France et les USA," *Libération*, 21 November 1984, 16.

51. Quotations in this paragraph are from Jack Lang, "The Higher the Satellite, the Lower the Culture," *New Perspectives Quarterly*, Fall 1991, 42–44.

52. Suffert, *Les Nouveaux Cow-boys*, 9.

53. One effort at mapping the world of intellectuals is Rémy Rieffel, *La Tribu des clercs: les intellectuels sous la Ve République, 1958–1990* (Paris: Éditions Calmann-Lévy, 1993).

54. Pierre Grémion, "Ecrivains et intellectuels à Paris," *French Politics and Society* 16 (1998): 5. See also Pierre Grémion, *Paris–Prague* (Paris: Éditions Julliard, 1985).

55. This is a major theme in Michael Scott Christofferson, *French Intellectuals against the Left* (New York: Berghahn, 2004).

56. See Jean-Philippe Mathy, *Extrême-Occident: French Intellectuals and America* (Chicago: University of Chicago Press, 1993).

57. See *Tel Quel*, nos. 71–73 (1977).

58. "L'Américain Connection, ou un peau-rouge en France," *Le Canard Enchaîné*, 10, 17, 24, 31 August and 6 September 1977.

59. Even if the thesis about the shift to Americanophilia is a bit overstated, a still useful exposition is Diana Pinto, "De l'anti-américanisme à l'américanophilie: l'itinéraire de l'intelligentsia," *French Politics and Society* 9 (1985): 19–26. See also Diana Pinto, "The French Intelligentsia Rediscovers America" in Lacorne, Rupnik, and Toinet, eds., *The Rise and Fall of Anti-Americanism*, 97–107; and Pinto, "The Left, the Intellectuals, and Culture."

60. Edgar Morin, *Journal de Californie* (Paris: Éditions du Seuil, 1970).

61. Jean-François Revel, *Ni Marx, ni Jésus: de la seconde révolution américaine à la seconde révolution mondiale* (Paris: Éditions Robert Laffont, 1970), translated by J. F. Bernard as *Without Marx or Jesus: The New American Revolution Has Begun* (Garden City, NY: Doubleday, 1971). Thirty years later, after 9/11, Revel spoke out again, condemning anti-Americanism; see Jean-François Revel, *L'Obsession anti-américaine* (Paris: Plon, 2002).

62. Louis Pinot, *L'Intelligence en action: le Nouvel Observateur* (Paris: Éditions A.-M. Métailié, 1984), 195–99.

63. For the impact of American universities on the left see Jean Daniel, "Les mythes américains de la gauche française," in *Le Reflux américain: décadence ou renouveau des Etats-Unis?* (Paris: Éditions du Seuil, 1980), 111–13.

64. Michel Crozier, *La Société bloquée* (Paris: Éditions du Seuil, 1970), translated by Rupert Swyer as *The Stalled Society* (New York: Viking, 1973). Despite his sympathies for the United States, in the late 1970s Crozier found it complacent and insular; see Michel Crozier, *Le Mal américain* (Paris: Éditions Fayard, 1980), translated by Peter Heinegg as *The Trouble with America* (Berkeley and Los Angeles: University of California Press, 1984).

65. Daniel, "Les mythes américains," 109–10.

66. Jacques Arnault, "Réalités américaines," *L'Humanité*, 18–20, 25–28 January 1972, 2.

67. Jacques Chirac, *Discours pour la France à l'heure du choix: la lueur de l'espérance* (Paris: Livre de Poche, 1981), 392, 398–401.

68. As an early indicator of this trend, one of de Gaulle's former ministers, Alain Peyrefitte, published a best-seller in 1976 titled *Le Mal français* (Paris: Plon, 1976), translated by William R. Byron as *The Trouble with France* (New York: Knopf, 1981), that argued for a more open society and more competitive practices in the economy and education, which provoked some observers to suggest the Gaullists were giving in to the American model.

69. Jean-Pierre Chevènement, "Pour l'indépendance nationale," *Le Monde*, 11 May 1983, 2.

70. Anicet Le Pors, *Marianne à l'encan* (Paris: Éditions Sociales, 1980), 201.

71. Robert Solé, "M. Jean-Paul Sartre exprime…," *Le Monde*, 24 September 1977, 4.

72. Jacques Thibau, *La France colonisée* (Paris: Éditions Flammarion, 1980), 267.

73. Michel Jobert, *Les Américains* (Paris: Éditions Albin Michel, 1987), 105.

74. Jobert, *Les Américains*, 177.

75. The essential studies are: Anne-Marie Duranton-Crabol, *Visages de la nouvelle droite: le GRECE et son histoire* (Paris: Presses de Sciences Po, 1988) and Pierre-André Taguieff, *Sur la nouvelle droite: jalons d'une analyse critique* (Paris: Éditions Descartes et Cie, 1994).

76. GRECE and *Le Figaro Magazine* parted ways after 1981 when the latter, directed by Louis Pauwels, embraced Reaganism and Atlanticism; see Duranton-Crabol, *Visages,* 228–29).

77. Alain de Benoist, quoted in Taguieff, *Sur la nouvelle droite*, 57.

78. Guillaume Faye, "La culture-gadget," *Eléments* 46 (1983): 11.

79. Quoted by Taguieff, *Sur la nouvelle droite*, 303.

80. Cercle Héraclite, "La France de Mickey," *Eléments* 57–58 (1986): 9.

81. Jean-Louis Cartry, "French Culture kaput?" *Le Figaro Magazine*, 23 February 1980, 85.

82. Cercle Héraclite, "La France de Mickey," 8.

83. Quoted by Taguieff, *Sur la nouvelle droite*, 302.

84. Alain de Benoist, *Europe, Tiers Monde, même combat* (Paris: Éditions Robert Laffont, 1986), 219. See also Alain de Benoist, cited in Alain Rollat, "Le GRECE prêche la 'guerre culturelle' contre la civilisation 'américano-occidentale,'" *Le Monde*, 20 May 1981, 10.

85. Alain de Benoist, quoted in Duranton-Cabrol, *Visages*, 209.

86. Cercle Héraclite, "La France de Mickey," 8.

87. Olivier Dard, "La nouvelle droite et la société de consommation," *Vingtième Siècle* 91 (2006): 127.

88. Faye, "La culture-gadget," 2, 5–12.

89. Taguieff, *Sur la nouvelle droite*, 302.

90. Henri Gobard, *La Guerre culturelle, logique du désastre* (Paris: Éditions Copernic, 1979), 83.

91. Jean-Marie Benoist, *Pavane pour une Europe défunte* (Paris: Éditions Hallier, 1976), 87–89.

92. The quotations by Baudrillard that follow, unless otherwise noted, are from the American edition: Jean Baudrillard, *America*, trans. Chris Turner (London: Verso, 1988). The original text is *Amérique* (Paris: Éditions Bernard Grasset, 1986). Baudrillard reiterated his observations at a conference sponsored by New York University in 1991 in "L'Amérique, de l'imaginaire au virtuel," in *L'Amérique des Français*, ed. Christine Fauré and Tom Bishop (Paris: Éditions F. Bourin, 1992), 29–36.

93. See, for example, Robert Hughes, "Patron Saint of Neo Pop," *New York Review of Books*, 1 June 1989, 29–32; and Richard Poirier, "America Deserta," *London Review of Books* 11 (1989): 3, 5, 6.

94. Baudrillard, "L'Amérique, de l'imaginaire au virtuel," 33. Jacques Meunier, "Le roi Baudrillard au pays des Yankees," *Le Monde*, 28 February 1986, 13, scored *Amérique* as vain, trite, and sententious.

95. Baudrillard, "L'Amérique, de l'imaginaire au virtuel," 34.

96. Ibid., 35.

97. Julliard, "Cette souris est-elle dangereuse?" 20. What prompted this outburst was the announcement by the socialist government that Disney would construct a new theme park outside Paris, which Julliard accepted, even if he detested the park, as a repudiation of Jack Lang's earlier policies.

98. Jacques Julliard, quoted in Régis Debray, "Confessions d'un antiaméricain," in Fauré and Bishop, eds., *L'Amérique des Français*, 199.

99. Guy Scarpetta, "L'Anti-américanisme primaire," *Le Monde*, 5 November 1980, 2.

100. See Konopnicki, "A des années-lumière," and "Le poison français."

101. Nicolas Beau, "Les Français de l'Oncle Sam," *Le Monde*, 4–5 November 1984, iii–iv.

102. Meunier, "Le roi Baudrillard," 13.

103. Dominique Moïsi, "Le déclin de l'anti-américanisme," *Le Figaro*, 11 November 1984, 14. *Le Point*, in a special issue devoted to the United States (30 June 1986), presented a flattering portrait of a tolerant, free, optimistic society represented by yuppies that included an interview with Ronald Reagan.

104. Alain-Gérard Slama, "Anti-américanisme: la fin d'un mythe?" *Politique internationale* 37 (1987): 26.

105. See, for example, Paul Gagnon, "French Views of Postwar America, 1919–1932" (PhD diss., Harvard University, 1960), which he summarized in "French Views of the Second American Revolution," *French Historical Studies* 4 (1962): 431–49; and David Strauss, *Menace in the West: The Rise of French Anti-Americanism in Modern Times* (Westport, CT: Greenwood, 1978).

106. Michel Winock, "'U.S. go Home': l'antiaméricanisme français," *L'Histoire* 50 (1982): 7–20. Winock was responding to the early anxiety about Ronald Reagan and the rise of the New Right.

107. Collections from these colloquia are Denis Lacorne, Jacques Rupnik, and Marie-France Toinet, eds., *L'Amérique dans les têtes: un siècle de fascinations et d'aversions* (Paris: Hachette, 1986), translated by Gerry Turner as *The Rise and Fall of Anti-Americanism: A Century of French Perception* (New York: St. Martin's, 1990); and Fauré and Bishop, eds., *L'Amérique des Français*. Some select recent studies are Philippe Roger, *The American Enemy: The History of French Anti-Americanism*, trans. Sharon Bowman (Chicago: University of Chicago Press, 2005); Mathy, *Extrême-Occident*; Philippe Roger, *Rêves et cauchemars américains: Les Etats-Unis au miroir de l'opinion publique française, 1945–1953* (Villeneuve d'Ascq, France: Presses universitaires du septentrion, 1996); Jacques Portes, *Fascination and Misgivings: The United States in French Opinion, 1870–1914*, trans. Elborg Forster (Cambridge: Cambridge University Press, 2000); Seth Armus, *French Anti-Americanism, 1930–1948* (Lanham, MD: Lexington Books, 2007); Revel, *L'Obsession anti-américaine*; Pierre Rigoulot, *L'Antiaméricanisme: critique d'un prêt-à-penser rétrograde et chauvin* (Paris: Éditions Robert Laffont, 2004); Richard Kuisel, "The Gallic Rooster Crows Again: The Paradox of French Anti-Americanism," *French Politics, Culture and Society* 19 (2001): 1–16; and Sophie Meunier, "Anti-Americanism in France," *French Politics, Culture and Society* 23 (2005): 126–41.

108. See Marie-France Toinet, "Does Anti-Americanism Exist?" in Lacorne, Rupnik, and Toinet, eds., *The Rise and Fall of Anti-Americanism*, 219–35; and

Marie-France Toinet, "French Pique and Piques Françaises," *Annals of the American Academy of Political and Social Science* 497 (1988): 133–41.

109. The most forceful advocates of the psychological interpretation are André Kaspi, "By Way of Conclusion," in Lacorne, Rupnik, and Toinet, eds., *The Rise and Fall of Anti-Americanism*, 336–43; and Pierre Guerlain, *Miroirs transatlantiques: la France et les Etats-Unis entre passions et indifférences* (Paris: Éditions L'Harmattan, 1996).

110. What eluded these experts, however, was identifying the sources of American images: were they the media, education, intellectuals, politicians, contacts among peoples (or their absence), or simply the *air du temps*?

111. Kaspi, "By Way of Conclusion," 242.

112. Jacques Rupnik and Muriel Humbertjean, "Images of the United States in Public Opinion," in Lacorne, Rupnik, and Toinet, eds., *The Rise and Fall of Anti-Americanism*, 79. See also Jacques Rupnik, "Anti-Americanism and the Modern: The French Image of the United States in French Public Opinion," in *France and Modernisation*, ed. John Gaffney (Aldershot, England: Avebury, 1988), 189–205. The parlor game reference is from Pierre Guerlain, "Dead Again: Anti-Americanism in France," *French Cultural Studies* 3 (1992): 201.

113. Michel Crozier, "Remarques sur l'antiaméricanisme des Français," in Fauré and Bishop, eds., *L'Amérique des Français*, 197.

114. Franz-Olivier Giesbert and Jacques Mornand, "Pourriez-vous vivre à l'américaine?" *Le Nouvel Observateur*, 14 September 1984, 46–50.

115. Diana Pinto introduced these categories in "De l'anti-américanisme à l'américanophilie."

116. Léo Sauvage, *Les Américains: enquête sur un mythe* (Paris: Bibliothèque Mazarine, 1983), 70.

117. Suffert, *Les Nouveaux Cow-boys*, 172.

118. Ibid., 235.

119. Ibid., 8.

120. Jean-Jacques Servan-Schreiber, "Défi et autre défi," *Le Monde*, 4–5 November 1984, iv. Servan-Schreiber welcomed what he saw as a new appetite for American technology—especially computers—as a way of advancing French modernization.

121. Alain Minc, *L'Avenir en face* (Paris: Éditions du Seuil, 1984).

122. Pierre Nora, "Le Fardeau de l'histoire aux Etats-Unis," in *Mélanges Pierre Renouvin: études d'histoire des relations internationales* (Paris: Presses universitaires de France, 1966), 51–74. For his tour of the U.S. see the new biography: François Dosse, *Pierre Nora: Homo historicus* (Paris: Editions Perrin, 2011): 93–97.

123. Pierre Nora, "America and the French Intellectuals," *Daedalus* 107 (1978): 334.

124. Ibid., 325.

125. Pierre Nora, "La fascination de l'Amérique," *L'Histoire* 91 (1986): 5.

126. Ibid.

127. Jean-Marie Domenach, "Le monde des intellectuels," in *Société et culture de la France contemporaine*, ed. Georges Santoni (Albany: State University of New York Press, 1981), 331–32.

128. Jean-Marie Domenach, *Le Crépuscule de la culture française?* (Paris: Plon, 1995), 191.

129. Quotes in this paragraph are from Domenach, *Le Crépuscule*, 192.

130. Ibid., 191.

131. Ibid., 185.

132. Jean-Marie Domenach, "Dieu est moderne," *L'Expansion*, 19 October–1 November 1984, 261.

133. Jean-Marie Domenach, "Aider plutôt que défendre" *Le Monde*, 10 October 1981, 2.

134. Jean-Marie Domenach, *Europe, le défi culturel* (Paris: La Découverte, 1990), 128–29.

135. Régis Debray, "Confessions d'un antiaméricain" in Fauré and Bishop, eds., *L'Amérique des Français*; the article also appeared as "Pour en finir avec l'antiaméricanisme," *L'Evénement du jeudi*, 4 July 1991, iii–ix.

Chapter 3. Reverie and Rivalry: Mitterrand and Reagan-Bush

1. Evan Galbraith, *Ambassador in Paris: The Reagan Years* (Washington, DC: Regnery Gateway, 1987), 110.

2. Roland Dumas, *Affaires étrangères, 1981–1988* (Paris: Éditions Fayard, 2007), 94. Addressing an American audience in Paris, Galbraith allegedly told them that France would find a way to survive the new socialist president.

3. Renata Fritsch-Bournazel, "France: Attachment to a Nonbinding Relationship," in *The Public and Atlantic Defense*, ed. Gregory Flynn and Hans Rattinger (Totowa NJ: Rowman and Allanheld, 1985), 97.

4. Some 43 percent depended on television and 14 percent on the press for information about U.S.-European relations, and the rest received their information from radio, magazines, friends, etc. The less educated relied more on TV (48 percent) than newspapers (12 percent) while the better educated obtained their information from the press (24 percent) rather than television (19 percent); see Steven Smith and Douglas Wertman, *U.S.–West European Relations during the Reagan Years* (New York: St. Martin's, 1992), 193–97.

5. Leo Crespi, *Trends in Foreign Perceptions of U.S. Power*, 26 March 1981, U.S. International Communications Agency (henceforth USICA) Office of Research, National Archives, RG 306, USIA, Reports of the Office of Research, 1964–82, box 28, 1981 reports.

6. Fritsch-Bournazel, "France: Attachment," 74.

7. Ibid., 93–96. According to a SOFRES poll conducted in February 1983, only 29 percent believed a military alliance with the United States best ensured their country's safety, whereas 57 percent preferred either neutrality or membership in a Western alliance independent of the United States; see Elizabeth Hann Hastings and Philip Hastings, eds., *Index to International Public Opinion, 1983–1984* (New York: Survey Research Consultants International/Greenwood, 1985), 200.

8. Leo Crespi, *Trends in U.S. Standing in West European Public Opinion*, February 1982, USICA Office of Research, National Archives, RG 306, USIA, Reports of the Office of Research, 1964–82, box 29, 1982 Reports.

9. Régis Debray, "The Third World: From Kalashnikovs to God and Computers," interview, *New Perspectives Quarterly* 3, no. 1 (1986): 25–28. See also Régis Debray, *Les Empires contre l'Europe* (Paris: Éditions Gallimard, 1985).

10. Natalie La Balme, "L'Influence de l'opinion publique dans la gestion des crises," in *Mitterrand et la sortie de la guerre froide*, ed. Samy Cohen (Paris: Presses universitaires de France, 1998), 409–26.

11. François Mitterrand, *Ici et maintenant* (Paris: Éditions Fayard, 1980), 242.

12. Socialist Party, and François Mitterrand, quoted in Philip Gordon, *A Certain Idea of France: French Security Policy and the Gaullist Legacy* (Princeton, NJ: Princeton University Press, 1993) 107. For security issues, my discussion relies on Gordon's study.

13. Mitterrand, *Ici et maintenant*, 241–42.

14. François Mitterrand, quoted in Gordon, *Certain Idea*, 131.

15. Hubert Védrine, *Les Mondes de François Mitterrand: à l'Elysée 1981–85* (Paris: Éditions Fayard, 1996), 163.

16. Frédéric Bozo and Guillaume Parmentier, "France and the United States: Waiting for Regime Change," *Survival* 49 (2007): 181–98.

17. François Mitterrand, quoted in Védrine, *Les Mondes*, 184.

18. Galbraith, *Ambassador*, 48, 113. Galbraith was pleasantly surprised at the socialists' policies and in time came to think "it's popular [in France] to be pro-American."

19. François Mitterrand, "Excerpts from an interview with François Mitterrand," by James Reston, *New York Times*, 4 June 1981, A14.

20. Jacques Attali, *Verbatim*, vol. 1, *Chronique des années 1981–86, première partie, 1981–83* (Paris: Éditions Fayard, 1995), 62–66. Bush's visit to Paris is fully explored in Vincent Nouzille, *Dans le Secret des présidents: CIA, Maison-Blanche, Elysée, les dossiers confidentiels*, vol. 2, *1981–2010* (Paris: Éditions Fayard, 2010), 19–42.

21. Védrine, *Les Mondes*, 249.

22. Attali, *Verbatim*, 1:86. Attali is not an altogether reliable source and must be consulted with caution; many American officials found him opinionated, arrogant, and anti-American. For this espionage affair, see Pierre Favier and Michel Martin-Rolland, *La Décennie Mitterrand*, vol. 1, *Les Ruptures, 1981–84* (Paris: Éditions du Seuil, 1990), 94–6; Franz-Olivier Giesbert, *François Mitterrand, une vie* (Paris: Éditions du Seuil, 1996), 354–55.

23. Attali, *Verbatim*, 1:87.

24. Jean Lacouture, *Mitterrand: une histoire de Français*, vol. 2, *Les Vertiges du sommet* (Paris: Éditions du Seuil, 1988), 52.

25. Giesbert, *François Mitterrand*, 365.

26. Lou Cannon, *President Reagan: The Role of a Lifetime* (New York: Public Affairs, 2000), 409.

27. Robert Rudney, "Mitterrand's New Atlanticism: Evolving French Attitudes toward NATO," *Orbis* 28, no. 1 (1984): 87; and Gordon, *Certain Idea*, 121.

28. Védrine, *Les Mondes*, 256.

29. For a detailed analysis of French security policy, see Gordon, *Certain Idea*, chaps. 5 and 6.

30. Defense Minister Hernu, according to one expert, "openly admitted that any FAR operation in Europe would automatically come under SACEUR command and depend on NATO air support and logistics" even if it stood formally outside NATO orders; Rudney, "Mitterrand's New Atlanticism," 90.

31. François Mitterrand, *Réflexions sur la politique extérieure de la France* (Paris: Éditions Fayard, 1986), 9.

32. Claude Cheysson, "French Defense Policy and the U.S.," *Wall Street Journal*, 25 February 1983, 26.

33. Defense official, quoted in Rudney, "Mitterrand's New Atlanticism," 85.

34. Samuel Wells, "France and NATO under Mitterrand, 1981–89," in *La France et l'OTAN, 1949–1996, actes du colloque . . . 1996*, ed. Maurice Vaïsse, Pierre Mélandri, and Frédéric Bozo (Brussels: Éditions Complexe, 1996), 560; Gordon, *Certain Idea*, 119.

35. Richard Ullman, "The Covert French Connection," *Foreign Policy* 75 (1989): 3–33.

36. Jolyon Howorth, "Renegotiating the Marriage Contract: Franco-American Relations since 1981," in *Coming In from the Cold War*, ed. Sabrina Ramet and Christine Ingebritsen (Lanham, MD: Rowman and Littlefield, 2002), 75.

37. "La conférence de presse du Président de la République," *Le Monde*, 11 June 1982, 9.

38. For the Chirac and Giscard interviews, see Jim Hoagland, "Gaullist Endorses Reagan on Missiles," *Washington Post*, 14 January 1983, A21; Michael Dobbs, "Giscard Urges Phased Deployment," *Washington Post*, 8 April 1983, A14. One of the RPR defense experts even recommended establishing an inter-allied command staff in peacetime that would become operational after the beginning of hostilities, which "M. Aurillac favorable au déploiement . . . ," *Le Monde*, 10 August 1983, 7, observed would "purely and simply" mean the rein-tegration of France with NATO and a break with Gaullist orthodoxy.

39. Michael Harrison, "Mitterrand's France in the Atlantic System: A Foreign Policy of Accommodation," *Political Science Quarterly* 99, no. 2 (1984): 225–26.

40. On PCF dissent, see Rudney, "Mitterrand's New Atlanticism," 95. When the PCF sided with the Soviet Union in arguing that the force de frappe should be counted as part of NATO's arsenal, Mitterrand forcefully rejected it.

41. See, for example, Alain Besançon, "Reagan entre deux mandats," *L'Express*, 9–15 November 1984, 30.

42. Regarding opinion of deployment of intermediate-range missiles and U.S. leadership, see USICA, *West European Opinion on Security Issues*, October 1981, USICA Office of Research, National Archives, RG 306, USIA, Reports of the Office of Research, 1964–82, box 29, 1981 Reports; and Crespi, *Trends in U.S. Standing*, February 1982, 1982 Reports. According to one SOFRES poll, the favorable/unfavorable/no opinion responses to the deployment of intermediate-range missiles were, respectively, 33:33:34; see Daniel Vernet, "Les Français préfèrent M. Reagan au 'reaganisme,'" *Le Monde*, 6 November 1984, 1, 6.

43. According to a Louis Harris poll of May 1983, 44 percent opposed stationing the Pershing II even if the SS-20s remained; see Fritsch-Bournazel, "France: Attachment," 89.

44. Lacouture, *Mitterrand*, 2:132.

45. Gordon, *Certain Idea*, 119.

46. Bernard Guetta and Jean-Yves Lhomeau, "Accord franco-américain sur la re-prise du dialogue avec l'Union soviétique," *Le Monde*, 24 March 1984, 1, 3.

47. Henri de Kergorlay and Denis Legras, "Reagan-Mitterrand: assaut de cour-toisie," *Le Figaro*, 23 March 1984, 4.

48. Jean-Yves Lhomeau, "Quarante-huit heures consacrées aux industries de pointe et à la recherche technologique," *Le Monde*, 27 March 1984, 4.
49. "La visite du Président de la République aux Etats-Unis," *Le Monde*, 24 March 1984, 3.
50. "Mitterrand Leaving Problems Behind," *New York Times*, 21 March 1984, A14.
51. De Kergorlay and Legras, "Reagan-Mitterrand," 4.
52. Védrine, *Les Mondes*, 250.
53. Frédéric Bozo, "Before the Wall: French Diplomacy and the Last Decade of the Cold War, 1979–1989," in *The Last Decade of the Cold War*, ed. Olav Njølstad (London: Frank Cass, 2004), 288–316.
54. All quotes in this paragraph are from Bozo, "Before the Wall," 292–95. One official wrote, "whereas Western cohesion [is indispensable] . . . the [Atlantic] Alliance [should not be] a bloc at the service of the United States."
55. For an assessment of tiers-mondisme as a policy, see Marie-Claude Smouts, "La France et le Tiers-Monde ou comment gagner le sud sans perdre le nord," *Politique étrangère* 50, no. 2 (1985): 339–57.
56. Dumas, *Affaires étrangères*, 78–79. Speaking of the Third World in Mexico, Mitterrand said in 1981, "There is not and there cannot be political stability without social justice. And when inequalities, injustices or backwardness of a society go too far, there is no established order, repressive as it may be, that can resist the rising up of life. The East-West conflict cannot explain the struggles of the 'damned of the earth' for emancipation any more than it can help resolve them." See Mitterrand, *Réflexions*, 316.
57. U.S. Department of State, *French Public Opinion on Current Issues*, 2 April 1985, Department of State Office of Research, 1983–87, National Archives, RG 306, box 6, 1985 Briefing Papers; Sara Pais, "Plus ça change . . . ça change: A Survey of French-American Attitudes," *France Magazine* 6 (1986): 7.
58. George Schultz, *Turmoil and Triumph* (New York: Scribner's, 1993), 300.
59. For Reagan's use of Apollon to stop Mitterrand from aiding the Sandinistas, see Vincent Jauvert, "Mitterrand dans les dossiers secrets de la Maison-Blanche," *Le Nouvel Observateur*, 22 August 2010, 32–35.
60. John Vinocour, "Mitterrand Asks Streamlining of Annual Economic Meeting," *New York Times,* 12 October 1982, A14.
61. USIA, *French Public Opinion on Economic Summit Issues*, 18 April 1984, Office of Research, USIA, National Archives, RG 306, USIA, Research Memorandum, 1983–87, box 3, 1984; Smith and Wertman, *U.S.–West European Relations*, 224–29; L'Institut Français d'Opinion Publique (henceforth IFOP) poll, September 1981, cited in Fritsch-Bournazel, "France: Attachment," 92. As

late as 1986 a Gallup poll asking what issues most divided the two countries the French selected the dollar exchange rate as the number one difference— followed by problems in Latin America, the price of oil, and Africa; see Pais, "Plus ça change," 7.

62. SOFRES poll, November 1982, reported in Hastings and Hastings, eds., *Index to International Public Opinion, 1983–1984*, 214.

63. Smith and Wertman, *U.S.–West European Relations*, 225.

64. Alan Dobson, "The Reagan Administration, Economic Warfare, and Starting to Close Down the Cold War," *Diplomatic History* 29 (2005): 531–56.

65. See Antony J. Blinken, *Ally versus Ally: America, Europe, and the Siberian Pipeline Crisis* (New York: Praeger, 1987).

66. USIA, *French Public Opinion on Economic Summit Issues*. Opinion was divided over applying restrictions on high-tech trade.

67. For an insider's scathing account of the summit, see Dumas, *Affaires étrangères*, 81–95. A sharp analysis of the European position over sanctions is Holly Wyatt-Walter, *The European Community and the Security Dilemma, 1979–1992* (New York: St. Martin's, 1997), 76–81.

68. Védrine, *Les Mondes*, 297ff.

69. James Goldsborough, "Warfare among the Allies," *New York Times*, 20 July 1982, A23.

70. Claude Julien, "Une diplomatie écartelée," *Le Monde diplomatique*, August 1982, 1, 9; Claude Briançon, "Gazoduc," *Libération*, 18 July 1982, 9.

71. Schultz, *Turmoil and Triumph*, 145.

72. Blinken, *Ally versus Ally*, 105.

73. The quotations from Mauroy's office and from Védrine are in Védrine, *Les Mondes*, 220–22.

74. Favier and Martin-Rolland, *La Décennie Mitterrand*, 1:263.

75. Claude Cheysson, quoted in Védrine, *Les Mondes*, 221.

76. Ibid., 225.

77. Blinken, *Ally versus Ally*, 109.

78. IFOP, November 1981, cited in Fritsch-Bournazel, "France: Attachment," 90.

79. SOFRES poll, November 1982, reported in Hastings and Hastings, eds., *Index to International Public Opinion, 1983–1984*, 201.

80. Louis Harris poll, September 1982, cited in Fritsch-Bournazel, "France: Attachment," 97.

81. Attali, *Verbatim*, 1:692.

82. Védrine, *Les Mondes*, 243.

83. Ronald Reagan, *The Reagan Diaries* (New York: HarperCollins, 2007), 156.

84. Attali, *Verbatim*, 1:693. Attali said he didn't tell Mitterrand of this threat out of fear that the French president would immediately break off negotiations and bring on the most serious crisis in Franco-American relations since France left the integrated command of NATO in 1966.

85. Officials later clarified that France was not partner to the Geneva talks and had no obligation for Japan's defense.

86. Favier and Martin-Rolland, *La Décennie Mitterrand*, 1:279.

87. Maurice Delarue, "La déclaration de Williamsburg . . . ," *Le Monde*, 31 May 1983, 1, 6.

88. Védrine, *Les Mondes*, 247.

89. Ibid., 175, 179.

90. Attali, *Verbatim*, 1:85.

91. Ibid., 1:697.

92. USIA, *West European Opinion of the U.S. Remains More Favorable . . .* , 13 November 1987, USIA, Research Memorandum, National Archives, RG 306, box 7, 1987; Smith and Wertman, *U.S.–West European Relations*, 116–18.

93. Smith and Wertman, *U.S.–West European Relations*, 116–18.

94. Opinion progressed from good versus bad ratio of 30:51 in 1982 to 40:38 in March 1984 and then to 43:27 in November 1985; SOFRES polls, reported in Elizabeth Hann Hastings and Philip Hastings, eds., *Index to International Public Opinion, 1984–1985* (New York: Survey Research Consultants International/Greenwood, 1986), 232, and Elizabeth Hann Hastings and Philip Hastings, eds., *Index to International Public Opinion, 1985–1986* (New York: Survey Research Consultants International/Greenwood, 1987), 223.

95. Smith and Wertman, *U.S.–West European Relations*, 125.

96. It was reported that the French would have backed a more serious effort at removing Ghadafi and objected to a "pin prick." For the reputed French tough talk, see Bernard Guetta, "Les grandes manœuvres du Président Reagan," *Le Monde*, 23 April 1986, 1–2; and William Safire, "Vive le Pinprick," *New York Times*, 18 April 1986, A35. For a well-informed contemporary account of French policy, see Michel Colomès, Kosta Christitch, and Jean Joulin, "Reagan: objectif Kadhafi," *Le Point*, 21 April 1986, 27–34.

97. Jacques Chirac, *Mémoires: chaque pas doit être un but*, vol. 1 (Paris: NiL Éditions, 2009), 344.

98. Dumas, *Affaires étrangères*, 320–21.

99. Judith Miller, "America's Ire Leaves the French in a Pique," *New York Times*, 1 May 1986, A9.

100. Survey data is from "Gallup Poll finds the French Approve of U.S. Raid on Libya," *New York Times*, 20 April 1986, 14; and Smith and Wertman, *U.S.– West European Relations*, 205–11.

101. Jérôme Dumoulin, "Libye: la loi de la guerre," *L'Express*, 18–24 April 1986, 36.

102. Marc Kravetz, "Autopsie d'une guerre annoncée," *Libération*, 16 April 1986, 3; André Fontaine, "Une lutte de longue haleine," *Le Monde*, 16 April 1986, 1, 3.

103. Mitterrand explains his reasons for opposing SDI in Mitterrand, *Réflexions*, 50–66. See also Rachel Utley, *The French Defense Debate: Consensus and Continuity in the Mitterrand Era* (London: Macmillan, 2000), 118–22. For the European response to SDI see Robert E. Osgood, "The Implications of SDI for U.S.-European Relations," in *SDI and U.S. Foreign Policy*, ed. Robert W. Tucker, George Liska, Robert E. Osgood, and David P. Calleo, SAIS Papers in International Affairs no. 15 (Boulder, CO: Westview, 1987), 59–100; and David P. Calleo, "SDI, Europe, and the American Strategic Dilemma," in the same volume, 101–26.

104. Jacques Isnard, "M. Mitterrand au salon du Bourget," *Le Monde*, 1 June 1985, 24.

105. Pierre Favier and Michel Martin-Rolland, *La Décennie Mitterrand*, vol. 2, *Les Epreuves* (Paris: Éditions du Seuil, 1991), 300.

106. François Mitterrand, quoted in Dumas, *Affaires étrangères*, 246.

107. Reagan, *Reagan Diaries*, 322.

108. Favier and Martin-Rolland, *La Décennie Mitterrand*, 2:307.

109. Robert Solé, "M. Reagan relance les recherches . . . ," *Le Monde*, 25 March 1983, 1.

110. Védrine, *Les Mondes*, 367.

111. USIA, *West Europeans Expect Little from the November Meeting . . . SDI Research*, 21 October 1985, Office of Research, USIA, National Archives, RG 306, USIA, Regular and Special Reports, 1983–87, box 6, Briefing Papers; Pais, "Plus ça change," 6.

112. USIA, *West European Attitudes on the Eve of Geneva*, 13 November 1985, Office of Research, USIA, National Archives, RG 306, USIA, Regular and Special Reports, 1983–87 box 6, Briefing Papers. On continuing French skepticism toward Gorbachev and the USSR, see USIA, *West European Opinion of the U.S. Remains More Favorable . . .* , 13 November 1987, Office of Research, USIA, National Archives, RG 306, USIA, Regular and Special Reports, 1983–87, box 7, 1987 Research Memoranda.

113. John Morrison, "Chirac Calls on Western Europe . . . ," *International Herald Tribune*, 3 December 1986, 1.

114. Jean-Pierre Joulin, "Reykjavik: la douche islandaise," *Le Point*, 20 October 1986, 35–37; Michel Tatu, "Washington et Moscou . . . ," *Le Monde*, 16 October 1986, 1–3.

115. Chirac, *Mémoires*, 367–68.

116. Utley, *French Defense Debate*, 128. The former head of policy planning, Thierry de Montbrial, cautioned Washington against succumbing to Gorbachev's pressure for "complete denuclearization" because Moscow's aims had not changed; it still wanted to consolidate its grip on Eastern Europe and extend its hegemony over the entire continent. Thierry de Montbrial, "Security Requires Caution," *Foreign Policy* 71 (1988): 87, 98.

117. François Mitterrand, "La stratégie de la France," interview with Jean Daniel, *Le Nouvel Observateur*, 18–24 December 1987, 23–26.

118. One poll, taken in 1987, showed more people thought Iran and Libya were more dangerous than the Soviet Union. See USIA, *Western Europeans Worried . . . Zero-option*, 17 November 1987, Office of Research, USIA, National Archives, RG 306, USIA, Regular and Special Reports, 1983–97, box 7, 1987 Research Memoranda.

119. "L'effet Gorbachev," *Le Monde*, 25 February 1988, 12.

120. Smith and Wertman, *U.S.–West European Relations*, 89–90.

121. Mitterrand, "La stratégie de la France," 25.

122. Lacouture, *Mitterrand*, 2:258.

123. Jacques Attali, *Verbatim*, vol. 2, *Chronique des années 1986–1988* (Paris: Éditions Fayard, 1995), 272.

124. Samuel Wells, "From Euromissiles to Maastricht: The Policies of Reagan-Bush and Mitterrand," in *Strategic Triangle: France, Germany and the United States in the Shaping of the New Europe*, ed. Helga Haftendorn, Georges-Henri Soutou, Stephen Szabo, and Samuel Wells (Washington, DC: Woodrow Wilson Center Press, 2006), 299.

125. Jacques Renard, "Quand l'Amérique doute de Reagan," *L'Express*, 14–20 November 1986, 36.

126. François Schlosser, "Reagan dans le guêpier," *Le Nouvel Observateur*, 28 November–4 December 1986, 36–37.

127. "Europe faults Reagan Talk," *New York Times*, 15 November 1986, 5.

128. Bernard Guetta, "M. Schulz se prononce contre de nouvelles livraisons . . . ," *Le Monde*, 18 November 1986, 2.

129. Smith and Wertman, *U.S.–West European Relations*, 216–17.

130. Whereas good opinion of Reagan hovered around 60 percent in 1985–86 it began to decline in mid-1986, falling to 48 percent by mid-1987. Meanwhile

Gorbachev's good opinion rose steadily from 1985 so that by 1987 he ranked very close to the American president; see Brulé Ville Associés poll, March 1987, in "Opinion Roundup," *Public Opinion* 12, no. 1 (1989): 29.

131. Dominique Moïsi, "French Foreign Policy: The Challenge of Adaptation," *Foreign Affairs* 67, no. 1 (1988): 155.

132. USIA, *Opinion of Soviets in Industrialized Nations . . .* , 15 July 1988, USIA, Research Memorandum, National Archives, RG 306, box 4, 1988. The French ratio of approval versus disapproval was 68:18, compared to 65:24 for the West Germans and 70:27 for the British.

133. USIA, *American Image in France Remains Positive*, 28 January 1988, USIA, National Archives, RG 306, USIA, Regular and Special Reports, 1988–89, box 4, 1988 Research Memoranda.

134. Richard Burt, cited in Wells, "From Euromissiles to Maastricht." See also Geir Lundestad, *The United States and Western Europe since 1945* (Oxford: Oxford University Press, 2003), 231–32.

135. See, for example, the op-ed piece by onetime Reagan official Robert Hormats, "A 'Fortress Europe' in 1992," *New York Times*, 22 August 1988.

136. Wells, "From Euromissiles to Maastricht," 303.

137. Jacques Attali, *Verbatim*, vol. 3, *1988–91* (Paris: Éditions Fayard, 1995), 95.

138. George Bush and Brent Scowcroft, *A World Transformed* (New York: Alfred A. Knopf, 1998), 74–78.

139. Jean-Pierre Chevènement, quoted in Anand Menon, *France, NATO and the Limits of Independence, 1981–1997* (New York: St. Martin's, 2000), 122.

140. Howorth, "Renegotiating," 77.

141. François Hauter, "Accord pour aider l'Europe de l'Est," *Libération*, 17 July 1989, 3.

142. The French favorable versus unfavorable ratio was 69:23, compared to 79:14 for the West Germans and 72:24 for the British. In France the average of favorable opinion for the United States during 1987–89 was 69 percent, compared to 54 percent for 1981–82; see Smith and Wertman, *U.S.–West European Relations*, 100.

143. Frédéric Bozo had access to archives of the president and the Quai d'Orsay among others for his study; see Frédéric Bozo, *Mitterrand, the End of the Cold War, and German Reunification* (New York: Berghahn, 2009), xxii. This work is a translation by Susan Emanuel of Bozo's *Mitterrand, la fin de la guerre froide et l'unification allemande: de Yalta à Maastricht* (Paris: Éditions Odile Jacob, 2005). Another recent study also based on extensive archival

research similarly concludes that Mitterrand was "an uneasy but crucial facilitator of German unity, not its foe"; see Mary Elise Sarotte, *1989: The Struggle to Create Post–Cold War Europe* (Princeton, NJ: Princeton University Press, 2009), 3. Yet a third archival-based study concurs that France did not seek to slow down reunification; see Tilo Schabert, *How World Politics Is Made: France and the Reunification of Germany* (Columbia: University of Missouri Press, 2009), xi. Among the critics are American insiders: Robert Hutchings, Philip Zelikow, and Condoleezza Rice. Hutchings, who served on the National Security Council, called the French, compared to Margaret Thatcher, "more determined and effective in using their not inconsiderable influence to retard the process"; see Robert Hutchings, *American Diplomacy and the End of the Cold War* (Washington, DC: Woodrow Wilson Center Press, 1997), 96; Zelikow and Rice, who had access to records and sources unavailable to others, stress the reluctance and pessimism of the French, but see them as less obstructionist than Margaret Thatcher; see Philip Zelikow and Condoleezza Rice, *Germany Unified and Europe Transformed* (Cambridge, MA: Harvard University Press, 1995). Other experts are more muted in their criticism. Julius Friend argues that Mitterrand did not accept the inevitability of reunification until January 1990, and believes that Mitterrand's fumbling of reunification cost him the confidence of the French people; see Julius Friend, *The Long Presidency: France in the Mitterrand Years* (Boulder, CO: Westview, 1998), 211–21. Stanley Hoffmann stresses French fears of an unfettered Germany and finds Mitterrand's policy "somewhat erratic" until the middle of 1991; see Stanley Hoffmann, "French Dilemmas and Strategies in the New Europe," in *After the Cold War*, ed. Robert Keohane, Joseph Nye, and Stanley Hoffmann (Cambridge, MA: Harvard University Press, 1993), 130. Howorth, "Renegotiating the Marriage Contract," 73–96, argues that Mitterrand overplayed his hand, failing to recognize that France had become less indispensable to the United States after the fall of the Berlin Wall.

144. François Mitterrand, quoted in Zelikow and Rice, *Germany Unified*, 98.
145. Bozo, "Before the Wall," 304–10.
146. Marie-Noëlle Cremieux, *Les Français face à la réunification allemande, automne 1989–automne 1990* (Paris: Éditions L'Harmattan, 2004).
147. Bozo, *Mitterrand, the End of the Cold War, and German Reunification*, 130–31.
148. Zelikow and Rice, *Germany Unified*, 206. Brent Scowcroft worried, "The United States seemed largely absent in longer-term French calculations about Europe. These appeared to be focused on the outlines of a Europe in which

NATO would play a stagnant role, or even disappear, and the WEU as the defense component of the EC would gradually take over European security"; see Bush and Scowcroft, *World Transformed*, 266.

149. Zelikow and Rice, *Germany Unified*, 169.

150. Hutchings, *American Diplomacy*, 150.

151. Ibid., 157.

152. Bozo, *Mitterrand, the End of the Cold War, and German Reunification*, 246. Zelikow and Rice, *Germany Unified*, 169, stress that the continued presence of American troops was essential to make the United States a player in European politics. Or, as one high State Department official stated before Congress in 1990, the reasons for sustaining NATO were: first, the Soviet threat had not entirely disappeared; second, American leadership kept Germany under control and prevented the Europeans from returning to their bad old habits that had caused two world wars; third, it gave the United States a vital role in European affairs; and fourth, it curtailed isolationist impulse among the American people; James Dobbins testimony, summarized in Frank Costigliola, *France and the United States: The Cold Alliance since World War II* (New York: Twayne, 1992), 228.

153. Hutchings, *American Diplomacy*, 136.

154. Zelikow and Rice, *Germany Unified*, 206.

155. François Mitterrand, quoted in Sarotte, *1989*, 24.

156. George H. W. Bush to François Mitterrand, quoted in Bozo, *Mitterrand, the End of the Cold War, and German Reunification*, 249.

157. Attali, *Verbatim*, 3:460.

158. George H. W. Bush, quoted in Favier and Martin-Rolland, *La Décennie Mitterrand*, vol. 3, *Les Défis, 1988–1991* (Paris: Éditions du Seuil, 1998), 251.

159. Jacques Lanxade, quoted in Favier and Martin-Rolland, *La Décennie Mitterrand*, 3:256.

160. Bozo, *Mitterrand, the End of the Cold War, and German Reunification*, 257.

161. Ibid., 282.

162. Zelikow and Rice, *Germany Unified*, 324.

163. Frédéric Bozo, "'Winners and Losers': France, the United States, and the End of the Cold War," *Diplomatic History* 33 (2009): 948–49.

164. Bozo, *Mitterrand, the End of the Cold War, and German Reunification*, 356.

165. Hoffmann, "French Dilemmas," 146.

166. Hubert Védrine, quoted in Favier and Martin-Rolland, *La Décennie Mitterrand*, 2:290.

167. Schultz, *Turmoil and Triumph*, 356.

168. Dumas, *Affaires étrangères*, 269. De Gaulle, after initially refusing, deemed it necessary to attend the conference.

Chapter 4. The Adventures of Mickey Mouse, Big Mac, and Coke in the Land of the Gauls

1. John Georgas, quoted in "Coke's Never-Ending Journey," *Beverage World*, Fall 1993, 32.
2. Todd Gitlin, "World Leaders: Mickey, et al.," *New York Times*, 3 May 1992, 1.
3. "Coke's Never-Ending Journey," 32.
4. Ray Kroc, quoted in Max Boas and Steve Chain, *Big Mac: The Unauthorized Story of McDonald's* (New York: New American Library, 1976), 23.
5. Mark Pendergrast, *For God, Country and Coca-Cola* (New York: Scribner's, 1993), 93.
6. Alan Bryman, *Disney and His Worlds* (London: Routledge, 1995), 77.
7. "The Science of Alliance," *Economist*, 4 April 1998, 69–70. See also "Disney Signs Up McDonald's," *Leisure Week,* 31 May 1996, 6.
8. Walt Disney's father believed the family came from Burgundy; see Richard Schickel, *The Disney Version*, 3rd ed. (Chicago: Ivan R. Dee, 1997), 45. Disney also borrowed extensively from Europe—e.g., hiring European animators; see Robin Allan, *Walt Disney and Europe* (Bloomington: Indiana University Press, 1999).
9. For an explanation of McDonald's complicated and evolving franchise system, see John F. Love, *McDonald's: Behind the Arches* (New York: Bantam, 1986), 48–65.
10. Pendergrast, *For God, Country and Coca-Cola*, 62ff. Another recent history of the company is Frederick Allen, *Secret Formula* (New York: Harper Business, 1994).
11. The most comprehensive, if uncritical, account of Euro Disney up to 1994 is Andrew Lainsbury, *Once upon an American Dream: the Story of Euro Disneyland* (Lawrence: University of Kansas Press, 2000).
12. "Mickey Hops the Pond," *Economist*, 28 March 1987, 75.
13. Tim O'Brien, "Closing, Bankruptcy Fate of Many Ill-Planned French Theme Parks," *Amusement Business*, 9 September 1991, 5.
14. Tim O'Brien, "Futuroscope Combines Fun, Education," *Amusement Business*, 11 May 1992, 46; Claude Barjonet, "Des milliards pour s'amuser," *L'Expansion* 16 (1986): 134–41.
15. Julie Fingersh, "Disney in Europe: Is It by Invitation or Invasion?" *Amusement Business*, 9 March 1992, 3.

16. On Disney's setup and its subsequent brush with bankruptcy, see Ron Grover, *The Disney Touch: How a Daring Management Team Revived an Entertainment Empire* (Homewood, IL: Business One Irwin, 1991), 185–98; Joe Flower, *Prince of the Magic Kingdom: Michael Eisner and the Re-making of Disney* (New York: Wiley, 1991), 207–16; Bryman, *Disney and His Worlds*, 76–80; Michael Eisner, *Work in Progress* (New York: Random House, 1998), 270–92; Lainsbury, *Once upon an American Dream*, chaps. 1–3; Tim O'Brien, "Euro Disney: Can They Make It Work?" *Amusement Business*, 15 June 1992, 18. See also Roger Cohen, "When You Wish upon a Deficit," *New York Times*, 18 July 1993, sec. 2, pp. 1, 18–19; Roger Cohen, "Euro Disney in Danger of Shutdown," *New York Times*, 23 December 1993, D3; Alan Riding, "Rescue Set for Disney in France," *New York Times*, 15 March 1994, D1–2.

17. Marianne Debouzy, "Does Mickey Mouse Threaten French Culture? The French Debate about Euro Disneyland," in *Kazaam! Splat! Ploof! The American Impact on European Popular Culture since 1945*, ed. Sabrina Ramet and Gordana Crnković (Lanham, MD: Rowman and Littlefield, 2003), 16–17.

18. Debouzy, "Does Mickey Mouse Threaten French Culture?" 18–22, provides a good account of labor issues.

19. Shanny Peer, "Marketing Mickey: Disney Goes to France," *Tocqueville Review* 13, no. 2 (1992): 137.

20. Debouzy, "Does Mickey Mouse Threaten French Culture?" 22.

21. *Le Canard Enchaîné*, 19 August 1992, 4, cited in Debouzy, "Does Mickey Mouse Threaten French Culture?" 20.

22. Disney employees, quoted in Eisner, *Work in Progress*, 281. Eisner acknowledges his company did not manage the media well.

23. Disney communications manager, quoted in Peer, "Marketing Mickey," 128.

24. Gilles Smadja, *Mickey l'arnaque* (Paris: Messidor, 1988).

25. Isabelle Lefort, "Mickey ronge tout," *Le Nouvel Observateur*, 12–18 August 1988, 43; and Patrick Bonazza, "Disneyland: les dents longues de Mickey," *Le Nouvel Observateur*, 13 March 1987, 7–10; Jacques Julliard, "Cette souris est-elle dangereuse?" *Le Nouvel Observateur*, 3 January 1986, 20.

26. Robert Fitzpatrick, quoted in Steven Greenhouse, "Playing Disney in the Parisian Fields," *New York Times*, 17 February 1991, sec. 3, pp. 1, 6.

27. See the references in note 16.

28. Eisner said the alcohol policy "has been discussed every day, seven days a week, for the last seven years. It is probably the most discussed policy at [Euro Disney]." Michael Eisner, quoted in O'Brien, "Euro Disney: Can They Make It Work?" 5. He later defended his tough stand by arguing that when some alco-

holic beverages were introduced, it made little difference because Europeans acted like Americans in the park and did not consume much wine or beer; Eisner, *Work in Progress*, 283–84.

29. Nathaniel Nash, "Euro Disney Reports Its First Profits," *New York Times*, 26 July 1995, D 3. The resort's operations were actually in the black much earlier, but the heavy debt payment kept it in deficit; Lisa Gubernick, "Mickey n'est pas fini," *Forbes*, 14 February 1994, 42–43.

30. Laura Holson, "The Feng Shui Kingdom," *New York Times*, 25 April 2005, C1.

31. "Lost in France," *Independent* (London), 24 February 1994, 23. See also "Debt Traps an American Mouse in Paris," *Guardian*, 26 February 1994, 33.

32. Eisner, *Work in Progress*, 270. See also Lainsbury, *Once upon an American Dream*, 53.

33. Peer, "Marketing Mickey," 134.

34. Jean-Marie Gerbeaux, quoted in Lainsbury, *Once upon an American Dream*, 62.

35. Michael Eisner said one of his reasons for this change was because Bourguignon "truly understood the culture"; Eisner, *Work in Progress*, 285.

36. Eisner, *Work in Progress*, 292.

37. Peer, "Marketing Mickey," 130–34.

38. Michael Eisner, quoted in Lainsbury, *Once upon an American Dream*, 134.

39. Robert Fitzpatrick, quoted in Martha Zuber, "Mickey-sur-Marne: une culture conquérante?" *French Politics and Society* 10 (1992): 67.

40. This view continued to be voiced by Disney's management; see Holson, "The Feng Shui Kingdom." Roger Cohen, "When You Wish upon a Deficit," has observed the enthusiasm of French children for Mickey and company.

41. Alain Finkielkraut and Jean Cau, quoted in Alan Riding, "Only the French Elite Scorn Mickey's Debut," *New York Times*, 13 April 1992, 1, A13.

42. Jean-Yves Guiomar, "Le conservatoire du néant," *Le Débat*, January–February 1993, 152–61.

43. Pierre-André Taguieff, *Sur la nouvelle droite: jalons d'une analyse critique* (Paris: Éditions Descartes et Cie, 1994), 301.

44. Emmanuel de Roux, "L'ouverture d'Euro Disney," *Le Monde*, 12–13 April 1992, 9.

45. Debouzy, "Does Mickey Mouse Threaten French Culture?" 22–28.

46. Riding, "Only the French Elite Scorn Mickey's Debut."

47. Robert Fitzpatrick, quoted in de Roux, "L'ouverture d'Euro Disney."

48. Lang's views are cited in de Roux, "L'ouverture d'Euro Disney." He was also interviewed about the opening in Jacqueline Remy, "Lang: 'Une culture n'en menace pas une autre,'" *L'Express*, 27 March 1992, 44–45.

49. Roger Cohen, "Defy Disney? The Unmitigated Gaul!" *New York Times*, 9 April 1992, D1, D5; Riding, "Only the French Elite Scorn Mickey's Debut"; David Lawday, "Where All the Dwarfs Are Grumpy: Euro Disneyland Gives Paris a Run for the Money," *U.S. News and World Report*, 28 May 1990, 50–51.

50. Michel Serres, "La langue française doit faire de la résistance," *Le Point*, 21–27 March 1992, 57; and Jean-François Revel, "Culture, ne craignons pas l'Amérique," *Le Point*, 21–27 March 1992, 51.

51. André Glucksmann, "American Magic, in an Homage to its Roots," *New York Times*, 9 April 1992, 3.

52. François Reynaert, "Des citrouilles en or," *Le Nouvel Observateur*, 9–15 April 1992, 43.

53. Henri Haget, "Qui a peur de Mickey Mouse?" *L'Express*, 27 March 1992, 32–45.

54. Revel, "Culture, ne craignons pas l'Amérique," 51.

55. Christophe de Chenay, "Disney à la mode de chez nous," *Le Monde*, 12 April 1993, 11.

56. François Forestier, "On fait de l'art, ils font du spectacle," *L'Express*, 27 March 1992, 43.

57. Pierre Guerlain, "Qui diabolise Mickey?" *Esprit*, June 1992, 160–69.

58. One survey of about fifty college students in 1999 showed that virtually everyone of them had seen a Disney film or read a Disney book as a child and had good memories of the experience. Half thought Euro Disney was not a problem, but only 28 percent had actually visited the resort. See Jacques Guyot, "France: Disney in the Land of Cultural Exception," in *Dazzled by Disney? The Global Disney Audiences Project*, ed. Janet Wasko, Mark Phillips and Eileen Meehan (London: Leicester University Press, 2001), 121–34.

59. Eisner, *Work in Progress*, 399.

60. François Bostnavaron and Christophe de Chenay, "Gilles Péllison 'L'idéal serait . . . le deuxième parc . . . ,'" *Le Monde*, 29 January 1999, 16.

61. Capucine Lorai, "La malédiction d'Euro Disney," *Le Point*, 5 August 2004, 56; John Tagliabue, "Thrill Rides for Investors," *New York Times*, 4 July 2007, 1, 6.

62. Olivier de Bosredon, quoted in Tim O'Brien, "Parc Astérix Heading in New Direction with New Rides," *Amusement Business*, 18 May 1992, 1.

63. Nicolas Perrard, quoted in John Tagliabue, "Paris Journal: A Comic-Strip Gaul Valiantly Battles Disney," *New York Times*, 15 August, 1995, A4.

64. Nicolas Perrard, quoted in John Tagliabue, "International Business: Step Right Up, Monsieur!" *New York Times*, 23 August 1995, D1.

65. Jean Marie Deroy, "Rentrée tranquille au parc Astérix," *Le Monde*, 14 April 1992, 17.

66. Hervé Bentégeat, "Parcs de loisirs," *Le Point*, 30 December 1995, 41–43. Tim O'Brien, "With a Variety of Markets Europe Holds Great Potential," *Amusement Business*, 17 August 1998, 16, counts over one hundred parks with a total of 43 million visitors per year.

67. Steven Greenhouse, "McDonald's Tries Paris, Again," *New York Times*, 12 June, 1988, sec. 3, p. 1; Love, *McDonald's*, 409–11.

68. Economist Intelligence Unit, "Special Report No. 2: Fast Food in France," *Marketing in Europe: Food, Drink, Tobacco* 296 (1987): 37–49; Priscilla Andreiev, "Dayan Prepares O'Kitch," *Restaurant Business Magazine*, 10 April 1984, 264; Priscilla Andreiev, "Expanding European Markets," *Restaurant Business Magazine*, 1 November 1984, 152.

69. Michael Mueller, "European Fast Food," *Restaurant Business Magazine*, 1 May 1990, 90; "French Fast Food Boom Continues," *Eurofood*, April 1993, 6.

70. Economist Intelligence Unit, "Fast Food in France," 37.

71. Ibid., 40.

72. Love, *McDonald's*, 436–37.

73. Steve Barnes, quoted in Love, *McDonald's*, 434. For McDonald's global activities see Love, *McDonald's*, 413–56; and James L. Watson, ed., *Golden Arches East* (Stanford, CA: Stanford University Press, 1997).

74. Pascale Krémer, "Le hamburger n'a pas encore détroné le jambon-beurre," *Le Monde*, 20 January 1995, 14.

75. Rick Fantasia, "Fast Food in France," *Theory and Society* 24 (1995), 215–29.

76. In 1989, 83 percent of paying customers at fast food restaurants were under thirty-four years of age, according to a marketing survey; see Fantasia, "Fast Food in France," 217.

77. Hervé Jannic, "Les Français craignent l'envahissement américain," *L'Expansion*, 2–15 June 1994, 53.

78. Barry James, "Big Macs Watch Out," *International Herald Tribune*, 23 October 1992, 9; Suzanne Daly, "With ABC's of Dining, France Raises Epicures," *New York Times*, 27 October 2001, A4.

79. Jean-Yves Nau, "A l'école de bon goût," *Le Monde*, 17 October 1991, 16; Françoise Chirot, "Paris gastronomie l'école des goûts," *Le Monde*, 4 July 1993, 22; Judith Valente, "The Land of Cuisine Sees Taste Besieged by 'le Big Mac,'" *Wall Street Journal*, 25 May 1994, A1.

80. Denis Hennequin, Jean-Pierre Petit, and Philippe Labbé, *McDo se met à table* (Paris: Plon, 2002), 33.

81. Anonymous spokeswoman, quoted in Rone Tempest, "U.S. Firms in France try Counterattack," *Los Angeles Times*, 27 November 1992, A6.

82. "Burger King Bids Adieu to France," *Eurofood*, 14 August 1997, 9.

83. Jean-Michel Normand, "McDonald's, critiqué mais toujours frequenté," *Le Monde*, 24 September 1999, 29.

84. Laure Belot and François Bostnavaron, "McDonald's doit changer," *Le Monde*, 27 January 1999, 18.

85. "McDonald's Steps Up Rate of French Expansion," *Eurofood*, 28 February 1996, 10.

86. Economist Intelligence Unit, "Fast Food in France," 37–49.

87. This analysis is based on the work of Rick Fantasia. See Fantasia, "Fast Food in France"; and Rick Fantasia, "Everything and Nothing: The Meaning of Fast Food and Other American Cultural Goods in France," *Tocqueville Review* 15, no. 2 (1994): 57–88.

88. Love, *McDonald's*, 442–45.

89. Marianne Debouzy, "Working for McDonald's, France: Resistance to the Americanization of Work," *International Labor and Working Class History* 70 (2006): 126–42.

90. For the effects of McDonald's on consumers—e.g., eating habits, standards of hygiene—outside Europe, see Watson, *Golden Arches East*.

91. Economist Intelligence Unit, "Fast Food in France," 38. See also Paul Moreira, "De la Poule-au-pot au tandoori," in *Nourritures*, ed. Fabrice Piault (Paris: Autrement, 1989), 107–11.

92. Hennequin et al., *McDo se met à table*, 49.

93. Jean-Luc Volatier, *Le repas traditionnel se porte encore bien*, Report No. 132 (Paris: Centre de recherche pour l'étude et l'observation des conditions de vie, 30 January 1999); Krémer, "Le hamburger n'a pas encore détroné le jambon-beurre"; Véronique Cauhapé, "Les traditions de la table résistent au fast-food," *Le Monde*, 19 February 1999, 25.

94. Pascale Hébel and Gloria Calamassi Tran, *La Restauration hors foyer en 1994*, vol. 2, *Consommations alimentaires*, Collection des rapports no. 154 (Paris: Centre de recherche pour l'étude et l'observation des conditions de vie, September 1994), 144.

95. MKG Consulting, "*2003: une année morose pour la restauration*," *HTR Magazine*, 2003, http://www.htrmagazine.com/site_web/htr/fr/rubriques .asp?numero_mag=112&code_depeche=559.

96. Amanda Friedman, "Let Them Eat Sandwiches," *Nation's Restaurant News*, 11 October 1999, 94.

97. See José Bové and François Dufour, *Le Monde n'est pas une marchandise: des paysans contre la malbouffe* (Paris: Éditions La Découverte, 2000); Roger Cohen, "Fearful over the Future, Europe Seizes Food," *New York Times*, 29 August 1999, sec. 4, pp. 1, 3; Charles Trueheart, "A Beef with More than Big Mac," *Washington Post*, 1 July 2000, 1. For the success of Bové in transforming the cause of marginal farmers into popular resistance to globalization, see Sarah Waters, "Globalization, the Confédération paysanne, and Symbolic Power," *French Politics, Culture and Society* 28 (2010), 96–117.

98. Cohen, "Fearful over the Future."

99. Alain Duhamel, quoted in Cohen, "Fearful over the Future."

100. Suzanne Daly, "French Turn Vandal into Hero against U.S.," *New York Times*, 1 July 2000, A1.

101. Debouzy, "Working for McDonald's, France," 128.

102. Christophe Gallaz, "Comment s'est fabriqué l' 'effet Bové,'" *Le Monde*, 7 July 2000, 15.

103. Alain Rollat, "Vive le roquefort libre!" *Le Monde*, 9 September 1999, 32, quoted in Philip Gordon and Sophie Meunier, *The French Challenge: Adapting to Globalization* (Washington, DC: Brookings Institution Press, 2001), 53.

104. "Chirac Adds Voice to McDonald's Flap," United Press International, 17 September 1999.

105. John Tagliabue, "McDonald's Gets a Lesson in, Well, the French Fry," *New York Times*, 11 December 1999, 1.

106. Jean-Michel Normand, "Trois questions à Jean-Pierre Petit," *Le Monde*, 24 September 1999, 29.

107. Jack Greenberg, "McAtlas Shrugged," Interview with Moisés Naim, *Foreign Policy*, May–June 2001, 26–37.

108. Normand, "Trois questions à Jean-Pierre Petit."

109. Jean-Michel Normand, "Un vrai danger pour le fast-food: la 'ringardisation,'" *Le Monde*, 24 September 1999, 29.

110. "Burger and Fries à la française," *Economist*, 17 April 2004, 60–61; Carol Matlack and Pallavi Gogoi, "What's This? The French Love McDonald's?" *Business Week*, 13 January 2003, 50.

111. Jennifer Willging, "Of GMOs, McDomination and Foreign Fat: Contemporary Franco-American Food Fights," *French Cultural Studies* 19 (2008): 211.

112. Hennequin et al., *McDo se met à table*.

113. Marian Burros, "McDonald's France Says Slow Down on the Fast Food," *New York Times,* 30 October 2002, C7.

114. Tony Karon, "Adieu, Ronald McDonald," *Time*, 24 January 2002, http://www.time.com/time/columnist/karon/article/0,9565,196925,00.html.

115. John Tagliabue, "A McDonald's Ally in Paris," *New York Times*, 20 June 2006, C1, 5.

116. "How a Frenchman is Reviving McDonald's in Europe," *Economist*, 27 January 2007, 82; Julia Werdigier, "McDonald's, but with Flair," *New York Times*, 25 August 2007, 1, 4.

117. MKG Consulting, *2003*; "Delicious Irony," *Economist*, 27 April 2002, 65.

118. Data from *Le Figaro* cited in Anne Swardson, "A Paris Tradition Gets Sacked," *Washington Post*, 12 January 1998, A01.

119. For the "cosmopolitisme alimentaire" thesis, see Claude Fischler, *L'Homnivore: le goût, la cuisine et le corps* (Paris: Éditions Odile Jacob, 1990), 212–17.

120. For example, Gérard Pélisson, one of the founders of the Fondation Brillat-Savarin, an association created in 1986 for the protection of the national culinary patrimony, was also co-manager of a hotel group that owned burger outlets and *viennoiseries*; see Fantasia, "Fast Food in France," 231. Traditional restaurants and fast food had, of course, some differences: the one that most upset the former was the tax structure of the value-added tax, largely imposed by the EU, which weighed far more heavily on meals eaten at classic restaurants than at fast food outlets. In 1999, a thousand chefs wearing white aprons and tocques marched on the National Assembly trying, to no avail, to get the government to equalize the tax; see Charles Trueheart, "French Chefs Shell Police with Eggs," *Washington Post*, 12 October 1999, A13.

121. Robert Belleret, "La bataille du goût contre la 'malbouffe,'" *Le Monde*, 14 November 1999, 10.

122. Sophie Laurent, "Le McDo ne détrônera pas le pot-au-feu," *La Croix*, 22 October 1996, 7.

123. Richard Kuisel, "Coca-Cola and the Cold War: The French Face of Americanization, 1948–53," *French Historical Studies* 17 (1991): 96–116; Allen, *Secret Formula*, 1–17.

124. "La Société Coca-Cola," *Le Monde*, 30 December 1949, 8.

125. On Coke's expansion, see David Greising, *I'd Like the World to Buy a Coke: The Life and Leadership of Roberto Goizueta* (New York: Wiley, 1998), 172–85; Pendergrast, *For God, Country and Coca-Cola*, 391–92; and Roger Cohen, "For Coke, World Is Its Oyster," *New York Times*, 21 November 1991, D1, 5. The controversial role of Douglas Ivester is recounted in Constance L. Hays, *The Real Thing: Truth and Power at the Coca-Cola Company* (New York:

Random House, 2004). I wish to thank Philip Mooney, head of the Coca-Cola Company archives, for providing documentation.

126. For the company's phobia about France, see William Reymond, *Coca-Cola, l'enquête interdite* (Paris: Éditions Flammarion, 2006), 154–56. Reymond writes as a frustrated investigative reporter determined to unmask the secrets and legends of the company.

127. Thomas Kamm, "France's Pernod-Ricard to Sell to Coke," *Wall Street Journal*, 26 May 1989, 1.

128. For Hoffman's marketing, see William Dawkins, "C'est la Guerre for Coke and Pepsi," *Financial Times*, 18 February 1991, 15; "Coke Makes Monumental Continental Effort," *Beverage World Periscope Edition*, 31 March 1991, 6; and Greising, *I'd Like the World*, 184–85.

129. Bruce Crumley, "Bordeaux to Coke: 'Non' on Machines," *Fortune*, 30 July 1990, 14.

130. Jean-Sébastien Stehli, "Coca a soif de conquête," *Le Point*, 30 May 1992, 39.

131. Gary Hemphill, "Beachhead at Dunkirk," *Beverage Industry*, September 1990, 1–3.

132. "European Soft Drinks Up 6 Percent," *Eurofood*, March 1992.

133. John Georgas, quoted in "Coke's Never-ending Journey," *Beverage World*, Fall 1993, 32.

134. David Buchan, "Orangina Takes Some Fizz out of Coke," *Financial Times*, 30 January 1997, 2; Charles Fleming and Nikhil Deogun, "French Unit fines Coke $1.8 Million for Sales Practices," *Wall Street Journal*, 30 January 1997, B12.

135. "Coca-Cola Unit Fined," Bloomberg News, 29 January 1997.

136. Paul Hemp, "French EC Protestors Hope Things Go Better with Coke," *Boston Globe*, 27 November 1992, 89. A spokesman for the national young farmer's association said "Coca-Cola is the biggest symbol of an America that wants to extend its hegemony more and more"; quoted in "France Admits It Can't Legally Veto Trade Pact," *Atlanta Constitution*, 24 November 1992, A12.

137. Rone Tempest, "U.S. Firms in France Try Counterattack," *Los Angeles Times*, 27 November 1992. A6.

138. Eduardo Cue, "Sacrébleu! French Youth Prefer Coke," *U.S. News and World Report*, 9 March 1998, 38.

139. "Those Vulgar Markets," *Economist*, 22 January 2005, 48.

140. Hébel et al., *La Restauration hors foyer en 1994*, 148. Students, professionals, cadres and *employés* liked soft drinks far better than did farmers, merchants, workers, craftsmen, and retirees.

141. Gérard Mermet, co-author of a government report, quoted in Keith Richburg, "In France, Thirst for Wine Is Drying Up," *Washington Post*, 24 April 2001, A14.

142. Véronique Dahm, "Coca-Pepsi, la bataille de France," *L'Expansion*, 14–27 April 1995, 52–54.

143. Ibid., 54.

144. "Coca-Cola, soifs de demain," *Le Figaro économie*, 3 July 1995, 3–6.

145. Mickey Gramig, "Coca-Cola Wines, Dines the Paris Masses," *Atlanta Journal-Constitution*, 12 July 1998, C1.

146. "Going for Coke," *Economist*, 14 August 1999, 51–52; "Coke Is Hit Again," *Economist*, 24 July 1999, 60–61; "Coca-Cola's Style Offends European Regulators' Taste," *Financial Times*, 22 July 1999, 2.

147. Within a decade the French orange drink was the second-best seller in Europe and available in forty-three countries; see Michel Fontanes, "Orange You Glad," *Beverage World*, 30 September 1994, 14.

148. In Vietnam after the end of hostilities, for example, although the French beverage arrived first, the American cola giants quickly pushed it aside. Pernod-Ricard had chosen "the strategy of Coca-Cola" without the means; see Estelle Saget, "Combien de volumes d'Orangina pour sauver le Ricard?" *L'Expansion*, 7–20 December 1995, 66.

149. Pascal Galinier, "Pepsi-Cola propose à Orangina une alternative," *Le Monde*, 29 August 1998, 17.

150. Hays, *The Real Thing*, 194–95.

151. Laure Belot, "Orangina n'a aucun avenir en Europe," *Le Monde*, 30 July 1998, 15.

152. Pascal Galinier, "Négotiations à l'arraché . . . ," *Le Monde*, 17 September 1998, 16.

153. Laure Belot and Pascal Galinier, "M. Strauss-Kahn dit non à Coca-Cola," *Le Monde*, 19 September 1998, 1, 28.

154. The CEO of PepsiCo France, Charles Bouaziz, argued, "[I]f the board agrees with Coke, Pepsi will disappear from the French market and Coke will have an absolute monopoly"; quoted in Olivier Bruzek and Marc Landré, "Orangina, Pepsi secoue Coca," *Le Point*, 1 October 1999, 34. Some estimated that Coca-Cola's control over soft drinks consumed outside the home would reach 90 percent. Ivester unintentionally raised concern about the company's monopolistic pretensions when Atlanta bought out the soft drink brands owned by the Cadbury Schweppes group even though the deal excluded many countries—among them France.

155. The board's ruling and this quote are both in Betty Liu, "Coke's Orangina Bid Blocked," *Financial Times*, 25 November 1999, 25.

156. For the contamination fiasco, see Hays, *The Real Thing*, 263–76; Constance Hays, Alan Cowell, and Craig Whitney, "A Sputter in the Coke Machine," *New York Times*, 30 June 1999, C1, 6.

157. "Bad for You," *Economist*, 19 June 1999, 62–63.

158. "Coca-Cola, New Doug, Old Tricks," *Economist*, 11 December 1999, 55.

159. As of 1999, per-capita annual consumption of an eight-ounce servings was: Belgium, 260; Germany, 203; United Kingdom, 118; France, 88; see "Coke's Crisis," *Marketing News*, 27 September 1999. A report by Coca-Cola Enterprises in 1999 gave the following figures: Belgium, 260; Germany, 200; France, 96; see Constance Hays, "Coke Products Ordered Off Shelves," *New York Times*, 16 June 1999, C2. Relative market shares for Coke and Pepsi are reported in "The Bubbles Pop," *Economist*, 24 April 1999, 64–65.

160. Among the most ardent proponents of the appropriation/domestication/assimilation thesis has been: Richard Pells, *Not Like Us: How Europeans Have Loved, Hated and Transformed American Culture since World War II* (New York: Basic Books, 1997). Other scholars have proposed "glocalization" or "hybridization" as ways of stressing cultural negotiation; see, for example, Jan Nederveen Pieterse, "Globalization as Hybridization," in *Global Modernities*, ed. Mike Featherstone, Scott Lash, and Roland Robertson (London: Sage, 1995), 45–68; Roland Robertson, *Globalization: Social Theory and Global Culture* (London: Sage Publications, 1992) advances the notion of "unicity" as an alternative; yet another variation on this thesis is the semiotic interpretation proposed in Rob Kroes, *If You've Seen One You've Seen the Mall: Europeans and American Mass Culture* (Urbana: University of Illinois Press, 1996), and Rob Kroes, "American Empire and Cultural Imperialism," *Diplomatic History* 23 (1999): 463–77. For general assessments of Americanization as a process of cultural interaction, see Heide Fehrenbach and Uta Poiger, "Introduction: Americanization Reconsidered" in *Transactions, Transgressions, Transformations: American Culture in Western Europe and Japan*, ed. Heide Fehrenbach and Uta Poiger (New York: Berghahn, 2000), 208–23; and Richard Kuisel, "Debating Americanization: The Case of France," in *Global America? The Cultural Consequences of Globalization*, ed. Ulrich Beck, Natan Sznaider, and Rainer Winter (Liverpool, England: Liverpool University Press, 2003), 95–113.

161. Thomas Allin, quoted in Greenhouse, "McDonald's Tries Paris, Again," 1.

162. Grover, *The Disney Touch*, 190–95.

163. Eisner, *Work in Progress*, 289.

164. Amy Schwartz, "Good, Clean . . . Flop?" *Washington Post*, 18 August 1993, A21.

165. Gitlin, "World Leaders: Mickey, et al."

166. Anonymous Disney official, quoted in Bryman, *Disney and His Worlds*, 121.

167. Marc Fumaroli, "Le défi américain," *Le Nouvel Observateur*, 9–15 April, 1992, 43.

168. For this thesis see Fischler, *L'Hominvore*. According to Paul Moreira, by the early 1980s couscous was the fourth most popular dish for the French, following more traditional meals like boeuf bourguignon; Moreira, "De la poule-au-pot au tandoori," 107. See also Pascale Pynson, "Mangeurs fin de siècle," in *Nourritures*, ed. Fabrice Piault (Paris: Autrement, 1989), 186–92. James Watson, "Introduction" in *Golden Arches East*, 10, argues against any cultural consensus or essentialism in cuisine insisting that it is changing so rapidly that it is impossible to distinguish what is "local" from what is "foreign." For a somewhat different view, one that stresses how "industrial food" has standardized or globalized cuisine and taste, see Jack Goody, *Cooking, Cuisine and Class* (Cambridge: Cambridge University Press, 1982).

169. Belleret, "La bataille du goût."

170. Marlise Simons, "Starved for Customers, the Bistros Die in Droves," *New York Times*, 22 December 1994, A4.

Chapter 5. Taming the Hyperpower: The 1990s

1. Jacques Chirac, quoted in Gilles Delafon and Thomas Sancton, *Dear Jacques, cher Bill: Au coeur de l'Elysée et de la Maison Blanche, 1995–1999* (Paris: Plon, 1999), 55.

2. Michael Brenner and Guillaume Parmentier make this point in *Reconcilable Differences: U.S.-French Relations in the New Era* (Washington, DC: Brookings Institution Press, 2002), 23.

3. Pierre Favier and Michel Martin-Rolland, *La Décennie Mitterrand*, vol. 3, *Les Défis, 1988–1991* (Paris: Éditions du Seuil, 1998), 454.

4. Debates within the cabinet are reported in Favier and Martin-Rolland, *La Décennie Mitterrand*, 3:445ff.

5. For dissent over the Gulf War, see Rachel Utley, *The French Defense Debate: Consensus and Continuity in the Mitterrand Era* (London: Macmillan, 2000), 180–85; Anne-Marie Duranton-Crabol, "L'anti-américanisme français face à la guerre du Golfe," *Vingtième Siècle* 59 (1998): 129–39.

6. Elisabeth Dupoirier, "De la crise à la guerre du Golfe: un exemple de mobilisation de l'opinion," in *SOFRES-L'Etat de l'opinion, 1992*, ed. Olivier Duhamel and Jérôme Jaffré (Paris: TNS/SOFRES, 1992), 127. But this poll was something of an anomaly because the French quickly rallied to the war.

7. Favier and Martin-Rolland, *La Décennie Mitterrand*, 3:446.

8. Ibid., 3:449.

9. James A. Baker, *The Politics of Diplomacy: Revolution, War, and Peace, 1989–1992* (New York: Putnam's, 1995), 314.

10. François Mitterrand, quoted in Favier and Martin-Rolland, *La Décennie Mitterrand*, 3:479.

11. François Mitterrand, quoted in Jacques Attali, *Verbatim*, vol. 3, *1988–91* (Paris: Éditions Fayard, 1995), 598.

12. François Mitterrand, quoted in Favier and Martin-Rolland, *La Décennie Mitterrand*, 3:482.

13. Baker, *Politics*, 371.

14. Attali, *Verbatim*, 3:722–24.

15. George Bush and Brent Scowcroft, *A World Transformed* (New York: Knopf, 1998), 339.

16. Dupoirier, "De la crise," 130–36.

17. Duranton-Crabol, "L'anti-américanisme," 132.

18. Utley, *The French Defense Debate*, 186–87.

19. Dupoirier, "De la crise," 136.

20. Attali, *Verbatim*, 3:675–76.

21. François Mitterrand, quoted in Thierry Tardy, *La France et la gestion des conflits yougoslaves 1991–1995* (Brussels: Etablissements Emile Bruylant, 1999), 215.

22. Frédéric Bozo, "France," in *NATO and Collective Security*, ed. Michael Brenner (New York: St. Martin's, 1998), 46–47. Bozo reported that some French officials suspected the Americans wanted the Europeans to fail so that they could seize control and exclude them from the final settlement.

23. Claire Tréan, "M. Juppé relance l'idée," *Le Monde*, 24 February 1994, 6.

24. See Klaus Larres, "Bloody as Hell: Bush, Clinton and the Abdication of American Leadership in the Former Yugoslavia," *Journal of European Integration History* 10 (2004): 179–202.

25. Richard Holbrooke, *To End a War* (New York: Modern Library, 1999), 29.

26. François Mitterrand, quoted in Vincent Nouzille, *Dans le Secret des présidents: CIA, Maison-Blanche, Elysée, les dossiers confidentiels*, vol. 2, *1981–2010* (Paris: Éditions Fayard, 2010), 250. Taylor Branch, *The Clinton Tapes* (New York: Simon and Schuster, 2009), 217. Branch notes that Clinton believed the French and the British did not want an independent Muslim Bosnia in Europe (9–10).

27. Unidentified official, quoted in Ivo Daalder, *Getting to Dayton: The Making of America's Bosnia Policy* (Washington, DC: Brookings Institution Press, 2002), 22.

28. Elisabeth Guigou, quoted in Roger Cohen, "U.S.-French Relations Turn Icy after Cold War," *New York Times*, 2 July 1992, A10.

29. James Petras and Morris Morley, "Contesting Hegemonies: U.S.-French Relations in the 'New World Order,'" *Review of International Studies* 26 (2000): 55–56.

30. Alain Juppé, quoted in Alan Riding, "French Successfully Bluff Allies on Bosnia," *New York Times*, 13 December 1994, A8.

31. Joyce Kaufman, *NATO and the Former Yugoslavia* (Lanham, MD: Rowman and Littlefield, 2002), 113–17; Daalder, *Getting to Dayton*, 32.

32. Balladur received intelligence that the Americans were sending weapons and trainers to the Bosnian Muslims; see Édouard Balladur, *Le Pouvoir ne se partage pas: conversations avec François Mitterrand* (Paris: Éditions Fayard, 2009), 339.

33. Hubert Védrine, quoted in Pierre Favier and Michel Martin-Rolland, *La Décennie Mitterrand,* vol. 4, *Les Déchirements, 1991–95* (Paris: Éditions du Seuil, 1999), 512.

34. Bozo, "France," 67; Daalder, *Getting to Dayton*, 33.

35. David Halberstam, *War in a Time of Peace* (New York: Scribner's, 2001), 303–6, 316–17.

36. Daalder, *Getting to Dayton,* 163–64.

37. Kori Schake, "NATO after the Cold War, 1991–1995," *Contemporary European History* 7 (1998): 406.

38. Hubert Védrine, *Les Mondes de François Mitterrand* (Paris: Éditions Fayard, 1996), 652.

39. Richard Holbrooke, quoted in Delafon and Sancton, *Dear Jacques*, 131.

40. Ibid., 132–33.

41. Paul Gallis, *France: Current Foreign Policy Issues and Relations with the United States*, Library of Congress, Congressional Research Service, CRS Report for Congress, 26 September 1996, 11.

42. Tardy, *La France,* 326.

43. Warren Christopher, quoted in Derek Chollet and James Goldgeir, *America between the Wars, from 11/9 to 9/11* (New York: Public Affairs, 2008), 131.

44. Frédéric Bozo, *Mitterrand, the End of the Cold War, and German Unification*, trans. Susan Emanuel (New York: Berghahn, 2009), 249–50.

45. Philip Gordon, *French Security Policy after the Cold War* (Santa Monica, CA: RAND Arroyo Center, 1992), 14–17.

46. Roland Dumas, quoted in "M. Dumas prône la cohésion des douze face à la crise yougoslave," *Le Monde*, 6–7 October 1991, 5.

47. Mary Elise Sarotte, *1989 and the Struggle to Create Post–Cold War Europe* (Princeton, NJ: Princeton University Press, 2009), 175.

48. Philip Zelikow and Condoleezza Rice, *Germany Unified and Europe Transformed* (Cambridge, MA: Harvard University Press, 1995), 466.

49. Robert Hutchings, *American Diplomacy and the End of the Cold War* (Washington, DC: Woodrow Wilson Center Press, 1997), 136.

50. For post-1989 security policy, see Pascal Boniface, "Révolution stratégique mondiale, continuité et inflexions de la politique française de sécurité," in *Mitterrand et la sortie de la guerre froide*, ed. Samy Cohen (Paris: Presses universitaires de France, 1998), 157–85; Philip Gordon, *A Certain Idea of France* (Princeton, NJ: Princeton University Press, 1993); and Gordon, *French Security Policy after the Cold War*.

51. François Mitterrand, quoted in Favier and Martin-Rolland, *La Décennie Mitterrand*, 4:201–2.

52. Pierre Joxe, quoted in Paul Gallis, *France and the United States: New Tensions in an Old Partnership*, Library of Congress, Congressional Research Service, CRS Report for Congress, 9 June 1993, 21.

53. Mark Eyskens, quoted in Craig Whitney, "Gulf Fighting Shatters Europeans' Fragile Unity," *New York Times*, 25 January 1991, A11.

54. Jacques Delors, "European Integration and Security," Alastair Buchan Memorial Lecture, 7 March 1991, *Survival* 33, no. 2 (1991): 107–9.

55. Gallis, *France and the United States*, 21.

56. Gallis, *France: Current Foreign Policy Issues*, 3. Brent Scowcroft sought reassurances from Védrine that the WEU/EC scheme would not "diverge from NATO even in the long run"; Favier and Martin-Rolland, *La Décennie Mitterrand*, 4:206.

57. Patrick Tyler, "U.S. Strategy Plan Calls for Insuring No Rivals Develop," *New York Times*, 8 March 1992, 14.

58. Raymond Seitz, quoted in Bozo, *Mitterrand*, 336–37.

59. Bozo, *Mitterrand*, 344.

60. George H. W. Bush, quoted in Hutchings, *American Diplomacy*, 281.

61. François Mitterrand, quoted in Bozo, *Mitterrand*, 346.

62. Holly Wyatt-Walter, *The European Community and the Security Dilemma, 1979–92* (New York: St. Martin's, 1997), 227.

63. François Mitterrand to Helmut Kohl, July 1991, quoted in Bozo, *Mitterrand*, 321.

64. Unidentified American diplomat, quoted in Wyatt-Walter, *European Community*, 200.

65. James Baker, quoted in Cohen, "U.S.-French Relations Turn Icy." In his memoirs Baker recalled that French obstructionism within NATO incited him to complain to Dumas, "With no other country except France do we have this. . . . Nowhere else in Europe do we feel that we have to deal with such antipathy"; see Baker, *Politics of Diplomacy*, 170.

66. Gallis, *France and the United States*, 27.

67. Robert Hutchings, quoted in Samuel Wells, "From Euromissiles to Maastricht: the Policies of Reagan-Bush and Mitterrand," in *The Strategic Triangle: France, Germany, and the United States in the Shaping of the New Europe*, ed. Helga Haftendorn, Georges-Henri Soutou, Stephen Szabo, and Samuel Wells (Washington, DC: Woodrow Wilson Center Press, 2006), 301.

68. Robert Grant, "France's New Relationship with NATO," *Survival* 38 (1996): 58–80.

69. Michel Rocard, "Europe's Drive to Union is Irreversible," *International Herald Tribune*, 28 July 1992, 8.

70. Jacques Chirac, quoted in Grant, "France's New Relationship," 63.

71. Alain Juppé, "Quel horizon pour la politique étrangère de la France?" *Politique étrangère* 50 (1995): 251.

72. Jacques Chirac, *Mémoires: chaque pas doit être un but*, vol. 1 (Paris NiL Éditions, 2009), 47–54.

73. Bill Clinton, *My Life* (New York: Knopf, 2004), 656.

74. Pamela Harriman, quoted in Delafon and Sancton, *Dear Jacques*, 88.

75. Jacques Chirac, "Discours de M. Jacques Chirac, Président de la République, devant le Congrès des Etats-Unis d'Amérique, 1 February 1996," http://www .elysee.fr/français archives.

76. Alain Frachon and Laurent Zecchini, "M. Chirac appelle Washington . . . ," *Le Monde*, 3 February 1996, 2.

77. Four well-informed sources for the topic of NATO reform are: Bozo, "France," 39–80; Delafon and Sancton, *Dear Jacques*, 200ff; Brenner and Parmentier, *Reconcilable Differences*, 38–62; and Gallis, *France: Current Foreign Policy Issues*.

78. Gallis, *France: Current Foreign Policy Issues*, 7.

79. Jean-Claude Casanova, "Dissuasion concertée," *L'Express*, 28 September 1995, 26.

80. Delafon and Sancton, *Dear Jacques*, 139.

81. Brenner and Parmentier, *Reconcilable Differences*, 51.

82. John Kornblum, quoted in Delafon and Sancton, *Dear Jacques*, 157.

83. Bill Clinton, quoted in Jacques Amalric, "OTAN: comment Washington a coulé Paris," *Libération*, 27 February 1997, 9.

84. Pierre Messmer, quoted in Hubert Coudurier, *Le Monde selon Chirac* (Paris: Éditions Calmann-Lévy, 1998), 272.

85. William Drozdiak, "French Snub NATO Tribute to Christopher," *Washington Post*, 12 December 1996, A45.

86. NATO sources, quoted in "Paris Rift with U.S. Poisons Hopes for a Slimmer NATO," *Times* (London), 10 December 1996, 13.

87. Brenner and Parmentier, *Reconcilable Differences*, 53, points out a split between the French military, who thought they had a right to the southern command, and the Elysée, Quai d'Orsay, and civilian defense officials, who were more open to alternatives about Europeanizing this post.

88. Delafon and Sancton, *Dear Jacques*, 279.

89. Madeleine Albright, quoted in Petras and Morley, "Contesting Hegemonies," 57.

90. Pascal Boniface, "The NATO Debate in France," 7 October 1997, http://www.nato.int/acad/conf/enlarg97/boniface.htm.

91. Chirac's admission and quotes in this paragraph are from Delafon and Sancton, *Dear Jacques*, 305–6.

92. This is the assessment of Brenner and Parmentier, *Reconcilable Differences*, 61.

93. Anand Menon, *France, NATO and the Limits of Independence, 1981–1997* (New York: St. Martin's, 2000), 53–54. For specifics on the CJTF approach see Hans-Georg Ehrhart, "Change by Rapprochement?" in *The France-U.S. Leadership Race*, ed. David Haglund (Kingston, ON: Queen's Quarterly, 2000), 72–77.

94. Paul Quilès, "OTAN: la dérive," *Le Monde*, 11 June 1996, 14.

95. Pascal Boniface, "Un triomphe américain en trompe-l'œil," *Le Monde,* 10 July 1997, 14.

96. Jean-Yves Haine, "ESDP: An Overview," European Union Institute for Security Studies, http://www.iss-eu.org/esdp.

97. See Franco-British Summit, *Joint Declaration On European Defense*, http://www.atlanticcommunity.org/Saint-Malo%20Declaration%20Text.html.

98. Peter Schmidt, "Where's the Boeuf? Policy, Rhetoric and Reality in the EU's Decisions to Develop a Common Security and Defence Policy," in Haglund, ed., *France-U.S. Leadership Race*, 125–41; Frédéric Bozo, "The U.S. Changing Role and Europe's Transatlantic Dilemmas," in *Just Another Major Crisis? The United States and Europe since 2000*, ed. Geir Lundestad (New York: Oxford University Press, 2008), 102–3.

99. See Cologne European Council, *Presidency Conclusions*, http://www
.consilium.europa.eu/uedocs/cmsUpload/Cologne%20European%20
Council-Presidency%20conclusions.pdf.

100. By "decoupling," Madeleine Albright meant that "European decision-making
is not unhooked" from NATO; by "duplication" she referred to replicating
force planning, and procurement decisions, and finally she wanted to avoid
"discrimination against NATO members who were not EU members"; Madeleine Albright, "The Right Balance Will Secure NATO's Future," *Financial
Times*, 7 December 1998, 22. See also Jolyon Howorth and John Keeler, "The
EU, NATO, and the Quest for European Autonomy," in *Defending Europe:
The EU, NATO and the Quest for European Autonomy*, ed. Jolyon Howorth
and John Keeler (New York: Palgrave Macmillan, 2003), 3–21.

101. Paul Gallis, *France: Factors Shaping Foreign Policy, and Issues in U.S.-French
Relations*, Library of Congress, Congressional Research Service, CRS Report
for Congress, 4 February 2005, 13.

102. Hubert Védrine, quoted in Craig Whitney, "NATO at 50," *New York Times*, 15
February 1999, A7.

103. Hubert Védrine with Dominique Moïsi, *France in an Age of Globalization*,
trans. Philip Gordon (Washington, DC: Brookings Institution Press, 2001), 57.

104. Frédéric Bozo, "France and NATO under Sarkozy: End of the French Exception?" Working Paper, Fondation pour l'innovation politique, March 2008,
8–9.

105. Nicolas Sarkozy, quoted in "France Rejoins NATO's Integrated Command
Structure," *News from France*, 23 April 2009, 4.

106. Hutchings, *American Diplomacy*, 161.

107. George H. W. Bush, quoted in Wells, "From Euromissiles to Maastricht," 303.

108. For the views of Bush advisers, see Kevin Featherstone and Roy H. Ginsberg,
The United States and the European Union in the 1990s (New York: St. Martin's, 1996), 89–90.

109. Hutchings, *American Diplomacy*, 161.

110. George H. W. Bush, "Remarks at a Luncheon Hosted by Prime Minister
Ruud Lubbers of the Netherlands in the Hague," 9 November 1991, Administration of George Bush, Office of the Press Secretary, The White House, 1428.

111. Alan Riding, "French Farms Gird for War against U.S.," *New York Times*, 11
November 1992, A11.

112. Pierre Bérégovoy, "L'Amérique, l'Europe, la France," *Le Monde*, 6 January
1993, 8.

113. Elisabeth Guigou, quoted in Gallis, *France and the United States*, 13–14.

114. Pierre Bérégovoy, quoted in William Drozdiak, "France Threatens Global Trade Pact," *Washington Post*, 26 November 1992, A1. Legally France could only veto the entire GATT package, not the farm deal, but a veto of Blair House seemed plausible to other EU members.

115. Jacques Chirac, quoted in "Les réactions politiques," *Le Monde*, 24 November 1992, 8.

116. Alan Riding, "Europeans Agree with U.S. on Cutting Farm Subsidies," *New York Times*, 21 November 1992, 1, 36. Craig Whitney, "Kohl Silently Avoiding a Conflict with Mitterrand on Trade Accord," *New York Times*, 24 November 1992, A6.

117. *Le Monde* warned against such a drastic step because it would delight the British and upset the Germans; see Thierry Bréhier, "L'opposition pousse le gouvernement . . . ," *Le Monde*, 20 November 1992, 1, 8.

118. Sophie Meunier, *Trading Voices: The European Union in International Commercial Negotiations* (Princeton, NJ: Princeton University Press, 2005), 109–24.

119. Alain Juppé, quoted in Christian Leblond, "Le dossier agricole dans la phase finale de l'Uruguay Round, 1991–1993: un affrontement franco-américain?" in *Les Relations franco-américaines au XXe siècle*, ed. Pierre Mélandri and Serge Ricard (Paris: Éditions L'Harmattan, 2003), 223.

120. Alain Juppé, quoted in Andrew Hill, "Paris to Seek Fresh EC-U.S. Farm Deal," *Financial Times*, 6 April 1993, 5.

121. Anonymous farmer, quoted in Alan Riding, "Pitching GATT's Pluses to a Reluctant France," *New York Times*, 4 December 1993, 49.

122. Gerry van der Kamp-Alons, "Anti-Americanism in French Preference Formation on Trade Liberalization" (unpublished paper, Radboud University Nijmegen, 2010).

123. Poll conducted for *Le Point*, November 1992, reported in "French Farmers Reject EC-U.S. Farm Trade Deal," *News from France*, 4 December 1992.

124. Michel Noblecourt, "Le gouvernement continue de s'opposer à un accord agricole sur le GATT," *Le Monde*, 19 November 1992, 1, 21.

125. Christian Jacob, quoted in Leblond, "Le dossier agricole," 221–22.

126. Craig Whitney, "Germans Whisper Softly in Trade Rivals' Ears," *New York Times*, 14 December 1993, D7.

127. Roger Cohen, "Yielding, French Accept Farm Pact," *New York Times*, 9 June 1993 D1.

128. Alan Riding, "Months of Risk, Moments of Isolation, Now Boasts of Triumph," *New York Times*, 15 December 1993, D19. The last-minute deal be-

tween the EU and the United States granted concessions to European, especially French, grain and food exporters by delaying cuts in subsidized export agreed to at Blair House for the next six years. In exchange the United States won steep tariff cuts in a variety of food products opening the way for American exports; Riding, "Pitching GATT's Pluses to a Reluctant France."

129. Alain Juppé, quoted in Leblond, "Le dossier agricole," 225. Balladur also appraised the negotiations as a French success; see Balladur, *Le Pouvoir*, 166–67.

130. David Hanley, "France and GATT: the Real Politics of Trade Negotiations," in *France from the Cold War to the New World Order*, ed. Tony Chafer and Brian Jenkins (New York: St. Martin's, 1996), 140–49.

131. For a contrary interpretation that asserts that "French stubbornness had won the day," see Brenner and Parmentier, *Reconcilable Differences*, 77.

132. Hervé de Charette, quoted in Petras and Morley, "Contesting Hegemonies," 63.

133. Craig Whitney, "Ignoring U.S., France Signs Accord Protecting Cuba Ties," *New York Times*, 26 April 1997, 3.

134. Jacques Chirac, quoted in Gallis, *France: Current Foreign Policy Issues*, 19.

135. Jacques Chirac, quoted in Petras and Morley, "Contesting Hegemonies," 64.

136. Hervé de Charette, quoted in Gallis, *France: Current Foreign Policy Issues*, 19.

137. Unidentified official, quoted in Steven Erlanger and David Sanger, "On World Stage, Many Lessons for Clinton," *New York Times*, 29 July 1996, A15.

138. Madeleine Albright, quoted in Petras and Morley, "Contesting Hegemonies," 64.

139. Roger Cohen, "France Scoffs at U.S. Protest over Iran Deal," *New York Times*, 20 September 1997, A12.

140. Bill Clinton, "Second Inaugural Address of William J. Clinton; January 20, 1997," http://www.usa-presidents.info/inaugural/clinton-2.html.

141. Bill Clinton, "Address by the President to the Democratic National Convention," 29 August 1996, http://www.4president.org/speeches/clintongore 1996convention.htm.

142. A high French official ignited a brushfire when, on the eve of the 1996 presidential elections, he suggested in offhand remarks to the press that Warren Christopher's African tour might boost Clinton's vote among African Americans; Coudurier, *Le Monde selon Chirac*, 282–83. Christopher, always prickly about the French, later wrote, "The time has passed when outside powers could view whole groups of states as their private domain"; Warren Christopher, *In the Stream of History* (Stanford, CA: Stanford Univ. Press, 1998), 474.

143. Jacques Godfrain, former head of ministry for African cooperation, quoted in Tom Masland, "Fighting for Africa," *Newsweek*, 30 March 1998, 32.

144. In 1995, Herman Cohen, assistant secretary of state for African affairs, stated while addressing a U.S.-African trade conference that "the African market is open to everyone" and asserted the United States could "no longer afford to accept France's determination to maintain its privileged *chasse gardée* within the economic realm"; quoted in Asterias C. Huliaras, "The 'Anglo-Saxon Conspiracy': French Perceptions of the Great Lakes Crisis," *Journal of Modern African Studies* 36, no. 4 (1998): 603–4.

145. Huliaras, "The 'Anglo-Saxon Conspiracy,'" 594.

146. François Ngolet, "African and American Connivance in Congo-Zaire," *Africa Today* 47, no. 1 (2000): 75.

147. Jacques Chirac, quoted in Philip Gordon, *The Transatlantic Allies and the Changing Middle East*, Adelphi Paper 322 (London: International Institute for Strategic Studies, 1998), 21.

148. Gordon, *Transatlantic Allies*, 23–37; Petras and Morley, "Contesting Hegemonies," 60–61.

149. Drozdiak, "French Snub NATO Tribute to Christopher."

150. Quotes and data in this paragraph are from Delafon and Sancton, *Dear Jacques*, 259–60.

151. In this instance one diplomat's mistrust, cultural insecurity, and tetchiness encountered another's intentional, or unintentional, provocation. As the story goes, Charette—wanting to make up with Christopher, who was leaving office, for their past bickering—hosted a dinner at the Quai d'Orsay and, with the intention of honoring the American, offered him a selection of prize-winning French books wrapped in a tricolor ribbon even though the guest, as it was known, did not read French. Christopher, who chafed against French linguistic snobbery, took exception to the books, assuming Charette was purposely embarrassing him by a gift of "paperback novels—in French." The retiring diplomat thought he got the best of his host by ignoring the "elegantly contemptuous gesture." See Warren Christopher, *Chances of a Lifetime* (New York: Scribner, 2001), 28.

152. These paragraphs are based Philip Gordon, *Transatlantic Allies*, 53–58, and Philip Gordon and Jeremy Shapiro, *Allies at War: America, Europe and the Crisis over Iraq* (New York: McGraw-Hill, 2004), 39–44, 77–78.

153. Jacques Chirac, "M. Chirac plaide pour la fin des sanctions…," interview with Jean-Marie Colombani, Alain Frachon, Patrick Jarreau, and Mouna Naïm, *Le Monde*, 27 February 1998, 2.

154. The Russians were supposedly furious because the strikes were delivered just as the Security Council began its debate over Iraq; Barbara Crossette, "At the UN, Tensions of Cold War Are Renewed," *New York Times*, 18 December 1998, A23.

155. After Operation Desert Fox, Clinton signed legislation advocating regime change; Gordon and Shapiro, *Allies at War*, 43.

156. Claire Tréan, "Pourquoi la France n'ose pas afficher ses divergences avec les Etats-Unis," *Le Monde*, 20 December 1998, 4. See also Michel Noblecourt, "Les hommes politiques français critiquent l'intervention armée en Irak," *Le Monde*, 20 December 1998, 28.

157. Ivo Daalder and Michael O'Hanlon, *Winning Ugly: NATO's War to Save Kosovo* (Washington, DC: Brookings Institution Press, 2000), 44–45. My account relies on Daalder and O'Hanlon's study, as well as Kaufman, *NATO and the Former Yugoslavia*, 149–208.

158. Daalder and O'Hanlon, *Winning Ugly*, 75.

159. Chirac said Blair's recommendation was "neither useful nor reasonable"; Jacques Chirac, "Oui, c'est une capitulation," *Le Figaro*, 11 June 1999, B5.

160. Daalder and O'Hanlon, *Winning Ugly*, 162–64.

161. See Chirac, "Oui, c'est une capitulation." Scholars agree with Chirac; see Frédéric Bozo, "The Effects of Kosovo and the Danger of Decoupling," in *Defending Europe: The EU, NATO and the Quest for European Autonomy*, ed. Jolyon Howorth and John Keeler (New York: Palgrave Macmillan, 2003), 61–77; and Brenner and Parmentier, *Reconcilable Differences*, 62–64.

162. For the French response to Kosovo, see Michel Fortmann and Hélène Viau, "A Model Ally? France and the U.S. during the Kosovo Crisis of 1989–99," in Haglund, ed., *France-U.S. Leadership Race*, 87–109; Renéo Lukic, "The Anti-Americanism in France during the War in Kosovo," in *Culture, Politics, and Nationalism in the Age of Globalization*, ed. Renéo Lukic and Michael Brint (London: Ashgate, 2000), 145–81; and "The Mixed Feelings of Europeans," *Economist*, 17 April 1999, 53.

163. Régis Debray, "L'Europe somnambule," *Le Monde*, 1 April 1999, 1, 19; Régis Debray, "Lettre d'un voyageur au Président de la République," *Le Monde*, 13 May 1999, 1, 15.

164. Jean Baudrillard, "Duplicité totale de cette guerre," *Libération*, 29 April 1999, 6.

165. André Glucksmann, quoted in Roger Cohen, "In Uniting over Kosovo, a New Sense of Identity," *New York Times*, 28 April 1999, A15.

166. Michel Wieviorka, quoted in Thomas Ferenczi, "Les impasses de l'antiaméricanisme," *Le Monde*, 9 June 1999, 1, 22.

167. Pascal Bruckner, "Pourquoi cette rage anti-américaine?" *Le Monde*, 7 April 1999, 1, 21.

168. This case is made in Claire Tréan, "La diplomatie européenne aux commandes," *Le Monde*, 5 June 1999, 18.

169. Chirac, "Oui, c'est une capitulation."

170. Fortman and Viau, "A Model Ally," 105–6; Daalder and O'Hanlon, *Winning Ugly*, 161. Cohen, "In Uniting over Kosovo," A15, cites a poll showing 70 percent of French in favor of NATO intervention.

171. CSA-*Libération*, "C'est de plus en plus loin, l'Amérique," *Libération*, 10–11 April 1999.

172. Hubert Védrine, *Face à l'hyperpuissance: textes et discours, 1995–2003* (Paris: Éditions Fayard, 2003), 104.

173. Craig Whitney, "With a 'Don't Be Vexed' Air, Chirac Assesses U.S.," *New York Times*, 17 December 1999, A3.

174. Quotes in this paragraph are from Chollet and Goldgeir, *America between the Wars*, 232–33, 287.

175. Védrine, *France in an Age of Globalization*, 46–47, 50. The interview appeared originally as *Les Cartes de la France à l'heure de la mondialisation* (Paris: Éditions Fayard, 2000), but it was expanded for the American edition.

176. Jacques Andréani, *L'Amérique et nous* (Paris: Éditions Odile Jacob, 2000), 203, 289. Andréani was ambassador from 1989 to 1995.

177. Lionel Jospin, quoted in Jean-Michel Aphatie, Patrick Jarreau, Laurent Mauduit and Michel Noblecourt, "Lionel Jospin trace sa route," *Le Monde*, 7 January 1999, 6–7.

178. Andréani, *L'Amérique*, 196.

179. Hubert Védrine, quoted in Whitney, "With a 'Don't Be Vexed' Air," A3.

180. Jacques Chirac, quoted in Whitney, "With a 'Don't Be Vexed' Air," A3.

181. See, for example, Pascal Boniface, *La France est-elle encore une grande puissance?* (Paris: Presses de Sciences Po, 1998), 69–79.

182. Védrine, *Face à l'hyperpuissance*, 203.

183. Védrine, *France in an Age of Globalization*, 31.

184. Hubert Védrine, quoted in Richard Cohen, "France vs. U.S.: Warring Versions of Capitalism," *New York Times*, 20 October 1997, A10.

185. Védrine, *France in an Age of Globalization*, 131.

186. Védrine, quoted in Cohen, "France vs. U.S."

187. Védrine, *France in an Age of Globalization*, 45. Pascal Boniface, an analyst for the socialists, elaborated Védrine's argument, writing that France could no longer pretend to rival the American "mastodon" or act as the alterna-

tive pole for Europeans. He felt that French diplomats should stop harassing the U.S. government; win support from other Europeans and the UN;
voice their differences cogently, but without hysterics; and try to persuade
the Americans with serious arguments; Boniface, *La France*, 77–79.

188. Chirac, "M. Chirac plaide pour la fin des sanctions . . ."

189. Jacques Chirac, quoted in Craig Whitney, "France Presses for a Power Independent of the U.S.," *New York Times*, 7 November 1999, 9. With the
deployment of the U.S. missile shield in mind, Chirac said, "I deplore the
present American disengagement. . . . I wish the United States would once
again assume all its responsibilities on the international scene, and as soon as
possible. But the world is a fragile place. It won't wait." Jacques Chirac, "La
France dans un monde multipolaire," *Politique étrangère* 4 (1999): 806.

190. Jacques Chirac, "L'Europe selon Chirac," *Libération*, 25 March 1996, 2.

191. Chirac, "La France dans un monde multipolaire," 804–5.

192. Ibid., 807.

193. What was articulated in the late 1990s anticipated the French position in
2003. As Chirac declared to the UN General Assembly, referring to the U.S.
invasion of Iraq, "In an open world, no one can isolate oneself, no one can
act alone in the name of all, and no one can accept the anarchy of society
without rules. There is no alternative to the United Nations. . . . Multilateralism is essential. . . , it's effective. . . , it's modern." After urging a reformed and
strengthened UN Security Council, he added that it was up to the Council
"to frame the use of force. No one can appropriate the right to use it unilaterally and preventively." Jacques Chirac, "Nul ne peut agir seul," *Le Monde*, 24
September 2003, 2.

194. Andréani, *L'Amérique*, 292.

195. For mistrust of the French among Washington officials and pundits, see Simon Serfaty, *La France vue par les Etats-Unis: réflexions sur la francophobie à
Washington* (Paris: Institut français des relations internationales, 2003).

Chapter 6. The French Way: Economy, Society, and Culture in the 1990s

1. Jacques Chirac, quoted in Philippe Lemaître and Laurent Zecchini, "L'Europe
ne croit guère aux recettes libérales américaines," *Le Monde*, 24 June 1997, 2.

2. Jacques Chirac, quoted in Gilles Delafon and Thomas Sancton, *Dear Jacques,
cher Bill: au coeur de l'Elysée et de la Maison Blanche, 1995–1999* (Paris: Plon,
1999), 300.

3. See, for example, Clarisse Fabre and Eric Fassin, *Liberté, égalité, sexualité: actu-
alité politique des questions sexuelles* (Paris: Éditions Belfond/Le Monde, 2003).

4. "Ces fonds de pension qui font peur aux Français," *Le Monde*, 26 October 1999, 18.

5. Suzanne Berger, "Trade and Identity: The Coming Protectionism?" in *Remaking the Hexagon: The New France in the New Europe*, ed. Gregory Flynn (Boulder, CO: Westview, 1995), 195–210.

6. Sophie Pedder, "The Grand Illusion," *Economist*, 5 June 1999, 10–11.

7. Timothy Smith, *France in Crisis: Welfare, Inequality and Globalization since 1980* (Cambridge: Cambridge University Press, 2004), 129.

8. Mark Kesselman, "The Triple Exceptionalism of the French Welfare State," in *Diminishing Welfare: A Cross-National Study of Social Protection*, ed. Gertrude Schaffner Goldberg and Marguerite Rosenthal (New York: Greenwood, 2001), 201.

9. In 2002, French public spending as percent of GDP, about 53 percent, was higher than all other nations of the EU except for Sweden and Denmark; see Peter Hall, *The Economic Challenges Facing President Jacques Chirac*, U.S.-France Analysis Series (Washington, DC: Brookings Institution, July 2002), 3.

10. Andrew Jack, *The French Exception* (London: Profile Books, 1999), 67.

11. David Ross Cameron, "From Barre to Balladur: Economic Policy in the Era of the EMS," in Flynn, ed., *Remaking the Hexagon*, 117–57.

12. Pierre Rosanvallon, *L'Etat en France de 1789 à nos jours* (Paris: Éditions du Seuil, 1990), 262.

13. William James Adams, "France and Global Competition," in Flynn, *Remaking the Hexagon*, 88.

14. Christian Sautter, minister in the Jospin government, quoted in Gunnar Trumbull, *Silicon and the State: French Innovation Policy in the Internet Age* (Washington, DC: Brookings Institution Press, 2004), 6–7.

15. Secrétariat d'Etat auprès du Premier Ministre chargé du Plan, rapport du groupe "Horizon 2000" présidé par Emmanuel Le Roy Ladurie, *Entrer dans le XXIe siècle: essai sur l'avenir de l'identité française* (Paris: Éditions la Découverte et la Documentation française, 1990), 156.

16. Ibid., 163.

17. Jean Daniel, "L'Amérique ou rien?" *Le Nouvel Observateur*, 26 June–2 July 1997, 22.

18. Serge Marti, "Les dures leçons de l' 'arrogance' américaine," *Le Monde*, 2 September 1997, III.

19. See Jean Heffer, "Il n'y a pas de miracle économique!" *Les Collections de L'Histoire: L'Empire américain* 7 (2000): 88–90; Bernard Lalanne, "Voyage dans la job machine américaine," *L'Expansion*, 3–16 March 1994, 70–77;

Jacques Andréani, *L'Amérique et nous* (Paris: Éditions Odile Jacob, 2000), 205–21.

20. Andréani, *L'Amérique*, 81.

21. Daniel, "L'Amérique ou rien?" 23.

22. Jean Daniel, "Modernité de la gauche," *Le Nouvel Observateur*, 29 May–4 June 1997, 19.

23. Jean Daniel, "L'Europe racontée aux enfants," *Le Nouvel Observateur*, 19–25 June 1997, 22.

24. The contention is that the French welfare state merely serves the comfortable members of society at the expense of the weak: behind the rhetoric of *acquis sociaux*, powerful interests like pensioners, aided by left-wing intellectuals and timid politicians, protect their benefits while the young, women, the disabled, and immigrants go without jobs. Solidarity may have been celebrated as the antidote to American social policy but, from this perspective, it served the affluent. See Smith, *France in Crisis*.

25. Jean-Marie Le Pen wanted to confine the welfare state to "the French." Spurred by fear about crime and immigration, the Front National sought to deny equal social rights to immigrants—i.e., to give priority for all jobs and public housing to "the native French"; to create a separate medical benefits system for foreigners working in France so that French tax money would not go for their care; and, to halt all immigration. In its own nasty and reactionary way this agenda also undermined the French model.

26. Raymond Aron, quoted in Thierry Leterre: *La Gauche et la peur libérale* (Paris: Presses de Sciences Po, 2000), 28. Jack Hayward, *Fragmented France: Two Centuries of Disputed Identity* (New York: Oxford University Press, 2007), indicts the French for their long history of antipathy toward Anglo-American liberalism.

27. Viviane Forrester, *L'Horreur économique* (Paris: Éditions Fayard, 1996). One might read this polemic, which attacked globalization and ultraliberalism, and not realize the target was the United States. But in a later book, *Une Etrange Dictature* (Paris: Éditions Fayard, 2000), Forrester was more explicit in blaming Anglo-American mutual funds for making profits by firing employees.

28. Where 71 percent of Americans, 66 percent of the British, 65 percent of the Germans, and 59 percent of the Italians agreed with this proposition, only 36 percent of the French did. See "20 Nation Poll Finds Strong Global Consensus: Support for Free Market System . . . ," Program on International Policy Attitudes, University of Maryland, 11 January 2006, http://www.worldpublicopinion.org.

29. Alain Duhamel, *Les Peurs françaises* (Paris: Éditions Flammarion, 1993), 43.

30. For a concise and informed review of liberal thought and a plea for the Left to become more liberal, see Leterre, *La Gauche.*

31. Jérôme Jaffré, "La Gauche accepte le marché, la droite admet la différence," *Le Monde*, 18 August 1999, 5. In a SOFRES survey of June 1994 less than a third thought the theory of economic liberalism was a problem; see Hervé Jannic, "Les Français craignent l'envahissement américain," *L'Expansion*, 2–15 June 1994, 52. In the midst of the presidential election of 1995 one survey reported two of three wanted more state intervention in the economy, but also backed free trade; "Une majorité de Français souhaitent . . . ," *Le Monde*, 11 April 1995, 6.

32. Philip Gordon and Sophie Meunier, *The French Challenge: Adapting to Globalization* (Washington, DC: Brookings Institution Press, 2001), 14. Gordon and Meunier are the best guide to this process.

33. Erik Izraelewicz, *Le Capitalisme zinzin* (Paris: Éditions Bernard Grasset, 1999).

34. Gordon and Meunier, *French Challenge*, 31.

35. Trumbull, *Silicon and the State*, 105.

36. Pedder, "The Grand Illusion," 4.

37. Peter Hall, "Introduction: the Politics of Social Change in France," in *Changing France: The Politics that Markets Make*, ed. Pepper Culpepper, Peter Hall, and Bruno Palier (Basingstoke, England: Palgrave Macmillan, 2008), 21.

38. Jérôme Sainte Marie, "Nos derniers sondages publiés: l'image des Etats-Unis," *Paris-Match*, 20 February 2003.

39. Édouard Balladur, *Le Pouvoir ne se partage pas: conversations avec François Mitterrand* (Paris: Éditions Fayard, 2009), 426.

40. Édouard Balladur, quoted in "Putting the Brakes On," *Economist*, 4 August 2001, 43.

41. Édouard Balladur, "En réponse à Philippe Seguin Édouard Balladur défend sa politique économique," *Le Monde*, 6 June 1993, 7.

42. Édouard Balladur, *Deux Ans à Matignon* (Paris: Plon, 1995), 255.

43. Édouard Balladur, "Édouard Balladur multiplie les promesses," *Le Monde*, 2 April 1995, 7.

44. Jacques Chirac, speech at the Sorbonne given on the fiftieth anniversary of the plan in 1996, quoted in Jacques Michel Tondre, *Jacques Chirac dans le texte* (Paris: Éditions Ramsay, 2000), 105.

45. Jacques Chirac, speech of 1997, quoted in Tondre, *Jacques Chirac*, 114.

46. Jacques Chirac, quoted in Serge Marti, "Le G7 s'efforce de concilier mondialisation et cohésion sociale," *Le Monde*, 3 April 1996, 2.

47. Jean-Marie Messier, *J6M.COM: faut-il avoir peur de la nouvelle économie?* (Paris: Hachette, 2000), 73, 131.

48. Jacques Chirac, quoted in Roger Cohen, "For France, Sagging Self-Image and Esprit," *New York Times*, 11 February 1997, A1, 8.

49. Jacques Chirac, quoted in John Andrews, "A Divided Self: A Survey of France," *Economist*, 16 November 2002, 18.

50. Jacques Chirac, quoted in Pierre Péan, *L'Inconnu de l'Elysée* (Paris: Éditions Fayard, 2007), 459.

51. A. Chaillot, quoted in Steve Bastow, "Front National Economic Policy: From Neo-Liberalism to Protectionism," *Modern and Contemporary France* 5, no. 1 (1997): 65.

52. Jean-Marie Le Pen, quoted in Christiane Chombeau, "Jean-Marie Le Pen dresse la liste des candidats . . . ," *Le Monde*, 31 May 1997, 10.

53. Philippe Bernard and Luc Leroux, "La France exige des Etats-Unis le départ de cinq agents de la CIA," *Le Monde*, 23 February 1995, 1, 9. The *New York Times* reported the story the same day: "France Accuses 5 Americans of Spying," *New York Times*, 23 February 1995, A1, 12. The CIA later owned up to the botched espionage; Tim Weiner, "CIA Confirms Blunders during Economic Spying on France," *New York Times*, 13 March 1996, 8. See also Jean-François Jacquier and Marc Nexon, "Comment la CIA déstabilise les entreprises françaises," *L'Expansion*, 10–23 July 1995, 32–7; and Jean Guisnel, *Les Pires Amis du monde* (Paris: Éditions Stock, 1999), 183–213, 289–316.

54. "A Dangerous Skirmish," *Financial Times*, 18 August 1995, 13.

55. Alain Juppé, quoted in "Crise idéologique," *Le Monde*, 27 August 1995, 9.

56. For the Plan Juppé see Jean-Marie Domenach, Eric Fassin, Pierre Grémion, René Mouriaux, Pascal Perrineau, Michel Wieviorka, Paul Thibaud, and George Ross, "Debate: the Movements of Autumn—Something New or Déjà Vu," *French Politics and Society* 14 (1996): 1–27.

57. Jacques Chirac, quoted in Ibrahim Youssef, "As Strike Intensifies, French Government Stands Firm," *New York Times*, 5 December 1995, A1.

58. For the most part, the strikers represented the public sector with only nominal participation from private employees; see "Le secteur privé a peu suivi les appels de la CGT et de FO," *Le Monde*, 7 December 1995, 12.

59. Pascal Perrineau and Michel Wieviorka, "De la nature du mouvement social," *French Politics and Society* 14 (1996): 19.

60. Marc Blondel, quoted in Craig Whitney, "French Rail and Other Workers Ending their 3-Week Walkout," *New York Times*, 16 December 1995, 7.

61. Alan Riding, "France Questions Its Identity as It Sinks into 'Le Malaise,'" *New York Times*, 23 December 1990, 1.

62. "Between liberalism that increases social inequities in the name of freedom, and collectivism that asphyxiates freedom in the name of an imaginary equality," he stated, "there is a place for a society of responsibility and solidarity"; Pierre Bérégovoy, "L'Amérique, l'Europe, la France," *Le Monde*, 6 January 1993, 8.

63. Noël Mamère and Olivier Warin, *Non merci, Oncle Sam!* (Paris: Éditions Ramsay, 1999), 187. Another Green Party critic of the American Fordist economy was Alain Lipietz.

64. Lionel Jospin, "Changeons d'avenir, changeons de majorité: nos engagements," *Le Monde*, 3 May 1997, 8.

65. Quotations in this paragraph are from Lionel Jospin, "A ceux qui doutent de la gauche . . . ," interview with Edgar Morin, Alain Touraine, and Jean Daniel, *Le Nouvel Observateur*, 22–28 May 1997, 23–25. See also his address to the National Assembly for his views on republican solidarity; Lionel Jospin, "Le discours de Lionel Jospin," *Le Monde*, 21 June 1997, 8–10.

66. Édouard Balladur, "Nous devons inventer un libéralisme à la française . . . ," *Le Monde*, 28 May 1997, 7.

67. Lionel Jospin, *Modern Socialism*, Fabian Pamphlet 592 (London: Fabian Society, 1999), 1.

68. Ibid., 10.

69. Ibid., 8.

70. Ibid., 10.

71. Lionel Jospin, "Le Discours de Lionel Jospin à Rio," *Le Monde*, 18 April 2001, 16.

72. Jospin, *Modern Socialism*, 6.

73. Gilles Senges, "Création d'emploi: Lionel Jospin tire les leçons de l'expérience américaine," *Les Echos*, 19 June 1998; "Jospin Discovers America," *Economist*, 27 June 1998, 50.

74. Lionel Jospin, quoted in Andrews, "A Divided Self," 14.

75. "Still a Dirty Word," *Economist*, 8 June 2002, 48.

76. Pedder, "The Grand Illusion," 11.

77. Anonymous adviser, quoted in Pedder, "The Grand Illusion," 12. Pedder also quotes Tony Blair who, in contrast, at a meeting in Milan lectured the French

socialists, to their dismay, on the need to imitate America's flexible labor markets: "We can't argue with the fact that U.S. unemployment is lower, growth higher," the British Prime Minister said; "high unemployment is not social cohesion" (12).

78. Dominique Strauss-Kahn, quoted in Pedder, "The Grand Illusion," 11.

79. Lionel Jospin, "Ce monde a besoin de règles," *Le Monde*, 22 September 1999, 3; Lionel Jospin, "Concurrence à gauche pour la formation d'un front 'anticapitaliste,'" *Le Monde*, 23 September 1999, 6.

80. Dominique Strauss-Kahn, quoted in Philippe Lemaître and Laurent Zecchini, "L'Europe ne croit guère aux recettes libérales américaines," *Le Monde*, 24 June 1997, 2.

81. Michel Lallement, "New Patterns of Industrial Relations and Political Action since the 1980s," in Culpepper et al., eds., *Changing France*, 54–60.

82. For Minitel and the Internet, see Trumbull, *Silicon and the State*, 60–82. For the country's rapid progress see the World Bank's development indicators, http://www.google.com/publicdata?ds=wb-wdi&met=it_net_user&idim =country:FRA&dl=en&hl=en&q=france+internet+users+statistics.

83. Trumbull, *Silicon and the State*, 2. See also Gunnar Trumbull, "From Rents to Risks: France's New Innovation Policy," paper presented at the conference "The New Cleavages in France," Princeton University, October 2003. My discussion of information technology is derived from Trumbull's studies.

84. Alain Duhamel, "Droite: le handicap Seillière," *Libération*, 20 February 1998, 5; "Ernest-Antoine de Seillière, Boss of France's Bosses," *Economist*, 11 March 2000, 60–61. For the Mouvement des enterprises de France, see Isabelle Mandraud and Caroline Monnot, "Kessler égale Tocqueville," *Le Monde*, 25 June 2000, 11.

85. Gérard Desportes, "Un libéralisme sans complexe: le MEDEF . . . ," *Libération*, 6 April 2000, 4.

86. Alain Minc, *Www.capitalisme.fr* (Paris: Éditions Bernard Grasset, 2000). See also Messier, *J6M.com*.

87. Patrick Coquidé, "Mais où sont donc passés les libéraux?" *L'Expansion*, 19 May–1 June 1994, 50–52.

88. Gordon and Meunier, *French Challenge*, 24.

89. Michel Goyer, *The Transformation of Corporate Governance in France*, U.S.-France Analysis Series (Washington, DC: Brookings Institution, January 2003), 83.

90. Hervé Jannic, "U.S. Corp. in France," *L'Expansion* special issue, "Comment l'Amérique a changé la France," 2–15 June 1994, 54–58.

91. Joseph Quinlan, *Drifting Apart or Growing Together? The Primacy of the Transatlantic Economy* (Washington, DC: Center for Transatlantic Relations, 2003), 28.

92. Sophie Meunier, "Free-Falling France or Free-Trading France?" *French Politics, Culture and Society* 22 (2004): 102.

93. For general treatments besides Gordon and Meunier, *French Challenge,* see Vivien A. Schmidt, "French Capitalism Transformed, Yet still a Third Variety of Capitalism," *Economy and Society* 32 (2003): 526–54; Pepper Culpepper, "Capitalism, Coordination, and Economic Change: the French Political Economy since 1985," in Culpepper et al., eds., *Changing France,* 29–49; and Cait Murphy, "The Next French Revolution," *Fortune,* 12 June 2000, 157–68.

94. Marc Lassus, quoted in G. Pascal Zachary, "Yanks in Vogue," *Wall Street Journal,* 8 June 1998, 1, 10.

95. Samer Iskandar, "BNP Turns Up Heat in Bank Bid Battle," *Financial Times,* 26 July 1999, 20.

96. "Three Wiser Men," *Financial Times,* 30 August 1999, 13.

97. Samer Iskandar, "Regulators Block BNP's Bid for Société Générale," *Financial Times,* 30 August 1999, 1.

98. François Morin, "Transformation of the French Model of Shareholding and Management," *Economy and Society* 29, no. 1 (2000): 37.

99. Morin, "Transformation," 45, 49.

100. Jean-Luc Lagardère, quoted in Pedder, "The Grand Illusion," 4.

101. Pierre Briançon, "The Great French Shopping Spree," *France Magazine* 59 (2001): 34.

102. Small business owner, quoted in John Ardagh, *France in the New Century* (London: Penguin, 2000), 182.

103. Jean-Pierre Ponssard, *Stock Options and Performance-Based Pay in France,* U.S.-France Analysis Series (Washington, DC: Brookings Institution, March 2001); Jean-Baptiste Jacquin and Franck Dedieu, "Stock-Options: la France championne d'Europe," *L'Expansion,* 13 September 2001, 92–97.

104. Goyer, *The Transformation of Corporate Governance,* 2.

105. Ibid., 3.

106. Surveys showed that the French public had warmed to rewarding employees with stock options, but deputies in the National Assembly remained uncomfortable with the practice. As Trumbull, *Silicon and the State,* 27, notes, "France's political leaders . . . were out of touch with France's changing attitudes toward performance-based compensation."

107. Survey conducted in 2000–2001; See Mette Zølner, "French E-Managers: A Generation in the Making," *French Politics, Culture and Society* 20 (2002): 33–51.

108. Jean-Marie Messier, quoted in Martine Orange and Jo Johnson, *The Man Who Tried to Buy the World: Jean-Marie Messier and Vivendi Universal* (New York: Portfolio, 2003), xiii. See also William Emmanuel, *Le Maître des illusions: l'ascension et la chute de Jean-Marie Messier* (Paris: Éditions Economica, 2002).

109. Messier, *J6M*, 166.

110. Jean-Marie Messier, quoted in Alan Riding, "Remark by Vivendi Chief Unnerves French Film Industry," *New York Times*, 24 December 2001, 1.

111. Daniel Toscan du Plantier, quoted in Mark Landler, "In a French Mogul's Fall, A Warning for Globalists," *New York Times*, 7 July 2002, 4.

112. "A French Exception," *Economist*, 6 July 2002, 12–13.

113. Jean-Benoit Nadeau and Julie Barlow, *The Story of French* (New York: St. Martin's Griffin, 2006), 381; Jim Hoagland, "Attack of the Deux Raviolis," *Washington Post*, 22 July 1990, C4.

114. Maurice Druon, quoted in Jack, *French Exception*, 27.

115. Maurice Druon, quoted in Paul Cohen, "Of Linguistic Jacobinism and Cultural Balkanization: Contemporary French Linguistic Politics in Historical Context," *French Politics, Culture and Society* 18 (2000): 41, n. 6.

116. Édouard Balladur, quoted in Marlise Simons, "Bar English? French Bicker on Barricades," *New York Times*, 15 March 1994, A 1.

117. Balladur, *Le Pouvoir*, 196.

118. Lionel Jospin, quoted in Gordon and Meunier, *French Challenge*, 58.

119. Hubert Védrine with Dominique Moïsi, *France in an Age of Globalization*, trans. Philip Gordon (Washington, DC: Brookings Institution Press, 2001), 21–22.

120. Ardagh, *France in the New Century*, 704.

121. Alan Riding, "A bas l'Anglais!" *New York Times*, 11 July 1992, 3.

122. Jacques Toubon, quoted in Marcel Machill, "Background to French Language Policy and Its Impact on the Media," *European Journal of Communication* 2 (1997): 494.

123. Yves Berger, "La langue aux abois," *Le Monde des débats*, May 1994, 24; Bernard Cassin, "Parler français ou la 'langue des maîtres,'" *Le Monde diplomatique*, April 1994, 32; Bertrand Poirot-Delpech, "Défense et illustration du français," *Le Monde*, 17 April 1994, 22.

124. Simons, "Bar English?" A1.

125. Stella and Joël de Rosnay, "Honni soit qui mal y pense," *Libération*, 4 March 1994, 6.

126. Jack, *French Exception,* 36–37.

127. Jacques Toubon, quoted in "Well, Excuse Moi!" *Wall Street Journal*, 24 February 1994, A12.

128. Jacques Toubon, "Tempest in a Demitasse," *New York Times*, 4 April 1994, A15.

129. Lionel Jospin, quoted in Gordon and Meunier, *French Challenge*, 58.

130. "After Babel, a New Common Language," *Economist*, 7 August 2004, 42.

131. Ardagh, *France in the New Century*, 705.

132. The reasons for using English were to associate products with globalization, superior technology, or an American lifestyle and to attract attention or add humor. See Elizabeth Martin, "Cultural Images and Different Varieties of English in French Television Commercials," *English Today* 72 (2002): 8–20.

133. Denis Ager, *Identity, Security and Image: France and Language* (Cleveden, England: Multilingual Matters, 1999), 110–11. Those who objected to American influence on language rose slightly during the 1980s and '90s but at 34 percent was much less than that recorded in other areas of culture like television or the cinema. SOFRES and French-American Foundation, *France-Etats-Unis: regards croisés,* June 2000, 17–18.

134. "Babel Runs Backwards," *Economist*, 1 January 2005, 63.

135. Jack, *French Exception,* 43.

136. Some 97 percent chose English; Sandrine Blanchard and Stéphanie Le Bars, "L'hégémonie de l'anglais," *Le Monde*, 28 February 2000, 8.

137. "English Is Still on the March," *Economist*, 24 February 2001, 50.

138. Data compiled by the Centre National de la Cinématographie, reported in Jacques Buob, "Culture: l'assaut américain," *L'Express*, 7–13 October 1993, 73.

139. See the data collected by the Centre National de la Cinématographie in Patrick Messerlin, "La politique française du cinéma: l'arbre, le maire et la médiathèque," *Commentaire* 71 (1995): 595; and Centre National de la cinématographie, *CNC Info* 276 (May 2000): 5.

140. See the issue of *L'Express*, 7–13 October 1993, 70–88; and "La guéguerre des étoiles," *Le Nouvel Observateur*, 23–29 September 1993, 62–63.

141. Joseph Hanania, "Fleeing a Fallow France for Greener U.S. Pastures," *New York Times*, 22 October 1995, H14.

142. Vincent Malle, quoted in Paul Chutkow, "Who Will Control the Soul of French Cinema?" *New York Times*, 9 August 1992, 22.

143. Bernard Weintraub, "Directors Battle over GATT's Final Cut and Print," *New York Times,* 12 December 1993, 25. For the increase in American programs on

television see David Looseley, *The Politics of Fun: Cultural Policy and Debate in Contemporary France* (Oxford: Berg, 1997), 204–7.

144. For these negotiations, see Kerry Segrave, *American Television Abroad: Hollywood's Attempt to Dominate World Television* (Jefferson, NC: McFarland, 1998), 208–11; Laurent Burin des Roziers, *Du cinéma au multimédia: une brève histoire de l'exception culturelle* (Paris: Institut français des relations internationales, 1998); David Puttnam, *The Undeclared War: The Struggle for Control of the World's Film Industry* (London: HarperCollins, 1997), 339–44.

145. Alan Riding, "Paris Seeks to Rally Support," *New York Times*, 19 October 1993, A3.

146. Jacques Toubon, "Laisser respirer nos âmes," *Le Monde*, 1 October 1993, 1–2; Louise Stroud, "France and EU Policy-Making on Visual Culture," in *France in Focus: Film and National Identity*, ed. Elizabeth Ezra and Sue Harris (Oxford: Berg, 2000), 61–75.

147. François Mitterrand, quoted in Buob, "Culture: l'assaut américain," 71. See also Jean-Pierre Péroncel-Hugoz, "Les créations de l'esprit . . . de simples marchandises," *Le Monde*, 19 October 1993, 9.

148. Bertrand Tavernier, quoted in Jonathan Buchsbaum, "The *Exception Culturelle* is Dead," *Framework: The Journal of Cinema and Media* 47 (2006): 9; Alain Corneau, quoted in Alan Riding, "French Film Industry Circles the Wagons," *New York Times*, 18 September 1993, 11.

149. Nicolas Seydoux, quoted in Buob, "Culture: l'assaut américain," 74.

150. Frank Price, quoted in Weintraub, "Directors Battle," 25.

151. Jack Valenti, quoted in Keith Bradsher, "Big Cut in Tariffs: Movies, TV . . . ," *New York Times*, 15 December 1993, A1.

152. Jack Valenti, quoted in Segrave, *American Television*, 256.

153. "GATT: images et culture," *Le Monde*, 18 September 1993, 1. See also Marin Karmitz, interview with Dominique Simmonnet, *L'Express*, 7–13 October 1993, 84–85.

154. See the debate between Costa-Gavras and Michael Eisner, "From Magic Kingdom to Media Empire," *New Perspectives Quarterly* 12 (1995): 4–10.

155. "GATT: images et culture," 1.

156. Jack Lang, quoted in "La guéguerre des étoiles," 63.

157. Daniel Toscan du Plantier, quoted in Fabienne Pascaud, "Faut-il avoir peur de la culture américaine?" *Télérama*, 6 October 1993, 14.

158. "Attention au retour de l'anti-américanisme," *Quotidien de Paris*, 19 October 1991, n.p.

159. Mario Vargas-Llosa, "De l'exception culturelle française," *Libération*, 19 October 1993, 6.

160. Régis Debray, "Y a-t-il une sortie sur l'autoroute? Réponse à Mario Vargas Llosa," *El País*, 4 November 1993, 15.

161. Max Gallo, "Sauver l'homme-citoyen," *Le Monde des débats*, November 1993, 8.

162. This exchange is Mario Vargas-Llosa, "Cher Régis," *Libération*, 2 December 1993, 6; and Régis Debray, "Quelles Tribus? Cher Mario," *Libération*, 3 December 1993, 3.

163. Jacques Toubon, quoted in John Rockwell, "Making a Mark on French Culture," *New York Times*, 8 November 1993, C11.

164. Jack Lang, quoted in Alan Riding, "The French Strategy, Months of Risk," *New York Times*, 15 December 1993, D19.

165. Jack Lang, quoted in C. Anthony Gifford, "Culture versus Commerce: Europe Strives to keep Hollywood at Bay," in *Kazaam! Splat! Ploof! The American Impact on European Popular Culture since 1945*, ed. Sabrina Ramet and Gordana Crnković (Lanham, MD: Rowman and Littlefield, 2003), 46.

166. Harvey Feigenbaum, "Is Technology the Enemy of Culture?" *International Journal of Cultural Policy* 10, no. 3 (2004): 251–63.

167. Jack Valenti, "What U.S. Film Makers Really Wanted," *New York Times*, 3 January 1994, A22.

168. Henri de Bresson, "Les occidentaux guerroient sur le statut de l'investissement étranger," *Le Monde*, 18 February 1998, 2. David Henderson, a principal American negotiator, blamed France for ending the talks; see David Henderson, *The MAI Affair: A Story and Its Lessons* (London: Royal Institute of International Affairs, 1999), 4.

169. Gordon and Meunier, *French Challenge*, 75.

170. At Nice the cultural exception was explicitly included in EU law. France held out against granting the EU exclusive competence over trade in cultural and audiovisual services.

171. At the end of the decade French films held 32 percent of the domestic market, as opposed to 54 percent for the Americans; see http://www.cnc.fr/CNC_GALLERY_CONTENT/DOCUMENTS/statistiques/par_secteur_EN_pdf/Attendance.pdf. See also John Tagliabue, "Now Playing Europe: Invasion of the Multiplex," *New York Times*, 27 January 2000, C1.

172. Data from Gordon and Meunier, *French Challenge*, 50.

173. Anne Jäckel, "The Inter/Nationalism of French Film Policy," *Modern and Contemporary France* 15 (2007): 21–36.

174. Burin des Roziers, *Du cinéma*, 21. The comparable data are for Germany (43 percent to 85 percent), Spain (62 percent to 77 percent), United Kingdom (60 percent to 82 percent), and Italy (52 percent to 71 percent). The French stations in this sample were France 3 and TF1.

175. Gordon and Meunier, *French Challenge*, 49.

176. Laurent Creton, *Economie du cinéma: perspectives stratégiques* (Paris: Éditions Nathan, 1994), argues government support has been and is imperative for the industry to meet American competition. Eric Dubet, even though he believes subsidies risk hampering competitiveness, sees them as assisting the industry; see Eric Dubet, *Economie du cinéma européen: de l'interventionnisme à l'action entrepreneuriale* (Paris: Éditions L'Harmattan, 2000). See also Jonathan Buchsbaum, "After GATT: Has the Revival of French Cinema Ended?" *French Politics, Culture and Society* 23 (2005): 42; Jean-Pierre Jeancolas, "From the Blum-Byrnes Agreement to the GATT Affair," in *Hollywood and Europe*, ed. Geoffrey Nowell-Smith and Steven Ricci (London: British Film Institute, 1998), 56. For the importance of television acting as the banker for cinema see Buchsbaum, "The *Exception Culturelle*." Some European directors like Wim Wenders and David Puttnam wanted to extend the French subsidy system throughout Europe.

177. Harvey Feigenbaum, "America's Cultural Challenge Abroad," *Political Science Quarterly*, forthcoming.

178. Martine Danan, "From a 'Prenational' to a 'Postnational' French Cinema," in *The European Cinema Reader*, ed. Catherine Fowler (London: Routledge, 2002), 237–43; Kristin Hohenadell, "European Films Learn to Speak English," *New York Times,* 30 January 2000, 15. Other French directors who tried their hand at English films were Louis Malle, Bertrand Tavernier, Jean-Pierre Jeunet, and Jean-Jacques Annaud. On Hollywood remakes, see Lucy Mazdon, *Encore Hollywood: Remaking French Cinema* (London: British Film Institute, 2000).

179. Messerlin, "La politique," 597. Much of the critique in this paragraph comes from Messerlin's study.

180. Harvey Feigenbaum, "The Production of Culture in the Postimperial Era: The World Versus Hollywood?" in *Postimperialism in World Politics*, ed. David G. Becker and Richard L. Sklar (Westport, CT: Praeger, 1999), 105–24.

181. Alan Riding, "Where Is the Glory That Was France?" *New York Times,* 14 January 1996, 22.

182. Antoine de Baecque, "Il n'y a pas de cinéma français," *La Règle du jeu* 12 (1994): 234–40.

183. Data provided in Messerlin, "La politique," 587. Nevertheless, Messerlin stresses a decline in the French appetite for their own films since the late 1970s. As a percentage of ticket sales for American films, the French in 1991–93 selected local productions at a rate of 59 percent, compared to 22 percent for the Germans and Italians.
184. Alan Riding, "French Comic Book Heroes Battle Hollywood's Hordes," *New York Times*, 10 February 1999, E2.
185. Bruno Palier, "The Long Good Bye to Bismarck? Changes in the French Welfare State," in Culpepper et al., eds., *Changing France*, 127.

Chapter 7. The Paradox of the Fin de Siècle:
Anti-Americanism and Americanization

1. Patrick Gofman, *Le cauchemar américain* (Lausanne, Switzerland: Éditions l'Age d'homme, 2000); Noël Mamère and Olivier Warin, *Non merci, Oncle Sam!* (Paris: Éditions Ramsay, 1999).
2. Thierry de Montbrial, cited in Joseph Biden, "Unholy Symbiosis: Isolationism and Anti-Americanism," *Washington Quarterly* 23 (2000): 11.
3. Jane Perlez, "At Democracy's Picnic Paris Supplies Ants," *New York Times*, 27 June 2000, 6.
4. For investment data see Ambassade de France aux Etats-Unis, *Les Investissements directs français aux Etats-Unis*, December 1999.
5. Data from the Centre National de la Cinématographie website, http://www.cnc.fr/CNC_GALLERY_CONTENT/DOCUMENTS/statistiques/par_secteur_FR_pdf/Frequentation.pdf. In a nation of almost sixty million people, twenty million tickets were sold for the movie *Titanic*.
6. "English Is Still on the March," *Economist*, 24 February 2001, 50.
7. One survey showed that 61 percent of those consulted in France relied on TV for information on national and international issues, with the press and radio accounting for 18 percent and 17 percent, respectively. See Pew Global Attitudes Project, *Views of a Changing World* (Washington, DC: Pew Research Center for the People and the Press, 2003), T-96. The U.S. State Department, asking about how the French learned about "American culture," found almost half (46 percent) said it was from TV; and the rest were scattered among cinema (14 percent), the press (11 percent), schools (8 percent), visits to the United States (5 percent), books (3 percent), etc. See Anna Dean and Mary Demeri, U.S. Department of State, Office of Research, *Europeans and Anti-Americanism: Fact vs. Fiction* (Washington, DC: U.S. Department of State, September 2002), A-23. In general, polling agents like the Pew Center and the

State Department hold that in 19 out of 20 cases the sampling error is no more than about 4 percentage points.

8. For example, in the summer of 2002 one poll found 71 percent held either a "very" or "somewhat" favorable opinion of Americans. In 2002 the Germans (70 percent) and Italians (74 percent) held similar favorable views of Americans while the British recorded the high, at 83 percent. Pew Global Attitudes Project, *Views of a Changing World*, T-132–33.

9. CSA-Libération, "C'est de plus en plus loin, l'Amérique," *Libération*, 10–11 April 1999, 6.

10. When asked which people they felt more sympathy for, 39 percent chose the Germans; 20 percent the Americans, and only 15 percent the British. And few, given a choice between various Europeans and Americans, would select Americans. Jérôme Sainte Marie, "Nos derniers sondages publiés: l'image des Etats-Unis," *Paris-Match*, 20 February 2003, n.p.

11. U.S. Department of State, *Key West Europeans Mostly Negative* (Washington, DC: U.S. Department of State, May 2003), fig. 4. In the summer of 2002 the favorable view was endorsed by 63 percent of the French, 61 percent of the Germans, 70 percent of the Italians, and 75 percent of the British. Pew Research Center, *What the World Thinks in 2002: How Global Publics View Their Lives, Their Countries, the World, America* (Washington, DC: Pew Research Center for the People and the Press, 2002), 53.

12. A negative trend emerged in French opinion of the United States. Data are contradictory on this subject, but one set of polls conducted by a French agency demonstrated a modest deterioration after 1988. The question posed was, "Are you, with respect to the United States, rather sympathetic, rather antipathetic, or neither sympathetic nor antipathetic?" Given this limited choice, polls taken in 1988, 1994, 1996, showed "sympathy" steadily in decline (54 percent, 40 percent, 35 percent). In contrast, "antipathy" advanced from 6 percent, to 11 percent, to 17 percent. And the "neither/nor" option rose from 38 percent to 47 percent; SOFRES and French-American Foundation, *France-Etats-Unis: regards croisés*, June 2000, 6. In May 2000 the same question evoked slightly better results: 41 percent said they were "sympathetic"; 10 percent said "antipathetic"; and among the rest who answered, 48 percent said neither one nor the other; SOFRES and French-American Foundation, *France-Etats-Unis*, 1. In other words, sympathy for the United States slipped between 1988 and 2000 from 54 percent to 41 percent; and both antipathy and indifference toward the United States increased.

13. Sondages CSA, *Les Français et les Etats-Unis à l'approche de l'élection présiden-tielle américaine*, October 2000.

14. SOFRES and French-American Foundation, *France-Etats-Unis*, 1.

15. See U.S. Department of State, *Europeans and Anti-Americanism*, 11–12. The question was, "Does the United States have too much influence over domes-tic affairs?"

16. In 1996 *Le Monde* found that 64 percent of those polled regarded U.S. influ-ence in the world "excessive"; Alain Frachon, "L'image des Etats-Unis ne cesse de se dégrader en France," *Le Monde*, 31 October 1996, 1–3.

17. U.S. Department of State, *Europeans and Anti-Americanism*, A-24.

18. The percentages that assessed U.S. influence as excessive were: culture (61 percent), economics (60 percent), the military (56 percent), and politics (53 percent); CSA-Libération, "L'Amérique," 6.

19. Sondages CSA, *L'Approche de l'éléction*. Once George W. Bush took office the spread of "American ideas and customs" was considered undesirable by almost three-quarters of the French, the Germans, and the Spanish. Only half of the Italians and the British felt the same way (Pew Global Attitudes Project, *Views of a Changing World*, T-136).

20. U.S. Department of State, *Europeans and Anti-Americanism*, 10. The percent-ages of those who said the United States does not consult others were: French, 79 percent; British, 68 percent; Italians, 67 percent; and Germans, 63 percent. The Pew Center, *What the World Thinks*, 58, also found that the French led these four nations in the belief that the United States did not take the interests of others into account.

21. SOFRES and French-American Foundation, *France-Etats-Unis*, 12.

22. U.S. Department of State, *Europeans and Anti-Americanism*, 11–12.

23. Ibid., A-24. Some 92 percent of the French, 91 percent of the Italians, and 83 percent of the British, but only 68 percent of the Germans, found the United States "domineering."

24. Chicago Council on Foreign Relations and the German Marshall Fund of the United States, *Worldviews 2002: European Public Opinion and Foreign Policy* 29, http://www.thechicagocouncil.org/UserFiles/File/POS_Topline%20 Reports/POS%202002/2002_Europe_Report.pdf. Henceforth these orga-nizations will be abbreviated as CCFR and GMF.

25. U.S. Department of State, Office of Research, *Highlights from the Office of Research: Elite Surveys in France, Germany, Spain, Bulgaria and the Czech Re-public* (Washington, DC: U.S. Department of State, 2001), 3. There was yet

another surge (to 79 percent) with the coming of the Bush government in the winter of 2000–2001.

26. If a majority of the French approved of globalization, they also accounted for the largest negative minority opinion of any wealthy nation. A State Department poll for 2000–2001 also found that a majority in France thought globalization was good, but 33 percent of the public and 25 percent of the elite said it was bad. In Germany, 17 percent of the public and 31 percent of the elite found globalization bad. See U.S. Department of State, *Europeans and Anti-Americanism*, 23. And while 1 in 10 in Germany, and 2 in 10 in Britain and Italy, viewed globalization as a threat to their national culture, 4 in 10 did so in France; ibid., 23–24.

27. On the link with U.S. domination, see U.S. Department of State, *Europeans and Anti-Americanism*, 23. The data on who benefits from globalization are in SOFRES and French American Foundation, *France-Etats-Unis*, 3.

28. The question was, "How much confidence would you say you have in the ability of the United States to deal responsibly with world problems?" The "confident" choice represents the sum of those who said they had a "great deal" and those who said a "fair amount." Usually the former was small, around 10 percent. From 1981 to 1988 (Ronald Reagan), the average expressing confidence was 45 percent, with a dip in February 1987 to 34 percent. From 1989 to 1991 (George H. W. Bush), the average was 63 percent, with an unusual peak of over 70 percent in January 1991. From 1991 to 2000 (Bill Clinton), the average was over 50 percent until 1997 with high volatility in late summer 1995 (low 39 percent to high 62 percent) because of events in Bosnia; it then dropped to an average of 46 percent from 1998 to 2000. The most detailed sources are the A-2 tables in U.S. Department of State, *Europeans and Anti-Americanism*, and in graph form in U.S. Department of State, *Key West Europeans Mostly Negative*, 2, fig. 5.

29. Some 47 percent named trade and economics, followed distantly by American hegemony at 11 percent. See U.S. Department of State, Office of Research, Opinion Analysis, *Six in Ten French Elites Value U.S. Leadership* (Washington, DC: U.S. Department of State, 19 March 2001).

30. CSA-Libération, "L'Amérique."

31. Ibid.

32. SOFRES and French American Foundation, *France-Etats-Unis*, 15. The choice of ascribing motives to the United States were: to protect and extend its interests (63 percent); to impose its will on the world (51 percent); to preserve peace (28 percent); to promote democracy (11 percent).

33. As military intervention approached in the spring of 2003, half of those who had said they favored the United States the previous summer changed their mind, and the favorable vote dropped from 63 percent to 31 percent; U.S. Department of State, *Key West Europeans*, appendix, table 2. Similarly, the good reputation of Americans faded. Once the war began, "very" or "somewhat" favorable opinions of Americans plunged precipitously and unfavorable attitudes soared; Pew Global Attitudes Project, *Views of a Changing World*, T-133. But the president was the primary target. Among those holding unfavorable views of the United States in April–May 2003, when asked pointedly if this was "mostly because of President George Bush or is it a more general problem with "America," three-quarters charged the president while less than a quarter blamed America; Pew Global Attitudes Project, *Views of a Changing World*, T-134. French cynicism about U.S. motives is recorded in Pew Center, *What the World Thinks*, 3.

34. U.S. Department of State, *Europeans and Anti-Americanism*, 9, 48. On issues like trade and economic disputes and the environment over 60 percent of the public said (in 2001) that the two countries were working in different directions. The only issues where as many as 40 percent perceived similarity in policy were on questions like reducing international drug trafficking or preventing Iraq from developing a nuclear capacity.

35. CCFR and GMF, *Worldviews 2002*, 26.

36. SOFRES and French American Foundation, *France-Etats-Unis*, 7.

37. CCFR and GMF, *Worldviews 2002*, 15. Superpower status for the EU was the choice for 91 percent of the French; 76 percent of the Italians, 63 percent of the Poles, 59 percent of the Dutch; 56 percent of the British, and 48 percent of the Germans.

38. CSA-Libération, "L'Amérique." A common European defense without the United States was the choice of 43 percent, while 45 percent preferred a defense constructed with NATO. And 6 percent wanted an independent French defense.

39. CCFR and GMF, *Worldviews 2002*, 17.

40. SOFRES and French-American Foundation, *France-Etats-Unis*, 17–18. Objections to American influence from 1984 to 2000 increased by the following percentages: television (45 percent to 65 percent); cinema (36 percent to 57 percent); food (9 percent to 26 percent); language (28 percent to 34 percent); clothes (18 percent to 22 percent); advertising (34 percent to 35 percent). But for music, those who found influence excessive declined from 42 percent to 37 percent.

41. U.S. Department of State, *Europeans and Anti-Americanism*, 39. In 1995 those expressing unfavorable opinions of "American popular culture such as music, television and films" were: the French, 57 percent; the Germans, 50 percent; and the British, 39 percent. In 2000 the percentages were: the French, 48 percent; the Germans, 38 percent; the Italians, 33 percent; and the British, 30 percent.

42. U.S. Department of State, *Europeans and Anti-Americanism*, A-29. The comparable perceptions of a cultural threat were: British, 27 percent; Germans, 24 percent; Italians, 19 percent.

43. SOFRES poll of May 1994, reported in Hervé Jannic, "Les Français craignent l'envahissement américain," *L'Expansion*, 2–15 June 1994, 52–53.

44. In 2003, one survey found two-thirds of the French, similar to other West Europeans, declaring they "liked," rather than "disliked," these American imports. Pew Global Attitudes Project, *Views of a Changing World*, T-139.

45. Pew Center, *What the World Thinks*, 63. If 71 percent regarded the spread of American ideas as bad, 66 percent said they liked American popular culture.

46. Ibid., 63, 66.

47. Pew Global Attitudes Project, *Views of a Changing World*, T-18. In fact, 47 percent of Americans also believed fast food was a change for the worse.

48. In 1988 the choices were: *power* (56 percent), *dynamism* (32 percent), *wealth* (31 percent), and *liberty* (30 percent). In 1996 they had become: *violence* (59 percent), *power* (57 percent), *inequality* (45 percent), and *racism* (39 percent). *Liberty* fell to 18 percent and *imperialism* rose from 12 percent to 21 percent. SOFRES and French-American Foundation, *France-Etats-Unis*, 15.

49. Frachon, "L'image des Etats-Unis," 2.

50. SOFRES and French-American Foundation, *France-Etats-Unis*, 15. The numbers were: *violence* (67 percent), *power* (66 percent), *inequality* (49 percent), *racism* (42 percent), and *imperialism* (23 percent). *Liberty* fell to 16 percent. But more positive words like *wealth* (39 percent) and *dynamism* (34 percent) also increased over 1996.

51. SOFRES and French-American Foundation, *France-Etats-Unis*, 12, 14.

52. Sondages CSA, *L'Approche de l'élection*.

53. The percentages for the 1995/2001 polls were: *domineering* (90/92), *materialistic* (88/83), *democratic* (77/68), *violent* (74/82), *trustworthy* (68/53), *racist* (65/71), *cultured* (65/59), *religious* (62/69), *cooperative* (62/49), *isolationist* (54/51), and *hypocritical* (48/53). U.S. Department of State, *Europeans and Anti-Americanism*, A-24.

54. U.S. Department of State, *Europeans and Anti-Americanism*, A-27.

55. But this survey revealed considerable ignorance because almost 40 percent believed mistakenly that the unemployment rate in the United States was higher than in France when in fact it was 12 percent in France and 5 percent in the United States. Frachon, "L'image des Etats-Unis," 2.

56. SOFRES and French-American Foundation, *France-Etats-Unis*, 9–10.

57. U.S. Department of State, *Europeans and Anti-Americanism*, 37.

58. Ibid., A-27.

59. Ibid., 26–27.

60. SOFRES and French-American Foundation, *France-Etats-Unis*, 9.

61. Pew Global Attitudes Project, *Views of a Changing World*, T-138. Aversion for American corporate wrongdoing and reservations about the market may have been the cause of this criticism; Pew Center, *What the World Thinks*, 68.

62. Statement made by former ambassador Felix Rohatyn to the National Press Club, 25 October 1999.

63. Pew Global Attitudes Project, *Views of a Changing World*, 109; for specifics see T-7.

64. Ibid., T-53. In assessing failure, the French blamed the individual rather than society, at a percentage ratio of 68:28. For Americans the ratio was 82:12; for Germans it was 74:22; and for Italians it was 57:31.

65. Ibid., T-55. Some 87 percent of the French and 90 percent of the Germans professed this, but only 73 percent of Americans did.

66. Ibid., 105. While 62 percent of the French believed that government aid for the needy was more important than freedom of opportunity, only 34 percent of Americans held this view.

67. U.S. Department of State, Office of Research, Opinion Analysis, *West Europeans Positive Toward U.S.* (Washington, DC: U.S. Department of State, 2 November 2000), 5. But the Italians believed all of their values were even more different than the French did.

68. Pew Global Attitudes Project, *Views of a Changing World*, 115. In agreement with the proposition that belief in God is necessary for morality were: the British, 25 percent; the Italians, 27 percent; the Germans, 33 percent; and the Americans, 58 percent.

69. Ibid., T-142. Some 65 percent of the French, compared to 36 percent of the Germans, 33 percent of the British, 18 percent of the Spanish, and 14 percent of the Italians said America was too religious.

70. University of Michigan, *World Values Survey*, summarized in "Living with a Superpower," *Economist*, 24 January 2003, 18–20.

71. Details of the methodology for polling elites can be found in U.S. Department of State, *Six in Ten French Elites*, 5.

72. Ibid., 2. From 1999 on, the public was split almost 50/50 on the desirability of U.S. leadership in world affairs, but elites were far more positive; U.S. Department of State, *Europeans and Anti-Americanism*, 45.

73. U.S. Department of State, *Europeans and Anti-Americanism*, A-6.

74. U.S. Department of State, *Six in Ten French Elites*, 3.

75. U.S. Department of State, *Europeans and Anti-Americanism*, A-27.

76 A majority of the public, as opposed to less than a majority of the elite, for example, thought the two nations had conflicting views on both "family" and "democracy" ("democracy" apparently referred to social equality rather than political institutions). Three of four members of both elites and nonelites perceived differences over "work." But many more of the nonelite than the elite thought the countries differed with respect to both "morality and ethics" and "law and order." Above all, it was "lifestyle" that exposed the most glaring notion of Franco-American social dissimilarity. See U.S. Department of State, *Europeans and Anti-Americanism*, A-25.

77. U.S. Department of State, *Europeans and Anti-Americanism*, 39. See also U.S. Department of State, *Six in Ten French Elites*, 4.

78. Some 63 percent of the Communists and 35 percent of the Greens made the very negative choice. Data for elites and political affiliation come from U.S. Department of State, *Highlights from the Office of Research: Elite Surveys*, 11.

79. Data for elite subcategories come from U.S. Department of State, *Six in Ten French Elites*, 5. See also U.S. Department of State, *Highlights from the Office of Research: Elite Surveys*, 11.

80. The percentages were: educators, 17 percent; media elites, 21 percent; cultural leaders, 24 percent; religious leaders, 28 percent; and elite politicians, 30 percent. There were inconsistencies among religious and cultural elites who simultaneously registered strong positive and strong negative views.

81. SOFRES and French-American Foundation, *France-Etats-Unis*, 1.

82. Sondages CSA, *L'Approche de l'élection*. Women also chose, more highly then men, the category "tout est permis."

83. CSA-Libération, "L'Amérique."

84. U.S. Department of State, *Europeans and Anti-Americanism*, 6.

85. Pew Global Attitudes Project, *Views of a Changing World*, 78. Among those age 50 and over, 89 percent said they liked American popular culture, while 96 percent of the 18–29 cohort expressed the same preference.

86. SOFRES and French-American Foundation, *France-Etats-Unis*, 1, found that 44 percent of the oldest cohort, compared to 37 percent of the youngest cohort (18 to 24), expressed sympathy toward the United States. A survey conducted by the Institut BVA found that age correlated directly with a good opinion of Americans; Sainte Marie, "Nos derniers sondages."

87. Sondages CSA, *L'Approche de l'élection*.

88. CSA-Libération, "L'Amérique." For example, 45 percent of those over 65 said they felt close to the American people, but only 29 percent of those between 30 and 49 did and even fewer did among those younger than age 30.

89. One survey, taken in the midst of the Franco-American debate over Iraq in 2003, found that those between 18 and 24 were the only age group of whom a relative majority expressed a bad opinion of the American people. Among the young, the division between bad and good opinion of Americans was 46 percent to 44 percent; Sainte Marie, "Nos derniers sondages."

90. CSA-Libération, "L'Amérique."

91. Zogby International, *The Ten Nation Impressions of America Poll* (Washington, DC: Zogby International, March 23, 2002), 5. The national average of unfavorable views of the American people was 28 percent, while 35 percent of those between 18 and 29 spoke unfavorably.

92. The CSA poll, which offered the most detailed analysis of age, echoed the findings of the State Department and the Pew Center that it was not a significant variable, except for the older generation; Sondages CSA, *L'Approche de l'élection*.

93. The State Department concluded, after reviewing variables like age and gender for France, Britain, Germany and Italy, that "clear and consistent differences exist only along party lines"; U.S. Department of State, *Europeans and Anti-Americanism*, 6. An earlier Gallup survey reached the same conclusion about the importance of political preference; Gallup International, France-America Foundation and *L'Express*, *France and the United States: A Study in Mutual Image* (Washington, DC: Gallup International, 1986), 8.

94. SOFRES and French-American Foundation, *France-Etats-Unis*, 1.

95. Some 66 percent of the Right in contrast to 49 percent of the Left made this choice. Sainte Marie, "Nos derniers sondages." The CSA-Libération poll confirmed this finding: it reported that 70 percent of the Left, as opposed to 50 percent of the Right, said they did not feel close to the American people. CSA-Libération, "L'Amérique."

96. Sondages CSA, *L'Approche de l'élection*.

97. Sainte Marie, "Nos derniers sondages." Of the Right, 35 percent expressed a positive appreciation, but only 19 percent of the Left did.

98. Sondages CSA, *L'Approche de l'élection*. Those who associated themselves with the Left, more frequently than those on the Right, selected (respectively, in percentages) negative terms like *violence* (53/47), *strong social inequality* (49/43), and *racism* (38/27).

99. Data for this paragraph come from Sondages CSA, *L'Approche de l'élection*.

100. Martin A. Schain, "Immigration, the National Front and Changes in the French Party System," paper presented to the American Political Science Association, Boston, September 1998.

101. See Sondages CSA, *L'Approche de l'élection*; and Frachon, "L'image des Etats-Unis." National Front adherents attributed the death penalty to the United States far more frequently than any other party, probably because they wanted capital punishment restored in France. In the Iraq crisis, the Far Right showed more sympathy for the U.S. position than the Parliamentary Right or the Left, but it also believed (66 percent) more strongly than the Parliamentary Right (46 percent) and Left (54 percent) that the United States and France opposed each other on the major issues of the time. See Ipsos, "Que pensent les Français des Etats-Unis et de la crise irakienne?" 10 March 2003, http://www.ipsos.fr/CanalIpsos/poll/7746.asp.

102. CSA-Libération, "L'Amérique."

103. Charles Truehart, "A Beef with More Than Big Mac," *Washington Post*, 1 July 2000, A22.

104. See René Rémond, *Les Etats-Unis devant l'opinion française, 1814–1852* (Paris: Éditions Armand Colin, 1962); Jacques Portes, *Fascination and Misgivings: The United States in French Opinion, 1870–1914*, trans. Elborg Forster (Cambridge: Cambridge University Press, 2000); and Philippe Roger, *The American Enemy: The History of French Anti-Americanism*, trans. Sharon Bowman (Chicago: University of Chicago Press, 2002).

105. See Roger, *The American Enemy*, part 2; and Seth Armus, *French Anti-Americanism, 1930–1948* (Lanham, MD: Lexington Books, 2007).

106. Pierre Bourdieu and Loïc Wacquant, for example, savaged American social theory for its mental colonization of Europe. See Pierre Bourdieu and Loïc Wacquant, "La nouvelle vague planétaire," *Le Monde diplomatique*, May 2000, 6–7; and Pierre Bourdieu and Loïc Wacquant, "On the Cunning of Imperialist Reason," *Theory, Culture and Society* 16, no. 1 (1999): 41–58. Bourdieu and Wacquant denounced America for globalizing its analytical categories and po-

sitions and setting the agenda for how everyone debated social, economic and political questions.

107. Jacques Chirac, quoted in John Tagliabue, "Resisting Those Ugly Americans," *New York Times*, 9 January, 2000, 10.

108. Mickey Kantor, quoted in David Sanger, "Playing the Trade Card," *New York Times*, 17 February 1997, 43.

109. Editorial by Felix Rohatyn, *Washington Post*, 20 February 2001, A23.

110. Jean-Philippe Mathy, *French Resistance: The French-American Culture Wars* (Minneapolis: University of Minnesota Press, 2000), 16.

111. Mamère and Warin, *Non merci*, 175.

112. Denis Lacorne, "The Barbaric Americans," *Wilson Quarterly* 25 (2001): 54.

113. "Autour du malaise français" featured articles by Lucien Karpik, Philippe Raynaud, Michel Wieviorka, Paul Yonnet, and Brigitte Vial in *Le Débat* 75 (1993): 112–48. See also Alain Duhamel, *Les Peurs françaises* (Paris: Éditions Flammarion, 1993); Stéphane Marchand, *French Blues: pourquoi plus ça change, plus c'est la même chose* (Paris: First Editions, 1997); Jean-Claude Barreau, *La France va-t-elle disparaître* (Paris: Éditions Bernard Grasset, 1997); Stanley Hoffmann, "France, Keeping the Demons at Bay," *New York Review of Books*, 3 March 1994, 10–16; Secrétariat d'Etat au Plan, *Entrer dans le XXIe siècle: essai sur l'avenir de l'identité française* (Paris: Éditions la Découverte et la Documentation française, 1990). For a bibliographic guide, see Edward Knox, "Regarder la France: une réflexion bibliographique," *French Review* 72 (1998): 91–101. See also Alan Riding, "The French Funk," *New York Times Magazine*, 21 March 1993, 24, 51–54; Dominique Moïsi, "The Trouble with France," *Foreign Affairs* 77, no. 3 (1998): 94–104; Jean-Louis Bourlanges, *Le Diable est-il européen?* (Paris: Éditions Stock, 1992). Two British contributions to this discussion are Andrew Jack, *The French Exception: Still So Special?* (London: Profile, 1999); and Jonathan Fenby, *France on the Brink: A Great Civilization Faces the New Century* (New York: Arcade, 1998).

114. Hubert Haenel, "La France abîmée," *Le Figaro*, 26 September 1991, 2.

115. For a review of *Les Lieux de mémoire*, see Yves Lequin, "Une rupture épistémologique," *Magazine littéraire*, February 1993, 27–28. The original edition under the direction of Pierre Nora was published by Éditions Gallimard between 1984 and 1992 as *Les Lieux de mémoire*. The two multivolume English versions are: *Realms of Memory*, ed. Lawrence Kitzman, trans. Arthur Goldhammer (New York: Columbia University Press, 1996–98); and *Rethinking*

France, translation directed by David Jordan (Chicago: University of Chicago Press, 2001–10).

116. Unidentified deputy, quoted in Alan Riding, "France Questions Its Identity as It Sinks into 'Le Malaise,'" *New York Times*, 23 December 1990, 8.

117. Pierre Birnbaum, quoted in Roger Cohen, "For France, Sagging Self-Image and Esprit," *New York Times*, 11 February 1997, A8.

118. Riding, "France Questions Its Identity," 8.

119. Moïsi, "The Trouble with France," 103.

120. Alec Stone, "Ratifying Maastricht: France Debates European Union," *French Politics and Society* 11 (1993), 83–84; Paul Lewis, "Europeans Say French Vote Forces Delay," *New York Times*, 22 September 1992, A1, 16.

121. Jacques Lesourne, "Les enjeux du 'oui,'" *Le Monde*, 19 September 1992, 1.

122. Duhamel, *Les Peurs françaises*, 15–16.

123. For the transformation of the peasantry since 1950, see Annie Moulin, *Peasantry and Society in France since 1789* (Cambridge: Cambridge University Press, 1991), 165–99; and Henri Mendras, *La Fin des paysans suivi d'une réflexion sur La fin des paysans vingt ans après* (Arles, France: Actes Sud, 1984). For the recent past, see Bertrand Hervieu, "Un impossible deuil: à propos de l'agriculture et du monde rural en France," *French Politics and Society* 10 (1992): 41–59.

124. Hervieu, "Un impossible deuil," 58.

125. Laurence Wylie, "Roussillon, '87: Returning to the Village in the Vaucluse," *French Politics and Society* 7 (1989): 1–26.

126. Dominique Moïsi, quoted in Roger Cohen, "The French, Disneyed and Jurassick, Fear Erosion," *New York Times*, 21 November 1993, E2.

127. Alan Riding, "French Farmers Gird for War against U.S." *New York Times*, 11 November 1992, A11.

128. Some 47 percent said the two nations were either adversaries or adversarial partners. An equal number said the two were partners. Only 28 percent perceived the United States as acting to keep peace, and 11 percent to help democracy. SOFRES and French-American Foundation, *France-Etats-Unis*, 2.

129. U.S. Department of State, *Six in Ten French Elites*. Significantly, only 5 percent of the elite made this connection. On attitudes toward globalization, see Philip Gordon and Sophie Meunier, "Globalization and French Cultural Identity," *French Politics, Culture and Society* 10, no. 1 (2001): 22–41.

130. Hubert Védrine with Dominique Moïsi, *France in an Age of Globalization*, trans. Philip Gordon (Washington, DC: Brookings Institution Press, 2001), 3.

131. Daniel Vernet, "Les Français préfèrent M. Reagan au 'reaganisme,'" *Le Monde*, 6 November 1984, 1, 6.

132. For Germany, Mary Nolan contends, the rise of "political anti-Americanism" since the 1960s replaced the cultural, socioeconomic, antimodernist version of earlier decades; see Mary Nolan, "Anti-Americanism and Americanization in Germany," *Politics and Society* 33 (March 2005): 88–122. Alexander Stephan, addressing Europe, argues that traditional anti-Americanism, the emotional totalizing rejection of American culture and lifestyle, has given way to a conflict over political, socioeconomic, cultural systems; Alexander Stephan, "Cold War Alliances and the Emergence of Transatlantic Competition," in *The Americanization of Europe: Culture, Diplomacy and Anti-Americanism after 1945*, ed. Alexander Stephan (New York: Berghahn, 2006), 5.

133. Sophie Meunier, "The French Exception," *Foreign Affairs* 79, no. 4 (2000): 104–16.

134. See Jean-François Revel, *L'Obsession anti-américaine* (Paris: Plon, 2002); Guy Sorman, "L'antiaméricanisme se réchauffe," *Le Figaro*, 8 April 2001, 17; Pascal Bruckner, "La France, victime universelle?" *Le Monde*, 2 April 1998, 18.

135. In 1991 *Le Monde diplomatique* accepted its reputation as anti-American on the condition that "anti-Americanism begins with refusing submission"; see Vincent Dollier, "La croisade du *Monde Diplomatique*," *Les Collections de L'Histoire: L'Empire américain* 7 (2000): 100.

136. Craig Whitney, "Anxious French Mutter," *New York Times*, 2 December 1999, A12.

Reflections

1. Madeleine Albright, *Madam Secretary* (New York: Miramax Books, 2003), 447.

2. Marc Bloch, *Strange Defeat*, trans. Gerard Hopkins (New York: Norton, 1999), 149.

3. Jean-Marie Colombani, "Un Monde à part," *Le Monde*, 5 November 2004, 1.

4. Estimates vary in the range of 3.5 to 4.4 percent; some place France ahead, others the United States.

INDEX ∎

Note: Page numbers in italic indicate illustrations.

advertising: by American businesses, 155, 157, 188, 191, 195, 203, 204, *205*; as aspect of culture, 72–73, 204–5, 339; Bas-Lauriol Law and French language requirement for, 303, 308–9, 312

Afghanistan, 6, 82, 102, 105

Africa, 102, 116, 252–53, 254, 443n144

agriculture: Common Agricultural Policy of the EU, 245–46, 248–50; as cultural heritage and source of identity, 182, 244–45, 287, 361, 362, 365–67; EU import restrictions, 182, 245–50; food safety concerns about American products, 181–82, 369; GATT negotiations and, 128, 244–48, 249, 269, 356, 367; genetically modified crops, 336, 369, 376; McDonald's crop requirements, 179; protection and subsidies for French, 128, 244–50, 269, 276, 336, 356, 367, 375; protests against American companies, 153, 161–63, 193, *247*

AIDS epidemic, 2, 32–40, 44

Albert, Michel, 32

Albright, Madeline, 237, 240, 251, 252, 255, 377

Allègre, Claude, 312

Americanization, xiv, xvi, 7–9; adaptation of American businesses to other cultural contexts, 199–200; American businesses in France (*See* Coca-Cola; Euro Disney; McDonald's); anti-Americanism and, 329–30, 371–72, 389; consumer culture and, 6–7, 92–93; of French business practices, 299–306; French national identity and, 93, 208, 352–54, 360–67, 375, 382–83; global business environment and, 290–91, 327; influence on social order or civil society, 7, 290–91; Lang and efforts to curb, 45–46, 57–58, 71; and loss of global cultural diversity, 45–48, 53, 63–64, 72–73, 75–76, 78, 93–94, 316–21; as superficial, 52. *See also* cultural imperialism

Andréani, Jacques, 264–65, 268

Annan, Kofi, 252, 268

anti-Americanism, xix–xxii; academic study of phenomenon, 84–86; and America as "other," 91–92, 329, 372–73, 378; American enterprises and, 153; Americanization as context for, 330–31; among intellectuals, 48–53, 64–98, 330, 371, 380; *anti-américanisme primaire,*

473

trade *(continued)*
  Fortress Europe, 60, 134–35, 243–44; Franco-American bilateral, 387; French concerns about US trade and globalization, 336; import/export and French GDP, 275–76; Iran-Libya Sanctions Act, 250–51, 268; Single European Act (SEA) and, 134–35, 154, 242–44; trade sanctions, 250–51, 336. *See also* General Agreement on Tariffs and Trade (GATT); *specific sectors* (agriculture; audiovisual industries; *etc.*)
trade unions, 161–63, 180, 183, 289–90, 383
transatlantic community: common values and, 147, 210, 261, 279–280, 341–344, 357–360; continental drift and the French Way, xiii, xv–xvi, 383–90 (*See also* Americanization; investment; NATO; trade)
triumphalism, American, xiii, 251, 263, 271, 367, 369–70, 374, 389

UDF. *See* Union pour la Démocratie Française (UDF)
unemployment: as chronic and endemic in France, 274–75, 286, 387–88; and dollar exchange rate, 116; and French policies toward, 23–24, 30, 286, 295; and French response to US policies toward, 17, 278, 286, 343; McJobs and, 295; multinationals (American) as employers, 158, 178, 208; rates in America *vs.* France, 274
unilateralism, American: French responses to, 100, 149, 210, 250–51, 262–70; and trade sanctions, 118–20, 250–51. *See also* Iraq; Yugoslavia
Union pour la Démocratie Française (UDF), 111, 282, 286, 287, 350; and

anti-Americanism, 350, 394n11, 398n62; economic liberalism and, 21, 28, 282, 286, 398n62; reaction to American financial policy, 116; security policy and, 111, 127
United Kingdom (UK). *See* Great Britain
United Nations: and American unilateralism, 256–57, 264; French reliance on, 214, 216, 218, 255–57, 265, 268; and multilateralism, 267; reappointment of Boutros-Ghali as secretary general, 252; UNPROFOR and security in Yugoslavia, 217–21
Uruguay Round, GATT negotiations, 242–50, 315–22
USSR. *See* Soviet Union (USSR)

values: and American commercial enterprises in France, 152–53, 200–208; American *vs.* French or European, xv–xvi, xx, 8–9, 90–92, 279–80, 331, 341–44, 346, 358–59, 378–80; common values as foundation for alliances, 147, 210, 261; French national identity and, 381–82; republican solidarity as French, 358–59, 381–82
Vargas-Llosa, Mario, 319–21
Védrine, Hubert, 119, 121–23, 211, 219–20, 241, 262–66, 294, 308, 356, 369, 401
Vidal-Naquet, Pierre, 260

Waechter, Antoine, 213
Walters, Vernon, 126
Wanniski, Jude, 16
Warsaw Pact, 66–67, 104–5, 111, 120, 140, 144
welfare state: benefits of French, 276; deficiencies and economic costs, 274–75, 280, 388; French reform efforts, 276,